JUDGING COMPOSITE DECISION-MAKING

This book examines the European Court of Justice's principles relating to composite decision-making.

Through rigorous case law analysis, it shows how these rely on national and Union observance of rule of law requirements, under what the book calls the 'Unitary Protection' doctrine. It explores the theoretical dimension of this doctrine, illustrating how it represents a departure from the EU's foundational federalist approach to administrative law. This fills a longstanding gap in the literature and in our full understanding of composite decision-making, a key tenet of EU law. EU constitutional and administrative law scholars will be fascinated by this compelling study.

Volume 128 in the Series Modern Studies in European Law

Modern Studies in European Law

Recent titles in this series:

The Structural Transformation of European Private Law: A Critique of Juridical Hermeneutic
Leone Niglia

The Future of EU Constitutionalism
Edited by Matej Avbelj

The Changing Role of Citizens in EU Democratic Governance
Edited by Davor Jancic

The EU and the Baltic Sea Area
Edited by Allan Rosas and Henrik Ringbom

The Evolving Governance of EU Competition Law in a Time of Disruptions: A Constitutional Perspective
Edited by Carlo Maria Colombo, Kathryn Wright and Mariolina Eliantonio

The European Integrated Border Management: Frontex, Human Rights, and International Responsibility
Giulia Raimondo

Private Autonomy in EU Internal Market Law: Parameters of its Protection and Limitation
Rufat Babayev

Free Movement and Welfare Access in the European Union: Re-Balancing Conflicting Interests in Citizenship Jurisprudence
Victoria Hooton

EU Trade and Investment Treaty-Making Post-Lisbon: Moving Beyond Mixity
Gesa Kübek

The Normative Foundations for EU Criminal Justice: Powers, Limits and Justifications
Jacob Öberg

EU Neighbourhood Law: Wider Europe and the Extended EU's Legal Space
Alessandro Petti

The Dynamics of Powers in the European Union
Edited by Christina Eckes, Päivi Leino-Sandberg and Anna W Ghavanin

The European Convention on Human Rights and Private Law: Comparative Perspectives from South-Eastern Europe
Edited by Mateja Durovic and Cristina Poncibò

Judging Composite Decision-Making: The Transformation of European Administrative Law
Filipe Brito Bastos

For the complete list of titles in this series see www.bloomsbury.com/uk/series/modern-studies-in-european-law/

Judging Composite Decision-Making

The Transformation of European Administrative Law

Filipe Brito Bastos

•HART•

OXFORD • LONDON • NEW YORK • NEW DELHI • SYDNEY

HART PUBLISHING

Bloomsbury Publishing Plc

Kemp House, Chawley Park, Cumnor Hill, Oxford, OX2 9PH, UK

1385 Broadway, New York, NY 10018, USA

29 Earlsfort Terrace, Dublin 2, Ireland

HART PUBLISHING, the Hart/Stag logo, BLOOMSBURY and the Diana logo are trademarks of Bloomsbury Publishing Plc

First published in Great Britain 2024

A catalogue record for this book is available from the British Library.

A catalogue record for this book is available from the Library of Congress.

ISBN: HB: 978-1-50998-042-0
ePDF: 978-1-50998-044-4
ePub: 978-1-50998-043-7

Typeset by Compuscript Ltd, Shannon

À Sara

ACKNOWLEDGEMENTS

This book is the output of a long process of research that spanned the full course, and perhaps marks the end, of my years as an early-career scholar. The book grew from doctrinal insights originally developed in my doctoral thesis, defended at the European University Institute of Florence. It benefitted from additional conceptual refinement during my postdoctoral research at the Amsterdam Centre for European Law and Governance. Lastly, it builds on deeper theoretical work and methodological fine-tuning that I have conducted as assistant professor at NOVA School of Law and researcher at its research centre, CEDIS. Much of this research resulted in other publications, in journal articles as well as edited volumes, and are referred to in the book's text at different points.

All of the book's flaws, imprecisions, imperfections and mistakes are exclusively mine. But they would have been many more – and the book would not exist in its present and final form – were it not for the invaluable and countless exchanges I had with esteemed colleagues and friends over the years. I must make special reference to two. One is Deirdre Curtin, my doctoral supervisor and a friend to whom I owe a huge debt of gratitude, both academic and personal, for her constant encouragement and critique during my PhD and well beyond. The other is Michał Krajewski, one of the finest European Union lawyers of our generation, but also my most frequent, constructive and honest reader, and one whom I am proud to call a friend.

I also wish to acknowledge other colleagues with whom I discussed the argument in *Judging Composite Decision-Making* throughout the years – often in more than one of its incarnations. My sincere thanks go, among many others, to Athina Sachoulidou, Bruno de Witte, Fabrizio Esposito, Giulia Gentile, Herwig Hofmann, James Dennison, Jan Komárek, Joana Mendes, Marcin Baranski, Loïc Azoulai, Luis Arroyo Jiménez, Mariolina Eliantonio, Marta Morvillo, Martijn van den Brink, Melanie Fink, Miguel Poiares Maduro, Morten Rasmussen, Nausica Palazzo, Niovi Vavoula, Paul Craig, and Przemysław Pałka.

I would also like to thank Hart Publishing for agreeing to include this book in the prestigious *Modern Studies in European Law* series, as well as the book's two anonymous reviewers for their attentive reading and generous critique and Jo Choulerton for her superb work in editing the manuscript. During part of the research that led to this book, I benefitted from financial support from *Fundação para a Ciência e Tecnologia* (the Portuguese Foundation for Science and Technology) in the form of a doctoral grant (grant No. SFRH/BD/52120/2013).

Towards the final stages of its completion, the book benefitted from careful proofreading by six excellent students and research assistants at NOVA School of Law. For their great work, I would like to thank Guilherme Sousa, Isabel Costa, Jéssica Pereira, Leonor Ferreira, Mafalda Jardim and Rita Esteves.

On a personal note, I would like to express my gratitude to my friends – among others, Gui, Koen, Christophe, Marta, Cátia and André – and to my family. I would especially like to thank my father, Rui, and my brother, Miguel. I am more grateful to my very patient wife, Mariana, than I could possibly put into words, though I did try, albeit imperfectly, in the acknowledgements to my doctoral dissertation. It was naturally to Mariana that I dedicated the dissertation. This book, however, which has its early origins in the dissertation, I dedicate to our baby daughter, Sara.

Filipe Brito Bastos
April 2024

CONTENTS

TABLE OF CASES

Judgments of the Court of Justice

Opinions of Advocates General

Judgments of the General Court

Introduction

1

Unity and Dominance

I. Dualism, Cooperation, and Unity

The story of the Union's constitutional and political system can be told as one of a gradual transition. From a model of dual federalism, where Member State and the Union 'are co-equal and operate independently in their respective spheres', the Union came to evolve into a model of cooperative federalism, where both levels work together and share power.[1] The Union's administrative system has largely followed the same transition. There is, however, one exception. A substantial part of the Union administrative system can no longer be likened to cooperative federalism. Not because national and Union administration fail to cooperate, but because such cooperation, and above all its judge-made framework, has eroded the divide between national and Union administration to the point that, if one takes a minimum of separation between the state and the national levels as essential to federalism, their relations simply can no longer even qualify as federal at all.

This book makes a twofold contribution to the existing literature in European administrative law. One contribution is doctrinal. The book reconstructs a body of implicit principles gradually developed by the Court of Justice of the European Union (CJEU). The principles in question specifically aim to regulate composite decision-making (or 'composite administrative procedures'). Composite administrative procedures are administrative processes that are unique to European Union law and pervade all its policy areas, from bank supervision to the regulation of medicines, from data protection to food safety law. The distinctive feature of composite administrative procedures is decisional interdependence. They require national and Union authorities to exercise decision-making powers in a joint, interdependent fashion in order for a final decision to be taken.

The CJEU's implicit principles on composite decision-making rest upon the recognition of this feature, and together form a doctrine that is itself unique to European administrative law. That doctrine will be termed 'Unitary Protection'.

At its core, the Unitary Protection doctrine requires national and Union administration to observe procedural rights (such as the right to be heard) and

[1] R Schütze, *From Dual to Cooperative Federalism: The Changing Structure of European Law* (Oxford University Press, 2009), 5–7. See also S Alonso de Léon, *Composite Administrative Procedures in the European Union* (Iustel, 2017), 47.

to answer judicially as if they formed as a single, integrated administration. This basic notion is operationalised with a simple test. The test is termed in this book as 'decisional dominance'. The responsibility to ensure procedural rights will fall to national or Union administration, and judicial review to national or Union courts, depending on whether it is a national or Union authority that exercises the formal power to determine the final decision.

The second contribution of the book is theoretical. the book argues that the CJEU's principles on composite decision-making imply a shift in its conception of the relations between the Union and the Member States – in administrative law, at least. The CJEU's basic doctrine on the relations between national and Union administration, European Executive Federalism, emerged gradually right from the Union's early days. Influential jurists in the Community institutions – many of whom were German and/or Treaty drafters – adopted a federal conception of European integration. They advocated that the Treaties had implicitly enshrined, at the constitutional level, a federal model of administration made in the image of the German system. The Court agreed. Some of its (also German) judges openly stated that the CJEU's case law demonstrated the federal nature and German inspiration of the Union's administrative system.

While its early political origins may to have slipped into oblivion, European Executive Federalism is still good law. It entails principles of 'strict separation' and cooperation that apply to this day. One aims to preserve the ability of national and Union administrations to exercise their own powers independently of interference from the other; the other requires national and Union administrations to offer their mutual assistance. The two principles have always been able to accommodate *most* of the Union's administrative system, which overwhelmingly combines cooperation and formally independent powers. Indeed, practices of 'cooperative federalism', in the Union's administrative system, have always rested upon the principles of Executive Federalism, in the Union's administrative law.

However, mounting litigation confronted the CJEU with limitations of European Executive Federalism. European Executive Federalism rests upon an assumption that national and Union administrations decide independently from one another. Its principles therefore require separate observance of procedural rights by national and Union administration; and separate judicial review, by national and Union courts, of the decisions that they take. Starting with a string of rulings since the early 1990s, the CJEU ultimately realised that such principles were simply unable to ensure basic rule of law requirements whenever national and Union administrations decide jointly rather than separately.

The CJEU hence needed to fashion a new doctrinal framework specifically to preserve the rule of law in composite decision-making. The principles of that new doctrine, Unitary Protection, constitute a derogation from the principles of European Executive Federalism. Unitary Protection obliges the national and Union administration to observe procedural rights jointly and ensure that judicial review need only be carried out against one of the two. Yet this development was far more than purely doctrinal. The principles of composite decision-making crafted by the CJEU treat national and Union administration in a unitary fashion. Over time, the CJEU thus came to shed – not to promote – the federal conception upon which the foundations of the Union's administration, and administrative law, had been built.

This development was, however, *specific* to composite administrative decision-making. Executive Federalism and Unitary Protection today constitute two competing doctrines on how to order relations between the administrative powers of the Union and of the Member States. The former still applies to most instances of administrative decision-making in the European Union. It retains a federal – albeit cooperative – logic. The latter applies specifically to composite decision-making. By negating any real divide between national and Union administration, it is not only beyond dual federalism, or even cooperative federalism, but beyond the very idea of federalism itself.

Composite decision-making is shaped by the same political concerns that shape the Union's administrative system at large. That is, the concern to preserve a balance of power between the Union and the Member States, both of which strive to advance their own autonomy and power.[2] Ironically, it also represents a form of administration banned under federal constitutions, such as the American or the German, for calling into question the divide – the balance – between State and federal power. The CJEU, however, never came even close to rejecting the absence of divided powers. Instead, it fashioned a doctrinal framework for composite decision-making that treats national and Union administration as a continuum – as parts of one and the same unitary administration.

II. Composite Decision-Making and the Union's Rule of Law

The principle that the European Union constitutes a 'Union based on the rule of law' is an overarching ideal of European integration.[3] That principle constrains the power of the Member States over individuals, and of the Union, over both.[4] This notion is the bedrock of European administrative law.

[2] E Grande and M McCowan, 'The Two Logics of Multilevel Administration in the EU' in M Bauer and J Trondal (eds), *The Palgrave Handbook of the European Administrative System* (Palgrave, 2015), 55.

[3] Cases 294/83 *'Les Verts' v European Parliament* ECLI:EU:C:1986:166, para 23 and C-619/18 *European Commission v Republic of Poland* ECLI:EU:C:2019:531, para 46 and Case C-64/16 *Associação Sindical dos Juízes Portugueses v Tribunal de Contas*, ECLI:EU:C:2018:117, para 36. On the principle of the rule of law in the European Union see, of many, L Pech, 'The Rule of Law as a Well-Established and Well-Defined Principle of EU Law' (2022) 14 *Hague Journal on the Rule of Law* 107; K Lenaerts, 'New Horizons for the Rule of Law in the EU' (2020) 21 *German Law Journal* 29 and A von Bogdandy, 'Ways to Frame the European Rule of Law: Rechtsgemeinschaft, Trust, Revolution, and Kantian Peace' (2018) 14 *European Constitutional Law Review* 675.

[4] K Tuori, *European Constitutionalism* (Cambridge University Press, 2015), 214.

At its core, and across legal traditions, the rule of law aims to prevent arbitrary, unforeseeable, or excessive use of power.[5] Though some traditions comprise substantive requirements, such as human rights,[6] the Union's own version of the rule of law constitutes a legal principle, or perhaps more accurately, a cluster of legal principles,[7] of a formal and procedural nature.[8]

Such 'principles of the rule of law', according to the CJEU, include 'principles of legality, legal certainty, prohibition of arbitrariness of the executive powers, effective judicial protection and separation of powers'.[9] From the rule of law, the CJEU also derives procedural fundamental rights.[10] One, enshrined in Article 41 of the European Charter of Fundamental Rights (henceforth, 'the Charter'), is the right to good administration. Good administration requires the administration to consider all relevant interests carefully and impartially, hear the individuals affected by its decisions and give reasons for said decisions.[11] The other right, enshrined in Article 47 of the Charter, is the right to effective judicial protection. Effective judicial protection is, in the CJEU's own words, 'of the essence of the rule of law', and requires, among other things, judicial independence and that individuals enjoy appropriate judicial remedies.[12]

In Parts II and II, the book will offer a theoretical account of the scope and rule of law rationales of good administration and judicial control, of the challenges that composite decision-making posed to such requirements, and of the CJEU's solutions therefor. For now, may it suffice to observe that such challenges emerge from a mismatch: if applied to composite decision-making, the principles of European Executive Federalism lead to rule of law gaps.

[5] For a comparative view of the meaning of the rule of law across several countries, see M Loughlin, *The Foundations of Public Law* (Oxford University Press, 2010), 312 ff. See also J Raz, *The Authority of Law: Essays on Law and Morality* (Clarendon, 1979), 210 ff, 214–18 and B Tamanaha, 'A Concise Guide to the Rule of Law' in G Palombella and N Walker (eds), *Relocating the Rule of Law* (Hart Publishing, 2009), 3–6.

[6] B Tamanaha, *On the Rule of Law: History, Politics, Theory* (Cambridge University Press, 2004), 91 ff.

[7] See M Avbelj, *The European Union under Transnational Law: A Pluralist Appraisal* (Hart Publishing, 2018), 62 ff and T von Danwitz, 'The Rule of Law in the Recent Jurisprudence of the ECJ' (2014) 37 *Fordham International Law Journal* 1311, 1315 ff.

[8] L Pech, 'A Union Founded on the Rule of Law: Meaning and Reality of the Rule of Law as a Constitutional Principle of EU Law' (2010) 6 *European Constitutional Law Review* 359, 362.

[9] Case C-156/21 *Hungary v European Parliament and Council of the European Union*, ECLI:EU:C:2022:97, para 236.

[10] To this extent, it is an overgeneralisation to suggest that the link that the CJEU makes between effective judicial protection and the rule of law demonstrates that the Union subscribes to a substantive conception of the latter. In this regard, see J Raitio, 'Does the concept of rule of law have any material content? A Nordic point of view' (2017) 24 *Maastricht Journal of European and Comparative Law* 774.

[11] For the link between good administration and the rule of law, see Case T-165/15 *Ryanair DAC, formerly Ryanair Ltd and Airport Marketing Services Ltd v European Commission*, ECLI:EU:T:2018:953, para 53 and the Opinion of AG Pikamäe in Case C-894/19 P *European Parliament v UZ* ECLI:EU:C:2021:497, paras 65–67.

[12] Joined Cases C-357/19, C-379/19, C-547/19, C-811/19 and C-840/19 *Criminal proceedings against PM and Others*, ECLI:EU:C:2021:1034, para 219. See also Case C-430/21 *Proceedings brought by RS* ECLI:EU:C:2022:99, para 41.

The principles of European Executive Federalism presuppose a scenario of decisional independence between national and Union administration, whereas composite decision-making involves decisional interdependence between the two. The principle that national and Union administration may not interfere in each other's sphere of power would appear not to have any immediate impact on procedural fundamental rights. Yet the CJEU has extracted from such principle a notion of separate legal relations. Individuals are bound by legal relations *either* to national *or* to Union administration, depending on which of the two exercises powers in regard to them. When national and Union administrations decide separately from one another, this poses no problem – there is clarity as to which of the two is bound by a legal relation to an individual, and must therefore ensure observance, eg of her right to be heard. Yet if one applies this same reasoning to interdependent decision-making, it becomes entirely unclear whether individuals will be entitled to be heard by the Union administration, national administration, both, or neither.

Similar problems emerge in judicial review. The principle that only national courts may review national decisions, and Union courts review Union decisions, may be appropriate to ensure effective judicial control when national and Union decisional powers are exercised separately. Yet it has no minimally adequate solution to offer when decisions result from a single administrative procedure involving national and Union authorities alike.

In short, the rise of composite decision-making presented the CJEU with two choices. One was to cling on to the principles of European Executive Federalism, and to insist on treating national and Union administration as strictly separate – even where they were not, and even if to the detriment of basic rule of law principles. The CJEU took this formalistic road in many of its first rulings.

The other choice was more nuanced, complex and transformative. That was the choice to recognise the absence of decisional independence, to uphold rule of law principles, and to no longer preserve a strict separation between national and Union administration. The CJEU has taken this approach since the early 1990s. While it has remained fragmentary, the CJEU's case law gradually developed an implicit doctrine that settles most rule of law problems by composite decision-making.

III. Legal Doctrine and the 'Touch of Stateness'

Legal scholarship should avoid a risk well-known to empirical political science. The risk is that analysis of the Union's multilevel administration becomes distorted by 'applying established concepts from national contexts to the EU'.[13] Instead, one should seek to consider the Union's administration and

[13] E Grande and M McCowan, n 2, 49.

administrative law in their singular political and constitutional contexts.[14] This risk, which Shaw and Wiener have aptly termed the 'touch of stateness',[15] should be prevented when investigating European administrative law generally, and composite decision-making more specifically.

Indeed, the CJEU's case law on composite decision-making needed to address a reality for which no conceptual language had yet been made. However, the case law consistently resorts to the same argumentative patterns when resolving legal issues that specifically emerge from the structure of composite procedures. Said patterns have been applied across administrative procedures, rulings and policy areas. They encapsulate generalisable legal principles which, for want of similar phenomena in national administrative traditions, have largely remained only implicit and nameless. It is those principles that this book aims to excavate.

Reconstructing the CJEU's principles on composite decision-making is an exercise in legal-doctrinal analysis – in reformulating and systematising concepts and principles that lay implicit in legal sources.[16] Questions arise of how such analysis is to be carried out, at the methodological level, and what is intended by its end-product – a legal doctrine.

A. Methodology in the Administrative-Constitutional Continuum

The book's argument will deploy a methodological approach that I have previously advocated.[17] The approach involves extracting administrative law concepts and principles from 'subjects of reference' and testing their constitutional conformity and purpose. The basic premise of the 'subjects of reference' method is that doctrinal analysis should operate inductively. Rather than beginning in pre-existing, abstract and often outdated theories, doctrinal analysis should begin by identifying and comparing structurally similar administrative law issues that would appear to be specific to certain policy sectors – the 'subjects of reference' (*Referenzgebieten*). Doctrinal analysis should then test whether such issues are generalisable across other policy sectors.[18] Hence, as they provide 'raw material' from which existing doctrines can be reformed, and *novel doctrines* fleshed out,[19]

[14] See J Mendes, 'The Foundations of EU Administrative Law as a Scholarly Field: Functional Comparison, Normativism and Integration' (2022) 18 *European Constitutional Law Review* 706 and F Brito Bastos, 'Doctrinal Methodology in EU Administrative Law: Confronting the "Touch of Stateness"' (2021) 22 *German Law Journal* 593.

[15] J Shaw and A Wiener, 'The Paradox of the "European Polity"' in M Green Cowles and M Smith (eds), *Risks, Reform, Resistance, and Revival* (Oxford University Press, 2000), 64–65.

[16] W Kahl, *Wissenschaft, Praxis und Dogmatik im Verwaltungsrecht* (Mohr Siebeck, 2020), 78 ff.

[17] The following is a summary of F Brito Bastos, n 14.

[18] For a defence of this method, see F Brito Bastos n 14. See also A Voßkuhle, 'Neue Verwaltungsrechtswissenschaft' in W Hoffmann-Riem, E Schmidt-Aßmann and A Voßkuhle (eds), *Grundlagen des Verwaltungsrechts*, vol I, 2nd edn (CH Beck, 2012), 39.

[19] E Schmidt-Aßmann 'Cuestiones Fundamentales Sobre la Reforma de la Teoría General del Derecho Administrativo. Necesidad de la Innovación y Presupuestos Metodológicos' in J Barnes (ed), *Innovación y Reforma en el Derecho Administrativo* (Global Law Press, 2006), 75–76.

'subjects of reference' show particular analytical potential in an administrative law system, which, like the European Union's, is fragmentary, uncodified, and in need of a new doctrinal language of its own.[20]

The argument in the present book draws from a large body of case law, produced across policy sectors, for its 'subjects of reference'. What unifies said case law is the repeated use of argumentative patterns specifically relating to the nature of relations between national and Union decision-making. As it turns out, some such patterns are specific to instances of decisional independence between national and Union administration; others, unique to instances of decisional interdependence.[21] Both strands of argumentative patterns are generalisable and allow the reconstruction, respectively, of two competing doctrines – European Executive Federalism and Unitary Protection.

One thing is to identify generalisable administrative law doctrines. Another is to identify what purposes they must serve. The latter task requires administrative law to be analysed in a continuum with,[22] and as a concretisation of,[23] constitutional law. As it aims to regulate the exercise of all constituted powers, constitutional law necessarily shapes how legislatures and judges may frame the powers of administrative authorities. The Treaties and the Charter represent the Union's constitutional law. They fulfil the basic functions of any constitution, such as establishing the constitutional subject (the Union), defining its relations to other entities (member and third states) and restricting its powers (by enshrining

[20] E Schmidt-Aßmann, *Verwaltungsrechtliche Dogmatik* (Mohr Siebeck, 2013), 9 and L Arroyo Jiménez, 'Introduction: Quelle Théorie pour le Droit Administratif Européen?' in JB Auby and J Dutheil de la Rochère, *Traité de Droit Administratif Européen*, 3rd edn (Bruylant, 2022).

[21] Some readers will find the argument's scope too limited given that it chooses not to consider purely horizontal composite procedures – ie administrative procedures only involving authorities from different Member States, without any role for the Union administration. This is legitimate criticism. However, there are several reasons for the choice. Composite decision-making of the purely horizontal sort is rare. It has produced only limited case law, mainly confined to procedures for the request of information between national tax authorities (For many, see F Brito Bastos, '*Luxembourg v B*: How Far Should Jurisdictional Limits Be Eroded in the Name of Effective Judicial Protection?' (2020) 41 *EU Law Live* 10 and P Mazzotti and M Eliantonio, 'Transnational Judicial Review in Horizontal Composite Procedures: Berlioz, Donnellan, and the Constitutional Law of the Union' (2020) 5 *European Papers* 41). It is hence too early to determine to what extent the CJEU's few findings contain principles generalisable to other policy areas, as its findings on 'vertical' composite procedures are. Moreover, horizontal decision-making does not raise the same fundamental problems in terms of the division of power between the Union and the Member States which is at the heart of European Executive Federalism. However, some composite procedures which begin as merely horizontal may lead to a stage where the Union administration takes a final decision to settle disputes between the distinct national authorities involved. Such administrative procedures are termed 'arbitral' composite procedures and *do* come under the scope of the analysis here. See Chapter 3, section III.C.(ii).

[22] A Sandulli, 'The Double Face of the Rule of Law in the European Legal Order: an Administrative Law Perspective' (2020) 5 *European Papers* 237, 248.

[23] For the notion of administrative law as concretised constitutional law, see F Werner, 'Verwaltungsrecht als konkretisiertes Verfassungsrecht' in F Werner, KA Bettermann and CH Ule, *Recht und Gericht unserer Zeit* (Carl Heymanns, 1971). This view must be held valid in the context of European administrative law, too. In this respect, see T von Danwitz, *Europäisches Verwaltungsrecht* (Springer, 2008), 141.

fundamental rights and limits to the Union's competences that safeguard the Member States' autonomy).[24]

These considerations are relevant in the present argument because the doctrines of European Executive Federalism and Unitary Protection each serve their own, distinct, constitutional purpose. The exclusive focus of European Executive Federalism has been to preserve the separation of administrative power between the Union and the Member States. By contrast, Unitary Protection serves more ambitious constitutional purposes. It aims to uphold rule of law principles of particular importance to administrative law, such as effective judicial protection, in composite decision-making.

B. The Anatomy of Legal Doctrines – And of a Doctrinal Transition

The purpose of doctrinal methodology is to develop legal doctrine. While intuitively familiar to lawyers, the notion of a legal doctrine is rarely spelled out. However, distinguishing the constitutive components of legal doctrines provides legal scholars with a sharper analytical framework, and hence conceptual clarity, when advocating for a particular interpretation of the law. Understanding the general structure of legal doctrines will facilitate the reconstruction of each of the CJEU's two competing and largely implicit doctrines – European Executive Federalism and Unitary Protection. Understanding the general structure of legal doctrines will also facilitate isolating and pinpointing exactly where the differences between the two doctrines lie.

Legal doctrines represent clusters of legal concepts and principles. Legal concepts form the shared vocabulary of jurists and have a primarily descriptive function. They serve as linguistic shortcuts that enable jurists to refer to institutional facts, or to communicate about interpretation or application of the law, through abstract categories – 'duty', 'feed', 'public health', and the like.[25] 'Decisional interdependence', for example, is a concept that describes the relations between national and Union administrations within composite procedures.

Legal principles, by contrast, have a prescriptive function.[26] Yet the concept of a legal principle may mean a variety of different things. Alexy's influential account distinguishes between rules – 'definitive commands' which can either be complied with or not – and legal principles – 'optimisation commands' requiring their object to be realised to the greatest degree possible.[27] Not all norms termed

[24] K Tuori, n 4, 28 ff.

[25] See F Brito Bastos, n 14, 608. See also D von der Pfordten, 'About concepts in law' in J Hage and D von der Pfordten (eds), *Concepts in Law* (Springer, 2009), 18–19.

[26] While the two may admittedly not always be easily distinguishable, principles can often only be understood by reference to related concepts. For instance, 'separation of powers', as a principle, would not be intelligible without concepts such as 'legislative branch'.

[27] R Alexy, 'On the Structure of Legal Principles' (2000) 13 *Ratio Juris* 294, 295.

'principles' represent optimisation requirements. Some are interpretive norms and prescribe how lawyers must ascribe meaning to legal sources.[28] Others are 'general legal principles', ie a synthesis of the normative contents of legal sources which enhances coherence and predictability within a legal system or at least some of its branches.[29] All principles of European Executive Federalism and Unitary Protection constitute principles of this kind.

However, legal doctrines are not only composed of concepts and principles. They also consist in a conception of the real-world realities that the law intends to govern – in what Pöyhönen describes as the 'factual and value commitments about the (legally regulated) object of the theory' (brackets in the original).[30] Legal interpreters – indeed, much like legal sources themselves – are immersed in a concrete social, political and cultural environment. That environment shapes both how the object of a doctrine is understood and what value choices its regulation is expected to observe. The prohibition of unfair dismissal, as well as its doctrinal interpretations, rely on a factual commitment that workers are the weaker party to a labour contract, and on a value commitment that workers merit protection, even if at some expense to the employer's autonomy. In a similar intuition, Rawlings and Harlow note that '[B]eneath every theory of administrative law there lies a theory of the state'.[31] The key theoretical and conceptual point that this book has to offer is that beneath each of the two overarching theories of Union administrative law – European Executive Federalism and Unitary Protection – there lie distinct theories, or better, conceptions, of what the Union and its administrative system are about.

The question of how to determine the characteristics of the conceptions then follows. This is an exercise which cannot be purely juristic and must instead draw on interdisciplinary insights. One may infer much from the language of the CJEU's rulings and the conceptions it implies about the relation between national and Union administration. One must, however, understand the shift between such conceptions in their historical and political context. In particular, one cannot understand why the CJEU's departure from European Executive Federalism was so reluctant and tortuous without considering that, just like the leading federalist jurists, the CJEU had come to consider it as a doctrine of constitutional rank.

In contrast, one cannot understand the rationale of composite decision-making without considering the political and functional factors behind its expansion. This is why the analysis in the book's argument requires dialogue with

[28] K Tuori, *Ratio and Voluntas* (Ashgate, 2011), 189.

[29] K Tuori, n 28, 189 and 195 and E Schmidt-Aßmann, n 20, 47 ff. In the interest of clarity, one should point out that 'general legal principle', in this theoretical sense, differs from the notion of 'general principle *of Union* law' in the CJEU's case law, which tends to represent a constitutional principle that operates as an optimisation requirement in the Alexian sense.

[30] J Pöyhönen, 'On the Role of Theories in Legal Dogmatics' (1981) 2 *Rechtstheorie* 127, 131. A similar analytical perspective is adopted by A Aarnio, *Essays on the Doctrinal Study of Law* (Springer, 2011), 177–78 and K Tuori, n 28, 197–200.

[31] C Harlow and R Rawlings, *Law and Administration* (4th edn, Cambridge University Press, 2021), 1.

empirical research on the Union's multilevel administrative system. The concern with a balance between national and Union administrative power has remained the key political factor shaping composite decision-making. However, and paradoxically, the rise of composite decision-making pushed the CJEU to develop a legal doctrine that, rather than balancing distinct powers at national and Union levels, unifies them instead. Intuitively, one would think that a unitary conception of national and Union administration might be a distant cry from institutional and administrative reality. Yet, political science has shown that national and Union administration increasingly do function in a unified manner, in particular because national authorities are often 'absorbed' or 'co-opted' as 'parts' of the Union administration.[32] This is precisely how the CJEU treats national authorities in most composite administrative procedures.[33]

IV. The Inconspicuous Rise of a Unitary Protection Doctrine

The 1990s are sometimes said to have been a period of relative restraint in the CJEU's creativity (some would say activism).[34] This was not so in the realm of composite decision-making. Indeed, the CJEU began during this same period to develop a set of entirely novel set of principles to accommodate composite decision-making into the Union's constitutional order.

Nevertheless, and even though it has existed since the dawn of European integration, composite decision-making did not spark lawyers' interest until quite late. In a way, this is unsurprising. Until Schwarze's landmark treatise in the late 1980s,[35] and with few exceptions,[36] legal scholarship neglected European administrative law in favour of the greater 'constitutional glamour'[37] of issues such as primacy, fundamental rights, or the Communities' legal nature.[38] It was only in the 1990s, following several ground-breaking CJEU rulings, and by the

[32] See Chapter 10, section V.E.

[33] See Chapter 10, section IV.

[34] K Lenaerts, 'The Court's Outer and Inner Selves: Exploring the External and Internal Legitimacy of the European Court of Justice' in M Adams, H de Waele and J Meeusen and G Straetmans (eds), *Judging Europe's Judges: The Legitimacy of the Case Law of the European Court of Justice* (Hart Publishing, 2013), 16 ff.

[35] J Schwarze, *Europäisches Verwaltungsrecht: Entstehung und Entwicklung im Rahmen der Europäischen Gemeinschaft* (Nomos, 1988).

[36] See for instance G Sacchi Morsiani, *Il potere amministrativo delle Comunità europee e le posizioni giuridiche dei privati* (Giuffrè, 1965) and HW Rengeling, *Rechtsgrundsätze beim Verwaltungsvollzug des Europäischen Gemeinschaftsrechts* (Carl Heymanns, 1977).

[37] M Bobek, 'Thou shalt have two Masters: The Application of European Law by Administrative Authorities in the New Member States' (2008) 1 *Review of European Administrative Law* 51, 52.

[38] H Hofmann, 'Seven Challenges for EU Administrative Law' in K de Graaf, J Jans, A Prechal and R Widdershoven (eds), *European Administrative Law: Top-Down and Bottom-up: Proceedings of the First REALaw Research Forum* (Europa Law Publishing, 2010), 37 ff, 37–38.

impulse of Italian academics,[39] that composite decision-making finally caught the eye of legal scholarship.

A second wave of judicial breakthroughs since the mid-2010s has brought about a revival in legal scholarship. A growing interest in composite decision-making is apparent from numerous recent writings not only from a sectoral perspective,[40] particularly so in data protection or Banking Union law,[41] but also from more general administrative and constitutional law perspectives.[42] The term 'composite administrative procedure' now appears in some Union Agencies' soft law.[43] It has also appeared in some Advocate General Opinions.[44] And, in March of 2023, the General Court's ruling in *Satabank* was the CJEU's first ever to use the term 'composite administrative procedure'.[45]

Over the years, legal scholarship has remained overwhelmingly critical. It has suggested that the CJEU's case law is contradictory;[46] makes up 'bureaucratic

[39] See L Casini, S Cassese and G Napolitano, 'The New Italian Public Law Scholarship' (2011) 9 *International Journal of Constitutional Law* 301, 307. The pioneering study of composite decision-making was C Franchini, *Amministrazione Italiana e Amministrazione Comunitaria* (2nd edn, CEDAM, 1993), 174 ff. See also M Chiti, 'I Procedimenti Composti nel Diritto Comunitario e nel Diritto Interno' in *Quaterni del Consiglio di Stato: Attività amministrativa e tutela degli interessati. L'influenza del diritto comunitario* (Centro studi e documentazione del Consiglio di Stato, 1997) and G della Cananea, 'The European Union's Mixed Administrative Proceedings' (2003–2004) 68 *Law and Contemporary Problems* 197.

[40] For instance, one can find contributions concerning judicial control in composite decision-making in pharmaceutical licensing or the regulation of genetically modified organisms. See S Röttger-Wirtz and M Eliantonio, 'From Integration to Exclusion: EU Composite Administration and Gaps in Judicial Accountability in the Authorisation of Pharmaceuticals' (2019) 10 *European Journal of Risk Regulation* 393; and R Tavares Lanceiro and M Eliantonio, 'The Genetically Modified Organisms' Regime: A Playground for Multi-Level Administration and a Nightmare for Effective Judicial Protection?' (2021) 22 *German Law Journal* 371.

[41] See generally G Gentile and O Lynskey, 'Deficient by Design? The Transnational Enforcement of the GDPR' (2022) 71 *International and Comparative Law Quarterly* 799; L Wissink, *Effective Legal Protection in Banking Supervision* (Europa Law Publishing, 2020); M Simoncini, 'Challenges of Justice in the European Banking Union: Administrative Integration and Mismatches in Jurisdiction' (2021) 40 *Yearbook of European Law* 310; M Markakis, 'Composite Procedures and Judicial Review in the Single Resolution Mechanism: Iccrea Banca' (2021) 13 *Review of European Administrative Law* 109.

[42] From a general administrative law standpoint, see, for many, M Eliantonio, 'Judicial Review in an Integrated Administration: the Case of "Composite Procedures"' (2014) 7 *Review of European Administrative Law* 65; F Brito Bastos, 'Derivative illegality in European composite administrative procedures' (2018) 55 *Common Market Law Review* 101; H Hofmann and A Türk, 'Legal Challenges in EU administrative Law by the Move to an Integrated Administration' in H Hofmann and A Türk (eds), *Legal Challenges in EU Administrative Law: Towards an Integrated Administration* (Edward Elgar, 2009). For a European constitutional law perspective, drawing on the findings of literature in European administrative law, see N Lupo, 'The Advantage of Having the First Word in the Composite European Constitution' (2018) 10 *Italian Journal of Public Law* 186.

[43] See the European Data Protection Board's Guidelines 03/2021 on the application of Article 65(1)(a) of the General Data Protection Regulation.

[44] See for instance the Opinion of AG Bobek in Joined Cases C-59/18 and C-182/18 *Italy v Council*, ECLI:EU:C:2021:812 and the Opinion of AG Campos Sánchez-Bordona in Case C-219/17 *Berlusconi*, ECLI:EU:C:2018:502.

[45] Case T-72/20 *Satabank plc v European Central Bank*, ECLI:EU:T:2023:149, para 70.

[46] See C Eckes and J Mendes, 'The right to be heard in composite administrative procedures: lost in between protection?' (2011) 36 *European Law Review* 665; and S Alonso de León n 1, 235–38.

detours',[47] that it offers individuals insufficient judicial protection;[48] and either 'stubbornly' fails to ensure individuals' rights,[49] or adopts 'baroque' or 'artificial' solutions to do so.[50]

This book begs to differ. The CJEU's case law on composite decision-making is by no means flawless. Indeed, the CJEU's rulings expose alarming rule of law fissures. De facto, Union law now allows national authorities operating in most of the Union's composite procedures to evade judicial control when they violate national administrative law. Indeed, the principle of unitary judicial control in practice makes the CJEU competent to review the contribution of Union as well as national authorities within a composite procedure, yet the CJEU lacks the jurisdiction to enforce the national laws that apply to the latter's decision-making processes.[51] Nevertheless, even considering such weaknesses, the CJEU has often been unfairly criticised. The literature's starting point in approaching the CJEU's case law has tended to be distorted by misplaced expectations and imprecise assumptions – as argued below and further explained throughout the book's argument.

A. Misplaced Expectations

First, it should be stressed that no jurist is immune to preconceptions that result from her upbringing in a concrete national legal culture – to the 'touch of stateness', as described above. The founding 'jurist-fathers' of the European Union were certainly not immune, either. It is telling that it was specifically *German* federalist lawyers who, looking into the textual emptiness of the Treaties, advanced the view – successfully – that the Treaties had self-evidently adopted the *German* model. That view did not escape the criticism of contemporary colleagues and countrymen.[52]

Similarly, doctrinal analysis in European administrative law, including on composite decision-making, has often been influenced by an expectation that Union law will ensure individual rights and judicial control as effectively and in a similar manner to national laws. This expectation is often unspoken, but occasionally explicit. Gaztea's contention that judicial review should in principle

[47] HP Nehl, *Principles of Administrative Procedure in EC Law* (Hart Publishing, 1999), 79.

[48] See G della Cananea, n 39, 198; L Maeso Seco, 'I Procedimenti Composti Comunitari: Riflessioni Intorno alla Problematica della Impossibilità a Difendersi ed Eventuali Alternative' in G della Cananea and M Gnes (eds), *I Procedimenti Amministrativi dell'Unione Europea. Un'Indagine* (Giappichelli, 2004), 12 and 29; and B Giorgio Mattarella, 'Procedimenti e Atti Amministrativi' in M Chiti (ed), *Diritto Amministrativo Europeo* (Giuffrè, 2013), 338.

[49] HP Nehl, n 47, 78.

[50] S Cassese, 'European Administrative Proceedings' (2004–2005) 68 *Law and Contemporary Problems* 21, 31 and S Alonso de León, n 1, 227.

[51] See Chapter 9, section V.

[52] One critical view can be found in HP Ipsen, 'Deutsche Verwaltung und europäische Wirtschaftsintegration' (1968) 21 *Die Öffentliche Verwaltung* 441.

only take place after the *final decision* of a composite administrative procedure has been taken, *because* this is so in several national administrative law systems, provides a case in point.[53] However, European administrative law is not a defective version of national administrative law. For better and often for worse, it is concretised constitutional law *of the European Union*, a polity fundamentally different from a state. The Union's constitutional law, and logically its administrative law, reflect normative choices that would be alien to strictly national constitutional laws.[54]

In short, when analysing the CJEU's case law on composite decision-making, legal scholarship should bear in mind that it deals with legal issues unknown to national administrative laws, in a constitutional setting that is unlike that of national constitutional law. However, the literature has rarely confronted the serious constitutional dilemmas that the CJEU has had to face and eventually overcome. Nor has it considered the merits of alternative solutions that the CJEU could have found. In essence, the constitutional dilemmas in question concerned rule of law principles in administrative decision-making, on the one hand, and the principles of European Executive Federalism, on the other. Both had emerged from the same Union constitutionalisation process that Union law scholarship often celebrates. To renounce European Executive Federalism, even if just in part, was to renounce a part of the constitutionalisation process itself.

B. A Doctrine in Bits and Pieces

The argument in this book can only *strive* to resist the touch of stateness. As with any other jurist, the Author's views will inevitably tend to skew towards his own internalised national preconceptions and expectations of what administrative law should be. The argument will seek to excavate and systematise the CJEU's case law, considering not only its contextual constitutional constraints, but also what possible alternatives it could have chosen within them.

In so doing, the argument builds on the existing literature on composite decision-making. Yet, it also disagrees with one of its most common assumptions. The fragmentary nature of the CJEU's case law will certainly give the appearance that it is inconsistent and unpredictable. However, it is submitted that the claim that the CJEU's case law is contradictory, supported by leading authors such as Alonso de León,[55] is not borne out by an attentive reading of the case law. Indeed,

[53] J Fernández Gaztea, *Cooperación Procedimental en la Unión Europea* (Tirant lo Blanch, 2020), 335.

[54] Suffice it to give two examples. In national laws, it would be odd to regulate judicial remedies in extensive detail at constitutional level – as Union law does in Article 263 TFEU, for example – instead of leaving their regime to the legislator. Union constitutional law also accepts a lowering of fundamental rights protection when necessary to ensure effectiveness and uniformity of Union legislation, which would be abhorrent from a national constitutional law standpoint (Case C-469/17 *Funke Medien NRW GmbH v Bundesrepublik Deutschland* ECLI:EU:C:2019:623, paras 30–32).

[55] See S Alonso de León, n 1, 318–19.

Alonso de León's comprehensive monograph carefully analyses distinct composite administrative procedures in distinct policy sectors. Yet it does not infer or deconstruct possible typologies of composite administrative procedures which, owing to their similar structure, raise practically identical legal issues, regardless of the policy sector to which they belong;[56] and the key to making sense of the CJEU's rulings is precisely to identify patterns of its reasoning that specifically engage with the varying structure of composite administrative procedures in terms of how they involve and allocate power between national and Union administration.

If such patterns are factored in, the CJEU's case law reveals not systemic inconsistency, but rather a fairly consistent line of reasoning, across policy areas and time. For all its undisputable analytical rigour, Nehl's 2002 pathbreaking monograph on general principles of administrative procedure in Union law overlooked the extent and implications of such consistency. The book analyses general principles of administrative law 'with particular consideration' of composite decision-making,[57] much as though it were the backdrop for such principles to be applied – rather than the source of novel, judge-made principles. However, in fairness, Nehl and Alonso de León could not have foreseen the CJEU's momentous case law after 2018. Due to litigation in the European Banking Union, new rulings pushed the crafting of such principles further and settled interpretative doubts that prior rulings had hitherto left unresolved.

In one of the first studies on the subject, della Cananea claimed that composite decision-making 'does not have its own legal framework, distinct from that of the entire universe of European administration' – that it constitutes a notion of mere 'cognitive value'.[58] This claim can no longer hold. The CJEU's case law, gradually and implicitly, created such a framework.

The basic rationale for that framework, the Unitary Protection doctrine, is that the division of composite decision-making into national and Union procedural stages cannot compromise observance of rule of law requirements. The doctrine comprises two principles which concretise this same idea, and a test to operationalise them.

The principle of unitary procedural protection requires procedural rights to be ensured throughout a composite administrative procedure, rather than separately by national and Union authorities. The principle of unitary judicial protection posits that decisions taken pursuant to a composite administrative procedure should be subject to a single, overall judicial review, rather than separately by national and Union courts (which are exclusively competent to review national and Union decision-making, respectively).

[56] S Alonso de León, n 1, 151 ff, does rightly acknowledge that defining such typologies is a difficult task, given the significant diversity of composite administrative procedures.

[57] HP Nehl, *Europäisches Verwaltungsverfahren und Gemeinschaftsverfassung. Eine Studie gemeinschaftsrechtlicher Verfahrensgrundsätze unter besonderer Berücksichtigung "mehrstufiger" Verwaltungsverfahren* (Duncker & Humblot, 2002).

[58] G della Cananea, n 39, 215.

The application of the two principles relies on the same test. That test consists in the location of decisional dominance within a composite administrative procedure – ie of the ability to define its final outcome. Indeed, even though composite administrative procedures always involve joint decision-making power, they never allocate such power equally between national and Union administration. One of the two will dominate. The ultimate responsibility to ensure that procedural rights are respected throughout the composite procedure falls to the national or Union administration, depending on which of the two exercises decisional dominance. The judicial competence for the review of the whole composite procedure falls to national courts or to the CJEU, depending on whether decisional dominance is located at the level of national or Union administration.

The Unitary Protection doctrine shows that composite decision-making is more than a mere combination of national and Union decision-making. The doctrine's two principles and test treat the national and Union procedural stages, and indeed the very functioning of the authorities involved in them, as a continuum; not as separate administrations, but as a unified whole that is more than the sum of its parts.

V. Structure of the Book

Besides this Introduction (Chapter one), the present book comprises three parts and a conclusion. Part I (Chapters two and three) explains the significance of European Executive Federalism and why its basic principles are unable to account for composite decision-making. Part II (Chapters four to six) and Part III (Chapters seven to nine) reconstitute and analyse the judicial development of the Unitary Protection doctrine – the former in terms of administrative procedural rights, the latter in terms of judicial control. The Conclusion (Chapter ten) summarises the findings and reflects upon the higher-level implications of the Unitary Protection doctrine.

Chapter two sets out the doctrinal structure and – largely still uncharted – origins of European Executive Federalism. Its principles, which aim to preserve a dual separation between national and Union administration, have deep roots in early federal conceptions of European integration. Such principles, though applicable in other cases, have been abandoned (and replaced) in composite decision-making. The supposed constitutional status of European Executive Federalism may explain why its dualistic logic was so reluctantly abandoned by the CJEU in cases concerning procedural rights and only makes it more striking that such a logic was never applied in cases concerning judicial review.

Chapter three outlines the concept and structure of composite decision-making. The chapter further distinguishes composite decision-making from other realities within the Union's system of multilevel administration, with which it tends to be conflated despite having very different legal implications. What sets composite administrative procedures apart is decisional interdependence, ie that certain decisions require decision-making by both national and Union administration. Yet the fact that such decisions equally require the exercise of power by national and Union administration does not mean that those administrations share power equally, or that power is equally distributed across different administrative procedures. The chapter will thus introduce the concept of decisional dominance and a typology of how composite administrative procedures arrange relations between national and Union administration. Decisional dominance, and its location within distinct types of administrative procedures, are crucial to making sense of the CJEU's case law.

Part II of the book (Chapters four, five and six) turns to the problems that composite procedures raise from the perspective of procedural rights. Chapter four explains the rise of the principle of unitary procedural protection from a theoretical standpoint. The chapter considers the role of procedural rights as rule of law requirements and sets out why they can be violated if national and Union administration are treated as strictly separate, as European Executive Federalism requires. Unitary procedural protection, in contrast, requires the observance of procedural rights throughout the administrative procedure so that individuals are not affected by its composite structure. To that end, the CJEU applies a test of decisional dominance to determine which administration is ultimately responsible for protecting procedural rights. The CJEU further requires the non-dominant administration to assist the dominant administration in discharging that burden. Chapters five and six show how this doctrinal framework applies in composite decision-making, respectively, in terms of the right to be heard and of the right to a reasoned decision. The choice of these two rights results from their particular importance in ensuring the rule of law in administrative procedures as well as from their having been the subject of extensive CJEU case law involving composite decision-making.

Part III (Chapters seven, eight and nine) concerns the rise of a principle of unitary judicial protection. Like Part II, Part III begins by first offering a theoretical account of that principle and its role within the Union's rule of law. The aim of unitary judicial protection – or the 'concept of a single judicial review', in the CJEU's words – is that individuals enjoy effective judicial protection despite the fact that the EU's judicial system is meant for situations where national and Union administration decide separately, rather than jointly. To allocate judicial jurisdiction to national or Union courts, the CJEU applies the same basic test of decisional dominance as in the observance of administrative procedural rights. Chapters eight and nine consider the application of unitary judicial protection and decisional dominance in the domain of bottom-up composite procedures, ie where national authorities help to prepare a final decision at Union level. Judicial review has proven remarkably complex and sensitive in composite procedures of this structure. Chapters eight and nine consider the *Borelli* and *Berlusconi* doctrines, respectively. The former applies when decisional dominance lies with the national administration; the latter, when it lies with the Union's.

Chapter ten concludes the book's argument by summarising the Unitary Protection doctrine and its differences from the principles of European Executive Federalism. However, the concluding analysis will also step back from purely doctrinal issues. The CJEU's case law has profound implications from conceptual, political and constitutional standpoints. Said case law represents a choice to tear down jurisdictional divides between national and Union administration whenever necessary to preserve rule of law requirements. Whenever national and Union administration decide separately, such requirements are still well-served by the old principles of European Executive Federalism, to this day. Whenever national and Union administration decide jointly, rule of law requirements are observed through the principles of the Unitary Protection doctrine. In short, Union law today rests upon two parallel models of administrative law. One is federal and revolves around separation between national and Union powers. The other is post-federal. It is a model of administrative law based on a conception of unity between national and Union administration and on the insight that either may exercise dominance in Union decision-making processes.

PART I

European Executive Federalism and the Challenge of Composite Decision-Making

2

The Judicial Crafting of European Executive Federalism

I. Introduction: In the Beginning, there were Lawyers

The rule of law issues posed by composite administrative procedures emerge from their tension with European Executive Federalism, the basic EU law doctrine on the division and relations between national and Union authorities. This chapter will map the structure of European Executive Federalism and the process by which it emerged in Union case law not just as a legal, but as a *constitutional* doctrine that the CJEU gradually came to abandon in composite decision-making.

Section II begins by explaining what is generally intended with the model of 'European Executive Federalism' and why that model is only partly regulated in its explicit legal basis, Article 291 TFEU. Sections III and IV situate the rise of the doctrine of European Executive Federalism in the political and institutional context of the early decades of European integration. The CJEU has crafted such a doctrine since the Union's foundational period, in a manner woven with the Treaties' ongoing constitutionalisation process. Its key principles reflected the conception, shared by many lawyers in the Community institutions and Treaty drafters, that European integration was federal in nature. They conceived of national and Union power as independent from one another, and of the Commission in particular as an authority primarily meant to coordinate national authorities rather than to deal with individuals or firms. Section V considers how the CJEU began, around this same period, to develop the basic principles of European Executive Federalism. Those principles require (i) national and Union administrative powers to be reviewed separately by national and Union courts, (ii) that said powers be preserved as strictly separate from one another, and (iii) that national and Union authorities assist each other in the exercise of their own, respective powers. The CJEU presented such principles as flowing immediately from the Treaties – ie as components of a constitutional doctrine. Section VI provides a clearer overview of the doctrinal structure of European Executive Federalism in light of the CJEU's historical case law and sets out the linkages between that case law and the federalist and neofunctionalist thought of many influential actors, such as Commission President Walter Hallstein and leading CJEU judges. Section VII concludes the chapter with some reflections on the significance, paradoxes, and limitations of European Executive Federalism.

Crucially, European Executive Federalism constitutes a doctrine the core principles of which *presume* decisional power to be exercised by national and Union administration in a strictly separate manner. As subsequent chapters will illustrate, this assumption cannot apply to composite decision-making. Indeed, later case law was characterised by a tension between the CJEU's historical commitment to European Executive Federalism, on the one hand, and, on the other, its recognition that the unique nature of composite administrative procedures required the crafting of novel principles of administrative law.

II. The Lisbon Iceberg: Article 291 TFEU

The phrase 'Executive Federalism' conjures different meanings. This book does not use the phrase in the sense used by Habermas to denote how the European Union's political process is dominated by members of national executives – especially the Council.[1] The book concerns 'Executive Federalism' exclusively in the sense used in European administrative law, ie the EU's characteristic decentralised model of administrative enforcement.

In a nutshell, 'European Executive Federalism' tends to be associated with the two following notions. First, the legislative competences exercised by the Union – ie its competence to make policy and enshrine it in ordinary legislation – are not coextensive with its competences of administrative enforcement. The vast powers of the European Parliament and of the Council to legislate on matters ranging from the internal market to environmental law do not correlate with similarly vast powers of the European Commission to enforce legislation through individual administrative decisions.[2] This represents a significant difference from other composite political systems, such as the United States of America, where enforcement of federal legislation falls to the federal administration.[3] Under the anti-commandeering doctrine, 'the Federal Government may neither issue directives requiring the States to address particular problems, nor command the States' officers … to administer or enforce a federal regulatory program'.[4] All Congress may do is to make federal funding to States conditional upon implementation of

[1] J Habermas, *Zur Verfassung Europas: ein Essay* (Suhrkamp, 2011).

[2] Indeed, one should recall that, given the fragmented structure of European executive power, no body exists in the European Union – not even the European Commission – that can claim the role of acting as a supreme, comprehensive European government. See D Curtin, 'Challenging Executive Dominance in European Democracy' (2014) 77 *Modern Law Review* 1, 6.

[3] R Schütze, *European Constitutional Law* (2nd edn, Cambridge University Press, 2016), 327.

[4] *Printz v United States*, 521 US 898, 935 (1997).

federal legislation or to threaten to pre-empt regulation in a given policy field if States do not willingly follow federal standards.[5]

Second, it is not simply that the Member States' administrations are required to implement Union law. Rather, the implementation of Union law is *primarily* a matter for the national authorities, acting in accordance with their own national law,[6] and only exceptionally a matter for the Union's own administration. Such decentralised enforcement, long recognised as a key distinctive feature of European Executive Federalism,[7] is perhaps the aspect in which it most obviously resembles *German* Executive Federalism (*Vollzugsföderalismus*), upon which it is modelled.[8]

Until Lisbon, the Treaties historically lacked any explicit constitutional framework for public administration. Today, as Schütze writes, Article 291 TFEU 'confirms and constitutionalizes the decentralized application of European law by the Member States – and with it the idea of executive federalism'.[9] The case law of the CJEU since 2009, when the provision entered into force, has emphasised the central role of national administrations, and the fact that their closeness to local realities makes them far better placed than the Commission to carry out many EU policies, such as the Common Agricultural Policy.[10] In contrast, the CJEU has held that, while the Commission's powers may include the discretion to take 'all the measures which are necessary or appropriate' to enforce Union legislation,[11] the circumstances in which such powers may be delegated at all are limited.[12] Article 291 TFEU *does* textually recognise that the Commission may be endowed with implementing powers 'where uniform conditions for implementing legally binding Union acts are needed'. However, what it does *not* say, as the Court repeatedly states, and as some of its members appear to suggest,[13] is that the Commission

[5] J Bulman-Polzen, 'Federalism as a Safeguard of the Separation of Powers' (2012) 112 *Columbia Law Review* 472, 473.

[6] R Schütze, 'From Rome to Lisbon: "Executive Federalism" in the (New) European Union' (2010) 47 *Common Market Law Review* 1385, 1405–06 and M Chamon, 'Institutional Balance and Community Method in the Implementation of EU Legislation Following the Lisbon Treaty' (2016) 53 *Common Market Law Review* 1501, 1505.

[7] T von Danwitz, *Europäisches Verwaltungsrecht* (Springer, 2008), 307. See also S Kadelbach, 'European Administrative Law and the Law of a Europeanized Administration' in C Joerges and R Dehousse (eds), *Good Governance in Europe's Integrated Market* (Oxford University Press, 2002); Jacques Ziller, 'Multilevel Governance and Executive Federalism: Comparing Germany and the European Union' in P Birkinshaw and M Varney (eds), *The European Union Legal Order after Lisbon* (Wolters Kluwer, 2010), 270.

[8] See U Stelkens, 'Art. 291 AEUV, das Unionsverwaltungsrecht und die Verwaltungsautonomie der Mitglied-staaten – zugleich zur Abgrenzung der Anwendungsbereiche von Art. 290 und Art. 291 AEUV' (2012) 47 *Europarecht* 511, 540.

[9] R Schütze, n 6, 1397–98.

[10] See Case T-384/14 *Italian Republic v European Commission*, ECLI:EU:T:2016:298, para 32 and the case law quoted there.

[11] Case C-65/13 *European Parliament v European Commission*, ECLI:EU:C: 2014:2289 paras 43–44.

[12] Case C-521/15 *Kingdom of Spain v Council of the European Union*, ECLI:EU:C:2017:982 para 47.

[13] This is partly illustrated by the writings of individual judges in extrajudicial capacity. See T von Danwitz, n 7, 316.

may receive those powers 'only' when such a need for uniformity arises.[14] The classic view that the Commission's exercise of administrative powers is the exception in respect of a rule of national enforcement seems still to inform the CJEU's interpretation of Article 291 TFEU.

Nevertheless, the regime brought about by Article 291 TFEU is elusive in its simplicity – it is, so to say, the tip of an iceberg. Some have noted that its wording is unhelpful in addressing many fundamental questions, such as where bodies not foreseen by the Treaties, such as EU Agencies, fit into the EU's administrative system.[15] But the laconic account of the division of administrative labour between Union and national authorities is problematic as well. Crucially, and notwithstanding the importance of decentralised enforcement, Article 291 does not exhaust all aspects of the doctrine of European Executive Federalism that emerged in the Court of Justice's case law over half a century. That doctrine gradually began its development in a time of deep, complex tensions between competing historical justifications for decentralised administration: the federalist reading of the Treaties, on the one hand, and the Member State's desire to preserve 'administrative sovereignty' over national bureaucracies and its laws against Union interference, on the other.[16]

III. The Original Treaties and the Federal Administrative System

The Treaty of Rome was born in the aftermath and largely shaped by the failure of the European Political Community (EPC) Treaty in 1954. Among others, one of the key reasons for the Treaty's defeat, in the French *Assemblée Nationale*, was that the EPC would have instituted a European Executive Council with far-reaching powers.[17]

The European Executive Council would have coordinated and supervised a multitude of European 'specialised' administrative agencies established 'in the European public interest'.[18] The Community's legislature enjoyed a large degree of discretion in shaping the federal administration.[19] Article 88(1) of the EPC

[14] Cases C-427/12 *European Commission v European Parliament and Council*, ECLI:EU:C:2014:170, para 34 and C-146/13, *Kingdom of Spain v European Parliament and Council*, ECLI:EU:C:2015:298, para 77.

[15] A point also made by A Volpato, 'Controlling the Invisible Accountability Issues in the Exercise of Implementing Powers by EU Agencies and in Harmonised Standardisation' (2019) 12 *Review of European Administrative Law* 75.

[16] D Curtin and M Egeberg, 'Tradition and innovation: Europe's accumulated executive order' (2008) 31 *West European Politics* 649.

[17] R Griffiths and A Milward, *The Beyen Plan and the European Political Community*, EUI Working Paper 85/199 (1985).

[18] See Article 43 of the EPC Treaty.

[19] See Article 88(4) EPC.

Treaty provided: 'the Community may set up, or sponsor the creation of, administrative bodies, institutions, public services or services in the European public interest, or self-governing and financially independent organizations, centralized or decentralized'. In addition, the Executive Council would even have enjoyed the option of making use of already existing (national) administrative services in order to pursue the Community's aims.[20] The EPC Treaty thus reflected the consensus of its drafters that 'the question of federal execution should be ruled by the Community itself'.[21]

The Treaty of Rome, by contrast, seemed to abandon any ambitions for a powerful European Executive. Indeed, the EEC Treaty was practically silent on administrative matters. The few provisions it *did* entail were aimed at containing the Community's own administration. One member of the Treaty's *groupe de rédaction* reported that the position of the Executive had been 'the most sensitive question' haunting the drafting of the Treaty.[22] Protective of their sovereignty, the Member States wanted to avoid an overly powerful European administration. Unlike the EPC Treaty, the Treaty of Rome did not contain any provisions allowing the Community to establish its own administrative bodies, or to create its own administrative laws.

The Member States' reluctance to empower the Commission becomes apparent not only from the provisions of the EEC Treaty themselves, but also from the political dynamics of the early years of the EEC's functioning.[23] Though the scope of the EEC's legislative competences was far wider than that of the European Coal and Steel Community, formed in 1951, the Commission's administrative powers were far more limited than those of the ECSC's High Authority.[24] Competition policy one of very few areas where the EEC Treaty explicitly did grant such powers to the Commission.[25] According to the Treaty, any other administrative decision-making powers would have to be conferred by the Council on the Commission on a case-by-case basis.[26] Moreover, even where the Commission was conferred implementing powers at all, the Member States placed their exercise under the

[20] See Article 88(3) EPC.

[21] Historical Archives of the European Union Document AH-154, *Session 2 – Onzième séance, le 6 décembre*, 1952AA/CC/SCP (2) PV 11, at 5.

[22] P Pescatore, 'Les Travaux du "groupe juridique" dans la négociation des traités de Rome' (1981) 34 *Studia Diplomatica* 159, 169.

[23] See W Loth and MT Bitsch, 'The Hallstein Commission 1958–67' in M Dumoulin (ed), *The European Commission 1958–1972: History and Memories* (Office for Official Publications of the European Communities, 2007).

[24] K Seidel, *The Process of Politics in Europe: the Rise of European Elites and Supranational Institutions* (Tauris, 2010), 68.

[25] E Chiti, 'La Costruzione del Sistema Amministrativo Europeo' in M Chiti (ed), *Diritto Amministrativo Europeo* (Giuffrè, 2013), 48–50 and S Cassese, 'La signoria comunitaria del diritto amministrativo' (2002) 12 *Rivista Italiana di Diritto Pubblico Comunitario* 291, 292–93.

[26] The Commission's powers of implementation of EC legislation had to be conferred by the Council, as provided for in Article 155, 4th indent, EEC. The provision, as Craig argues, was a 'decidedly shaky basis for the assertion of authority or autonomy' that the Commission required. See P Craig, *EU Administrative Law* (2nd edn, Oxford University Press, 2012), 112.

close supervision of committees of national experts: the comitology system.[27] The unwillingness of the Member States to empower the Commission even extended to the pettiest of its routine bureaucratic tasks, which occasionally resulted in the creation of rigid and cumbersome administrative procedures.[28]

Given the Commission's intended limited role, and given the lack of Treaty provisions not only concerning Community, but also national administration, the EEC was to operate – with few exceptions – under the normal rules of international law. It was for the Member States to define the bodies enforcing Community law at national level, the administrative procedures that they would need to follow, and the remedies that could be used against them.

Having ceded part of their sovereignty 'upstream', to the Community's legislative powers, the Member States were unwilling to renounce their sovereignty 'downstream', at the stage of administrative enforcement. By preserving their control over national administration, the Member States could remain in control of the integration process itself.[29]

The words of Andreas Donner, the Dutch judge who presided over the European Court of Justice from 1958 to 1964, are noteworthy in this regard. 'Member States', he wrote, 'have taken back with their left hand what they gave with the right one'.[30] Given such a concern of the Member States with national sovereignty, Donner criticised the Commission's federalist ambitions – with a good measure of irony, if not sarcasm. Co-opting national authorities into the EEC's own administration, as the EPC Treaty would have allowed, was off the table: 'a swift take-over of national public servants by the community would have been too exhausting even for people like Professor Hallstein and his colleagues and would certainly have seemed in bad taste to member governments'.[31]

Nevertheless, and regardless of whether or not the take-over of national authorities was his preferred option, Professor Hallstein had different views on the meaning of the Treaties' decentralised model of administration. In fact, that model actually went hand in glove with the political vision that Hallstein, as Commission President, was advancing in Brussels.

[27] CF Bergström, *Comitology: Delegation of Powers in the European Union and the Committee System* (Oxford University Press, 2005), 46 ff.

[28] One good example is Regulation 459/1968, the EEC's first antidumping regulation. Due to the 'reluctance on the part of some Member States to concede any strengthening of the Commission's role in the Community', the Regulation included certain features which can only be described as being 'somewhat bizarre' (JF Beseler and N Williams, *Anti-Dumping and Anti-Subsidy Law: The European Communities* (Sweet & Maxwell, 1986), 174). While the key decision-making powers fell to the Commission, all complaints had to be addressed to the national authorities. If the Commission received a complaint directly, it was obliged to (pointlessly) forward it back to the Member States.

[29] *Cf* S Cassese and G della Cananea, 'The Commission of the European Economic Community: the administrative ramification of its political development' (1992) 4 *Jahrbuch für europäische Verwaltungsgeschichte* 75, 79–80.

[30] A Donner, *The Role of the Lawyer in the European Communities* (Edinburgh University Press, 1968), 12–13.

[31] Ibid.

IV. Federalist 'Eurolawyers' and the Community Administration

In the first decades of European integration, one of the most powerful engines of the Union's political development was a broad, influential network of pro-integration, and indeed federalist, jurists. These 'Eurolawyers', as Vauchez names them, were often involved in the drafting of Treaties. Some later proceeded to occupy key positions in national governments or in the legal services of the Commission and the Council. Other became ECJ judges or Commissioners. Together, they crafted the legal doctrines needed to strengthen the Community's political and institutional framework.[32]

Walter Hallstein, legal academic, drafter of the Treaties and Commission President, was one such Eurolawyer. It was in the field of public administration – in the Commission's bureaucratic structure and relations to national authorities – that Hallstein first put his federalist political vision for the Community into practice.[33] Like many, in the Commission, in the Council, and in the Court, he held that the Communities' founding Treaties had set in motion an unstoppable march towards Europe's political unification in federal form. Such unification, it was claimed, was even the will of the Member States, as expressed in the Treaties' supposedly federalist aim of 'ever closer union among the peoples of Europe'.[34]

The shared belief in the federal destiny of European integration may explain why so many Eurolawyers maintained that the Treaties had founded a federal administrative system. This belief ran counter to the fact that the Treaties made no explicit mention of the Community's administrative system – let alone of its putative federal nature. That belief seems to have been especially strong among German drafters of the Treaty of Rome, which they considered to follow a model based on German executive federalism.[35] This is apparent if one considers the writings of von der Groeben and Hallstein – both of whom became Commission Members – of Ophüls, considered by some as Hallstein's 'right hand man'[36] – and of Wohlfahrt, later director of the Council's legal service and author of one of the most influential commentaries to the EEC Treaty.

[32] A Vauchez, *Brokering Europe: Euro-lawyers and the Making of a Transnational Polity* (Cambridge University Press, 2015), 24 ff.

[33] D Preda, 'Hallstein e l'amministrazione pubblica europea (1958–1967)' (2000) 8 *Storia Amministrazione Costituzione: Annale dell'Instituto per la Scienza dell'Amministrazione Pubblica* 79, 86.

[34] W Hallstein, *Die Europäische Gemeinschaft* (ECON, 1979), 36 and 364.

[35] E Noël, 'Témoignage: l'administration de la Communauté européenne dans le rétrospective d'un ancien haut fonctionnaire' (1992) *4 Jahrbuch für europäische Verwaltungsgeschichte* 145, 156. Some contemporary public lawyers were sceptical of this approach. Ipsen in particular cautioned against reading the relationship between national administrations and the Community under the Community Treaties as if the latter were the German Basic Law – *cf* HP Ipsen, 'Deutsche Verwaltung und europäische Wirtschaftsintegration' (1968) 24 *Die öffentliche Verwaltung* 441, 442.

[36] A Boerger and M Rasmussen, 'Transforming European Law: The Establishment of the Constitutional Discourse from 1950 to 1993' (2014) 10 *European Constitutional Law Review* 199, 203.

One may identify three concrete aspects in which the early Eurolawyers' conception of the Community's administration clearly drew on their broader political conception of the Community itself. The three aspects in question concern the roles of national administration, Community administration, and the nature of the relation between the two.

First, the federalist conception of European integration was not in any way based on a desire to supplant or dismantle the Member States. Rather, the emerging political order was to grow symbiotically around their existing institutions. Hallstein, for instance, held that that the Communities had 'never been conceived to make the states disappear, but as a form of Union between them'.[37] Quite the contrary, Member States were 'the pillars on which integration rests'.[38] In the drafters' views, by adopting the German model, which strongly emphasised decentralised administration,[39] the Treaties made it possible to preserve national autonomy and statehood.[40] The principle of loyal cooperation made it easier to support the idea that the role of national administration in the Community's system was of a federal nature. That principle, which still today requires national authorities to enforce Union law, was a feature that the EEC Treaty kept in practically identical terms from the defunct European Political Community Treaty. For that reason, Ophüls held, the EEC Treaty recovered the EPC's federal model, which, 'as has long been the case in German federal law, in essence leaves [the execution of Community law] to the administration of the Member States'.[41]

A second aspect concerned the role of Community administration. In the founding years of the Community, federalist and neofunctionalist ideas coexisted in a continuum. For the neofunctionalists, European integration was to be incremental and technical – 'some kind of federalism by instalments'.[42] Continual cooperation between Community and national officials was considered crucial. As Bignami put it, 'European integration was to be achieved through administration'.[43] Gradually, national authorities would see beyond parochial interests and embrace their new European role.[44] The Commission was shaped to

[37] W Hallstein, 'L'Évolution des Communautés Européennes' (1959) 6 *Annuaire Européen* 1, 6–7.

[38] See the speeches reproduced and the analysis in M Schönwald, 'Hallstein and the "Empty Chair" Crisis 1965/66' in W Loth (ed), *Crises and Compromises: the European Project 1963–1969* (Nomos, 2001), 159.

[39] E Wohlfahrt, U Everling, HJ Glaesner and R Sprung (eds), *Die Europäische Wirtschaftsgemeinschaft, Kommentar zum Vertrag* (Vahlen, 1960), 12 and 517.

[40] W Hallstein, n 34, 61–62 and 376–77.

[41] CF Ophüls, 'Zur ideengeschichtlichen Herkunft der Gemeinschaftsverfassung' in E von Caemmerer et al (eds), *Festschrift Walter Hallstein* (Vittorio Klostermann, 1966), 404.

[42] J White, 'The Neofunctionalists and the Hallstein EEC Commission' (2003) 9 *Journal of European Integration History* 111, 114 and 120.

[43] F Bignami, 'Three Generations of Participation Rights before the European Commission' (2004–2005) 68 *Law and Contemporary Problems* 61, 61. Evocatively, some have conceptualised the functionalist vision as one of a 'Europe of Offices'. See L van Middelaar, *The Passage to Europe: how a Continent became a Union* (Yale University Press, 2013), 2–3.

[44] See also W Hallstein, *Die echten Probleme der europäischen Integration* (Kieler Vorträge, 1965), 10–11.

become a 'great administration' and future federal government.[45] Its intended role under the Treaties, however, was understood quite differently from the constitutional role of other federal governments. In the United States, States cannot be compelled to enforce Congressional legislation – as a Supreme Court opinion reads, 'the Framers explicitly chose a Constitution that confers upon Congress the power to regulate individuals, not States'.[46] The Commission's intended role was the exact opposite. As a rule, the Commission was not to exercise powers directly over individuals or firms, but rather to supervise the national administrations that did.[47] It was intended to function not as administration for citizens, but as an 'administration for administrations' – as a *second-order* administration.[48]

Lastly, how the early Eurolawyers conceived of relations between national and Community administration was shaped by their broader conceptions of the Community institutions' constitutional status. Without effective powers, independent from the Member States, the Community's institutions would be unable to lead the integration process. Without such independence, the Commission in particular would be unable to secure an institutional position in respect of national administrations sufficiently robust to realistically expect their cooperation.[49] One doctrinal view, shared by German lawyers in the Community institutions – including Hallstein – offered an answer.[50] The view was that, precisely as in a federal state, the Member States had transferred their powers, *along with said powers' sovereign character*, to the Community institutions.[51] Consequently, the Treaties instituted an order constituted by two independent spheres of power: the sphere of the Member States, sovereign in its origin, and the sphere of the Community's institutions, sovereign within the scope of its received competences. The Community was structured to create an 'immediately binding order' at European level, while allowing the Member States to continue as such – a dual structure which, in Hallstein's view, mirrored 'the essence of the federation'.[52] For the Community administrative system, the

[45] E Noël, n 35, 152 and 'Comment fonctionnent les Institutions de la Communauté Économique Européenne' (1963) 5 *Revue du Marché Commun* 14; and K Seidel, n 24, 69.

[46] *New York v United States*, 505 US 144 (1992).

[47] S Cassese and G della Cananea, n 29, 79–80 and 89; E Noël, n 35, 157; and CF Ophüls n 41, 405.

[48] The notion of the 'second-order' character of Union administration draws on an expression, perhaps imperfectly translated from Italian ('second grade' administration, presumably from *di secondo grado*), found in S Cassese, 'Divided Powers: European administration and national bureaucracies' in S Cassese (ed), *The European Administration/L'Administration Européenne* (International Institute of Administrative Sciences/European Institute of Public Administration, 1987), 10.

[49] E Noël, n 35, 152 and 156; and D Preda, n 33, 86–87.

[50] See, for instance, CF Ophüls, 'La Relance Européenne' (1958) 4 *Annuaire Européen* 3, 11 and H von der Groeben, *The European Community: the formative years: the struggle to establish the Common Market and the Political Union (1958–66)* (Office for Official Publications of the European Communities, 1987), 26.

[51] W Hallstein, n 34, 41 and W Hallstein, 'Zu den Grundlagen und Verfassungsprinzipien der Europäischen Gemeinschaften' in W Hallstein and H-J Schlochauer (eds), *Zur Integration Europas. Festschrift für Carl Friedrich Ophüls* (Müller, 1965), 15.

[52] W Hallstein, n 34, 365.

duality of Community and Member State power translated to the Community administration's discretion to exercise independent powers which coexisted with the power of national authorities in a federal, dualistic scheme.

In conclusion, federal conceptions of European integration were ubiquitous in the early years of European integration. Such conceptions were widely shared within the 'Eurolawyer' community, in academic commentary,[53] and in the Commission's own legal service, which exerted a profound influence on how the CJEU interpreted the Treaties.[54] While the secrecy of ECJ deliberations – and the difficulty of reconstituting the contents of judges' bookshelves half a century ago – makes it impossible to find 'smoking gun' evidence, it is extremely likely that the CJEU also drew on such views. The CJEU's case law certainly does appear to reflect that it did.

V. European Executive Federalism and the Discreet Administrative Dimension of the European Constitutionalisation Process

Hallstein was not the only federalist at the helm of the Commission. Even after him, 'Mansholt and Rey were openly pursuing federalist objectives'.[55] It can be assumed that the vision of executive federalism endorsed by the Hallstein Commission was passed down through the decades.

However, while the Commission was beginning to define its place in the European integration process, the Court of Justice was busy at work. In Luxembourg, the founding Treaties were undergoing a process of judicial constitutionalisation.[56] Well-known as it may be, the EU's constitutionalisation process entailed an administrative side that has tended not to draw as much attention. The Court of Justice gradually crafted a doctrine of European Executive Federalism; a constitutional doctrine that revolved around a divide between the powers of the Union and its Member States.

That process began with the *Humblet* ruling of 1960. Humblet, an official of the ECSC, challenged before the ECJ a decision of the Belgian tax administration which supposedly violated the Protocol on the Privileges and Immunities of the ESCS. While the Court dismissed the application, the *Humblet* ruling came to define two fundamental principles. So fundamental are those principles, that most EU lawyers today would probably deem them too obvious to state.

[53] A Boerger and M Rasmussen, n 36, 201.

[54] A Vauchez, n 32, 29 ff and M Rasmussen, 'Revolutionizing European law: A history of the *Van Gend en Loos* judgment' (2014) 12 *International Journal of Constitutional Law* 136.

[55] H von der Groeben, n 59, 31.

[56] F Mancini, 'The Making of a Constitution for Europe' (1989) 26 *Common Market Law Review* 595; K Lenaerts, 'Constitutionalism and the Many Faces of Federalism' (1990) 38 *American Journal of Comparative Law* 205, 208 ff; and J Weiler, 'The Transformation of Europe' (1991) 100 *Yale Law Journal* 2403, 2413.

First, the Court of Justice held that the ECSC Treaty was based on 'the principle of a strict separation of the powers of the Community institutions and those of the authorities of the Member States'.[57] Even though the issue was of no relevance to the case, it added that the High Authority of the ECSC had no power to annul or revoke national decisions.

Second, the *Humblet* ruling held that such a line of reasoning also applied to the Court of Justice itself. The Court could not annul national measures. Only national courts could do so. The reason is the second principle set out in *Humblet*: the 'principle of the strict separation between the powers of the Court on the one hand and of the national courts on the other'.[58]

The following subsections consider the two distinct aspects of *Humblet* – judicial competences strictly separated between national and Community courts; and decisional powers strictly separated between national and Community administration. Both principles have been further developed in the case law over time and joined by a third – the principle of loyal cooperation between the two levels of administration.

A. Double Exclusivity

Humblet provided the Court of Justice with a first opportunity to clarify that a 'strict separation' existed not only between the powers of national and Union administration, but between the jurisdiction of national and Union courts as well. In order to avoid confusion between the two, the term *principle of separation* will be reserved for the former, whereas the latter will be referred to as the *principle of double exclusivity*. Double exclusivity has been a term aptly proposed by some scholars, such as Marchetti, to allude to the fact that national and Union courts each exercise exclusive jurisdiction in reviewing national and Union action respectively.[59]

Even though it applies beyond the domain of administration, the clear-cut separation between national and Union judiciaries is an integral part of European Executive Federalism.[60] Double exclusivity largely developed in the interstices of the divide between national and Union administration. The case law, as well as individual members of the Court, consider double exclusivity to reflect that divide.[61]

[57] Case 6/60 *Humblet v Belgian State*, ECLI:EU:C:1960:48.

[58] Ibid.

[59] B Marchetti, 'Il Sistema Integrato di Tutela' in L de Lucia and B Marchetti (eds), *L'Amministrazione Europea e le sue Regole* (Il Mulino, 2015), 198.

[60] *Cf* M Eliantonio, 'Judicial Review in an Integrated Administration: the Case of "Composite Procedures"' (2014) 7 *Review of European Administrative Law* 65, 96.

[61] See Cases T-93/95 *Laga v European Commission*, ECLI:EU:T:1998:22, para 33 ff and T-94/95 *Landuyt v European Commission*, ECLI:EU:T:1998:23, paras 33 ff. See also T von Danwitz, n 7, 612.

Often expressed as 'clear separation of functions' in preliminary rulings,[62] or 'strict separation of judiciaries' in liability cases,[63] the scope of double exclusivity only emerged clearly in case law spanning over many decades and far too extensive to summarise here. Chapter seven will explain that scope in detail, along with its mismatch with composite decision-making and the implications for the Union's rule of law raised by that mismatch.

B. The Separation Principle

When establishing the Union's constitutional groundwork, one of the most important early steps for the Court of Justice was to assert the principle of autonomy. The principle posits that the exercise of Union power is immune from national legal constraints. The Court clarified that national and Union law 'constitute two separate and distinct legal orders'.[64] On the one hand, the Court held that the Union constituted an entity 'composed of States, each of which *retains its own legal system*' (emphasis added).[65] On the other, the Union, too, was declared to enjoy 'its own legal system' as well as 'institutions endowed with sovereign rights'.[66] The new European institutions enjoyed 'real powers' stemming from a 'transfer of powers' by which the states had 'limited their sovereign rights'.[67] It is hard to miss the obvious similarity of this account, of the Union's legal independence and ostensibly sovereign powers, to the views of Hallstein and other early federalists.

Ever since its foundational period, the independence of the Union legal order has been linked to the independence of the power of the Union's institutions.[68]

[62] See for instance Cases C-119/05 *Ministero dell'Industria, del Commercio e dell'Artigianato v Lucchini SpA*, ECLI:EU:C:2007:434, para 43; C-220/05 *Auroux and Others v Commune de Roanne*, ECLI:EU:C:2007:31, para 25; C-341/05 *Laval un Partneri Ltd v Svenska Byggnadsarbetareförbundet and Others*, ECLI:EU:C:2007:809, para 45; C-11/07 *Eckelkamp Eckelkamp and Others v Belgische Staat*, ECLI:EU:C:2008:489, para 27; C-373/08 *Hoesch Metals and Alloys GmbH v Hauptzollamt Aachen*, ECLI:EU:C:2010:68, para 59; Joined Cases C-165/09 to C-167/09 *Stichting Natuur en Milieu and Others v College van Gedeputeerde Staten van Groningen*, ECLI:EU:C:2011:348, para 47; C-618/10 *Banco Español de Crédito SA v Calderón Camino*, ECLI:EU:C:2012:349, para 76; C-62/14 *Gauweiler and Others v Deutscher Bundestag* ECLI:EU:C:2015:400, para 15; and Joined Cases C-283/14 and C-284/14 *CM Eurologistik GmbH v Hauptzollamt Duisberg*, ECLI:EU:C:2016:57, para 44.

[63] See Case C-275/00 *European Community, represented by the European Commission v First NV*, ECLI:EU:C:2002:711, para 33. A similar idea had surfaced in an earlier judgment. See Joined Cases 12/77, 18/77 and 21/77 *Debayser SA v European Commission*, ECLI:EU:C:1978:42, para 25.

[64] Case 13/61 *Kledingverkoopbedrijf de Geus en Uitdenbogerd v Robert Bosch GmbH*, ECLI:EU:C:1962:11, at 49. See also K Tuori n 4, 53 ff.

[65] Case 33/67 *Kurrer v European Council*, ECLI:EU:C:1968:16.

[66] Case 26/62 *NV Algemene Transport- en Expeditie Onderneming van Gend en Loos v Netherlands Inland Revenue Administration*, ECLI:EU:C:1963:1.

[67] See Case 6/64 *Costa v ENEL (Ente Nazionale Energia Elettrica)*, ECLI:EU:C:1964:66. See also Cases *Van Gend en Loos*, n 66, and 14/68 *Walt Wilhelm and Others v Bundeskartellamt*, ECLI:EU:C:1969:4.

[68] See R Barents, *The Autonomy of Community Law* (Kluwer Law International, 2004), 226.

The principle of separation proclaimed in the *Humblet* ruling had already made that same link in respect to the administrative power of national and Union authorities.[69]

When the separation principle first appeared, in the *Humblet* ruling, its content appeared to be vague. The only concrete implication that the Court explicitly drew from it was that the Community's authorities could not annul or repeal national decisions. In later rulings the Court also refrained from openly referring to the principle.

Even so, the Commission itself occasionally pleaded for legal provisions on administrative enforcement to be interpreted taking into consideration 'their inspiration from a strict requirement for the separation of the Commission's powers from those of the Member States'.[70] Moreover, and despite the absence of textual references as clear as in *Humblet*, the development of an implicit separation principle can indeed be inferred form the Court's case law since the early decades of European integration. As will be shown below, that case law has consistently implied that national and Union authorities enjoy independent spheres of power that should be preserved as such.

(i) Distinct Responsibilities and Non-interference

The Court has long regarded national and Union authorities as exercising their own powers under Union law as a matter of their own responsibility. The Union administration does not answer for the illegal exercise of national administrative powers. One example of this is *FERAM*, a case concerning national certificates of origin for scrap metal, on which the High Authority of the ECSC relied to take certain decisions. The Court held that, when a

> wrongful act is committed by a national official who acts neither in accordance with orders given by the High Authority nor on behalf or in the name of that institution but in the performance of purely national duties, the wrongful act cannot be imputed to the High Authority.[71]

The same finding clearly still applies today to the Union administration (not least because the Commission is the High Authority's successor).

In *Wünsche*, delivered in 1971, the Court went a step further. Asked whether the Commission could adopt decisions confirming or revising illegal national decisions under a common agricultural policy regulation, the Court began by recalling that national and Union authorities performed 'on *their own* initiative

[69] Indeed, the *Humblet* judgment is occasionally mentioned as a precursor to the two seminal rulings of 1963 and 1964 (*Van Gend en Loos* and *Costa*). *Cf* R Barents, n 68, 423.

[70] See Case C-476/93 P *Nutral SpA v European Commission*, ECLI:EU:C:1995:401, para 6.

[71] Case 23/59 *Acciaieria Ferriera di Roma (FERAM) v High Authority of the ECSC*, ECLI:EU:C:1959:33. See also Joined Cases 46/59 and 47/59 *Meroni & Co v High Authority of the ECSC*, ECLI:EU:C:1962:44, [1962] ECR 411, 421–22.

their duties under Community law' (emphasis added). Consequently, it held that 'since the validity of such decisions does not depend on the view taken thereof by the Commission' the latter has no power to validate or rectify 'errors which the national authorities may commit'.[72]

The CJEU has held since the 1970s that the Commission, in principle, may not send binding instructions to national authorities. In *Société des Grands Moulins des Antilles*,[73] the applicant brought actions to the Court of Justice, demanding that the Commission pay agricultural aid that it claimed was owed by the French authorities. However, the Court held that the Commission *could not* be held liable, as under the applicable regulation 'only the Member States, and not the Community, [had] authority to pay the sums in question'.[74] As the 'requisite powers' to decide on payments were exclusively those of national administration, it was not for the Commission to substitute itself for national authorities in their exercise or for the Court of Justice to review them.[75]

A similar ruling followed in *Société pour l'Exportation des Sucres*. The Court emphasised that a given regulation 'entrusted the administration of the rules concerned to the Member States and gave them a wide discretion, making them responsible for [a] decision' adopted in exercise of that administration.[76] For that reason, the Commission could not be responsible for an 'independent decision' taken by a national authority that had merely received its non-binding advice.[77] To this day, national authorities bear 'sole and entire responsibility' for their decisions, even where they act by following information shared by the Union administration.[78]

(ii) Conferred Union Powers versus Residuary National Powers

Other lines of case law applied the logic of separateness by emphasising that decision-making power was exercised *either* by national *or* by Union bodies. In numerous rulings since the early 1970s, the Court affirmed a 'principle of law',[79] according to which the administrative procedures that national authorities follow to enforce Union law,[80] and the judicial review of said enforcement by

[72] Case 76/70 *Ludwig Wünsche & Co v Hauptzollant Ludwigshafen-Rhein*, ECLI:EU:C:1971:51, paras 9–11.

[73] Case 99/74 *Société des Grands Moulins des Antilles v European Commission*, ECLI:EU:C:1975:161.

[74] Ibid, paras 13 and 16.

[75] Ibid, paras 22–24. See also Case 96/71 *R & V Haegeman v European Commission*, ECLI:EU:C: 1972:88, paras 6–7 and 10–12.

[76] Case 132/77 *Société pour l'Exportation des Sucres SA v European Commission*, ECLI:EU:C:1978:99, para 13.

[77] See also *Debayser*, n 63.

[78] Case T-193/04 *Tillack v European Commission*, ECLI:EU:T:2006:292, para 7.

[79] Case 94/71 *Schlüter & Maack v Hauptzollamt Hamburg-Jonas*, ECLI:EU:C:1972:45, paras 10–11.

[80] Case 39/70 *Norddeutsches Vieh- und Fleischkontor v Hauptzollamt Hamburg-St Annen*, ECLI:EU: C:1971:16, para 4; 77/71 *Gervais-Danone AG v Hauptzollamt München-Mitte*, ECLI:EU:C:1971:129, para 12; *Haegeman*, n 75, para 7; 3/73 *Hessische Mehlindustrie Karl Schöttler KG v Einfuhr- und Vorratsstelle*

national courts, are both governed by national law.[81] The powers that national administration exercises cannot not be less effective than when enforcing purely domestic legislation.[82] For the rest, the choice of the national authorities competent for the enforcement of Union law is 'solely a matter for the constitutional system of each State'.[83]

The Union administration, for its part, is only subject to Union law.[84] Unless explicitly provided otherwise, the Court has held, the requisite powers to enforce Union law are exercised by national authorities.[85]

In short, the decisional powers to enforce Union legislation are dualistic – they can be either national or European. Said powers will be national unless Union legislation states otherwise. In the latter case, national authorities may not interfere with the Union administration's enforcement powers.[86]

Though they initially emerged in the context of the earlier policy areas of Union law, such as the common agricultural policy, it is striking how such findings resurfaced more explicitly, over time. One example is the regulation of medicines. The Court has maintained that, 'in the absence of express provision to the contrary', ie one that confers the Commission with decision-making powers, the power to adopt a given decision will fall under the remit of an 'exclusive residual competence of the Member States'.[87] In such a case, the Commission may not take a decision that would 'deprive the Member States of their *exclusive competences* … under *purely national* procedures' (emphasis added).[88]

(iii) Separate Legal Relations

One additional aspect of separation is that, according to the case law of the CJEU, the Union administration is bound by legal relations *either* to private

für Getreide und Futtermittel, ECLI:EU:C:1973:81, paras 6 ff; 230/78 *SpA Eridania-Zuccherifici nazionali v Minister of Agriculture and Forestry and Others*, ECLI:EU:C:1979:216, para 34; and Joined Cases 119/79 and 126/79 *Lippische Hauptgenossenschaft eG v Bundesanstalt für landwirtschaftliche Marktordnung*, ECLI:EU:C:1980:154, para 5.

[81] Cases 34/67 *Firma Gebrüder Lück v Hauptzollamt Köln-Rheinau*, ECLI:EU:C:1968:24 and 13/68 *SpA Salgoil v Italian Ministry of Foreign Trade*, ECLI:EU:C:1968:54, [1969] ECR 453, 463. See also Case 26/74 *Société Roquette Frères v French State*, ECLI:EU:C:1974:108, para 11.

[82] Joined Cases 66/79, 127/79 and 128/79 *Amministrazione delle finanze dello Stato v Srl Meridionale Industria Salumi and others*, ECLI:EU:C:1980:101, para 18.

[83] Joined Cases 51/71 to 54/71 *International Fruit Company NV and others v Produktschap voor groenten en fruit*, ECLI:EU:C:1971:128, para 4. See also Cases 9/74 *Casagrande v Landeshauptstadt München*, ECLI:EU:C:1974:74 and 31/78 *Bussone v Ministro dell'agricoltura e foreste*, ECLI:EU:C:1978:217.

[84] *Cf* Case 1/58 *Friedrich Stork & Cie v High Authority of the ECSC*, ECLI:EU:C:1959:4, para 4.

[85] Case 133/79 *Sucrimex SA v European Commission*, ECLI:EU:C:1980:104, para 16 and Case 217/81 *Compagnie Interagra SA v European Commission*, ECLI:EU:C:1982:222, para 8.

[86] Case 41/69 *ACF Chemiefarma NV v European Commission*, ECLI:EU:C:1970:71, paras 10–12.

[87] Case T-273/03 *Merck Sharp & Dohme Ltd and Others v European Commission*, ECLI:EU:T:2006:36, para 97. In this sense, see also Joined Cases T-74/00, T-76/00, T-83,00 to T-85/00, T-132/00, T-137/00 and T-141/00 *Artegodan GmbH and Others v European Commission*, ECLI:EU:T:2002:28, paras 143–144 and Case T-147/00 *Les Laboratoires Servier v European Commission*, ECLI:EU:T:2003:17, paras 61–62.

[88] *Merck*, n 87, para 90.

parties *or* to national authorities, depending on who the addressees of its decisions are. Most of its decisions are not taken directly in respect of individuals, but rather of national administrations. In the Court of Justice's case law, such will tend to result in a duplication of legal relations: that between the Union and national administration, on the one hand, and that between national administration and the individuals affected by its decisions, on the other.

In *Sucrimex*, the CJEU recalled that the Commission merely assisted national authorities by sending them non-binding opinions on agricultural export refunds. Those authorities, in turn, were solely competent to grant such refunds. From there, the Court of Justice concluded that the Commission's guidance 'is part of the internal co-operation between the Commission and the national bodies responsible for applying Community rules in this field' and that 'as a general rule this co-operation cannot make the Community liable to individuals'.[89] Put differently, it was not only that the Commission's guidance was not binding; such guidance constituted an exchange within a purely inter-administrative relationship between the Commission and national authorities, with individuals as mere third parties.

C. Loyal Cooperation

A divide between national and Union administration was never incompatible with cooperation between the two. In fact, the Court has long considered that 'close *cooperation* between the Member States and the Community Institutions, both performing *on their own* initiative *their duties* under Community law', went hand in hand with 'the *structure of the Community*' (emphasis added).[90]

Loyal cooperation is by no means a principle *specific* to European Executive Federalism or indeed to European administrative law. Nevertheless, it provided the Court with a normative standard from which it derived numerous specific duties for national and Union authorities.[91] National authorities must not obstruct, but indeed proactively enforce Union legislation.[92] They must set aside provisions of national law that conflict with Union legal rules.[93] National and

[89] *Sucrimex*, n 85, para 22. See also Cases *Interagra*, n 85, para 8; and 109/83 *Eurico Srl v European Commission* ECLI:EU:C:1984:321, para 20.

[90] Case 76/70 *Wünsche*, ECLI:EU:C:1971:51, para 10.

[91] See Case 78/70 *Deutsche Grammophon Gesellschaft mbH v Metro-SB-Großmärkte GmbH & Co KG*, ECLI:EU:C:1971:59, para 5 and the Opinion of AG Dutheillet de Lamothe in Case 39/70 *Norddeutsches Vieh- und Fleischkontor v Hauptzollamt Hamburg-St Annen*, ECLI:EU:C:1971:16, especially at 113 ff. In the literature, see J Temple Lang, 'Community Constitutional Law: Article 5 EEC Treaty' (1990) 27 *Common Market Law Review* 645 and J Temple Lang, 'The Duties of National Authorities under Community Constitutional Law' (1998) 23 *European Law Review* 109.

[92] Case 66/86 *Saeed Flugreisen v Zentrale zur Bekämpfung unlauteren Wettbewerbs eV*, ECLI:EU:C:1989:140.

[93] Case 103/88 *Fratelli Costanzo SpA v Comune di Milano*, ECLI:EU:C:1989:256 and Joined Cases C-171/07 and C-172/07 *Apothekerkammer des Saarlandes v Saarland and Ministerium für Justiz, Gesundheit und Soziales*, ECLI:EU:C:2009:316.

Union administrations must assist each other and exchange information in the exercise of their own competences.[94] As the Commission never had a general power to direct national authorities, the Court expects the latter to offer their cooperation spontaneously.[95] Lastly, and importantly, the Court of Justice's traditional understanding of administrative cooperation is, as mentioned before, that it exists within a relation strictly 'internal' to the national and Union bodies involved, where individuals play no role.[96]

D. The *Deutsche Milchkontor* Formula: Codification and Constitutional Status

While echoing *Humblet* and its affirmation of the separation principle, the rulings described above were delivered in a fragmentary fashion. The Court of Justice refrained from suggesting any broader, unified conception of the division of power between national and Union administration. The 1983 *Deutsche Milchkontor* ruling provided the Court of Justice with the opportunity it needed to do so and to explicitly situate administrative enforcement within the Union's general constitutional framework in the Treaties. It was in *Deutsche Milchkontor* (*DM*) that the CJEU adopted European Executive Federalism as a constitutional doctrine.

The plaintiff in the main proceedings had received financial aids for the processing of skimmed milk powder. The national authority deciding on the granting of those aids, the German Federal Office for Food and Forestry, had found that the beneficiary had not processed the powder in accordance with the applicable Union rules. It therefore demanded repayment of the aid even though, under Germany's general provisions on administrative law, the conditions were not met for the decision granting aid to be withdrawn. The preliminary questions submitted by the referring German court, in essence, concerned whether the general rules of the German Administrative Procedure Act applied in full to cases involving Union law or, instead, needed to be adapted in such cases. The CJEU could have simply based the answer on the rather technical rules on milk powder. Instead, it thought fit to draw the answer from general arguments of a constitutional nature. The Court declared that:

> According to the general principles on which the institutional system of the Community is based and which govern the relations between the Community and the Member

[94] D Curtin and I Dekker, 'The Constitutional Structure of the European Union: Some Reflections on Vertical Unity-in-Diversity' in P Beaumont, C Lyons, and N Walker (eds), *Convergence and Divergence in European Public Law* (Hart Publishing, 2002), 70.

[95] *Cf* DU Galetta, 'Coamministrazione, reti di amministrazioni, *Verwaltungsverbund*: modelli organizzativi nuovi o alternative semantiche alla nozione di "cooperazione amministrativa" dell'art. 10 TCE, per definire il fenomeno dell'amministrazione intrecciata?' (2009) *Rivista Italiana di Diritto Pubblico Comunitario* 1689, 1695–95.

[96] See eg *Sucrimex*, n 85.

> States, it is for the Member States, by virtue of Article 5 of the Treaty [ie the principle of loyal cooperation], to ensure that Community regulations … are implemented within their territory.[97]

This passage of *DM* will be referred to as 'the *DM* formula'. With little variation, numerous rulings have restated it ever since. The *DM* formula, as used in such rulings, codifies and constitutionalises the implicit reading of the relations between national and Union administration that CJEU case law had only implied until 1983.

(i) Deutsche Milchkontor: *Decentralised Enforcement, Separation, and Cooperation*

Since *DM*, the CJEU has stated that, according to the Treaties' principles, in the absence of provisions stating otherwise, 'it is for the Member States … to ensure that Community regulations … are implemented within their territory'.[98] This holding has been cited on multiple occasions to restate many of the central aspects of European Executive Federalism that had been implied in the CJEU's case law hitherto.

On the one hand, *DM* reaffirms the Union's system of decentralised enforcement. The competence to enforce Union law primarily falls to national administrations. Such a competence must be exercised actively, as prescribed by the principle of loyal cooperation,[99] 'in accordance with the procedural and substantive rules of their own national law',[100] and under control of national courts.[101] In contrast, the Union administration is only competent in the exceptional cases where the Union legislator decides to delegate – typically, limited – enforcement powers.[102]

On the other hand, *DM* has reinforced the understanding that cooperation between national and Union administration exists within the context of a relation 'internal' to them. Exchanges that may occur between national and Union administration, such as Commission guidance on how certain national decisions should be taken, are of no concern to the individuals affected by such decisions.[103]

[97] Joined Cases 205/82 to 215/82 *Deutsche Milchkontor GmbH and Others v Federal Republic of Germany*, ECLI:EU:C:1983:233, para 17.

[98] See also Joined Cases 89/86 and 91/86 *L'Etoile Commerciale v European Commission*, ECLI:EU:C:1987:337, para 11.

[99] See also Cases C-366/95 *Landbrugsministeriet – EF-Direktoratet v Steff-Houlberg Export I/S*, ECLI:EU:C:1998:216, para 14 and C-298/96 *Oelmühle Hamburg AG v Bundesanstalt für Landwirtschaft und Ernährung*, ECLI:EU:C:1998:372.

[100] *Deutsche Milchkontor*, n 97, para 17.

[101] *Deutsche Milchkontor* n 97, para 17 and Joined Cases C-383/06 to C-385/06 *Vereniging Nationaal Overlegorgaan Sociale Werkvoorziening v Minister van Sociale Zaken en Werkgelegenheid*, ECLI:EU:C:2008:165, para 48.

[102] Case T-244/00 *Coillte Teoranta v European Commission*, ECLI:EU:T:2001:124, para 42. See L Azoulai, 'The Judge and the Community's Administrative Governance' in C Joerges and R Dehousse (eds), *Good Governance in Europe's Integrated Market* (Oxford University Press, 2002), 110.

[103] Case T-54/96 *Oleifici Italiani SpA v European Commission*, ECLI:EU:T:1998:204, para 51.

DM has also been cited in CJEU case law to support an interpretation of Union legislation that entrenches several aspects of the separation principle. This is striking, as the *DM* formula itself does not refer to relations between national and Union administration at all.

First, *DM* has reinforced the notion that the Union administration cannot be held accountable for the mistakes of national authorities. When the Commission is not vested with enforcement powers, such powers consequently remaining with national authorities, an 'autonomous conduct' of the latter,[104] made on the basis of their 'independent choice', cannot be 'attributed to the Commission's services'.[105]

Second, *DM* has reinforced the notion that the Union administration generally lacks the ability to interfere with, or direct, the decisions of national authorities. Similarly to the very first use of the separation principle in *Humblet*, where the Court had found that the Union administration cannot annul or repeal national authorities' decisions, the *Nutral* ruling applied the *DM* formula, as a generic expression of the 'division of powers' between the two, to further support the argument that the Commission could not suspend national administrative decisions.[106] The *Oleifici Italiani* ruling cited the *DM* formula to support, as in several rulings from the 1970s, the finding that the Commission has no power to send binding instructions to national authorities.[107]

Lastly, the most overt use of *DM* to interpret legislation in conformity with the separation principle was in *Regione Siciliana I* and *II*, two cases concerning withdrawal of EU structural funding. Indeed, the General Court derived from *DM* an explicit 'principle of the separation of legal relations' between the Commission and the Member States, on the one hand, and between the Member States and individuals, on the other.[108] Vilaça rightly notes that the emphasis on such separation, or on the 'general principles which govern the relations between the Member States and the Union', was irrelevant to the legal questions at stake – namely, whether the plaintiffs had the standing to bring actions for annulment.[109] Indeed, reading the case, it is difficult to escape the impression that the General Court simply used the discussion of fairly technical procedural issues as a chance to make a generic point on the structure of the Union's administrative system.

[104] Ibid, paras 54 and 57.

[105] Ibid, para 67.

[106] Joined Cases T-492/93 and T-492/93 R *Nutral SpA v European Commission*, ECLI:EU:T:1993:85, paras 26 and 30 (admissibility decision).

[107] *Oleifici Italiani*, n 103, para 51.

[108] Cases T-60/03 *Regione Siciliana v European Commission (Regione Siciliana II)*, ECLI:EU:T:2005:360, para 33; and T-341/02 *Regione Siciliana v European Commission (Regione Siciliana I)*, ECLI:EU:T:2004:228, para 38.

[109] In this sense, see also JL da Cruz Vilaça, 'Effective Judicial Protection with Regard to Community Funds – May One be Directly Concerned by a Decision Addressed to a Member State?' in JL da Cruz Vilaça, *EU Law and Integration: Twenty Years of Judicial Application of EU Law* (Hart Publishing, 2014), 178.

And yet, the same logic of separate legal relations has kept resurfacing ever since in rulings on standing in similar structural funds cases.[110]

(ii) Deutsche Milchkontor *and Constitutional Embeddedness*

Despite substantial continuity with prior case law, there was one aspect of *Deutsche Milchkontor* that constituted a significant development. For the first time, the Court of Justice represented the division of administrative power between national and Union authorities as *flowing directly from the Treaty* – it represented European Executive Federalism as a doctrine of constitutional rank.

It is because of the 'principles which govern the relations between the Community [read: the Union] and the Member States', and 'the institutional structure' of the Union, that the Union and the national administration must be treated as separate from one another, and that the latter is responsible for implementation unless the EU legislature decides otherwise.[111]

That European Executive Federalism is, like the German model which inspired it, a constitutional doctrine, should not obscure one key difference between the two.[112] Unlike its German relative, European Executive Federalism does not generally *require* Union legislation in discrete policy areas – such as, say, product safety – to be implemented by national or Union administration. Under Union law, the choice to allocate the responsibility for administrative decision-making either to the Union or the national level (the default option) is, and has always been, a political choice with few constraints.[113] Rather than defining how administrative power should or should not be distributed between the two levels, the implicit principles of European Executive Federalism are intended to *govern* administrative power as it is *actually* distributed. The Court has never *struck down* legislation on the grounds that national and Union administration did not exercise sufficiently separated powers. (But, then again, neither has the Court ever invalidated legislation on grounds of subsidiarity, a principle which, though also politically malleable, has never been denied to be of constitutional rank.) As the previous sections have shown, however, the Court will often rely on such a reasoning of separation or cooperation to *interpret* existing legislation. It has done so often to preserve the powers of national or Union administration against undue interference from each other and to ensure they work together effectively.

[110] See eg Case T-403/15 *JYSK sp z o.o. v European Commission*, ECLI:EU:T:2017:300, paras 28–37.

[111] See Cases 262/87 *Kingdom of the Netherlands v European Commission*, ECLI:EU:C:1989:50; C-290/91 *Peter v Hauptzollamt Regensburg*, ECLI:EU:C:1993:220, para 8; C-285/93 *Dominikanerinnen-Kloster Altenhohenau v Hauptzollamt Rosenheim*, ECLI:EU:C:1995:398, para 26; C-292/97 *Karlsson*, ECLI:EU:C:2000:202, para 27; T-166/98 *Cantina sociale di Dolianova soc coop rl v European Commission*, ECLI:EU:T:2004:337, para 66; C-495/00 *Visentin v Azienda di Stato per gli interventi nel mercato agricolo*, ECLI:EU:C:2004:180, paras 39–40; T-341/02 *Regione Siciliana I* n 108, para 59; and C-402/13, *Cypra Ltd v Kypriaki Dimokratia*, ECLI:EU:C:2014:2333, para 23.

[112] I am grateful to Professor Paul Craig for drawing my attention to this critical difference.

[113] One of few constraints is eg the Commission's powers in State aid review under the Treaties.

Even with this in mind, it may appear puzzling that in *Deutsche Milchkontor* the Court maintained that the Union's model of administration derived immediately from Treaties – that European Executive Federalism was constitutionally embedded in them. Indeed, the Treaties' text at the time did not regulate public administration at all. As will be shown below, the context of the case law may offer some explanation.

VI. The Doctrinal Structure of European Executive Federalism

Like any doctrine in law, European Executive Federalism is composed of a network of principles and legal concepts and a conception of the real-life realities that it intends to regulate. As the previous section illustrates, European Executive Federalism consists of three key principles. One of these, the separation principle, is exclusive to EU administrative law and concerns the status that national and EU authorities respectively enjoy in the European administrative order. The two other principles are 'shared' with other branches of government in the EU. The second principle – 'double exclusivity' – concerns the allocation of jurisdiction for the judicial control of the different levels of administration. The third, loyal cooperation, provides the general normative standard that is intended to guide the relations between Union and national administrations.

European Executive Federalism also includes some legal concepts. The concepts refer to the structure of Europe's administration and distinguish between *indirect administration* – ie the Member States' authorities at local, regional and state level, when enforcing Union law – and *direct administration* – ie the Union's own administration, composed of the Commission, Union Agencies, and, more rarely the EU Council.[114] The concepts of indirect and direct administration have nonetheless remained more in use within legal scholarship – in fact, often with conflicting meanings[115] – than in the Court's case law, usually in written submissions by parties or in the Opinions of Advocates General.[116] For this reason, the remainder of the analysis will instead prefer the terms 'national' and 'Union' administration.

[114] H Hofmann, G Rowe, and A Türk, *Administrative Law and Policy of the European Union* (Oxford University Press, 2011), 13.

[115] See F Brito Bastos, 'Doctrinal Methodology in EU Administrative Law: Confronting the "Touch of Stateness"' (2021) 22 *German Law Journal* 593, 610 ff.

[116] See the Opinion of AG Léger in Case C-5/94 *R v Ministry of Agriculture, Fisheries and Food, ex parte Hedley Lomas*, ECLI:EU:C:1995:193, para 93 and of AG Trstenjak in Case C-19/05 *European Commission v Kingdom of Denmark*, ECLI:EU:C:2007:418, para 61. A 'principle of indirect administration' was invoked by the Council in Case C-147/13 *Kingdom of Spain v Council*, ECLI:EU:C:2015:299, para 77.

However, from a historical point of view, the most intriguing aspect of European Executive Federalism might not be the doctrine's constitutive principles and concepts but rather the conception of administration on which it relies. It is likely because of that conception that one may understand one of the most paradoxical features of European Executive Federalism. That is the fact that the Treaties' silence on administration was interpreted as a choice for a federal administrative system.

Executive Federalism was not a self-evident reading of the Treaties. Entirely different models could have been devised. Some ambivalent Treaty provisions could have perhaps been read as the legal basis for a far more centralised system. On the one hand, Schütze contends that a much greater role could have been accorded to the Council, founded upon its harmonising competences under Article 95 EC.[117] On the other, and although such would require quite some interpretive creativity, it has been suggested that the Commission itself could have claimed a much broader competence to enforce Union law directly, by invoking its general responsibility under Article 155 EEC to ensure 'that the provisions of [the] Treaty and the measures taken by the institutions pursuant thereto are applied'.[118]

And yet, the CJEU chose to build a constitutional doctrine of decentralised, federal enforcement, based on a generic, nebulous reference to the 'general principles of the Union's institutional system'. To understand why this the case – why the CJEU concluded that European Executive Federalism flowed directly from the Treaties – one must consider the political context in which the CJEU's case law emerged.

That political context will be set out in Chapter four. The context is one where an elite of federally-minded lawyers profoundly influenced the direction of the European Institutions at their seminal stages. Such 'Eurolawyers' disseminated their federal conception of European integration either by publication or, crucially, as they circulated between positions in different European Institutions. Despite the Treaties' silence on administration, these lawyers read into their provisions a certain balance of power between the Union and the Member States that they thought was self-evident. If one considers the Court of Justice's inevitable exposure to such ideas,[119] several aspects of its case law quite plainly resonate with the political and constitutional thought of the early federalists.

First, the case law reflects a conception, advanced by the German 'Eurolawyers', of a federal dual order of power. This is visible in the separation principle, as developed in the case law, as well as in the principle of double exclusivity. Both

[117] *Cf* R Schütze, n 6, 1425.

[118] *Cf* P Craig, *UK, EU and Global Administrative Law: Foundations and Challenges* (Cambridge University Press, 2015), 391. However, as R Schütze, n 6, concedes (at 1394), the qualification 'in the manner provided for in this Treaty' would have made such an interpretation less plausible.

[119] Pescatore is often mentioned as a paradigmatic example of a federalist 'Eurolawyer' judge. For an overview of his enduring influence, see V Fritz, 'Activism on and Off the Bench: Pierre Pescatore and the Law of Integration' (2020), 57 *Common Market Law Review* 475.

rested upon an assumption that national and Union bodies do, as a matter of actual fact, exercise their own powers independently from one another.

Second, ECJ judges interpreted Article 5 EEC, enshrining the principle of loyal cooperation, as a 'provision of a federal character', because of which 'the Member States constitute, in a way, *bodies of the Community*'.[120] That characterisation is practically a word-for-word replica of how at least one federalist Treaty drafter described that same provision. Wohlfahrt and co held that Article 5 EEC transformed national administrative authorities into 'executive bodies of the Community'.[121]

Lastly, the Court's case law seems to have been influenced by the assumption, shared by many key officials, that the Commission was constitutionally intended to function as a sort of *second-order administration*. Put differently, its primary business is coordinating and managing issues pertaining to national administrations rather than first-order administrative activity – ie directly taking decisions on the individual cases of citizens and firms. One example concerns the restrictive access of individuals to the CJEU. At times, some judges appeared to relativise – if not to approve – the limited locus standi of plaintiffs, arguing that they only rarely are affected by Commission decisions, usually addressed to the Member States' governments.[122]

This reasoning is, however, also present in the case law's increasingly explicit notion of a principle of separate legal relations between the Commission and national authorities, on the one hand, and between national authorities and individuals, on the other. It is equally present in the view that cooperation between national and Union authorities is 'internal' to them and of no concern to individuals.

One will concede that it is impossible to produce any conclusive evidence of a direct influence of federalist thought in the CJEU's case law on administrative law. CJEU rulings do not cite doctrinal sources. Detailed inventories of ECJ judges' personal libraries over the decades would be exceedingly difficult to reconstitute.

One may, however, find important clues that show how federalist views influenced the judicial development of European Executive Federalism. In the relatively scarce academic commentary on the *Deutsche Milchkontor* ruling, one finds the analysis of Ulrich Everling. Everling was none other than the judge-rapporteur for that case. As a junior law professor, he had previously co-authored one of the most influential commentaries on the EEC Treaty with Treaty drafter Wohlfahrt, regarded in his time as the leading federalist jurist.[123]

[120] In the words of former ECJ judge O Due, 'Article 5 du traité CEE. Une disposition de caractère fédéral?' in F Emmert (ed), *Collected Courses of the Academy of European Law* (Martinus Nijhoff, 1991), 23.

[121] E Wohlfahrt, U Everling, HJ Glaesner and R Sprung, n 39, 12 and 517.

[122] A Donner, n 30, 74–75.

[123] HP Ipsen, 'The Relationship between the Law of the European Communities and National Law' (1966) 3 *Common Market Law Review* 379, 385.

Writing in an extrajudicial capacity, Everling claimed that the *Deutsche Milchkontor* judgment (which he had drafted) demonstrated the Union's 'federal structure'. The division of administrative power between the Union and the Member States was just one example of that structure. He further argued that the EU's decentralised model of administrative implementation had 'certainly oriented itself under the influence of the German federal experience'.[124] In short, in Everling's view, the institutional system established since the Treaty of Rome was, and remains,[125] federal in structure. And the Union's administrative system was to be understood in that light.

Principles of European Executive Federalism in CJEU case law (derived from the 'the general principles on which the institutional system of the Community is based and which govern the relations between the Community and the Member States')	**Conception of the Community and of the Community administrative system supported by federalist and neofunctionalist 'Eurolawyers'** (such as Hallstein, Ophüls, von der Groeben, Wohlfahrt, etc.)
1. Strict separation between national and Union administrative power (separation principle) • The two levels of administration are exclusively responsible and liable for the exercise of their own powers (e.g. the Union administration may generally not send binding instructions to national authorities on how to enforce Union law; the Union administration is not liable for unlawful behaviour of national authorities). • Separation of legal relations: unless Union administration is given the power to decide directly in respect of individuals, which is the exception, there are typically legal relations between individuals and national authorities, on the one hand, and between national authorities and the Union administration, on the other.	**Division of power between the Community and the Member States** • The Community is based on a federal order of power, with a dualistic overlap of Community and Member State power. • Community institutions, including the Commission, exercise powers 'independent' from interference from the Member States. • The Community administrative system is based on the German federal model: the Member States' authorities act as bodies of the Community in that they enforce Community law. • The Commission is primarily designed to decide in respect of Member States (and their authorities) rather than in respect of individuals.

(continued)

[124] U Everling, 'Zur föderalen Struktur der Europäischen Gemeinschaft' in K Heibronner, G Ress and T Stein (eds), *Staat und Volkerrechtsordnung. Festschrift für Karl Doehring* (Springer, 1989), 183 and 186–87.

[125] The former judge reiterated this view decades after *Deutsche Milchkontor*. See U Everling, 'Die Europäische Union als föderaler Zusammenschluss von Staaten und Bürgern' in A von Bogdandy and J Bast, *Europäisches Verfassungsrecht: theoretische und dogmatische Grundzüge* (Springer, 2009), 991.

(Continued)

Principles of European Executive Federalism in CJEU case law (derived from the 'the general principles on which the institutional system of the Community is based and which govern the relations between the Community and the Member States')	**Conception of the Community and of the Community administrative system supported by federalist and neofunctionalist 'Eurolawyers'** (such as Hallstein, Ophüls, von der Groeben, Wohlfahrt, etc.)
2. Strict separation between national and Union courts ('double exclusivity' principle) • National authorities are not subject to judicial review by Union courts; Union authorities are not subject to judicial review by national courts.	
3. Principle of loyal cooperation The principle itself is not exclusive to European Executive Federalism. However: • Loyal cooperation is the constitutional basis for the most important duty of national authorities under European Executive Federalism: the duty to actively enforce Union law. • Loyal cooperation shapes the relation between national and Union administration which the CJEU traditionally understood as a 'purely internal' relation of cooperation.	**Importance of administrative cooperation** • National administrations must actively enforce Community legislation, similarly to state administrations enforcing federal legislation in Germany – Particular concern of neofunctionalists: Commission has a 'pedagogical' mission of engaging national administrations. • European integration led by administration: political integration is to advance gradually through interconnected sectoral areas – emphasis on technocratic governance and cooperation

VII. Federalism with Neofunctionalist Characteristics

The early history of the European legal order has been described as 'one of federalist political and legal forces promoting, through different actors at different points in time, a particular constitutional thinking about the Treaties and the ECJ'.[126] The judicial crafting of European Executive Federalism, seem as a

[126] M Rasmussen, 'The Origins of a Legal Revolution: The Early History of the European Court of Justice' (2008) *14 Journal of European Integration History* 77, 98.

doctrine constitutionally embedded in the Treaty's 'institutional system' and 'general principles', was a process permeated by this broader political context. Its constituent principles bear striking similarity to the early Eurolawyers' mix of federalist and neofunctionalist ideals. Especially given the opinions expressed by ECJ judges writing extrajudicially, it is highly implausible that this similarity is mere coincidence.

Nevertheless, and notwithstanding its supposed constitutional status, European Executive Federalism is largely a product of the Court's own creativity. The Treaties have never been *textually* as strict in dividing national and Union judicial jurisdiction as the CJEU suggests. And the principle of strict separation between national and Union administration seems to have lacked any textual basis at all.

What is perhaps most remarkable about the judicial crafting of European Executive Federalism is that it resulted from a peculiar and even paradoxical interpretation of the Treaties. The lack of references to administration, due in part to Member States' desire to keep their administrative powers intact despite the integration process, was read as a sign that the Treaties had constitutionalised a decentralised federal administrative system. The least ambitious legal regime was interpreted as the most ambitious of political choices. The federalist administration that was read into the Treaties was a paper tiger. But a long-lived paper tiger, nonetheless.

And yet, the reality of Europe's administrative system proved far more complex than the early federalist lawyers would have imagined. The principles of European Executive Federalism, which rested upon the conception of a strictly dual order of power, soon had to coexist with an intricate and multi-layered administrative order. They were directly called into question by the rise of joint administrative decision-making, that is, of composite administrative procedures. The Court of Justice was forced to confront its historical case law, along with increasingly outdated notions of any rigid divide between national and Union authority. This was a long, complex process. As Harlow put it, 'the split-level, dual competence solutions devised by the ECJ were arguably inadequate to deal with the [emerging] problems and the ECJ was slow to face up to them'.[127]

[127] C Harlow, 'Three Phases in the Evolution of EU Administrative Law' in P Craig and G de Búrca (eds), *The Evolution of EU Law* (Oxford University Press, 2011), 450.

3

Multilevel Administration and Composite Decision-Making

I. Introduction: What Makes Composite Decision-Making So Special?

The deepening of European integration required national and Union administrations to cooperate in many different ways to enforce a growing body of legislation. A complex multilevel system began to form.

Composite administrative decision-making is only one form of multilevel administration, though it is often conflated with others. This is no wonder given that, as political scientists have noted, the literature on multilevel administration still lacks a 'differentiated analytical framework' of generalisable, cross-sectoral typologies to capture the ways in which it works.[1]

The chapter aims to contribute to filling this gap. It proposes a conceptual framework aimed at bringing greater clarity to the analysis of three crucial issues. The first issue concerns the structural features of composite decision-making. The second concerns how composite decision-making compares to other types of European multilevel administrative cooperation. The third concerns whether existing forms of multilevel administration can be reconciled with the dualistic divide of European Executive Federalism, between national and Union administration, as envisaged by the CJEU. Counterintuitively, most forms can. Composite decision-making, however, cannot.

Section II sets out the basic conceptual and contextual underpinnings of European multilevel administration. It contends that multilevel administration is too diverse to argue, as most of the literature does, that it renders the notion of separation between national and Union administration obsolete. The debate should rather refocus on whether *specific forms of cooperation* within multilevel administration contradict such a separation and on what test should be used to determine whether a contradiction exists at all. The proposed test is the CJEU's own separation principle. Section III sets out the concept, structure, rationales and types of composite decision-making and explains why it is logically incompatible with the CJEU's separation principle. The proposed typologies of

[1] A Benz, 'European Public Administration as Multilevel Administration: A conceptual Framework' in M Bauer and J Trondal (eds), *The Palgrave Handbook of the European Administrative System* (Palgrave Macmillan, 2015), 35 and 45.

composite decision-making will be applied throughout the remainder of the book's argument. Composite administrative procedures are characterised by decisional interdependence, ie they require joint decision-making between national and Union administration, and by the allocation, to one of the two levels, of decisional dominance, ie the ability to decide the procedure's final outcome. Section IV offers a typology of forms of multilevel administration from which composite decision-making should be distinguished in that they are not just compatible with, but indeed presuppose, the separation between national and Union administrative power.[2] This distinction is precisely what makes composite administrative procedures so unique. It is why the CJEU had to abandon its historical doctrine of European Executive Federalism in composite decision-making, whereas in other forms of administration it did not. Section V concludes by outlining how the mismatch between composite decision-making and European Executive Federalism raises two sets of rule of law problems – procedural and judicial. The CJEU's doctrinal answer to said problems will be considered in Parts II and III of the book, respectively.

II. The Concept(s) of Multilevel Administration

Some of ECJ Judges cautioned that the Court's principle of 'strict separation' should not be regarded as so strict after all. '[Where] the textbooks preached separation of legal powers and responsibilities', Judge Donner wrote, 'reality demonstrated that their cumulation and integration corresponded more to the facts of political life'.[3] Similarly, Pescatore cautioned that the Court's reference to a principle of 'strict' separation seemed exaggerated given the extent of cooperation between national and Community bureaucracies.[4]

Indeed, already in its early years, intense cooperation occurred across all areas under the remit of the Community's competence. The High Authority of the ECSC relied heavily on flows of information from national bodies.[5] The first antitrust enforcement Regulation required the Commission to act in 'close and constant liaison with the competent authorities of the Member States'.[6] Though

[2] The categorisation draws on an earlier and more tentative version in F Brito Bastos, 'Composite Procedures in the SSM and SRM – an Analytical Overview' in C Zilioli and KP Wojcik (eds), *Judicial Review in the European Banking Union* (Edward Elgar, 2021). The categorisation, in turn, builds upon that proposed in E Schmidt-Aßmann, 'Strukturen des Europäischen Verwaltungsrechts: Einleitende Problemskizze' in E Schmidt-Aßmann and W Hoffmann-Riem (eds), *Strukturen des Europäischen Verwaltungsrechts* (Nomos, 1999), 9.

[3] A Donner, *The Role of the Lawyer in the European Communities* (Northwestern University Press 1968) 14.

[4] P Pescatore, 'Distribución de competencias y de poderes entre los estados miembros y las comunidades europeas' (1967), 1 *Derecho de la Integración* 108, 111.

[5] E Reuter, 'L'engagement général de coopération des Etats Membres avec la Haute Autorité et les nécessités de contrôle dans le domaine des prix' (1966) *Cahiers de Droit Européen* 52.

[6] Council Regulation (EEC) 17/1962 of 6 February 1962: First Regulation implementing Articles 85 and 86 of the Treaty, Recital (7).

based on a 'rather rigid division of power between the national authorities and the Commission', the first anti-dumping Regulation 'worked out in practice through a spirit of cooperation'.[7] Lastly, some authors writing on the cooperative administration of the Common Agricultural Policy noted that 'nothing would be more inaccurate than conceiving the relations between the Communities and their members in accordance to a scheme of dualistic inspiration'.[8]

Fifty years later, many scholars would subscribe to similar views. Yet, even the terminology of cooperative enforcement remains unsettled. Many legal scholars have opted for terms such as 'shared government';[9] 'coadministration';[10] 'intertwined administration';[11] 'shared administration';[12] 'integrated administration';[13] 'composite administration';[14] or 'shared management'.[15] Political science literature, by contrast, has tended to locate cooperative administration in theories of 'multilevel administration' or 'multilevel governance'.[16] Whereas both have the virtue of emphasising the involvement of subnational authorities,[17] 'multilevel governance' proves less analytically appropriate. Rather than researching the dynamics specific to administrative *policy implementation*, the proponents

[7] I van Bael, 'The EEC Anti-dumping Rules – A practical approach' (1978) 12 *International Lawyer* 523, 530.

[8] JM Martinière, *Collaboration entre l'ordre juridique communautaire et les ordres juridiques nationaux dans le secteur de l'agriculture: rapport français présenté à la Commission I (Agriculture) du Vième congrès international de droit européen* (Fédération Internationale Pour Le Droit Européen (FIDE), 1970) 10.

[9] R Widdershoven, 'European Administrative Law' in R Seerden (ed), *Administrative Law of the European Union, its Member States and the United States* (Intersentia, 2012), 245 and 250.

[10] C Franchini, *Amministrazione Italiana e Amministrazione Comunitaria. La Coamministrazione nei Settori di Interesse Comunitario* (CEDAM, 1993).

[11] P Chirulli, 'Amministrazioni Nazionali ed Esecuzione del Diritto Europeo' in L de Lucia and B Marchetti (eds), *L'Amministrazione Europea e le sue Regole*, (Il Mulino, 2015), 167 and J Ziller, 'Multilevel Governance and Executive Federalism: Comparing Germany and the European Union' in P Birkinshaw and M Varney (eds), *The European Union Legal Order after Lisbon* (Wolters Kluwer, 2010) 257–75, 257.

[12] C Harlow, 'Three Phases in the Evolution of EU Administrative Law' in P Craig and G de Búrca (eds), *The Evolution of EU Law* (Oxford University Press, 2011), 450.

[13] H Hofmann and A Türk, 'The Development of Integrated Administration in the EU Consequences' (2007) 13 *European Law Journal* 253, 253–54.

[14] D Curtin, *Executive Power in the European Union: Law, Practices, and the Living Constitution* (Oxford University Press, 2009) 65 ff; E Schmidt-Aßmann, 'Introduction: European Composite Administration and the Role of European Administrative Law' in O Jansen and B Schöndorf-Haubold (eds), *The European Composite Administration* (Intersentia 2011), 1–22; J Reichel, 'Communicating with the European Composite Administration' (2014), 15 *German Law Journal* 883, 886 ff.

[15] P Craig, *EU Administrative Law*, 3rd edn (Oxford University Press, 2018), 7.

[16] Respectively, J Trondal and M Bauer, 'Conceptualizing the European multilevel administrative order: capturing variation in the European administrative system' (2017) 9 *European Political Science Review* 73 and H Wockelberg, 'Why 'Multi-Level' and 'Governance' are Concepts of Relevance for our Understanding of Member State Implementation of EU Law' in AS Lind and J Reichel (ed), *Administrative law beyond the State: Nordic perspectives* (Martinus Nijhoff, 2013).

[17] L Hooghe and G Marks, *Multi-Level Governance and European Integration* (Rowman & Littlefield, 2002) and G Pagoulatos and L Tsoukalis, 'Multilevel Governance' in E Jones, A Menon and S Weatherill (eds), *The Oxford Handbook of the European Union* (Oxford University Press, 2012), 62–73.

of multilevel governance theory have a much broader focus; indeed, often even a primary focus on policy-*making* processes between the Commission and national or regional governments.[18]

For all their variation, the terminologies of law and political science all refer to the systemic cooperation in the exercise of distinct tasks by national and Union authorities across Union policy areas. Yet the remainder of this book will prefer the political science term 'multilevel administration' to describe that system. It does so despite acknowledging that 'multilevel' may be understood to have hierarchical overtones,[19] and that networked administrative relations within the EU are usually not hierarchical. It does so because 'multilevel administration' is not a legal-normative concept, but an empirical-descriptive concept.[20] A purely empirical-descriptive concept seems more appropriate given that the Union's system is, in its entirety, one of multilevel administration. Its shifting administrative practices are too diverse to raise identical legal issues; too elusive to be categorised exhaustively; too different to fit into an abstract, all-encompassing legal doctrine; and often too deprived of a firm legal basis to catch the eye of lawyers. Lastly, multilevel administration theory can be particularly helpful in explaining the contextual factors which determine the emergence and distinct shapes of cooperative relations between national and Union administration.

In what follows, the argument will consider how such factors are reflected in sectoral legislation. It will be argued that, given the diversity of forms of cooperation between national and Union administrations, it would be hasty to assume that *any* such form of cooperation is necessarily inconsistent with the powers of national and Union administration remaining separate.

A. Politics and Function

National administration (ministries, municipalities, directorates-general, regulatory agencies, regional bodies, just to name a few) and Union administration (the Commission, the EU Agencies, the ECB and occasionally the Council) constitute the building blocks of a complex European administrative system. That system may be broken down into discrete forms of administrative cooperation – into typical patterns of how the building blocks are arranged and fit with one another.

While there is no consensus in political science as to which factors are the more decisive,[21] it appears clear that functional as well as political factors play a

[18] A Benz, n 1, 35. See for instance N Bernard, *Multilevel Governance in the European Union* (Kluwer Law International, 2002).

[19] G della Cananea, 'The European Administration: *Imperium* and *Dominium*' in C Harlow, P Leino and G della Cananea (eds), *Research Handbook on EU administrative Law* (Edward Elgar, 2017), 64.

[20] Similarly, G Britz, 'Vom Europäischen Verwaltungsverbund zum Regulierungsverbund? Europäische Verwaltungsentwicklung am Beispiel der Netzzugangsregulierung bei Telekommunikation, Energie und Bahn' (2006) *Europarecht* 46, 47.

[21] See M Blauberger and B Rittberger, 'Orchestrating Policy Implementation: EU Governance Through Regulatory Networks' in K Abbott, P Genschel, D Snidal and B Zangl (eds), *International Organizations as Orchestrators* (Cambridge University Press, 2015), 44–46.

role in the Union's legislative choices when selecting and shaping distinct forms of cooperation.[22] Functional factors concern the institutional characteristics of national and Union authorities in view of, eg their resources and expertise. When designing European multilevel administration, the Union legislator will seek to exploit or mitigate the comparative institutional strengths and weaknesses specific to national or Union authorities – put differently, it will engage in what is termed 'comparative institutional analysis'.[23] National administration enjoys a much better grasp of relevant domestic circumstances, and is typically much better resourced. The Union administration, by contrast, is better placed to promote the exchange of national authorities' combined information and expertise; to advance the Union's own interests; and to make decisions without interference from parochial political pressures. Crucially, and unlike national authorities, whose powers are spatially confined within national borders, the Union administration may make decisions valid throughout the EU.[24] All these characteristics make the Union administration especially well-placed to ensure uniform enforcement of Union law,[25] as well as to pursue the Union's general interest and mediate between conflicting national interests.[26]

Nevertheless, functional factors alone cannot explain all legislative choices made in the design of EU administrative governance. Political considerations become apparent when one form of multilevel administration is promoted over others even where no evident functional advantages exist.[27] Typically, such political factors concern the Member States' dilemma between, on the one hand, reaping the benefits of interdependent governance and common policies, and, on the other, protecting national control over administration,[28] historically regarded as the preserve of national sovereignty.[29]

[22] The following passages in the main text draw on F Brito Bastos, 'Repurposing Administrative Procedures to Meet Novel Challenges in EU Competition Law' in C Colombo and M Eliantonio (eds), *The Evolving Governance of EU Competition Law in a Time of Disruptions: a Constitutional Perspective* (Hart Publishing, 2023).

[23] See eg N Komesar, *Imperfect Alternatives: Choosing Institutions in Law, Economics, and Public Policy* (University of Chicago Press, 1997), 3 and J Zglinski, *Europe's Passive Virtues: Deference to National Authorities in EU Free Movement Law* (Oxford University Press, 2020), 162.

[24] M Scholten, 'Mind the trend! Enforcement of EU law has been moving to "Brussels"' (2017) 24 *Journal of European Public Policy* 1348, 1354.

[25] J Trondal, 'National Agencies in the European Administrative Space: Government Driven, Commission Driven or Networked?' (2009) 87 *Public Administration* 779, 789.

[26] E Grande and M McCowan, 'The Two Logics of Multilevel Administration in the EU' in M Bauer and J Trondal (eds), *The Palgrave Handbook of the European Administrative System* (Palgrave Macmillan, 2015), 50.

[27] A Tarrant and D Kelemen, 'Reconceptualising European Union Regulatory Networks: A response to Blauberger and Rittberger' (2017) 11 *Regulation & Governance* 213.

[28] For many, see E Mastenbroek and D Martinsen, 'Filling the gap in the European Administrative space: the Role of Administrative Networks in EU Implementation and Enforcement' (2018) 25 *Journal of European Public Policy* 422, 424 and T Bach and E Ruffing, 'The Transformative Effects of Transnational Administrative Coordination in the European Multi-level System' in E Ongaro and S van Thiel (eds), *The Palgrave Handbook of Public Administration and Management in Europe* (Palgrave Macmillan, 2017), 748–51.

[29] P Genschel and M Jachtenfuchs, 'Introduction: beyond market regulation: analysing the European integration of core state powers' in P Genschel and M Jachtenfuchs, *Beyond the Regulatory Polity?: The European Integration of Core State Powers* (Oxford University Press, 2013), 2.

B. Multilevel Administration and 'Strict Separation' of Administrative Powers

One of the great debates in EU administrative law scholarship is whether the rise of multilevel administration has eroded the division between indirect (ie national) and direct (ie Union) administration. There have broadly been two views on the question. This section proposes a third.

The first, near-unanimous view is taken by some of the leading scholars of European administrative law. The view is that it is 'necessary to bid farewell to the idea that there is a clear distinction between direct and indirect administration';[30] that the distinction ignores or oversimplifies administrative reality;[31] or that the distinction has been 'abandoned' and 'hardly does justice' to how intertwined national and Union administration have become.[32]

The second, minority view is the opposite. Ziller, another leading scholar, contends that multilevel administration is 'not exactly a third category of Community administration, which would have chronologically appeared after direct administration and indirect administration [but] rather the coordination of the two types of administration, direct and indirect'.[33] Similarly, von Danwitz points out that, despite extensive cooperation, any decision can be traced back to an administrative procedure concluded either by a Union or a national authority.[34]

It is nonetheless submitted that the first as well as the second view overlook something fundamental. They seem to assume that multilevel administration, *in its entirety and in abstract*, can or cannot call into question the strict division between national and Union administrative power. A third, different view is taken here. This 'middle way', one could call it, can be summarised in two propositions.

First, European multilevel administration is too diverse and complex for any single, binary judgement to be made as to whether it may be reconciled with a dual

[30] See H Hofmann and A Türk, n 13, 254 and 270; and H Hofmann, 'Composite decision making procedures in EU administrative law' in H Hofmann and A Türk (eds), *Legal Challenges in EU Administrative Law: towards an integrated administration* (Edward Elgar, 2009), 137. For a similar view, see B Schöndorf-Haubold, *Die Strukturfonds der Europäischen Gemeinschaft: Rechtsformen und Verfahren europäischer Verbundverwaltung* (CH Beck 2005), 38 ff.

[31] E Chiti, 'The Administrative Implementation of European Union law: a Taxonomy and its Implications' in H Hofmann and A Türk (eds), *Legal Challenges in EU Administrative Law: towards an integrated administration* (Edward Elgar, 2009), 9–34, 11.

[32] M Eliantonio, 'Judicial Review in an Integrated Administration: the Case of "Composite Procedures"' (2014) 7 *Review of European Administrative Law* 66, and H Hofmann and A Türk, n 13, 255–56.

[33] J Ziller, 'Introduction: les concepts d'administration directe, d'administration indirecte et de co-administration et les fondements du droit administrative européen' in JB Auby and J Dutheil de la Rochère (eds), *Droit Administratif Européen* (Bruylant, 2007), 243. See also DU Galetta, 'Coamministrazione, reti di amministrazioni, *Verwaltungsverbund*: modelli organizzativi nuovi o alternative semantiche alla nozione di «cooperazione amministrativa» dell'art 10 TCE, per definire il fenomeno dell'amministrazione intrecciata?' (2009) *Rivista Italiana di Diritto Pubblico Comunitario* 1689, 1694–95.

[34] T von Danwitz, *Europäisches Verwaltungsrecht* (Springer, 2008), 612–13.

divide of administrative power. At best, one may only make such a judgement in respect of specific forms of cooperation.

Second, such a judgement requires clear yardsticks. Scholars risk talking past each other unless they agree on a test of what it would mean for the dual divide to be undermined. The yardstick proposed here is the separation principle – the key principle of Union Executive Federalism as crafted in the case law of the CJEU.

Separation of administrative powers and cooperation are *both* 'complementary constitutive principles' of the Union's administrative order.[35] Extensive cooperation between administrations does not deprive them of their own, exclusive competences.[36] The separation principle requires national and Union administration to be able to exercise their own powers, free from involvement or interference from one another. Separation thus remains intact for as long as either retains that ability. That is overwhelmingly the case in European multilevel administration. It is not the case in composite decision-making.

III. Composite Administrative Procedures: Conceptual Aspects

Composite administrative procedures can be defined as administrative decision-making procedures where national and Union authorities must exercise interdependent decisional powers in successive procedural stages in order for a final decision to be taken. Composite decision-making, thus defined, has existed for as long as multilevel administration itself has existed. Which is to say that it has existed since the very beginning of European integration. For example, under the first regulations of the Common Agricultural Policy, national administrations could, if faced with rapid fluctuations in agricultural produce prices, eg in the market for poultry, decide on the suspension of imports, subject to subsequent approval by the European Commission.[37] One Advocate General aptly characterised such administrative procedures as multilevel legal action (*mehrstufiges rechtliches Handeln*).[38] Nevertheless, the concept of composite procedure has largely remained elusive. The following subsections will attempt to clarify the constitutive characteristics of composite administrative procedures, to set out the

[35] See E Schmidt-Aßmann, 'Cuestiones fundamentales sobre la reforma de la Teoría General del Derecho Administrativo. Necesidad de la innovación y presupuestos metodológicos' in J Barnes (ed), *Innovación y Reforma en el Derecho Administrativo* (Global Law Press, 2006), 108. See in this sense also J Schwarze, 'Europäisches Verwaltungsrecht, 2nd edn (Nomos, 2005) CII–CIII and ff and A von Bogdandy and P Dann, 'International Composite Administration: Conceptualizing Multi-Level and Network Aspects in the Exercise of International Public Authority' (2008) 9 *German Law Journal* 2013, 2016.

[36] Case T-273/03 *Merck Sharp & Dohme Ltd v European Commission*, ECLI:EU:T:2007:288.

[37] See Article 12 of Council Regulation 22/62/EEC of 4 April 1962 on the progressive establishment of a common organisation of the market in poultry.

[38] Joined Cases 106/63 and 107/63 *Alfred Toepfer and Getreide-Import Gesellschaft v European Commission*, ECLI:EU:C:1965:65, [1965] ECR 405, 411.

roles that national and Union administration typically exercise within them, and to sketch out some of their most common structural types.

A. What is Meant by 'Composite', 'Administrative', and 'Procedure'?

The concept of 'composite administrative procedure' should be clarified by reference to its constituent operative terms. Composite procedures are *administrative* in the sense that they enforce, rather that define, Union policy priorities.

Composite procedures are administrative *procedures*. Like any administrative decision-making procedure, they consist of a legally prescribed order of stages, wherein different steps and preparatory acts lead to the adoption of a final decision.[39] The overarching function of administrative procedure is to promote decisional rationality. Procedural requirements limit authorities' powers and prevent their arbitrary or ill-informed exercise,[40] oblige authorities to investigate and consider opposing interests,[41] and steer them towards pursuing the policy goals determined by the legislator in an effective manner while respecting individuals' rights.[42] Such aims, which also pervade European administrative law,[43] illustrate why administrative procedure is indispensable to the process of ensuring that administrative decision-making observes the fundamental demands of the rule of law.[44]

Lastly, composite administrative procedures are administrative procedures of a *composite* structure. National laws, as well as Union law, often provide for complex administrative procedures which require the involvement of several distinct authorities.[45] What sets composite procedures apart from other complex administrative procedures is that they involve *different jurisdictions*. The pre-established order of procedural stages that must be followed for a decision to be

[39] G della Cananea, *Due Process of Law beyond the State: Requirements of Administrative Procedure* (Oxford University Press, 2016), 22.

[40] Ibid, 34. See also S Cassese, *Le Basi del Diritto Amministrativo* (Garzanti, 2000), 307–9.

[41] G della Cananea, n 39, 19.

[42] See J Barnes, 'Sobre el Procedimiento Administrativo: Evolución y Perspectivas' in J Barnes (ed), *Innovación y Reforma en el Derecho Administrativo* (Global Law Press, 2006), 261; H Pünder, 'Administrative procedure – mere facilitator of material law versus cooperative realisation of commonwelfare' in H Pünder and C Waldhoff (eds), *Debates in German Public Law* (Hart Publishing, 2014), 240.

[43] HC Röhl, 'Procedures in the European Composite Administration' in J Barnes, *Transforming Administrative Procedure* (Global Law Press, 2008), 79 ff.

[44] See F Brito Bastos and A de Ruijter, 'Break or Bend in Case of Emergency? Rule of Law and State of Emergency in European Public Health Administration' (2020) 10 *European Journal of Risk Regulation* 611, 615 ff.

[45] Suffice it to mention that complex administrative procedures are well-known to German, Italian, and Portuguese administrative law. See S Detterbeck, *Allgemeines Verwaltungsrecht mit Verwaltungsprozessrecht*, 18th edn (CH Beck, 2020), 162–63; and E Casetta, *Manuale di Diritto Amministrativo*, 11th edn (Giuffrè, 2009), 487–88; and FP Oliveira and JE Figueiredo Dias, *Noções Fundamentais de Direito Administrativo*, 5th edn (Almedina, 2022), 227.

taken requires the cumulative involvement of both national and Union authorities, which are created by the legal systems of the Member States and of the Union, respectively.[46] Composite procedures may be 'bottom-up', 'top-down', or hybrid, depending on how such stages are organised – depending on whether a Union stage follows a national stage, a national stage follows a Union stage, or whether bottom-up and top-down elements are combined.[47]

The concept of composite procedure adopted here requires one further clarification. Namely, that it differs from the substantive version of the concept followed by Hofmann and Lottini,[48] which includes information exchanges occurring outside of a pre-established procedure. A related version, supported by León, suggests a test based on a contribution by an authority being 'so relevant that it has a decisive effect on the outcome',[49] and that the core of the notion of composite decision-making is 'intensive cooperation between national and European authorities [that] is reflected in a procedural arrangement with different degrees of formalism'.[50] Instead, this book adopts a purely formal version, drawing on the views of Mendes and Eckes, as well as Schütze.[51] In that version, the defining test to identify composite decision-making is the presence of what this book's author has previously termed as 'decisional interdependence'.[52]

Decisional interdependence means that the Union administration may not exercise its own competences within the administrative procedure before the national administration has exercised its own, or the over way around. Put differently, composite procedures require the joint exercise of decision-making powers by national and Union administration. The notion of decisional interdependence is present in the ReNEUAL Draft Model Rules on EU Administrative Procedures,

[46] Given that a plurality of distinct authorities may act within the same composite procedure, it may appear simplistic to refer simply to national or Union 'authorities', 'procedural stages', or 'administration'. As the CJEU's case law shows, however, the constitutional issues that composite decision-making raises, and which set it apart from other multi-stage but 'single-level' administrative procedures, all concern the interaction between levels of administration, rather than of authorities as such. For a distinct view, emphasising the distinct authorities involved at the Union level, see SA Alonso de León, *Composite Administrative Procedures in the European Union* (Iustel, 2017), 173 ff.

[47] The distinction can be traced to G della Cananea, 'The European Union's Mixed Administrative Proceedings' (2004–2005) 68 *Law and Contemporary Problems* 193, 199.

[48] H Hofmann and A Türk, n 30, 141 and M Lottini, 'From "Administrative Cooperation" in the Application of European Union Law to "Administrative Cooperation" in the Protection of European Rights and Liberties' (2012) 18 *European Public Law* 127, 134.

[49] S Alonso de León, n 46, 153.

[50] Ibid, 341.

[51] See R Schütze, 'From Rome to Lisbon: "Executive Federalism" in the (New) European Union' (2010) 47 *Common Market Law Review* 1385, 1420–22 and 1426; C Eckes and J Mendes, 'The right to be heard in composite administrative procedures: lost in between protection?' (2011) 36 *European Law Review* 651.

[52] F Brito Bastos, 'Derivative Illegality in European Composite Administrative Procedures' (2018) 55 *Common Market Law Review* 105. This view has also been supported by S Röttger-Wirtz and M Eliantonio, 'From Integration to Exclusion: EU Composite Administration and Gaps in Judicial Accountability in the Authorisation of Pharmaceuticals' (2019) 10 *European Journal of Risk Regulation* 393, 394.

where a 'composite procedure' is defined as 'an administrative procedure where EU authorities and the authorities of a Member State or of different Member States have distinct functions which are inter-dependent'.[53] However, more importantly, the notion of decisional interdependence is clearly present in CJEU case law, even if expressed in other terms. The CJEU recognises that, in some administrative procedures, national authorities take measures which 'constitute a necessary step in the procedure for adopting an EU act';[54] that the Commission 'is neither obliged nor authorised' to exercise its powers until national authorities have previously adopted certain measures;[55] or that 'national authorities adopt acts that are preparatory to a final decision of an EU institution'.[56] Composite administrative procedures ought to be distinguished from mere information exchange precisely because the CJEU treats instances of such decisional interdependence differently from mere information-sharing. The point will be taken further below, in subsection IV.C.

B. Decisional Interdependence and Decisional Dominance

Like any other aspect of multilevel administration, decisional interdependence is shaped by functional and political factors. From a functional standpoint, national and Union administration must intervene at the stages of a decision-making process that can best exploit their respective institutional advantages. From a political standpoint, decisional interdependence promotes an adequate balance of power between national and Union administrative power.

Decisional interdependence can exist in many forms. Functional and political factors may require different allocations of decisional power between national and Union administration. Such power is always allocated unequally. One of the two, depending on the relevant sectoral legislation, will exercise *decisional dominance.*

Decisional dominance means that, within different administrative procedures, a national or a Union authority has the power to define the content of the final decision. Such may occur at the conclusion of the administrative procedure, with the adoption of the final decision itself, but also at preparatory stages, if the authority adopts binding opinions which in effect predetermine the content of the procedure's final decision. The following subsections will aim to offer an overview of how the roles played by national and Union administration may differ depending on which of the two exercises decisional dominance.

[53] See Article I-4 (3) of the Draft Model Rules.

[54] Case C-785/18 *GAEC Jeanningros v Institut national de l'origine et de la qualité (INAO)*, ECLI:EU:C:2020:46, para 25.

[55] Case C-31/13 P *Hungary v Commission*, ECLI:EU:C:2014:70, paras 61–62.

[56] Case C-414/18 *Iccrea Banca SpA Istituto Centrale del Credito Cooperativo v Banca d'Italia*, ECLI:EU:C:2019:1036, para 41.

(i) National Decisional Dominance

National decisional dominance is rare in composite procedures. In such cases, the Union administration is typically confined either to deciding in accordance with a binding national preparatory act, or to adopting non-binding instruments to guide national authorities in exercising their own powers. It is the national administration which takes a final decision or which, in the earlier preparatory stages, performs binding preparatory acts which predetermine the content of the final decision taken at Union level. The limitation of powers exercised by the Union administration may derive, eg from a lack of political will among the Member States to give up binding regulatory powers; or from a judgement that decisions will require the local knowledge of national authorities.

One example of the former concerns regulatory administrative procedures in telecommunications.[57] National regulatory authorities take decisions to impose specific regulatory requirements on operators with significant market power. The Commission's role, exercised in coordination with the Body of European Regulators for Electronic Communications (BEREC), is confined to giving national regulators recommendations as to how to proceed in a given case. Such must be understood in a context where Member States historically resisted extensive transfers of power to Union administration in the regulation of telecommunications.[58]

National authorities also exercise decisional dominance at the preparatory stage of composite procedures for the registration of protected designations of origins (PDOs) or geographic indications (PGIs). National authorities, which are familiar with local production practices and traditions, receive applications from groups for the classification and registration of food products as PDOs or PGIs (eg Tuscan prosciutto or Lübeck marzipan). After they make a positive assessment of the products' compliance with the EU requirements for registration, and if no objection is raised by any legal or natural person, national authorities support the applications and forward them to the Commission. The Commission is then obliged to register the products for EU-wide protection, without enjoying any margin of discretion.[59] The CJEU justifies the preeminence of national authorities in the administrative procedure as a result of the fact that the registration of geographic indications 'requires, to a large extent, detailed knowledge of matters particular to that Member State, which the competent authorities thereof are best placed to check'.[60]

[57] Article 33 of European Parliament and Council Directive (EU) 2018/1972 establishing the European Electronic Communications Code.

[58] See M Massaro, 'Between Integration and Protection of National Sovereignty in the European Union's Radio Spectrum Policy' (2019) 9 *Journal of Information Policy* 174, 191 and 193.

[59] The same obligation arises if there *are* objections but the persons raising them, and the applicants, come to an agreement. See Article 53(2)(a) of Regulation No 1151/2012 of 21 November 2012, on quality schemes for agricultural products and foodstuffs.

[60] Case C-53/20 *Hengstenberg Gmbh & Co KG v Spreewaldverein eV*, ECLI:EU:C:2021:279, para 37.

(ii) Union Decisional Dominance

Decisional dominance overwhelmingly falls to the Union administration – eg the Commission, Union Agencies, or the European Central Bank. Union decisional dominance is often justified due to its comparative institutional advantages in respect of national administration, which are broadly the same ones that shape its place in the European administrative system as a whole.[61] Such advantages include, for instance, the Union administration's independence from national parochial pressures,[62] or its EU-wide jurisdiction when licensing certain products or the entire internal market.[63]

Even in cases of Union decisional dominance, national authorities have a relevant role to play. That role varies both in terms of the stage of the procedure at which national authorities intervene and in terms of the influence that they may have within it.

In some composite procedures, the national administration is involved from the very beginning. It may have the sole competence to initiate the procedure, or serve as a 'reception desk' which receives applicants' requests and documents and forwards them to the Union authorities responsible for the final decision. It may also serve as a 'gatekeeper' with the power to filter – ie to reject – applications for decisions, such as licences, so that the Union administration only needs to engage with potentially successful applications. Just to give an example, this is a role that national competent authorities exercise in the licensing of new credit institutions by the ECB.[64]

In other composite procedures, national authorities act as 'rapporteurs' by preparing draft measures, occasionally termed as 'proposals',[65] or as 'reports'.[66] While non-binding, such measures may serve as the basis for the Union administration's final decision. For instance, national authorities prepare reports on the environmental risks of detergents; but the Commission may make a very different assessment when authorising their placing on the market.[67] Occasionally, the Union administration itself designates a national authority as a rapporteur for

[61] See section II.A. above.

[62] For example, given its independence, the European Central Bank is considered sufficiently insulated from the influence of national 'champion' credit institutions to exercise supervisory tasks more effectively than national supervisors did in the past. See E Wymeersch, 'The European Banking Union, a First Analysis', *Financial Law Institute Working Paper Series* WP 2012-07, available at SSRN: https://ssrn.com/abstract=2171785, at 2–3.

[63] For instance, the Commission and the European Food Safety Authority, when authorising novel foods. See, in this regard, Recitals (20) to (24) of Regulation (EU) 2015/2283 of the European Parliament and Council on novel foods.

[64] See Article 14 of Regulation (EU) No 806/2014 of the European Parliament and of the Council of 15 July 2014 (Single Resolution Mechanism Regulation).

[65] Case T-228/02 *Organisation des Modjahedines du peuple d'Iran* (OMPI) *v European Council*, ECLI:EU:T:2006:384, para 76.

[66] See Article 13(1) of Directive 2001/18/EC of the European Parliament and Council on the deliberate release into the environment of genetically modified organisms.

[67] See Articles 5(3)–(4) and 6 of Regulation No 648/2004 of the European Parliament and the Council of 31 March 2004 concerning detergents.

a decision it must take (eg the European Chemicals Agency, when assessing the safety of chemicals).[68]

Two other kinds of roles should still be mentioned. In certain composite procedures, national authorities must be consulted for an opinion before a final decision is taken.[69] Lastly, at the very conclusion of the administrative procedure, it may occur that national authorities are under a duty to merely implement – or as some authors suggest, 'ratify' – a prior Union decision into national law;[70] or even be limited in their role to simply notifying such a decision to affected parties.[71]

(iii) 'Second Life' Acts and Union Decisional Dominance

When considering decisional dominance, one should also mention a special class of composite procedures. Those are composite procedures where the national administration takes measures which, within the national legal order, are technically not preparatory, and indeed, not even necessarily administrative. Beyond their purely national existence, those measures are given a 'second life' as measures forming part of a European administrative procedure where the Union administration takes a final decision. Three examples may be given for this category.

First, administrative procedures for the 'blacklisting' of individuals and entities supporting terrorism end with a Council Regulation freezing their assets within the EU. However, Council blacklists may only be adopted based on proposals by national authorities. Such proposals are final decisions that have already been taken by domestic authorities – which may even be judicial authorities.[72]

Second, under procedures for state aid review, Member States cannot grant or implement aid unless notified and then approved by the Commission as compatible with the internal market. If granted without prior notification – and therefore unlawfully – the Commission may require Member States to recover aid. State aid is not granted by the Member States through preparatory acts, but

[68] See Articles 85 and 87 of Regulation (EC) No 1907/2006 of the European Parliament and of the Council of 18 December 2006 concerning the Registration, Evaluation, Authorisation and Restriction of Chemicals (REACH), establishing a European Chemicals Agency.

[69] For instance, national governments must be consulted before the Union administration approves requests for access to documents which it originally received from the Member States. See Article 4(5) of Regulation (EC) No 1049/2001 of the European Parliament and of the Council of 30 May 2001 regarding public access to European Parliament, Council and Commission documents. The composite administrative procedure in question has given rise to important case law on the duty to give reasons and is therefore analysed in greater detail in Chapter 6, section III.

[70] E Brosset, 'The Prior Authorisation Procedure Adopted for the Deliberate Release into the Environment of Genetically Modified Organisms: the Complexities of Balancing Community and National Competences' (2004) 10 *European Law Journal* 555, 565.

[71] Article 5(2) of Council Implementing Regulation 2015/81, specifying uniform conditions of application of Regulation (EU) No 806/2014 of the European Parliament and of the Council with regard to ex ante contributions to the Single Resolution Fund.

[72] See Article 1(4) of Council Common Position of 27 December 2001 on the application of specific measures to combat terrorism.

rather through final measures. Though often even of a legislative nature (eg tax exemptions), such measures are reviewed within an administrative procedure and cannot take effect before Commission approval.[73]

Lastly, in certain composite procedures, the Commission has the power to convert provisional national decisions taken urgently to address immediate risks to public health – eg those potentially posed by a medicine – into final Union decisions. Such administrative procedures exist in many sectors under 'safeguard clauses', which will be analysed separately in the ensuing subsection.

C. Prototypical Procedural Models

The diversity of composite procedures does not lend itself to exhaustive taxonomies. Nevertheless, for analytical purposes, it is worth setting out some basic models of composite procedures which are especially pervasive across policy fields. The Union legislator often repurposes pre-existing types of administrative procedures and adapts them when introducing legislation in a different policy sector.[74] The most common procedural models will be termed 'back-and-forth' procedures; arbitral procedures; safeguard clause procedures; and 'reception desk' procedures.

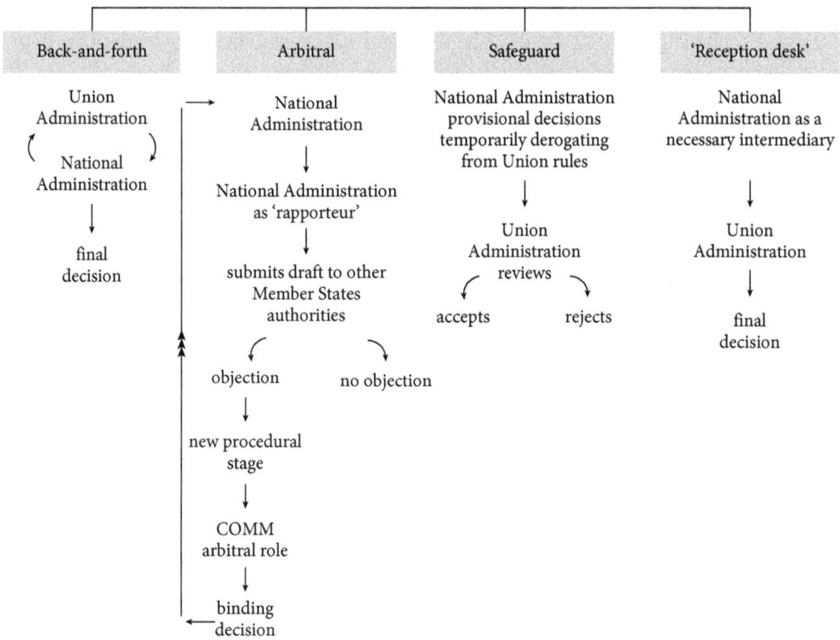

[73] See Case T-103/14 *Frucona Košice a.s. v European Commission*, ECLI:EU:T:2016:152, para 52.
[74] See F Brito Bastos, n 22.

(i) Back-and-forth Procedures

Numerous composite procedures are 'back-and-forth' procedures, as Eliantonio has aptly termed them.[75] They begin and end at the level of national administration, with a procedural stage at the Union level in-between.

The rationale is that enforcement of Union law remains, to the greatest extent possible, in the hands of national authorities, and that the Union administration only intervenes to take binding decisions on the issues that it is best placed to address. In administrative procedures aimed at determining whether the conditions for repayment or remission of customs debt are met, the Commission intervenes to ensure that those conditions are interpreted uniformly by national customs authorities.[76] One prominent example of a back-and-forth composite procedure emerged during the Covid-19 pandemic. National authorities receive initial applications and take the final decision as to whether to authorise the export of vaccines to third countries. However, in the interest of consistent protection of public health, the Commission may issue binding opinions which, in effect, veto authorisations.[77]

(ii) Arbitral Procedures

Arbitral composite procedures exist across several policy sectors.[78] In domains such as the regulation of financial markets,[79] biocides,[80] medicines,[81] the cross-border transportation of waste,[82] or data protection,[83] national authorities are required to refer to the Union administration if a legal, technical, or scientific disagreement emerges between them.

If intending to take a decision which will affect other Member States – eg licensing a drug or fining a data controller – a national authority (the rapporteur

[75] M Eliantonio, 'Judicial Review in an Integrated Administration: the Case of "Composite Procedures"' (2014) 7 *Review of European Administrative Law* 65, 73.

[76] See Articles 116, 119, and 120 of the Union Customs Code (Regulation (EU) No 952/2013 of the European Parliament and of the Council as regards detailed rules concerning certain provisions of the Union Customs Code) and Articles 98–102 of the UCC delegated act (Commission Delegated Regulation (EU) 2015/2446 of 28 July 2015).

[77] See Recitals (5)–(7) and Article 2 of Commission Implementing Regulation (EU) 2021/111 making the exportation of certain products subject to the production of an export authorisation.

[78] On composite procedures of this type, see the analysis carried out by L de Lucia, 'Conflict and Cooperation within European Composite Administration (Between Philia and Eris)' (2012) 5 *Review of European Administrative Law* 49.

[79] See Article 19 of Regulation (EU) 1095/2010 of the European Parliament and of the Council establishing a European Supervisory Authority (European Securities and Markets Authority).

[80] Article 36 of Regulation No 528/2012 of the European Parliament and the Council of 22 May 2012 concerning the making available on the market and use of biocidal products.

[81] Article 29 of Directive 2001/83/EC of 6 November of the European Parliament and the Council on the Community code relating to medicinal products for human use; and Article 54 of Regulation (EU) 2019/6 of the European Parliament and of the Council of 11 December 2018 on veterinary medicinal products.

[82] Article 11(3) of Regulation No 1013/2006 of the European Parliament and the Council of 14 June 2006 on shipments of waste.

[83] See Article 65(1)(a) of Regulation (EU) 2016/679 of the European Parliament and of the Council on the protection of natural persons with regard to the processing of personal data and on the free

authority) must first submit a draft decision to those states' competent authorities. Union legislation tends to entitle the authorities concerned to comment on or object to the decision, in what some have called a 'choral' procedure.[84] If no objection is made, then the rapporteur authority takes the decision as intended. If an objection is made and no compromise is reached, national authorities are required to initiate a new procedural stage which unfolds at Union level.[85] The Commission – often based on an Agency's opinion – will exercise an arbitral function by settling the disagreement with a binding decision, which the rapporteur national authority (and sometimes, the remaining authorities involved as well), is required to implement in the final decision of the administrative procedure.

(iii) Safeguard Clause Procedures

The oldest type of composite administrative procedure concerns so-called safeguard clauses. Under Article 114 TFEU, the Union legislator enjoys a general competence to establish such procedures when introducing harmonisation legislation. Safeguard clauses, which do not always bear that name in the legislation, constitute two-step administrative procedures. They enable national authorities to take provisional decisions that temporarily derogate from Union rules and are subsequently reviewed by the Union administration.

Safeguard procedures are available, for example, when data protection authorities need to take urgent measures to protect data subjects' rights.[86] Yet the bulk of such procedures can be found in economic sectors where immediate environmental or public health risks may arise. National administrations may, for instance, take urgent decisions to restrict the marketing of unsafe machinery,[87] foods,[88] medicines,[89] food supplements,[90] medical devices,[91] or genetically modified organisms.[92]

movement of such data (General Data Protection Regulation, henceforth 'GDPR'). See also the European Data Protection Board's (EDPB) Guidelines 03/2021 on the application of Article 65(1)(a) GDPR.

[84] S Cassese, 'European Administrative Proceedings' (2004–2005) 68 *Law and Contemporary Problems* 21, 28.

[85] The CJEU has emphasised that referral to the Union administration is mandatory. See Case C-452/06 *R (on the application of Synthon BV) v Licencing Authority of the Department of Health*, ECLI:EU:C:2008:565, paras 28–33.

[86] Article 66 GDPR.

[87] Article 11 of Directive 2006/42/EC of the European Parliament and of the Council of 17 May 2006 on machinery.

[88] Article 54 of Regulation (EC) No 178/2002 of the European Parliament and of the Council of 28 January 2002 laying down the general principles and requirements of food law, establishing the European Food Safety Authority and laying down procedures in matters of food safety.

[89] Article 20 of Regulation (EC) No 726/2004 of the European Parliament and of the Council of 31 March 2004 laying down Community procedures for the authorisation and supervision of medicinal products for human and veterinary use and establishing a European Medicines Agency. For a mechanism of this kind in the market of detergents, see Article 15 of Regulation No 648/2004 of the European Parliament and the Council.

[90] Article 12 of Directive 2002/46/EC of the European Parliament and of the Council on the approximation of the laws of the Member States relating to food supplements.

[91] Article 95 of Regulation (EU) 2017/745 of the European Parliament and of the Council of 5 April 2017 on medical devices.

[92] Article 23 of Directive 2001/18/EC of the European Parliament and of the Council of 12 March 2001 on the deliberate release into the environment of genetically modified organisms.

It was noted before that national safeguard decisions lead a sort of 'double life'. Within the national legal order, a safeguard decision is the final decision in an administrative procedure, albeit one that is only intended to remain in force temporarily. However, it also constitutes a preparatory act at the beginning of a European administrative procedure – a single administrative procedure which, in the CJEU's own words, 'takes place partly at national level and partly at European Union level'.[93] Indeed, the Union administration is in no way bound by national safeguard decisions and enjoys a wide margin of assessment.[94] It is empowered 'to review whether [safeguard] measures are justified, by satisfying itself in particular of the merits of the legal and factual grounds for the adoption of the measures', and ultimately to decide whether they should be rejected – in which case they must be disapplied and repealed[95] – or confirmed – and thus made definitive.[96]

(iv) 'Reception Desk' Procedures

A fourth common model of composite decision-making barely involves national administration at all. In composite procedures leading to authorisations relating, eg to GMO food and feed,[97] smoke flavourings in food,[98] or the use of certain nutritional or health claims made on foods,[99] national administration merely acts as a kind of 'reception desk' for Union Agencies or for the Commission.[100] National administration performs a purely formal role. It forwards initial applications, documents and information to the Union administration, which is solely competent to decide on the substance of a case.

[93] See Case T-465/11 *Globula a.s. v European Commission*, ECLI:EU:T:2013:406, para 32 and Article 36(8) of Directive 2009/73/EC of the European Parliament and of the Council concerning common rules for the internal market in natural gas.

[94] Case C-236/01 *Monsanto Agricoltura Italia SpA and Others v Presidenza del Consiglio dei Ministri*, ECLI:EU:C:2003:431.

[95] Case C-130/78 *Salumifficio di Cornuda SpA v Amministrazione delle Finanze dello Stato*, ECLI:EU:C:1979:60.

[96] Joined Cases 106/63 and 107/63 *Toepfer*, n 38, [1965] ECR 405, at 411, and Cases T-152/19 *Brunswick Bowling Products LLC v European Commission*, ECLI:EU:T:2021:539, para 66; T-168/16 *Grizzly Tools GmbH & Co KG v DEuropean Commission*, ECLI:EU:T:2018:246, para 51; C-41/93 *French Republic v European Commission*, ECLI:EU:C:1994:196, paras 25–28, C-6/05 *Medipac-Kazantzidis* ECLI:EU:C:2007:337, paras 46 and 59; and C-120/14 P *Klein*, ECLI:EU:C:2015:252, paras 64 and 76.

[97] See Articles 5(2)(a) and 17(2) of Regulation 1829/2003 of the European Parliament and of the Council of 22 September 2003 on genetically modified food and feed.

[98] Regulation (EC) 2065/2003 of the European Parliament and of the Council on smoke flavourings used or intended for use in or on foods.

[99] See Article 15 of Regulation No 1924/2006 of the European Parliament and of the Council of 20 December 2006 on nutrition and health claims made on foods.

[100] M Friant-Perrot, 'The European Union Regulatory Regime for Genetically Modified Organisms and its Integration into Community Food Law and Policy' in L Bodiguel and M Cardwell (eds), *The Regulation of Genetically Modified Organisms: Comparative Approaches* (Oxford University Press, 2010), 90.

The literature has rightly regarded national administration as serving as 'no more than an intermediary'.[101] The *Hagenmeyer* ruling has also made unequivocal that it constitutes a *necessary* intermediary. The Court held there that, contrary to what one of the parties had claimed, national authorities are more than a mere 'post-box' for applications and documents. They *do* enjoy a minimal degree of decisional power – to check if applications are in conformity with formal requirements, and can therefore be forwarded to the Union administration, as legally required, 'in order to proceed to the next stage in the procedure'.[102] Despite exercising decisional dominance, the Union administration may not take a final decision without the prior involvement of national authorities, formal as their role may be. 'Reception desk' procedures are thus just as based on decisional interdependence as any other instance of composite decision-making.

IV. Multilevel Administration: A Non-Exhaustive Typology

Multilevel administration raises a host of legal problems. Some such problems are systemic and pervade the EU's entire administrative system. It becomes difficult to ensure the overall transparency and accountability of that system when a multitude of different authorities are involved, and often interact by informal and opaque means.[103] However, European multilevel administration also lends itself to a possible taxonomy of distinct forms of cooperation, each raising specific legal issues of its own.

The following subsections sketch out an updated version of taxonomy first proposed by Schmidt-Aßmann. It should be noted, however, that the various forms of cooperation are not mutually exclusive and, in fact, tend to coexist. This is particularly true in EU Agency networks, as will be explained in subsection IV.F. Most forms of administrative cooperation set out below confirm a finding made in empirical political science. All forms of multilevel administration discussed below – with the exception of composite decision-making and perhaps one more – confirm the finding made in empirical political science. The finding is that, for all their extensive cooperation, the relations between national and Union authorities 'are characterised by a formal separation of powers'.[104]

[101] D Chalmers, 'Risk, anxiety and the European mediation of the politics of life' (2005) 30 *European Law Review* 649, 653.

[102] Case T-17/12 *Hagenmeyer v European Commission*, ECLI:EU:T:2014:234, paras 133–36.

[103] For many, see M Scholten, 'Shared Tasks, but Separated Controls: Building the System of Control for Shared Administration in an EU Multi-Jurisdictional Setting' (2019) 10 *European Journal of Risk Regulation* 538.

[104] A Benz, A Corcaci and JW Doser, 'Unravelling multilevel administration. Patterns and dynamics of administrative co-ordination in European governance' (2016) 23 *Journal of European Public Policy* 999, 1006.

A. Authentic Second-order Administration

National authorities are the primary enforcers of Union law. Yet the Union administration often performs a coordinating role with regard to them. In that role, Union administration may address binding measures to national authorities (such as decisions, implementing regulations, or instructions); it may adopt soft law acts (such as 'interpretive guidance' or recommendations);[105] or it may provide services of operational support (such as the management of information-sharing networks).[106]

Chapter two noted that, from its early days, the European Commission was believed to be constitutionally required to function as a second-order administration. Rather than administering the everyday issues of businesses and citizens, the Union administration was intended merely to *administer national administrations*.

This account will often be simplistic and counterproductive. Union administrative decisions often require national authorities to take specific decisions with immediate detrimental effects to the legal position of individuals. Such decision-making processes, in fact, constitute composite administrative procedures. The final decision taken by national administration results from a prior binding measure taken at Union level. These are instances of *merely apparent* second-order administration which, as Part II will show, have raised numerous problems of their own in terms of the protection of procedural rights.

Nevertheless, there are *also* instances of *authentic* second-order administration. Quite often, the Union administration performs tasks and exercises powers which are only addressed to and only affect national authorities, without requiring the latter to adopt any specific measure in respect of private parties. In such cases – eg in the management of most EU funds – there is no composite administrative procedure.[107] Instead, there is an administrative procedure where the Union administration, alone, adopts decisions which do not need any subsequent national measure to produce legal effects. Those legal effects exhaust themselves in the legal position of the Member States or their authorities. The latter may initiate their own administrative procedures, but those will be autonomous from the first, Union procedure, and lead to entirely separate decisions. Only those national decisions, not the earlier Union decisions, will produce legal effects which may affect private parties.

[105] On interpretive guidance, see C van Dam, 'Guidance documents of the European Commission: a typology to trace the effects in the national legal order' (2017) 10 *Review of European Administrative Law* 75.

[106] The CJEU has recognised that Union bodies may be created with the purpose of adopting 'non-binding supporting and framework measures' as 'services' provided to national authorities (and operators) to facilitate uniform implementation. See Case C-217/04 *United Kingdom v European Parliament and Council*, ECLI:EU:C:2006:279.

[107] Differently, León appears to consider *all* administrative procedures in EU funding to represent composite decision-making, whereas in the view supported here this is generally not the case given that decisional interdependence is typically lacking. See generally S Alonso de León, n 46.

The Recovery and Resilience Facility Regulation (RRFR) provides a good example.[108] The RRFR was adopted to address the economic fallout of the Covid-19 pandemic. It establishes an authentic second-order administrative procedure. National recovery and resilience plans (RRPs) are submitted by the Member States, then assessed by the Commission, and then finally approved (or rejected) by the Council. RRPs foresee large-scale investments and reforms which certainly require countless national administrative procedures – eg for the allocation of subsidies or for public procurement. However, the Council decision as such does not condition the independent power of national authorities to decide on the outcome of those procedures. It only affects the financial legal relations between the Member State and the Union.

B. Institutional Cooperation

Institutional cooperation, also referred to as organisational cooperation, concerns the creation of Union administrative bodies, where representatives of national, and sometimes also Union, authorities meet and deliberate. This is the case with Union Agencies – such as the European Data Protection Board,[109] or the European Union Agency for the Cooperation of Energy Regulators –[110] and the plethora of specialised comitology committees in the orbit of the European Commission.

The composite nature of institutional cooperation has tended to be overestimated. What *is* composite, if anything, is the diversity of national administrations represented in comitology committees and Agency boards. However, both kinds of administrative bodies are *bodies established by the European Union itself*. Their decisions are not imputed individually to each of the represented national authorities, but rather to the relevant Agencies or committees as such, subject exclusively to the EU's own rules on administrative procedure and to judicial review by the CJEU.

To put it perhaps provocatively, comitology committees and Agency boards are no more 'composite' than the Council, the legal status of which as an institution *of the EU* cannot be seriously disputed. Indeed, as Schütze has pointed out, the decisions of Agencies and comitology committees result from the exercise of power at Union level *only* and 'will be fully assimilated to European law'.[111] In short, even though they serve as a forum of multilevel administrative cooperation, Agency boards and comitology committees exercise powers separately from national administration.

[108] See eg Article 24 of Regulation (EU) 2021/241 of the European Parliament and of the Council of 12 February 2021 establishing the Recovery and Resilience Facility.

[109] See Article 68 GDPR, n 83.

[110] See Article 18 of Regulation (EU) 2019/943 of the European Parliament and of the Council establishing a European Union Agency for the Cooperation of Energy Regulators.

[111] R Schütze, n 51, 1424.

C. Informational Cooperation

It has been rightly pointed out that European administration is increasingly an 'administration of information'.[112] The European Union's administrative system is characterised by pervasive informational cooperation – ie information-sharing between the different levels of administration involved.[113]

The Union's own authorities, and Agencies in particular,[114] often serve as a hub for information gathered by national administrations to be received, stored and disseminated back to the Member States or to Union institutions. Yet the forms of information-sharing vary significantly.[115] Information may be exchanged vertically, between national and Union authorities, or horizontally, between authorities belonging to various Member States, as when potential cross-border effects are disclosed in environmental impact assessment procedures.[116] Information may be shared in a spontaneous and informal manner,[117] or shared to fulfil a specific legal obligation of mutual assistance.[118] Increasingly, information is shared within highly structured interoperable information systems, managed by Union Agencies as a service to competent national authorities in law enforcement, asylum, and internal border protection.[119]

Informational cooperation promotes effective enforcement without expanding Union administration or removing power away from national administration.[120] For this reason, Member States often favour informational cooperation as an approach to administrative integration, which is typically only abandoned if mere information exchanges prove ineffective (as for example when the European Markets and Securities Authority was created).[121]

[112] H Hofmann, G Rowe, and A Türk, *Administrative Law and Policy of the European Union* (Oxford University Press, 2011), 411.

[113] H Hofmann, 'Seven Challenges for EU administrative law' in K de Graaf et al (eds), *European Administrative Law: Top-Down and Bottom-up* (Europa Law Publishing, 2009), 53.

[114] E Chiti, 'An important part of the EU's institutional machinery: features, problems and perspectives of European agencies' (2009) 46 *Common Market Law Review* 1395, 1403.

[115] For an overview of European information-sharing mechanisms, see JP Schneider, 'Basic Structures of Information Management in the European Administrative Union' (2014) 20 *European Public Law* 89.

[116] See Article 7 of Directive 2011/92/EU of the European Parliament and of the Council of 13 December 2011 on the assessment of the effects of certain public and private projects on the environment.

[117] DU Galetta, 'Informal Information Processing in Dispute Resolution Networks: Informality Versus the Protection of Individual's Rights?' (2014) 20 *European Public Law* 71.

[118] See Article 12 of Council Regulation (EC) 1/2003 on the implementation of the rules on competition laid down in Articles 81 and 82 of the Treaty.

[119] See F Brito Bastos and D Curtin, 'Interoperable Information Sharing and the Five Novel Frontiers of EU Governance: A Special Issue' (2020) 26 *European Public Law* 59. For the view that interoperable data-sharing systems constitute composite procedures, rather than, as argued here, an altogether distinct form of administrative cooperation, see S Alonso de León, n 46, 209.

[120] See DU Galetta, H Hofmann, and JP Schneider, 'Information Exchange in the European Administrative Union: An Introduction' (2014) 20 *European Public Law* 65, 68 and D Curtin, n 14, 106 ff.

[121] See Recital (8) of founding act of the European Security Markets Authority (ESMA) (Regulation (EU) No 1095/2010 of the European Parliament and of the Council of 24 November 2010).

The distinction between informational cooperation and procedural cooperation (ie composite administrative procedures) has remained rather blurry. Hofmann considers information-sharing to be 'the substance' of composite decision-making.[122]

The view supported here, however, is very different from Hofmann's. Hofmann adopts a substantive conception of composite decision-making, where the use of information shared by another administration suffices for a decision-making process to qualify as composite. The version of the concept of decision-making endorsed in this book, by contrast, is formal in nature. It requires authorities to interact within an administrative procedure, in the sense previously described of a legally predefined sequence of steps and stages; and that those authorities exercise interdependent decisional powers. Hofmann writes that the *Tillack* case showcases the legal problems raised by composite procedures.[123] However, if one takes a formal conception, then the case concerned mere information-sharing rather than composite decision-making. In fact, *Tillack* illustrates precisely why the two are different and ought to be clearly distinguished.

The facts surrounding *Tillack* can be summarised as follows.[124] OLAF (the EU's anti-fraud office) forwarded a report to German and Belgian prosecuting authorities in which it claimed that Tillack, a journalist, had obtained OLAF confidential information with bribes. The Belgian federal police opened an investigation which ultimately led to Tillack's home being searched and to some documents and belongings in his possession being seized. Tillack brought an action for annulment of the decision to send information from OLAF to the national prosecuting authorities.

The General Court dismissed the action. It held that, because it does not entail binding legal effects, the mere forwarding of information cannot qualify as a reviewable decision under Article 263 TFEU. But even more importantly, the ruling emphasised that national authorities exercise their powers independently from interference from the EU administration. National authorities '*remain free*, in the context *of their own powers*, to assess the content and significance of that information'; and the '*only authorities* having the power to adopt decisions capable of affecting [an individual's] legal position'. Accordingly national decisions were 'the *sole and entire responsibility* of the national authorities' (emphasis added).[125]

In short, *Tillack* shows that, rather than requiring it to take any specific decisions, mere information-sharing simply provides the recipient authority with an adequate factual basis to take its own decisions.[126] A formal conception of

[122] H Hofmann and A Türk, n 30, 136, 141.

[123] H Hofmann, 'Decision-Making in EU Administrative Law – The Problem of Composite Procedures' (2009) 61 *Administrative Law Review* 199.

[124] See Cases T-193/04 R *Tillack v Commission*, ECLI:EU:T:2004:311; C-521/04 P(R) *Tillack v Commission*, ECLI:EU:C:2005:240; and T-193/04 *Tillack v Commission*, ECLI:EU:T:2006:292.

[125] Case T-193/04 R *Tillack v Commission*, ECLI:EU:T:2004:311, paras 69 and 70.

[126] Similarly, R Schütze, n 51, 1421.

composite decision-making prevents such information-sharing from being confused with the very different scenario where national and Union authorities decide interdependently and within a single administrative procedure. In that scenario, the sole one that falls under a formal conception of composite decision-making, the preparatory acts taken by one administration condition the exercise of decisional power by another administration. On the one hand, the administration that receives a preparatory act from another is required to take specific steps, like initiating a new procedural stage or adopting a final decision that implements that preparatory act. On the other hand, the final decisions in a composite procedure may not be validly adopted by one administration unless they are preceded by legally mandated preparatory acts issued by another administration. In short, and unlike composite decision-making, information-sharing does not deprive national or Union administration from the ability to exercise their own powers independently.

Lastly, the issues of judicial control raised by information-sharing and composite decision-making are also entirely different. A complex, nuanced body of case law emerged from the CJEU's attempt to square composite decision-making with the EU's dual system of judicial review. By contrast, the CJEU straightforwardly strikes down Union decisions based on flawed information provided by national authorities.[127]

This is not to say that judicial control of information exchanges is simple – indeed, it is not.[128] But this has little to do with composite decision-making, or indeed with multilevel administration more generally. The EU's judicial system revolves around the review of binding legal acts. It is entirely inadequate to scrutinise factual conduct, such as information exchanges.[129] Indeed, it is as ill-equipped to review information exchanges taking place exclusively within Union administration as it is to review information exchanges between national and Union administration.

D. Teamed-Up, Seconded and Collegial Cooperation

Three more forms of cooperation must be added. Though still underexplored, all three are of growing practical importance.[130] One may term as 'teamed-up' cooperation the practice of instituting informal, ad hoc teams of officials from different levels of administration. The role of teams is to assist other authorities

[127] Case C-375/96 *Zaninotto*, ECLI:EU:C:1998:517, paras 34 ff.

[128] H Hofmann and A Türk, n 30, 137; and M Eliantonio, 'Information Exchange in European Administrative Law: a Threat to Effective Judicial Protection?' (2016) 23 *Maastricht Journal of European and Comparative Law* 531.

[129] See N Xanthoulis, 'Administrative factual conduct: Legal effects and judicial control in EU law' (2019) 12 *Review of European Administrative Law* 39.

[130] The analysis in the main text draws on F Brito Bastos, 'Doctrinal Methodology in EU Administrative Law: Confronting the "Touch of Stateness"' (2021) 22 *German Law Journal* 593.

in taking their own decisions. For instance, the European Central Bank (ECB) is assisted in the supervision of each significant bank by a Joint Supervisory Team, composed of staff members of both the ECB and national supervision authorities.[131] In other areas of EU law, one also finds Migration Management Support Teams, and Asylum Support Teams.[132]

Seconded cooperation consists in the temporary deployment of individual national officials to the functioning of other authorities. Seconded national experts within the framework of European Union Agency for Law Enforcement Cooperation (Europol).[133]

Lastly, one can describe as 'collegial cooperation' those instances where representatives of different national administrations decide jointly within a single body which *is not* a body that belongs to the Union's own administration (a feature which distinguishes them, for example, from comitology committees). In the Single Resolution Mechanism, regulators from national resolution authorities convene in so-called resolution colleges to adopt a single resolution plan for a credit institution with cross-border activities.[134] In the framework of European Territorial Cooperation (Interreg), Member States create joint inter-state committees to manage applications for structural funds financing in border regions.[135]

Neither teamed-up nor seconded cooperation interfere with the autonomy of other levels of administration in taking their own decisions. Both are therefore compatible with the separation principle. The same cannot be said, however, of collegial cooperation. Instances of such cooperation, albeit rare, raise entirely new legal issues that emerge from the inability to ascribe colleges' decisions to any single administration – be it the Union administration or any of the national administrations involved in them.

E. EU Agency Networks as Cooperation Clusters

The forms of cooperation set out above are not mutually exclusive and in fact often coexist within the same policy field. Administrative networks – typically

[131] Regulation (EU) No 468/2014 of the European Central Bank of 16 April 2014 establishing the framework for cooperation within the Single Supervisory Mechanism between the European Central Bank and national competent authorities and with national designated authorities, Articles 3 ff.

[132] Article 18 of Regulation (EU) 2016/1624 of the European Parliament and of the Council of 14 September 2016 on the European Border and Coast Guard and Articles 13 ff of Regulation No 439/2010 of the European Parliament and of the Council of 19 May 2010 establishing a European Asylum Support Office.

[133] See Article 56 of Regulation (EU) 2016/794 of the European Parliament and of the Council of 11 May 2016.

[134] Article 88 and ff of Directive 2014/59/EU of the European Parliament and of the Council of 15 May 2014 establishing a framework for the recovery and resolution of credit institutions and investment firms.

[135] For a case illustrating the doubts posed by these committees, see Case C-562/12 *Liivimaa Lihaveis MTÜ v Eesti-Läti programmi 2007–2013 Seirekomitee* ECLI:EU:C:2014:2229.

regulatory agency networks – do not constitute a form of cooperation of their own. Rather, such networks combine clusters of distinct forms of cooperation.

The network of national data protection authorities (DPAs) governed by the General Data Protection Regulation (GDPR) provides a good illustration. The European Data Protection Board (EDPB) is an instance of institutional cooperation – it is a Union agency where DPAs are represented.[136] DPAs, in turn, are responsible for national implementation of the EDPB's guidelines and recommendations (ie the EDPB fulfils a role of second-order administration in assisting DPAs).[137] Informational cooperation is required of all DPAs.[138] Lastly, the GDPR establishes a composite administrative procedure (ie procedural cooperation) where the EDPB decides to settle a disagreement between DPAs.[139]

V. The Road to Unitary Protection

Cooperation between national and Union administration is as old as European integration itself. The Union's administrative system, in that sense, has been a multilevel administrative system from its very beginning. The cooperative relations between national and Union authorities became ever more complex and intertwined. This process occurred just as the CJEU proceeded in crafting its constitutional doctrine of European Executive Federalism. Besides setting out their rationale and variety, the present chapter sought to show that practically none of the EU's forms of multilevel administration actually calls into question the separation between national and Union administration which that doctrine aims to uphold.

Composite procedures represent the exception, even if future additional exceptions cannot be ruled out. Indeed, because they are based on decisional interdependence of national and Union administration, composite procedures 'do not mirror a constitutional structure based on separated powers'.[140] Composite administrative procedures are diverse in their structure – in how they connect national and Union authorities in interdependent decision-making. Their typologies illustrate the scale of difference between the roles of national and Union administration, depending on how decisional dominance is allocated. The role of national authorities ranges from adopting binding opinions to serving as mere reception desks; the role of Union administration ranges from the merely advisory to the exercise of arbitral powers over national authorities. Admittedly, one finds the occasional interpretive doubt as to whether Union legislation, in defining their respective roles, aims to confer decisional dominance to the national or

[136] Article 68 GDPR.
[137] Article 70(1) GDPR.
[138] Article 60(1) GDPR.
[139] Article 65(1)(a) GDPR.
[140] G della Cananea, n 47, 199.

the Union administration.[141] Nevertheless, what all such roles have in common is that they are not exercised in isolation by national and Union authorities, in discrete administrative procedures, but within the context of one and the same administrative procedure – of a unitary administrative procedure, as Gaztea rightly points out.[142] In short, in one form or another, composite decision-making involves joint, not separate, decision-making.

Composite decision-making thus represents a form of administration which the doctrinal framework of European Executive Federalism is not designed to regulate. This mismatch between composite decision-making and European Executive Federalism raises two sets of rule of law problems – procedural and judicial. In addressing them, the CJEU came to gradually develop a novel doctrine, Unitary Protection, which accordingly entails procedural as well as judicial aspects. The rise of unitary judicial protection, analysed in Part III of this book, was extraordinary in its own right. Even though many of its solutions proved counterintuitive, the CJEU surprisingly never hesitated to set aside the same strict division between national and Union courts that still applies to the judicial review of any administrative decision-making that does not occur within composite procedures. As Part II will show, however, the CJEU proved far more reluctant to compromise the strict federal separation between the powers of national and Union administration in the name of individuals' procedural rights.

[141] Under Article 6(10) of Regulation 2019/942 of the European Parliament and of the Council, ACER, the European Union Agency for the Cooperation of Energy Regulators, is 'competent to adopt individual decisions on regulatory issues having effects on cross-border trade or cross-border system security which require a joint decision by at least two regulatory authorities'. In Case T-607/20 *Austrian Grid*, ECLI:EU:T:2023:65, the General Court was called upon to determine whether ACER is free to decide independently from the national regulatory authorities' requests (in which case it would enjoy decisional dominance) or bound to decide in conformity to them (in which case is would not). In para 50 of the Case, the General Court took the former view: 'ACER exercises its competence independently and on its own responsibility … it cannot be bound by the position taken by the competent NRAs on some of the regulatory issues … in particular where it considers that that position is not in conformity with EU energy law'.

[142] J Fernández Gaztea, *Cooperación Procedimental en la Unión Europea: Límites Jurisdiccionales* (Tirant lo Blanch, 2020), 163 ff.

PART II

Good Administration Rights

4

Unitary Procedural Protection

I. Protecting the Individuals In-between

In the early decades of European integration, as Harlow aptly puts it, the 'Commission steered but did not row'.[1] While early ECJ rulings had implied individuals to be bound to the Union by direct legal links,[2] the Union administration remained overwhelmingly limited to coordinating enforcement by national administrations. Indeed, the absence of powers exercised immediately over individuals was even taken by some renowned scholars to demonstrate that a community administrative law was conceptually impossible.[3] And yet, even operating insulated by a dense web of legal relations with only national authorities, the Union's administrative power profoundly affected individuals' lives. As one commentator noted, 'the person finally concerned … will *never meet the community authorities who decide his fate*' (emphasis added).[4]

Part II of the book examines the judicial development of procedural rights requirements in composite administrative decision-making. The legal framework of many composite procedures focuses almost exclusively on regulating relations between national and Union administrations. It is often silent on the procedural rights that individuals enjoy in relation to either. For this reason, the CJEU often had to grapple with broader questions on the place of individuals in the relations between Union and national administrations.

The present chapter fulfils a threefold aim. It considers why procedural rights have proved difficult to square with composite decision-making – not least because the Union administration was historically thought not to be bound by legal relations to individuals, let alone obliged to observe their procedural rights. The chapter further discusses the distinct alternatives that the CJEU had to address that issue and sets out the key requirements of two rights, the right to be heard and the right to a reasoned decision, which were especially hard to respect. Lastly, the

[1] C Harlow, 'Three Phases in the Evolution of EU Administrative Law', in P Craig and G de Búrca (eds), *The Evolution of EU Law* (Oxford University Press, 2011), 444.

[2] See Case 26/62 *NV Algemene Transport- en Expeditie Onderneming Van Gend en Loos v Netherlands Inland Revenue Administration*, ECLI:EU:C:1963:1 and D Chalmers and L Barroso, 'What van Gend en Loos stands for' (2014) 12 *International Journal of Constitutional Law* 105, 108.

[3] MS Giannini, 'Profili di un diritto amministrativo delle Communità europee' (1967), published posthumously in (2003) *Rivista Trimestrale di Diritto Pubblico* 979, 985.

[4] A Donner, *The Role of the Lawyer in the European Communities* (Edinburgh University Press, 1968), 12.

chapter provides an overview of the doctrinal transformation in the CJEU's overall approach – from European Executive Federalism towards a novel principle of unitary procedural protection.

Section II considers the constitutional foundations of procedural rights as elements of the rule of law and the right to good administration. The CJEU had two alternative approaches from which it could choose to establish how procedural rights ought to be observed in composite procedures. Section III considers the first approach, which ignores the unique nature of composite procedures and interprets them in the light of the rigid, dualistic logic of European Executive Federalism. The result is what can be described as a purely *inter-administrative approach*, according to which the Union authorities are only bound by legal relations with national authorities, and only national authorities are bound by legal relations – including duties of procedural protection – in respect of individuals. The second approach, explained in section IV, recognises that composite decision-making requires specific solutions to ensure that the procedural protection of affected parties is not lost between national and Union procedural phases. It requires national and Union administrations to act jointly to that end – to function, in practice, as one. This approach constitutes what will be termed a *principle of unitary procedural protection*. The development of unitary procedural protection, a unique, implicit principle of the law of composite decision-making, will be considered in greater depth regarding the right to be heard and the right to a reasoned decision (in Chapters five and six, respectively).

II. Good Administration and the Rule of Law

Public interests could never be pursued effectively if every administrative measure required the agreement of every affected individual. Put differently, public administration requires authority. It requires the delegation of decisional power to change the legal order and the legal position of individuals without their consent.[5] Given that the legislature cannot predict how best to balance public and private interests in every individual case, such decisional power will usually entail a variable margin of discretion for the administration to make its own value choices.[6]

In the EU, as in its Member States, courts may not review the merits of the value choices behind administrative decision-making.[7] Yet it is precisely due to

[5] My views draw on the Razian 'service conception' of authority (see for instance Joseph Raz, 'Authority, Law and Morality' (1985) 68 *The Monist* 295, 299) and on the conceptualisation of legal power developed by A Somek, 'Individualism' (Oxford University Press, 2008), 17 ff and A Halpin, 'The Concept of a Legal Power' (1996) 16 *Oxford Journal of Legal Studies* 129, 140–47.

[6] BG Matarella, 'Indeterminacy and Legal Uncertainty in EU Law' in J Mendes (Ed), *EU Executive Discretion and the Limits of Law* (Oxford University Press, 2019), 32 ff.

[7] For many, see J Mendes, 'Discretion, Care and Public Interests in the EU Administration: Probing The Limits Of Law' (2016) 53 *Common Market Law Review* 421.

the limited scope of judicial control, and to the breadth of administrative discretion, that procedural requirements are so essential. Procedural requirements, ie the rules governing *how* administrative decisions should be made, typically aim to steer authorities toward well-informed, rational, and balanced decision-making. In such requirements, one can distinguish two different, albeit often overlapping purposes.[8] One is of an objective or institutional nature. Procedural requirements prompt the administration to attempt to gather and evaluate all the relevant information it needs to take decisions in a manner that carefully considers all interests and policy issues at stake.[9] The other purpose is rather of a subjective nature. Many procedural requirements fall into the category of procedural guarantees, ie individual rights intended to ensure that the persons affected by administrative decisions will have adequate opportunities to defend their own interests and influence the decision-making process.

Given its role in rationalising and limiting administrative power, respect for administrative procedure represents an important requirement of the Union's rule of law.[10] Indeed, as stated in the CJEU's case law, it is in the rule of law that the Union's constitutional ideal of administrative procedure – the general principle of the right to good administration – is grounded.[11] The CJEU insists on respect for that principle in all administrative decision-making, but especially so when the Union administration exercises discretion.[12]

The exact boundaries of what constitutes good administration are disputed. Some scholars have argued that it includes both legal and non-legal aspects; not all of which can be pinned down to a single Treaty provision.[13] What appears certain, however, is that the normative core of good administration as a general

[8] Similarly, H Pünder, 'Administrative procedure – mere facilitator of material law versus cooperative realisation of common welfare' in H Pünder and C Waldhoff (eds), *Debates in German Public Law* (Hart Publishing, 2014), 239–40.

[9] J Barnes, 'Sobre el Procedimiento Administrativo: Evolución y Perspectivas' in Javier Barnes (ed), *Innovación y Reforma en el Derecho Administrativo*, 261, 270–71.

[10] M Simoncini, *Administrative Regulation beyond the Non-Delegation Doctrine: A study on EU Agencies* (Hart Publishing, 2018), 132 ff; J Mendes, *Participation in EU Rule-Making: A Rights-Based Approach* (Oxford University Press, 2011), 32 ff; F Brito Bastos and A de Ruijter, 'Break or Bend in Case of Emergency? Rule of Law and State of Emergency in European Public Health Administration' (2020) 10 *European Journal of Risk Regulation* 611, 615 ff; T von Danwitz, 'The Rule of Law in the Recent Jurisprudence of the ECJ' (2014) 37 *Fordham International Law Journal* 1311, 1316.

[11] Case T-54/99 *max.mobil Telekommunikation Service GmbH v European Commission*, ECLI:EU:T:2002:20, para 48; Joined Cases T-228/99 and T-233/99 *Westdeutsche Landesbank Girozentrale v European Commission*, ECLI:EU:T:2003:57, para 167; and Cases T-138/14 *Randa Chart v European External Action Service*, ECLI:EU:T:2015:981, para 112; T-292/15 *Vakakis kai Synergates – Symvouloi gia Agrotiki Anaptixi AE Meleton v European Commission*, ECLI:EU:T:2018:103, para 55; T-165/15 *Ryanair DAC v European Commission*, ECLI:EU:T:2018:953, para 53.

[12] Case T-835-17 *Eurofer, Association Européenne de l'Acier, AISBL v European Commission*, ECLI:EU:T:2020:96.

[13] See for instance I Koivisto, 'From Moral Rules to Individual Rights – and Beyond? The Institutionalization of Good Administration in Finland and in Europe' (2018) 1 *Förvaltningsrättslig Tidskrift* 71, and P Leino, 'Efficiency, Citizens and Administrative Culture. The Politics of Good Administration in the EU' (2014) 20 *European Public Law* 681.

principle has been enshrined in primary law since the Treaty of Lisbon. Article 41(1) and (2) of the EU's Charter of Fundamental Rights now codifies a fundamental right to good administration as a cluster of procedural rights which had hitherto remained unwritten principles in Union case law and are sometimes interchangeably referred to as 'rights of the defence'.[14]

The right to good administration encompasses 'the right of every person to be heard, before any individual measure which would affect him or her adversely is taken' (the right to be heard); 'the right of every person to have access to his or her file' (the right of access to the casefile);[15] the 'obligation of the administration to give reasons for its decisions' (the right to a reasoned decision); and the administration's duties of care, of impartiality, and the right to a decision without unreasonable delay[16] It is more controversial whether, in providing for a right to have one's affairs 'handled fairly', Article 41(1) of the Charter allows for the development of additional procedural rights which have not historically formed part of the CJEU's case law on good administration. Some scholars hold that Article 41 provides 'merely a non-exhaustive list of pre-existing rights';[17] others consider it to be sufficiently open-ended to generate novel procedural guarantees.[18]

Unlike other provisions of the Charter, Article 41, as such, only applies to the Union administration.[19] This has, however, not prevented the CJEU from continuing to hold the right to good administration to be binding on national administrations as a general principle of law, just as before the Charter entered into force.[20] The practical implications of this double life of the right to good administration as a Charter-enshrined fundamental right, applicable only to the Union, and as a general principle of law, applicable to both the Union

[14] Cases C-230/18 *PI v Landespolizeidirecktion Tirol*, ECLI:EU:C:2019:383, para 57; and T-226/18 *Global Silicones Council v European Commission*, ECLI:EU:T:2021:403, paras 313–16. Article 41(3) and (4) enshrine the right of individuals to reparation of damage caused by Union authorities and the right to communicate with the Unions' institutions in any of the EU official languages. Technically, however, these are neither procedural requirements nor rights that the CJEU has historically associated to the notion of good administration. For an overview of the fundamental administrative procedural rights enshrined in Article 41 of the Charter, see K Kańska, 'Towards Administrative Human Rights in the EU. Impact of the Charter of Fundamental Rights' (2004) 10 *European Law Journal* 296.

[15] The right is generally seen by the CJEU as implied in the right to be heard. See Case C-358/16, *UBS Europe SE v DV*, ECLI:EU: C:2018:715, para 61 ff.

[16] On the three duties see, respectively, Case T-279/11, *T & L Sugars Ltd v European Commission*, ECLI:EU:T:2016:683; Case T-783/17, *GE Healthcare A/S v European Commission*, ECLI:EU:T:2019:624; and Cases T-389/10 and T-419/10, *Siderurgica Latina Martin SpA v European Commission*, ECLI:EU:T: 2015:513.

[17] R Bhousta, 'Who Said There is a "Right to Good Administration"? A Critical Analysis of Article 41 of the Charter of Fundamental Rights of the European Union' (2013) 19 *European Public Law* 481, 482.

[18] L Perfetti, 'Diritto ad una buona amministrazione, determinazione dell'interesse pubblico ed equità' (2010) 3–4 *Rivista Italiana di Diritto Pubblico Comunitario* 789, 818.

[19] Case C-482/10 *Cicala v Regione Siciliana*, ECLI:EU:C:2011:868, para 28.

[20] Cases C-604/12 *H.N. v Minister for Justice, Equality and Law Reform*, ECLI:EU:C:2014:302, paras 49–50; and C-249/13 *Boudjlida v Préfet des Pyrénées-Atlantiques*, ECLI:EU:C:2014:2431, paras 32–34.

and the Member States, are still being fleshed out in the literature and judicial practice.[21]

In short, national and Union authorities alike are subject to the various procedural requirements flowing from good administration, a principle which is essential to the Union's rule of law. And yet, the observance of such requirements has historically proven difficult whenever national and Union administration do not decide in isolation from one another, but jointly. Indeed, the rise of composite administrative procedures confronted the CJEU with the question of how the burden of fulfilling the requirements of good administration should be divided between national and Union authorities, given their involvement at distinct but interdependent procedural stages.

Overwhelmingly, the issues addressed in CJEU's case law on good administration in composite decision-making concerned the observance of the right to be heard and, to a lesser degree, the right to a reasoned decision. Only recently, as will be shown, have there been significant developments concerning the observance of the duty of impartiality as well as the creation of an entirely new procedural right.

Given its prominence and complexity, the CJEU case law concerning the right to be heard and the right to a reasoned decision will be examined in depth in Chapters five and six. However, before doing so, the remainder of this chapter will briefly map the scope and function of both rights, in particular those aspects of them that represented a special challenge to European Executive Federalism.

A. Right to be Heard

The right to be heard, right to a fair hearing, or administrative obligation of *audi alteram partem*, has long been considered by Union courts as a 'fundamental' general principle rooted in the constitutional traditions common to the Member States.[22] The right requires that every person has an opportunity 'to be heard,

[21] The Opinion of AG Bobek in Case C-298/16 *Ispas v Direcția Generală a Finanțelor Publice Cluj*, ECLI:EU:C:2017:650, is a remarkable illustration of this issue. In the literature, see H Hofmann and B Mihaescu, 'The Relation between the Charter's Fundamental Rights and the Unwritten General Principles of EU Law: Good Administration as the Test Case' (2013) 9 *European Constitutional Law Review* 73.

[22] See Cases 17/74 *Transocean Marine Paint Association v European Commission*, ECLI:EU:C:1974:91, para 15; Case 136/79 *National Panasonic (UK) Ltd v European Commission*, ECLI:EU:C:1980:169, para 21; Case 85/87 *Dow Benelux NV v European Commission*, ECLI:EU:C:1989:379, para 25; C-204/00–205/00 P C-211/00 P, C-213/00 P, C-217/00 P and C-219/00 P *Aalborg Portland A/S v European Commission*, ECLI:EU:C:2004:6, para 64; and T-410/06 *Foshan City Nanhai Golden Step Industrial Co Ltd v European Council*, ECLI:EU:T:2010:70, para 109. In general, on the Court's case law on procedural rights, see D Curtin, 'Constitutionalism in the European Community. The Right to Fair Procedures in Administrative Law' in B Walsh and J O'Reilly, *Human Rights and Constitutional Law. Essays in Honour of Brian Walsh* (Round Hall Press, 1992); and J Schwarze, 'The Procedural Guarantees in the Recent Case-law of the European Court of Justice' in D Curtin and T Heukels (eds),

before any individual measure which would affect him or her adversely is taken' (Article 41(2)(a) of the Charter).[23] It is recognised in EU law to have important implications for the rule of law.[24] The reasons for this are easy to grasp.

The CJEU itself speaks of a 'dual objective' of the right to be heard.[25] On the one hand, the right to be heard promotes decisional rationality. It obliges the administration to be confronted with opposing points of view and to consider additional information brought by interested parties which may be relevant for the final decision. On the other hand, the right to be heard fulfils a protective function. It provides interested parties with an opportunity to correct errors in the information used against them, and to state their views as to whether a decision should have a specific content or not be taken at all.[26]

As a result of its nature as a general principle of Union law, the right to be heard is required by the CJEU to be respected '*in all circumstances*';[27] and *even in the absence of any legal provisions providing for that right*.[28] Accordingly, the right to be heard has often been applied to fill gaps of procedural protection in administrative procedures unfolding at the Union level and, though only more recently, at the national level as well.[29]

Institutional Dynamics of European Integration: Essays in Honour of Henry G. Schermers, vol II (Martinus Nijhoff, 1994).

[23] As the wording suggests, the protection offered by the right to be heard before the adoption of an 'individual measure' indicates that, in principle, there is no right to be heard before the enactment of measures of general application, such as Commission implementing regulations. See Cases T-337/18 and T-347/18 *Laboratoire Pareva v European Commission*, ECLI:EU:T:2021:594, para 221.

[24] See the Opinion of AG Poiares Maduro in Joined Cases C-402/05 P and C-415/05 P *Kadi v European Council*, ECLI:EU:C:2008:11, para 49 and, more recently, the General Court's ruling in Case T-138/14 *Randa Chart v European External Action Service*, ECLI:EU:T:2015:981, para 112. See also Takis Tridimas, *The General Principles of EU law*, 2nd edn (Oxford University Press, 2006), 371 and H Hofmann, G Rowe and A Türk, *Administrative Law and Policy of the European Union* (Oxford University Press, 2011), 204.

[25] Case T-510/17 *Del Valle Ruiz v European Commission*, ECLI:EU:T:2022:312, para 120.

[26] See the Opinion of AG Bot in Case C-277/11, *M.M. v Minister for Justice, Equality and Law Reform*, ECLI:EU:C:2012:253, paras 34–46 and Case C-189/18, *Glencore Agriculture Hungary Kft. v Nemzeti Adó- és Vámhivatal Fellebbviteli Igazgatósága*, ECLI:EU:C:2019:861, para 41, and, more recently, T-351/18 *Ukreslhosprom PCF LLC and Versobank AS v European Central Bank*, ECLI:EU:T:2021:669, para 371.

[27] See Cases 322/81 *NV Nederlandsche Banden Industrie Michelin v European Commission*, ECLI:EU:C:1983:313, para 7 and T-30/91 *Solvay SA v European Commission*, ECLI:EU:T:1995:115, para 59.

[28] For rulings concerning Union-level decision-making, see Cases 85/76 *Hoffmann-La Roche & Co AG v European Commission*, ECLI:EU:C:1979:36, para 9; 40/85 *Kingdom of Belgium v Commission*, ECLI:EU:C:1986:305, para 28; 259/85 *French Republic v Commission*, ECLI:EU:C:1987:478, para 12; 301/87 *French Republic v Commission*, ECLI:EU:C:1990:67, para 29; and T-260/11 *Kingdom of Spain v Commission*, ECLI:EU:T:2014:555, paras 62–63. For rulings concerning national decision-making, see Case C-383/13 PPU, *M.G. v Staatssecretaris van Veiligheid en Justitie*, ECLI:EU:C:2013:533, para 32; and Joined Cases C-129/13 and C-130/13 *Kamino*, ECLI:EU:C:2014:2041, para 39.

[29] See Case C-349/07 *Sopropé*, ECLI:EU:C:2008:746. For a prior decision, see Case C-28/05 *Dokter*, ECLI:EU:C:2006:408. For an analysis of the influence of EU law in the introduction of rights of the defence at national level, see T Duijkersloot, 'Consequences of the Violation by Administrative Authorities of the Right to be heard under EU Law: the Case M.G. and N.R.' (2014) 7 *Review of European Administrative Law* 81, 90 ff.

The test to determine *when* the right applies has given rise to much debate.[30] The Charter as well as CJEU case law require the right to be respected 'in all proceedings *initiated against a person* which are liable to culminate in a measure *adversely affecting* that person' (emphasis added).[31] The wording – 'initiated against' – should be understood as a remnant of the origins of the right to be heard in case law relating to administrative sanctions, such as disciplinary sanctions in the EU civil service or penalties in EU competition law.[32] More recently, CJEU case law has made explicit that the right broadly applies when the administration is minded to take a decision which may adversely affect the interests of an individual.[33] Accordingly, such a decision may be a sanction, but also, among many others, the refusal to renew an authorisation or the exclusion of a market operator from a tender.[34]

It is crucial that the persons affected by a decision must 'be placed in a position in which they may *effectively* make known their views' (emphasis added).[35] Whatever form the hearing takes – and it will typically be in writing, given the absence of a right to an *oral* hearing in EU law[36] – it must offer the individual a genuine opportunity to influence the outcome of the procedure. In this regard, the CJEU has delimited the issues on which interested parties must be able to state their views. In the CJEU's words, while the right to be heard extends 'to *all the matters of fact and of law* which form the basis for the decision-making act', it does not extend to '*the final position* which the administration intends to adopt' (emphasis added).[37] EU law does not generally require the administration to hear affected parties on purely preparatory acts.[38] Indeed, and unlike some national

[30] See the contribution of I Rabinovici, 'The Right to Be Heard in the Charter of Fundamental Rights of the European Union' (2012) 18 *European Public Law* 149.

[31] Case C-161/15 *Bensada Benallal v État Belge*, ECLI:EU:C:2016:175, para 33.

[32] Case 32/62 *Alvis v European Council*, ECLI:EU:C:1963:15. See for instance R Lauwaars, 'Rights of Defence in Competition Cases' in D Curtin and T Heukels (eds), *Institutional Dynamics of European Integration: Essays in Honour of Henry G. Schermers*, vol II (Martinus Nijhoff, 1994).

[33] Case C-152/19 P *Deutsche Telekom AG v European Commission*, ECLI:EU:C:2021:238, para 105 and case law cited there. See also Case C-189/18 *Glencore Agriculture Hungary*, ECLI:EU:C:2019:861, para 39.

[34] Case T-719/17 *FMC Corporation v European Commission*, ECLI:EU:T: 2021:143, para 183, and Case C-387/19 *RTS infra BVBA v Vlaams Gewest*, ECLI:EU:C:2021:13, para 34.

[35] Case C-418/11 *Texdata Software GmbH*, ECLI:EU:C:2013:588, para 83. In the literature, see E Barbier de la Serre, 'Procedural Justice in the European Community Case-law concerning the Rights of the Defence: Essentialist and Instrumental Trends' (2006) 12 *European Public Law* 225, 233.

[36] See for instance Case T-202/12, *Bouchra Al Assad v European Council*, ECLI:EU:T:2014:113, para 79. Oral hearings are, however, an important aspect of the Commission's competition law enforcement proceedings. See Wouter Wils, 'The Oral Hearing in Competition Proceedings before the European Commission' (2012) 35 *World Competition* 397.

[37] For many, see Cases T-15/02 *BASF AG v European Commission*, ECLI:EU:T:2006:74, para 94; T-18/05 *IMI plc v European Commission*, ECLI:EU:T:2010:202, para 104; and T-392/09 *1. garantovaná a.s. v European Commission*, ECLI:EU:T:2012:674, para 74.

[38] Case C-276/12 *Sabou v Finanční ředitelství pro hlavní město Prahu*, ECLI:EU:C:2013:678, para 46. This point is well-established in EU competition law cases. See eg Cases T-395/94 *Atlantic Container Line AB v European Commission*, ECLI:EU:T:2002:49, para 417; and T-357/06 *Koninklijke Wegenbouw Stevin BV v European Commission*, ECLI:EU:T:2012:488, para 227.

legal orders, there is no right to be heard on *the likely outcome* of the procedure or on the contents of a *draft decision*.[39]

B. Right to a Reasoned Decision

The right to a reasoned decision constitutes an 'essential principle' of Union law which requires the administration to justify its own decisions.[40] In CJEU case law, the right is generally treated as instrumental to judicial control.[41] Much like judicial control itself, the right to a reasoned decision serves to place administrative power under the rule of law.[42] It fulfils the same dual purpose as judicial control.[43]

One aim is to ensure the protection of individuals – to ensure 'that the person adversely affected by the measure in question has the right to an effective remedy'.[44] Statements of reasons enable the person concerned to examine whether a decision was taken based on flawed reasoning and to weigh whether a judicial challenge against it could potentially succeed.[45] Statements of reasons also fulfil 'a more general objective, namely to ensure that the EU Courts are able to review the legality of the measure challenged before them'.[46] Indeed, statements of reasons assist courts in checking whether the administration has committed manifest errors of appraisal or misuse of power in the exercise of its discretion, or whether the factual and legal conditions for the adoption of the decision have been met.[47]

However, the purpose of reasons-giving transcends judicial control. It also contributes to exposing authorities' poor judgement, partiality, or maladministration.

[39] See, for instance, Article 122(2) of the Portuguese Code of Administrative Procedure.

[40] See Cases T-218/02 *Napoli Buzzanca v European Commission*, ECLI:EU:T:2005:343 para 57; T-159/09 *Biofrescos – Comércio de Produtos Alimentares, Lda v European Commission*, ECLI:EU:T:2012:307, para 37; and F-73/13 *AX v European Central Bank*, ECLI:EU:F:2015:9, para 188.

[41] Case T-15/20 *Skyliners GmbH v European Union Intellectual Property Office*, ECLI:EU:T:2021:401, para 75. Variations of this formula can be found in numerous rulings. See Cases T-306/00 *Conserve Italia Soc coop. rl. v European Commission*, ECLI:EU:T:2003:338, para 45; C-76/01 P *Comité des industries du coton et des fibres connexes de l'Union européenne (Eurocoton) v European Council*, ECLI:EU:C:2003:511, para 88; and Joined Cases T-44/01, T-119/01 and T-126/01 *Eduardo Vieira SA v European Commission*, ECLI:EU:T:2003:98, para 193; and C-564/16 P *European Union Intellectual Property Office v Puma SE*, ECLI:EU:C:2018:509, paras 64–65.

[42] See the Opinion of AG Kokott, in Case C-413/06 P *Bertelsmann AG v European Commission*, ECLI:EU:C:2008:392, paras 97–98 and KD Classen, *Gute Verwaltung im Recht der Europäischen Union* (Duncker & Humblot, 2006), 321.

[43] The purposes of judicial control are analysed in further detail in Chapter 6.

[44] See Case T-461/08 *Evropaïki Dynamiki – Proigmena Systimata Tilepikoinonion Pliroforikis kai Tilematikis AE v European Investment Bank*, ECLI:EU:T:2011:494, para 122.

[45] See Cases T-181/08 *Pye Phyo Tay Za v European Council*, ECLI:EU:T:2010:209, para 94; T-159/09 *Biofrescos*, ECLI:EU:T:2012:307, para 37; and T-509/10 *Manufacturing Support and Procurement Kala Naft v European Council*, ECLI:EU:T:2012:201, para 72.

[46] Case T-145/15 *Romania v European Commission*, ECLI:EU:T:2017:86, para 43.

[47] See inter alia Cases 42/84 *Remia BV v Commission*, ECLI:EU:C:1985:327, para 34; and T-260/11 *Kingdom of Spain v Commission*, ECLI:EU:T:2014:555, para 63.

It facilitates public scrutiny and promotes a culture of administrative transparency and accountability.[48] Importantly, the duty to give reasons serves as a guarantee of decisional rationality or, as others put it, as a form of self-discipline or self-regulation for decision-makers.[49] Indeed, if legally obliged to formally justify decisions, administrators cannot avoid a self-conscious examination of the reasonableness of their own choices.[50]

In European administrative law, three questions are particularly important when considering the duty to give reasons: first, which authorities are bound by it; second, when it applies; and third, what must be the content of statements of reasons.

Article 296(2) TFEU has long established a general obligation on the part of Union authorities to state reasons for all their legal acts. Today, the duty is enshrined in Article 41(1)(c) of the Charter as a fundamental right, though only in respect of *individual decisions*.[51] Even though Articles 296(2) TFEU and 41(1)(c) of the Charter only apply to EU authorities, the duty to give reasons also applies to national administration. This has never resulted from any explicit requirement in primary law, but rather from the CJEU's understanding of good administration and, before that, of the principle of effective judicial protection.[52]

As for when the duty to give reasons applies, a nuanced answer is needed. Given the breadth of Article 296 TFEU, Union authorities must give reasons whenever they adopt measures entailing binding legal effects,[53] regardless of whether they are preparatory or final; regardless of whether they are of individual or general application;[54] regardless of their legislative or administrative nature; and regardless

[48] See D Curtin, *Executive Power in the European Union: Law, Practices, and the Living Constitution* (Oxford University Press, 2009), 208–9. See also G Majone, 'From the Positive to the Regulatory State: Causes and Consequences of Changes in the Mode of Governance' (1997) 17 *Journal of Public Policy* 139, 160; C Harlow, *Accountability in the European Union* (Oxford University Press, 2002), 160; J Mashaw, 'Reasoned Administration: the European Union, the United States and the Project of Democratic Governance' (2007) 76 *George Washington Law Review* 99, 115; and O Brouwer and D Curtin, 'Why? The Giving Reasons Requirement of EU Administration' in M Bulterman, L Hancher, A McDonnell and H Sevenster (eds), *Views of European Law from the Mountain – Liber Amicorum Piet Jan Slot* (Kluwer Law International, 2009), 135–36.

[49] For a sophisticated discussion of this point, see J Mendes, 'The Foundations of the Duty to Give Reasons and a Normative Reconstruction' in E Fisher, J King and A Young (eds), *The Foundations and Future of Public Law: Essays in Honour of Paul Craig* (Oxford University Press, 2020), 299–322. See also R Thomas, 'Reasons-giving in English and European Community Administrative Law' (1997) 3 *European Public Law* 213, 213.

[50] See M Shapiro, 'The Giving Reasons Requirement' (1992) 92 *University of Chicago Legal Forum* 179, 180.

[51] For the 'double status' of the duty to give reasons as an objective requirement of legality under Article 296 TFEU and as a right of individuals vis-à-vis the administration, see Joined Cases C-584/20 P and C-621/20 P *SRB v Landesbank Baden-Württemberg*, ECLI:EU:C:2021:601, para 102.

[52] Joined Cases C-225/19 and C-226/19 *R.N.N.S. v Minister van Buitenlandse Zaken*, ECLI:EU:C:2020:951, paras 33–34 and 43.

[53] See G della Cananea, *Due Process of Law Beyond the State: Requirements of Administrative Procedure* (Oxford University Press, 2016), 77.

[54] P Craig, *EU Administrative Law*, 2nd edn (Oxford University Press, 2012), 341.

of whether they are favourable or adverse to private parties,[55] though in the latter case, and especially in the case of decisions involving sanctions, the bar is set higher for how detailed the reasons must be.[56]

The duty of national authorities to give reasons, by contrast, 'concerns only individual decisions adversely affecting individuals against which the latter must have some remedy of a judicial nature'.[57] This is why, as was already implicit in *Heylens*,[58] a landmark ruling on the principle of effective judicial protection, national administration is only under a duty to reason final decisions. National administration is not under a duty to give reasons for purely preparatory acts.[59] Nor is it under a duty to reason any other measures which national courts are not required to review in the name of effective judicial protection.[60]

Finally, every statement of reasons must observe several cumulative requirements, which must be assessed according to its wording as well as the specific legal and factual context of the case.[61] Statements of reasons must: be *appropriate to the act* at issue; disclose in a *clear and unequivocal fashion* the reasoning followed by the deciding authority; enable *the persons concerned* to ascertain the reasons of fact and law behind the decision; and enable the competent *court* to exercise its power of review. However, not all reasons need to be stated. Authorities need only disclose those which were of *decisive* importance for the decision they took.[62]

[55] See the Opinion of AG Kokott in Case C-413/06 P, *Bertelsmann*, n 42 above, para 98.

[56] See for instance T-199/99 *Sgaravatti Mediterranea Srl v European Commission* ECLI:EU:T:2002:228, para 101. The General Court emphasised the Commission's responsibility to clearly set out its reasons for adopting a decision reducing the amount of ESF assistance, given that decisions of that character cause serious consequences for beneficiaries. See also Cases C-181/90 *Consorgan*, ECLI:EU:C:1992:244, paras 16–18; C-41/00 P *Interporc Im- und Export GmbH v European Commission*, ECLI:EU:C:2003:125, para 55; T-196/01 *Aristoteleio Panepistimio Thessalonikis v European Commission*, ECLI:EU:T:2003:249, paras 52–53; and C-417/11 P *Bamba*, ECLI:EU:C:2012:718, para 49. In cases involving penalties, the General Court has required the European Central Bank and European Commission to set out the specific criteria and methodology used to evaluate the severity of the infraction and calculate the fine. See Case T-576/18 *Crédit Agricole SA v European Central Bank*, ECLI:EU:T:2020:304, paras 131–36.

[57] Case C-70/95 *Sodemare SA v Regione Lombardia*, ECLI:EU:C:1997:301, para 19.

[58] See Case 222/86 *Union nationale des entraîneurs et cadres techniques professionnels du football (Unectef) v Heylens*, ECLI:EU:C:1987:442, para 15. The same interpretation is made by HP Nehl, *Europäisches Verwaltungsverfahren und Gemeinschaftsverfassung. Eine Studie gemeinschaftsrechtlicher Verfahrensgrundsätze unter besonderer Berücksichtigung 'mehrstufiger' Verwaltungsverfahren* (Duncker & Humblot, 2002), 407–9.

[59] Case C-127/95 *Norbrook Laboratories Ltd v Ministry of Agriculture, Fisheries and Food*, ECLI:EU:C:1998:151, para 103.

[60] There is, for instance, no duty on the part of national authorities to give reasons for measures of general application, which is consistent with the fact that EU law generally does not require the Member States to establish remedies against national measures of general application. See *Sodemare* (n 57 above), paras 19–20 and Case C-432/05 *Unibet (London) Ltd v Justitiekanslern*, ECLI:EU:C:2007:163, para 65.

[61] See eg Cases T-24/05 *Alliance One International, Inc v European Commission*, ECLI:EU:T:2010:453, para 149; T-89/07 *VIP Car Solutions SARL v European Parliament*, ECLI:EU:T:2009:163, para 62; and T-165/12 *European Dynamics Luxembourg SA v European Commission*, ECLI:EU:T:2013:646, para 64.

[62] Cases C-131/15 P *Club Hotel Loutraki AE v European Commission*, ECLI:EU:C:2016:989, paras 46–47 and T-108/18 *Universität Koblenz-Landau v Education, Audiovisual and Culture Executive Agency*, ECLI:EU:T:2021:104, para 97.

III. The Inter-Administrative Approach to Procedural Rights

Good administration constitutes the rule of law backbone of the Union's administrative procedural law. Its constituent rights must be observed by both national and Union authorities. And yet, such observance has often proved problematic in composite decision-making.

The root of the problem is that, more often than not, Union legislation focuses almost exclusively on linking national and Union administrations, while saying little about the rights of individuals.[63] Chapter three noted that multilevel administration is shaped by complex considerations pertaining to the functional characteristics of national and Union administrations as well as to the aim of attaining an adequate balance of power between them. The legal position of the individual often seems to come as somewhat of an afterthought. This is true for all forms of multilevel administration, but especially so for composite decision-making. The provisions governing many composite procedures – though not all[64] – completely omit any reference to the rights of the defence of individuals, be it at the national or Union stages of the administrative procedure.[65]

Chapter three also noted that most forms of multilevel administration can be accommodated under the precepts of European Executive Federalism. Chapter two explained the development of some of those precepts, such as the principle of loyal cooperation and the separation principle. First, relations of cooperation between national and Union authorities tended to be regarded by the Court of Justice as purely internal to them. Second, the separation between national and Union administrations translates into a principle of separation of legal relations between individuals and national authorities, on the one hand, and between national and Union authorities, on the other. The separation principle also translates into a requirement that either level of administration remains exclusively responsible for its own tasks and that, in the absence of

[63] C Eckes and J Mendes, 'The Right to be Heard in Composite Administrative Procedures: lost in between protection?' (2011) 36 *European Law Review* 665.

[64] Indeed, some scholars have argued that some composite procedures not only provide for procedural rights, but have even proven to be 'remarkably applicant-friendly' 'beyond any practicability' (F Shirvani, 'Verfahrensgrundrechte in mehrstufigen, das EU-Recht vollziehenden Verwaltungsverfahren – Dargestellt am Beispiel des Arzneimittelzulassungs- und Gentechnikrechts' (2011) 126 *Deutsches Verwaltungsblatt* 674, 678 and 681).

[65] Composite procedures which *do not* provide for the participation of affected private parties are legion. As a few examples from the internal market alone, one could list the EU's administrative procedures for the authorisation of food additives, food enzymes and food flavourings (Regulation 1331/2008), the authorisation procedure for permissible detergents in the internal market (Regulation 648/2006), and the authorisation procedure for GMO food and feed (Regulation 1829/2003). There are also no provisions on individual procedural rights in the procedure for granting exclusive access to gas storage facilities to operators in the gas market (see Directive 2009/73/EC of the European Parliament and of the Council of 13 July 2009 concerning common rules for the internal market in natural gas), or in granting authorisations to set up aquaculture facilities with potential cross-border environmental effects (see Regulation 708/2007 concerning use of alien and locally absent species in aquaculture).

explicit provisions to the contrary, administrative decision-making for the enforcement of Union law falls only to national – not Union – authorities.

When put together, these precepts support a *purely inter-administrative* approach to procedural rights whenever Union legislation provides for Union administration only to take decisions addressed to, or at the request of national authorities – not individuals. According to this inter-administrative approach, such legislation should be interpreted as confining the Union administration to legal relations with national authorities, and as exempting it from any legal relations with – including procedural duties toward – citizens.

However, exempting the Union administration from any duty to observe procedural rights is only sensible in certain cases. It is a convincing solution where the Union administration functions as an *authentic* second-order administration, in the sense explained in Chapter three – ie when it adopts decisions which do not affect the legal position of individuals and are genuinely *only* of concern to national authorities. The European Regional Development Fund is a case in point. The CJEU invokes a 'principle of the separation of legal relations' to prevent the Commission from being bound by any 'direct link' to funding beneficiaries when it decides to impose financial corrections on Member States.[66] Because the Commission's decisions are only addressed to the Member States and do not require their administrations to recover funds irregularly paid to beneficiaries, the latter have no right to be heard before a financial correction is imposed.[67] The same can be said of when the Commission approves national implementation measures in Greenhouse Gas emission allowance trading schemes. Given that its role is but to consider whether national implementation measures comply with Union law, the Commission only decides in respect of the Member State. It does not decide, even indirectly, on individual allowances – which is the reason why the right to be heard must be observed at national level, by the Member States' environmental protection authorities that grant such allowances.[68]

By contrast, an inter-administrative approach should not apply in instances of merely *apparent* second-order administration. Put differently, the Union administration should not be exempt from observing procedural rights when it can require national authorities to take specific decisions in respect of individuals, and therefore exercises powers over individuals in all but form. In such cases, the Court of Justice *should have* always recognised that individuals must enjoy procedural protection even when they are not the formal addressees of the Union administration's decisions (indeed, much as they have always enjoyed *judicial* protection against such decisions).[69]

[66] Cases T-60/03 *Regione Siciliana v Commission (Regione Siciliana II)*, ECLI:EU:T:2005:360, para 33 and T-512/14 *Green Source Poland sp. z o.o. v European Commission*, ECLI:EU:T:2017:299, para 47.

[67] Case C-414/08 P *Sviluppo Italia Basilicata SpA v European Commission*, ECLI:EU:C:2010:165, paras 87–89.

[68] Case T-269/21 *Arctic Paper Grycksbo AB v European Commission*, ECLI:EU:T:2023:429, paras 88–90.

[69] Article 263 TFEU grants locus standi not only to the addressee of a decision, but also to persons who are directly concerned by it. The standard definition of 'direct concern' in CJEU case law is that

And yet, the Court of Justice in fact followed the formalistic inter-administrative approach in composite decision-making until 1993. That approach resulted in a denial of procedural protection which was – and still is – irreconcilable with the CJEU's own standards of good administration.

As was mentioned before, the right to be heard entitles individuals to *effectively* state their views. The right applies simply by virtue of individuals being *adversely affected* by a decision, and even when the applicable legislation is silent on whether hearings should be offered. In early case law on composite procedures, every one of these requirements was breached. Rather than detecting a gap in procedural protection, the Court held that the absence of references to procedural rights in legislation reflected a conscious political choice only to require the Commission to interact with national administration.[70] It treated national and Union stages of composite procedures as separate procedures, governing the exercise of separate powers at national and Union levels, and involving two separate legal relationships. Considering that the legislation only established legal relations between individuals and national authorities, on the one hand, and national and Union administrations, on the other, the Court concluded that the Commission only needed to deal with national authorities. The Commission was therefore not required to hear individuals and firms, regardless of how deeply affected they were by its decisions. Similarly, the CJEU only required the Union administration to discharge its duty to give reasoned decisions in a manner that would be understandable to national administration – and not necessarily to the individuals affected by them.

In short, the inter-administrative approach dominated the CJEU's early rulings on composite decision-making and procedural rights. Its endurance may reflect the CJEU's increasingly explicit view that the principles of European Executive Federalism, from which that approach was drawn, were constitutionally embedded in the Treaties.

IV. Unitary Procedural Protection, Decisional Dominance and the Unitary Administration

Eventually, the Court of Justice abandoned the formalistic inter-administrative approach to procedural rights. With one exception,[71] the case law reveals a

a measure is able to 'affect directly the legal situation of the individual and leave no discretion to its addressees, who are entrusted with the task of implementing it, such implementation being purely automatic and resulting from European Union rules without the application of other intermediate rules' (see Joined Cases T-454/10 and T-482/11 *Associazione Nazionale degli Industriali delle Conserve Alimentari Vegetali (Anicav) v European Commission*, ECLI:EU:T:2013:282, para 36).

[70] Some Commission pleadings explicitly state that this was precisely what the Union legislator had intended. See Case T-260/94 *Air Inter SA v European Commission*, ECLI:EU:T:1997:89, para 58.

[71] The exception is State aid review, as Chapters 5 and 6 will explain.

transition towards an entirely different approach. The overarching principle of the case law today is that the division of decisional power between Union and national administrations within composite decision-making should not impair individuals' procedural protection. Both administrations must work together to ensure such protection. The Union administration is considered to be bound by direct links to individuals and by a duty to observe their procedural rights. For this reason, the CJEU's second approach will be referred to as the *principle of unitary procedural protection*.

The aim of unitary procedural protection is attained by two components. Both stand in stark contrast with the principle of 'strict separation' between the powers of national and Union administration.

First, the CJEU relies on a test of *decisional dominance*. The ultimate responsibility for procedural rights falls to the level of administration having the power to define a composite procedure's final outcome. This is logical in view of the justification of good administration requirements in the rule of law. The greater the discretionary powers of administration, the more it should be subject to procedural safeguards to prevent their arbitrary use. The test of decisional dominance represents a departure from the separation principle in two ways. On the one hand, it does not treat national and Union administrations as strictly separate; only the dominant administration bears final responsibility for the observance of procedural rights *throughout the entirety* of the composite administrative procedure. On the other hand, decisional dominance implies a departure from the notion of separate legal relations. If it exercises decisional dominance, the Union administration is obliged to respect the rights of individuals. It is bound by legal relations to them – even if only required by the relevant sectoral legislation to interact with national authorities.

The second component of unitary procedural protection specifically concerns cases where decisional dominance falls to the Union administration. The Union administration may discharge its own duty to observe procedural rights with the assistance of national authorities. Yet it does so at its own peril, as any violation of procedural rights by national authorities may become imputable to Union administration and therefore be reviewable by the CJEU.[72] This implies a departure from the separation principle as well. Instead of requiring either level of administration to be exclusively responsible for its own legal obligations, the case law allows the Union administration to *share* its burden to comply with procedural rights with national authorities. Moreover, by ensuring that the Union administration observes procedural rights *through* and *with* national authorities, the CJEU preserves the latter as the primary interlocutor of individuals, as is often intended by the Union legislator.

[72] See B Mihaescu Evans, *The Right to Good administration at the Crossroads of the Various Sources of Fundamental Rights in the EU Integrated Administrative System* (Nomos, 2015), 293.

The principle of unitary procedural protection as developed by the CJEU encompasses multiple implicit rules which are unique to composite decision-making. They are unique in two senses. On the one hand, unitary procedural protection departs from the CJEU's normal interpretation of good administration. Section II.A. noted that, under Union law, the right to be heard only entitles adversely affected parties be heard on points of fact and law that will support the decision, but not on the decision itself. It does not entitle individuals to a hearing before the adoption of purely preparatory acts. Neither assertion holds in composite decision-making. National and Union authorities may be required to hear affected individuals on the content of their intended decisions. National authorities, in particular, must hear individuals before sending preparatory acts, such as proposals or opinions, to the Union administration.

On the other hand, the case law developing the principle of unitary procedural protection is unique in the sense that its rules, by definition, can *only* apply in composite decision-making. Chapters five and six will examine several of these rules in greater detail from the point of view of the rights to be heard and to a reasoned decision. However, it should be emphasised that unitary procedural protection is not restricted to those rights and has, in fact, already permeated the case law on other procedural requirements. Chapter eight will consider one peculiar new right that is intended to facilitate effective judicial protection. One other right that ought to be mentioned from the outset concerns the guarantee of administrative impartiality.

In *August Wolff*,[73] German pharmaceutical regulation authorities had rejected the renewal of a marketing authorisation for a medicine. They also initiated the referral procedure set out in the Community Code of medicinal products for human use.[74] The procedure in question may be initiated by a national regulator, after which the European Medicines Agency's Committee for Medicinal Products for Human Use prepares a reasoned opinion. That opinion serves as the basis for the Commission's final decision. The Committee appoints one of its members – who represent national regulators[75] – as rapporteur. In *August Wolff*, the rapporteur had been an employee of the same German authority which had initially rejected the renewal of the authorisation. The Court of Justice found that the appointment of the rapporteur violated the objective component of the principle of impartiality, a requirement of good administration, according to

[73] Case C-680/16 P *Dr August Wolff GmbH & Co v European Commission*, ECLI:EU:C:2019:257.

[74] Articles 31–33 of Directive 2001/83/EC of the European Parliament and of the Council of 6 November 2001 on the Community code relating to medicinal products for human use.

[75] Article 61(1) of Regulation (EC) 726/2004 of the European Parliament and of the Council of 31 March 2004 laying down Community procedures for the authorisation and supervision of medicinal products for human and veterinary use and establishing a European Medicines Agency.

which any legitimate doubt as to possible bias of the administration must be excluded.[76] The Court recalled that

> where a number of EU institutions or bodies are given separate responsibilities of their own in the context of a procedure …, each of those institutions and bodies is required, in respect of its own activities, to comply with the requirement of objective impartiality,

and that the final decision of the procedure may be illegal 'even where only one of them has breached that requirement'.[77]

The CJEU extended this requirement of impartiality of all 'EU institutions or bodies' throughout the same administrative procedure to include the *national* bodies involved in composite decision-making.[78] Remarkably, the CJEU expressly applied Article 41 of the Charter to national administration, despite the provision's scope being limited to the Union administration only. This is reflective of a broader trend in the case law which Chapter ten will consider in greater depth – a trend for the CJEU to treat national administration as integrated with, or indeed *into*, Union administration.

V. Unity, Dominance, and Doctrinal Transition

The present chapter has highlighted that the EU's core ideal of administrative procedure lies in good administration, a general principle and fundamental right that is inextricable from the Union's rule of law. It has also highlighted that CJEU case law can be divided into two distinct approaches as to how good administration rights should be observed in composite decision-making. The first approach is based on the precepts of European Executive Federalism. It is a purely inter-administrative approach, according to which composite procedures are assumed to involve separate powers of national and Union administrations, and therefore separate legal relations between individuals and national authorities, on the one hand, and between national authorities and the Union administration, on the other. The implication is that the Union administration is not required to observe procedural rights – even if its decisions, though formally addressed to national authorities, have a profound impact on individuals' legal positions. While the Court of Justice often used the inter-administrative approach as if it constituted no more than a literal application of the legislation, it is no coincidence that such an approach was developed in a period that overlapped with

[76] See eg Case C-521/15 *Spain v European Council*, ECLI:EU:C:2017:982, para 91. The subjective component of the principle of impartiality requires the freedom of individual members of authorities from bias or prejudice.

[77] *August Wolff*, n 73 above, para 28.

[78] Similarly, S Röttger-Wirtz, 'Fine-tuning the Impartiality of EMA Procedures: Case C-680/16 P Dr. August Wolff GmbH vs European Commission' (2019) 3 *European Pharmaceutical Law Review* 192, 194–95.

the *Deutsche Milchkontor* jurisprudence – the jurisprudence that crystallised European Executive Federalism as a constitutional doctrine.

The second approach is termed the principle of unitary procedural protection. It holds that the protection of procedural rights cannot suffer because of the structure of composite procedures, where national and Union administrations exercise interdependent powers.

Both levels of administration must now cooperate to ensure procedural rights. Two implicit notions are especially important. The first is the test of decisional dominance. Ultimate responsibility for the observance of procedural rights falls to the level of administration which exercises the decisive powers within a composite procedure. The second notion is that, in cases where decisional dominance belongs to Union administration, the latter may rely on the assistance of national authorities to fulfil its duties of procedural protection. Chapters five and six will illustrate in detail how the principle of unitary procedural protection was developed in the case law on the rights to be heard and to a reasoned decision.

5

The Principle of Unitary Procedural Protection and the Right to be Heard in Composite Decision-Making

I. Hearing Through the Screen of States

Early observers noted that the distinguishing feature of European integration was the *immediacy* of supranational power. Immediacy was the EU institutions' novel ability to 'pierce the screen of states', and to 'address themselves directly' to individuals.[1] Ironically, European Executive Federalism encouraged an approach to administrative law that was quite the opposite. The preconception of strictly separate legal powers at national and Union levels misled the Court of Justice into a purely inter-administrative approach to composite decision-making. It absolved the Commission from any duty to respect the fundamental procedural rights of individuals. No line of case law illustrates the tensions between immediacy and the limitations of Executive Federalism better than the Court's rulings on the right to be heard.

Many have pointed out that composite procedures raise significant problems concerning the exercise of this right.[2] The division of decisional tasks between national and Union administration makes it difficult to determine which level, if any, is obliged to respect the procedural rights of the parties affected by the procedure's final outcome. The CJEU's rulings illustrate its difficulties in solving this problem and have attracted much criticism for being inconsistent or affording an insufficient level of procedural protection.[3] Yet, as the chapter will aim to demonstrate, the case law reflects, more than anything, the hesitation of Union courts to

[1] P Pescatore, *The Law of Integration: emergence of a new phenomenon in international relations, based on the experience of the European Communities* (AW Sijthoff, 1974), 53–54.

[2] For many, see H Hofmann and M Tidghi, 'Rights and Remedies in Implementation of EU Policies by Multi-Jurisdictional Networks' (2014) 20 *European Public Law* 147, 151; C Eckes and J Mendes, 'The Right to be Heard in Composite Administrative Procedures: Lost in between Protection?' (2011) 36 *European Law Review* 665; HP Nehl, 'Legal Protection in the Field of EU Funds' (2011) 10 *European State Aid Law Quarterly* 629, 633 ff, S Cassese, 'European Administrative Proceedings' (2004–2005), 68 *Law and Contemporary Problems* 21, 31 ff; G della Cananea, 'The European Union's Mixed Administrative Proceedings' (2004–2005) 68 *Law and Contemporary Problems* 197, 211 ff, and G Sydow, *Verwaltungskooperation in der Europäischen Union* (Mohr Siebeck, 2004), 265–66.

[3] See for instance G Sydow, n 2, 275.

entirely abandon the constitutional doctrine of European Executive Federalism in composite decision-making.

Section II maps a period of the case law which followed the inter-administrative approach to composite decision-making to its logical conclusions. Based on a rigid understanding of separation between national and Union administrations, the Court held the latter not to be bound by individual procedural rights.

Section III sets out how, since the early 1990s, the case law has shifted entirely in its approach. It adopted the approach that Chapter four conceptualised as a principle of unitary protection. The approach aims to ensure that the division of administrative tasks between national and Union authorities does not harm the procedural protection of individuals. To that end, the case law assigns the duty to hear affected individuals to the administration exercising decisional dominance in a composite procedure. It is to ensure unitary procedural protection, too, that the Union administration, if dominant, may rely on the cooperation of national authorities to hear those individuals. The case law contains implicit rules in this regard – which will be referred to as the rules of primary contact, confirmation, and delegability.

One remarkable inconsistency in the handling of the right to be heard stands out in the case law on state aid. This last stronghold of the anachronic inter-administrative approach will be studied in section IV. Section V summarises the key findings.

II. An Excess of Doctrinal Zeal: The Inter-Administrative Approach

From 1983 to 1993, the Court ruled on a series of six cases relating to customs law. Some cases concerned requests for a specific exemption of customs duty on scientific instruments imported into the EU;[4] others concerned the repayment or remission (ie 'excusal') of customs duty.[5] The relevant administrative procedures begin and end at the level of national administration, with a Union administrative stage in between.[6] The importer submits an application to a

[4] Cases 294/81 *Control Data Belgium NV SA v European Commission*, ECLI:EU:C:1983:84; 98/83 and 230/83 *Van Gend en Loos NV and Expeditiebedrijf Wim Bosman v European Commission*, ECLI:EU:C:1984:342; 185/83 *Interfacultair Instituut Electronenmicroscopie of Universiteit Groningen v Inspecteur der Invoerrechten en Accijnzen, Groningen*, ECLI:EU:C:1984:331, 25 October 1984, [1984] ECR 3623; 203/85 *Nicolet Instrument GmbH v Hauptzollamt Frankfurt am Main-Flughafen (Nicolet I)* 26 June 1986, ECLI:EU:C:1986:269; 43/87 *Instrument GmbH v Hauptzollamt Frankfurt am Main-Flughafen (Nicolet II)*, 8 March 1988, ECLI:EU:C:1988:130; C-121/91 and C-122/91 *CT Control (Rotterdam) BV and JCT Benelux BV v European Commission*, ECLI:EU:C:1993:285.

[5] On these procedures, see M Gambardella, D Rovetta and S van Cutsem, *Remission and Repayment of customs duties in the EU* (Wolters Kluwer, 2014).

[6] The fitting of the Union stage into the procedure is designed to ensure that the conditions for repayment and remission, which involve indeterminate concepts such as 'good faith', 'negligence', and

national customs authority. The authority may be required to refer the case to the European Commission.[7] The Commission takes a decision on whether the requirements for duty-free importation, repayment or remission are met, which is addressed to the same authority that initially examined the application. That authority formally takes the final decision of the composite procedure, but is legally obliged to decide in accordance with the Commission's position.

In the six cases, the applicants in the customs procedures claimed that the Commission's decisions had been adopted in breach of their right to be heard. They had been afforded no opportunity to express their views during the Union stage of the procedures.

Time and again, the Court addressed these pleadings by giving reasons for the position supported by the Commission,[8] as well as by several Advocates General.[9] The argument, simple and terse, was that the legal framework of the procedures at stake did not establish a right to be heard before the Commission.[10]

In Nehl's words, the Court 'stubbornly' failed to observe the right to be heard.[11] The case law contradicted other rulings that the CJEU had delivered around the same time which required the Union administration to be 'scrupulous' in observing the right to be heard.[12]

It is important to note that Court never even questioned the fact that the applicants were *directly concerned* by the Commission's decisions – that is, that the Commission's powers in the customs procedures effectively *decided* the applicants' cases without leaving a margin of discretion to national authorities. The Court was fully aware that, even though only national authorities decided vis-à-vis applicants, it was the Commission, in effect, that decided on the substance of the applicants' cases. As some parties stressed,[13] the fact that they were directly concerned by the

'special situation', are interpreted and applied homogenously throughout the Union (*cf* K Limbach, *Uniformity of Customs Administration in the European Union* (Hart Publishing, 2015), 211–12). Such homogenous interpretation is instrumental to avoid discrimination between traders in different countries. In the case law, see Case C-419/04 *Conseil général de la Vienne v Directeur général des douanes et droits indirects*, ECLI:EU:C:2006:419, para 42.

[7] Currently, the applicable rules are found in Articles 116, 119, and 120 of the Union Customs Code (Regulation (EU) No 952/2013 of the European Parliament and of the Council as regards detailed rules concerning certain provisions of the Union Customs Code) and Articles 98–102 of the UCC delegated act (Commission Delegated Regulation (EU) 2015/2446 of 28 July 2015).

[8] For instance, *Van Gend en Loos and Bosman*, n 4 above.

[9] See the Opinion of AG Verloren van Themaat of 30 May 1984 [1984] ECR 3643 in *Universiteit Groningen*, n 4 above, of AG Mischo, 29 May 1986, ECLI:EU:C:1986:219, in *Nicolet I*, n 4 above, and AG Mancini, 21 January 1988, in *Nicolet II*, n 4, available at: https://curia.europa.eu/juris/showPdf.jsf?docid=95169&doclang=EN.

[10] *Universiteit Groningen*, n 4, paras 16 ff.

[11] HP Nehl, *Principles of Administrative Procedure in EC Law* (Hart Publishing, 1999), 78.

[12] Case C-49/88 *Al-Jubail Fertilizer Company (SAMAD) v Europen Council*, ECLI:EU:C:1991:276, para 16. Indeed, as some members of the Court from this period pointed out, the lack of references to procedural rights in the Treaties historically made the Commission reluctant to fully observe them. See O Due, 'Le respect des droits de la défense dans le droit administratif communautaire' (1987) *Cahiers de Droit Européen* 383, 384.

[13] See for instance *Nicolet I*, n 4, para 13.

Commission's decisions *should have* entitled them to an opportunity to be heard, in accordance with the Court's own case law.

Other parties claimed, though fruitlessly, that they should have been entitled to receive a level of protection similar to that in competition and anti-dumping law. There were two areas where the CJEU had previously filled gaps of procedural protection by applying the right to be heard as a general principle of law.[14] In *CT Control and JCT Benelux*, the sharp contrast to the liberal recognition of procedural rights in competition and anti-dumping cases led the applicants to beseech the Court to revise its previous case law on customs duty relief.[15] The comparison between these procedures and the composite procedures in customs was dismissed via two fundamental arguments.

First, the Court held that the degree of need for protection in different procedures had to be distinguished. In the customs procedures in question, the final decision was simply the rejection of an application for remission, repayment or duty-free admission. By contrast, in the procedures aimed at fining abuse of dominant position or dumping, the decision was a sanction. The Court held that in procedures of the latter kind, aimed at 'punishing' economic agents, the need to ensure the right to be heard 'assumes special importance'.[16]

However, the fact that it is of 'special importance' in such procedures does not mean that the right to be heard is not *also* of importance in other procedures. In fact, in the same period, the CJEU had already recognised that individuals have the right to be heard before any decisions 'adversely affecting them'.[17] It had abandoned earlier case law restricting that right to cases of sanctions, such as fines or penalties.[18] The nature of the decisions in the customs procedures could not therefore have been the main reason to reject the right to be heard.

The second and *decisive* argument is illuminating. What mattered in anti-dumping and competition cases was that final decisions were immediately addressed to an undertaking. By contrast, the Court emphasised, the Commission, in accordance with the provisions of the composite procedures on customs duty, was only supposed to interact with national administration.[19] It was national administration that requested a decision from the Commission.[20] That decision was 'addressed only to the Member States [and] notified only to the Member States', and, 'conversely', 'not notified to the applicant'.[21] The only contacts that

[14] See *Control Data*, n 4.

[15] C-121/91 and C-122/91 *CT Control and JCT Benelux*, n 4. AG Verloren van Themaat also proposed a revision of the Court's position on rights of the defence in customs relief cases, but to no avail. See his Opinion of 30 May 1984 in *Universiteit Groningen*, n 9 above.

[16] Case *CT Control and JCT Benelux*, n 4, 6 July 1993, paras 51–52. The same observation had been made in the Case by AG Gulman (see his Opinion of 11 November 1992, ECLI:EU:C:1992:429, at paras 14–15).

[17] See the case law cited in section II.A. of Chapter 4.

[18] See eg Case 85/76 *Hoffmann-La Roche*, EU:C:1979:36, para 9.

[19] *Van Gend en Loos and Bosman*, n 4, para 8.

[20] Cases *Nicolet I*, n 4, paras 11–17 and *Nicolet II*, n 4, para 13.

[21] *Universiteit Groningen*, n 4, paras 21–22.

the applicant had were with national authorities, which received and made a preliminary assessment of her application, and notified her of the final decision.[22]

In sum, the line of argument was based on the purely inter-administrative approach to composite decision-making, conceptualised in Chapter four.[23] The Commission was not obliged to hear affected parties *because* the legislation only provided for legal relations between the Commission and national authorities, on the one hand, and between national authorities and private parties, on the other. Even though it described the procedure as a single process, 'comprising several stages' at national and EU level,[24] the Court in practice treated the links between national and EU authorities as a sequence of two distinct administrative procedures, aimed at the exercise of distinct national and Union powers. In one procedure, national authorities adopted decisions in respect of private parties; and in the other, the EU administration decided in respect of national authorities. Following the logic of the separation of legal relations, the Court therefore held that there was a duplication of legal relations between the Commission and national administration, on the one hand, and national administration and the applicants, on the other. Moreover, much in line with its old understanding of cooperation between national and Union administration,[25] the Court did not contradict the Commission's argument that the procedure in question was purely 'internal' to the two.[26]

However, the Court was not completely indifferent to the applicants' position. It sought to justify why it was that the applicants' fundamental right to be heard had been respected, even though they could not present their views to the Commission.

That justification suggests that the Court struggled to find a place for procedural protection in the context of the inter-administrative approach. It held that the right to be heard had been satisfied because individuals had been able to forward their views in their *initial applications* to national authorities, the sole moment at which they could intervene in the administrative procedure.[27]

However, an initial application cannot replace the exercise of the right to be heard. That right requires individuals to have an opportunity to comment on the legal and factual basis for a decision, which becomes complete towards the end, not the beginning, of an administrative procedure. By absolving the Commission – and the national customs authorities – from the duty to provide such an opportunity, the Court effectively deprived affected parties of their right to be heard.

[22] *Van Gend en Loos and Bosman*, n 4, paras 8–9.
[23] See section III.
[24] *Van Gend en Loos and Bosman*, n 4, para 8.
[25] See Case 133/79 *Sucrimex SA v European Commission*, ECLI:EU:C:1980:104.
[26] *Control Data*, n 4.
[27] See Cases *Control Data*, n 4, para 17; *Van Gend en Loos and Bosman* n 4, para 9, *Universiteit Groningen*, n 4, paras 18–22; and CT *Control & JCT Benelux*, n 4, paras 48–49.

In conclusion, this period of the Court of Justice's case law reveals a deeply flawed approach to the right to be heard in composite decision-making. It reveals nothing short of an excess of doctrinal zeal towards European Executive Federalism. The inter-administrative approach led to private parties being regarded as mere onlookers to the administrative procedure and offered no opportunity to be heard at all.

It also failed to recognise the reality of composite decision-making. First, it failed to recognise that composite decision-making is not based on strictly divided power, but on its joint exercise by national and Union administration. For that reason alone, insisting on strictly separate legal relations was misplaced. Second, the Court failed to see that the Commission exercised decisional dominance – ie that even if the administrative procedures in question began and ended at the level of national administration, it was the Commission which determined their final outcome. As it entitles the individual to an opportunity to effectively influence the decision-making process, the right to be heard ought to be observed by the level of administration which enjoys decisional dominance.

In most composite procedures, the Union administration exercises decisional dominance and should therefore bear responsibility for the observance of the fundamental right to be heard.[28] It should not matter that the legal provisions governing the administrative procedure only foresee interactions between Union and national administrations. In time, the Court of Justice itself came to see this.

III. A Doctrinal U-Turn: The Rise of Unitary Procedural Protection

The Court's doctrinal U-turn began in 1991 with the *Technische Universität München* ruling (*TUM*).[29] The case concerned the composite procedure for the duty-free admission of scientific instruments into the internal market. The Technical University of Munich, which had imported a particular type of microscope, applied for a customs duty exemption.

The Commission rejected the application without giving the University the opportunity to be heard. Relying on the Court's previous rulings on the same procedure, explained in section III, and on the inter-administrative approach adopted in them, the Commission argued that individuals should seek to have their views heard by national authorities.[30] The Commission argued that the procedure was intended 'to be one between the Commission and the Member States only', and one whose 'applicable rules [were] not designed to establish a

[28] Similarly, H Hofmann and M Tidghi, n 2, 151.

[29] Case C-269/90 *Technische Universität München v Hauptzollamt München-Mitte*, ECLI:EU:C:1991:438.

[30] *TUM*, Report for Hearing, [1991] ECR I-5479.

procedure in which arguments are exchanged' with affected parties.[31] In its response, the Court *did* recognise that the procedure's provisions did not foresee any right to be heard by the Commission.[32] However, unlike what had occurred in the previous decade, the Court declared the Commission's decision to be vitiated by the breach of the University's right to be heard.[33] The inter-administrative approach had been abandoned.

Indeed, rather than preferring the strict separation of Union and national power over the protection of the right to be heard, the case law since *TUM* has been committed to the principle of unitary procedural protection, ie to ensuring that 'the protection of the individual should not suffer as a result of the division of the proceeding between two different administrations'.[34] The Commission, for its part, was slow to accept this shift, and continued to plead that where the applicable legislation only required it to interact with national authorities, it was thus not required to hear affected parties. It repeatedly failed to convince the CJEU in domains such as customs,[35] air transport,[36] and the European Social Fund.[37]

The case law developed unitary procedural protection with several more specific, implicit rules. Those rules require national and Union authorities to act in a concerted manner for affected parties to be effectively heard.[38] The basic test to determine which authority has the duty to hear such parties is the location, whether at the level of national or Union administration, of decisional dominance. The case law refers to this test by pointing out the

[31] Ibid.

[32] *TUM*, n 29, para 23.

[33] *TUM*, n 29, paras 24–25 and 28. For a view of the case, see J Schwarze, 'Developing principles of European administrative law' [1993] *Public Law* 229, 232.

[34] S Cassese, n 2, 34.

[35] Joined Cases T-186/97, T-187/97, T-190/97 to T-192/97, T-210/97, T-211/97, T-216/97 to T-218/97, T-279/97, T-280/97, T-293/97 and T-147/99 *Kaufring AG v European Commission*, ECLI:EU:T:2001:133, paras 141–42. For a more recent example, see the General Court's ruling in Case T-324/21 *Harley-Davidson*, EU:T:2023:101, para 166: '[the] Commission's argument that the procedure for adopting the contested decision envisages only a bilateral exchange between the Commission and the Member State concerned cannot succeed, in view of the fact [that the right to be heard] applies even in the absence of any specific rules'.

[36] Case T-260/94 *Air Inter SA v European Commission*, ECLI:EU:T:1997:89.

[37] See Case T-450/93 *Lisrestal – Organização Gestão de Restaurantes Colectivos Ldª v European Commission*, ECLI:EU:T:1994:290, para 40. The Commission sought to strengthen its argument by pointing out that the Court itself had recognised the 'central role' of the Member States in ESF procedures (see for instance C-334/91, *Innovation et Reconversion Industrielle ASBL v European Commission*, ECLI:EU:C:1993:211, para 24) and that the relevant legislation only foresaw a right *of Member States* – and not of the beneficiaries – to be heard. The General Court rejected this line of argument on several occasions, stressing that the fact that Member States have a right to be heard 'does not justify the conclusion that a principle of Community law as fundamental as that which guarantees every person the right to be heard before the adoption of a decision capable of adversely affecting him does not apply' (see Joined Cases T-194/97 and T-83/98 *Eugênio Branco, Ld.a v European Commission (Branco III)*, EU:T:2000:20, para 53).

[38] For a similar interpretation, see E Barbier de la Serre, 'Procedural Justice in the European Community Case-law concerning the Rights of the Defence: Essentialist and Instrumental Trends' (2006) 12 *European Public Law* 225, 241.

'exclusive authority' of the Commission,[39] the 'exclusive decision-making power' of national administration,[40] or that one of the two levels exercises discretion.[41]

Based on this test, the CJEU required the right to be heard to be respected in the same composite procedures in customs law where it had previously been denied.[42] The test later came to be extended to areas as varied as fisheries,[43] air traffic,[44] the European Social Fund,[45] counter-terrorism,[46] pesticides,[47] and telecommunications.[48]

Much of that case law is known to the academic debate. Scholars who have engaged with it have usually suggested that the CJEU oscillated somewhat erratically, over across time,[49] or across policy areas,[50] between requiring that the right to be heard be observed by national or by Union administration.[51]

In the view propounded here, these inconsistencies are more apparent than real. First, the question answered in the case law is not *if* respecting the right to be heard falls to the national or Union administration in the abstract, but *when* it must be observed by one or the other. The answer depends on how decisional power is concretely allocated between them within each particular composite procedure. Second, the appearance of inconsistency derives both from the textual ambiguity of the rulings and from the fact that the case law simultaneously addresses two distinct questions – *when* the duty to hear falls on the national or Union administration; and, in the event that the duty falls on the Union administration, *how* it may fulfil it.

Indeed, the notion that the procedural protection of individuals cannot be permitted to be lost between the various stages of composite procedures is merely the starting point for the principle of unitary procedural protection. The CJEU's challenge has been to square the effectiveness of the right to be heard with respect

[39] Case T-205/99 *Hyper Srl v European Commission*, ECLI:EU:T:2002:189, para 49.

[40] Case T-660/18 *VodafoneZiggo Group BV v European Commission*, ECLI:EU:T:2019:546, paras 71–72 and 109.

[41] See Case T-141/01 *Entorn – Societat Limitada Enginyeria i Serveis v European Commission*, ECLI:EU:T:2005:10, para 113; T-42/96 *Eyckeler & Malt AG v European Commission*, ECLI:EU:T:1998:40 paras 76–78 and *Kaufring*, n 35, para 155.

[42] Cases T-346/94 *France-Aviation v European Commission*, ECLI:EU:T:1995:187; *Eyckeler*, n 41; T-50/96 *Primex Produkte Import-Export GmbH & Co. KG v European Commission*, ECLI:EU:T:1998:223; T-290/97, *Mehibas Dordtselaan BV v European Commission*, ECLI:EU:T:2000:8; and *Kaufring*, n 35.

[43] Case C-135/92 *Fiskano AB v European Commission*, ECLI:EU:C:1994:267.

[44] *Air Inter*, n 36.

[45] See for example Cases C-462/98 P *Mediocurso – Estabelecimento de Ensino Particular Lda v European Commission (Mediocurso I)*, ECLI:EU:C:2000:480, para 36; T-199/99 *Sgaravatti Mediterranea Srl v European Commission*, ECLI:EU:T:2002:228, para 55; and T-159/07 *Cooperativa de Formação e Animação Cultural Cofac) v European Commission (Cofac II)*, ECLI:EU:T:2009:490, paras 33–34.

[46] See below at section IV.C.

[47] Case T-719/17 *FMC Corporation v European Commission*, ECLI:EU:T:2021:143.

[48] Eg in *VodafoneZiggo*, n 40.

[49] C Eckes and J Mendes, n 2, 655.

[50] S Alonso de Léon, *Composite Administrative Procedures in the European Union* (Iustel, 2017), 235 and 238.

[51] See for instance H Hofmann and M Tidghi, n 2, C Eckes and J Mendes, n 2, 655 and S Cassese, n 2, 31.

for the intended legislative design of composite procedures. Put differently, the CJEU's case law aims to ensure that ultimate responsibility for the observance of the right to be heard falls to whichever level of administration exercises decisional dominance, while deferring as far as possible to the Union legislator's choice to prioritise regulating the relations between the Union administration and its national counterparts.

The CJEU's answer to that balance is to allow the Union administration – if dominant – to discharge the duty to observe the right to be heard by exploiting its cooperative relationships with national authorities, and the latter's closer interactions with individuals on the ground. This is a concern that underlies all three rules drawn from the notion of unitary procedural protection. Those rules may be termed as the rule of primary contact, the rule of confirmation and the rule of delegability. The first refers to the right to be heard in national procedural stages. The latter two refer to the Union administration's ability to observe that right with the assistance of national authorities.

A. The Rule of Primary Contact

In earlier case law, all the CJEU was willing to afford to individuals was a dubious 'right of the application' before national authorities. This aspect of the inter-administrative approach resonated with the prerogative that the Member States enjoy, under European Executive Federalism, to regulate the legal relations between their own authorities and their own citizens.[52] By contrast, as the principle of unitary procedural protection developed, the CJEU shaped those relations by requiring the right to be heard to be respected by national authorities in composite decision-making.

The first rule developed by the CJEU establishes the national stages of composite procedures as the 'privileged moment' for the exercise of that right.[53] The rule can be termed as the rule of *primary contact*. It can be formulated as having one necessary and two alternative conditions for application (it is, admittedly, a rule difficult to formulate in simpler terms).

A national authority must observe the right to be heard in a composite administrative procedure

1. if, according to applicable legislation, the national authority is the first or only interlocutor of individuals; *and*
2. if that national authority either:
   a) exercises decisional dominance; *or*
   b) prepares the legal and factual basis, or a proposal for a final decision, in cases where decisional dominance is exercised by the Union administration.

[52] See Chapter 2, section V.B.(iii).
[53] *Cf* G della Cananea, *Diritto amministrativo europeo: principi e istituti*, 3rd edn (Giuffrè, 2011), 242.

The first condition for application is self-explanatory, but some more elaboration is required for the additional alternative two. The two alternatives will be considered in greater detail below (subsections III.A.(i). and (ii).). However, two other, preliminary issues should be clarified from the outset.

The first issue is that one may also infer some scenarios where national authorities would *not* be required to observe the right to be heard at all. First, national authorities are not required to observe the right to be heard in what were previously termed as 'reception desk' procedures.[54] In such procedures, national authorities do no more than to receive and examine the formal sufficiency of applications before they are forwarded to the Union administration for a decision on the substance of the case. Second, national authorities are not under a duty to hear affected individuals if they take a final decision which must entirely conform with a prior binding decision of the Union administration. In such composite procedures, eg in pharmaceutical regulation, it is the Union administration which exercises decisional dominance and is therefore under a duty to hear. Third, national authorities are not required to hear affected individuals if they may only adopt measures that as such have no effect upon the *substance* of the procedure's outcome and merely trigger the opening of a new phase of the procedure.[55] This is certainly the case for 'objections' raised by national authorities in the 'arbitral' composite procedures explained in Chapter three.[56]

The second issue concerns the appropriate level of procedural protection that national administrations must ensure. The right to be heard is ensured in the same terms as prescribed for the Union administration.[57] One implication is that the right to be heard may be restricted in national procedural stages just as in procedures which only involve Union administration. One example is that the CJEU considers that, just like the Union administration, national authorities are not required to hear affected parties before taking decisions intended to be urgent or not known in advance to those affected by them. Both explicitly and by analogy, the CJEU applied the same restrictions on the right to be heard as in 'dawn raids' – ie unannounced inspections – to composite procedures governing freezing the assets of individuals or entities that support terrorism.[58] In *OMPI*,

[54] See Chapter 3, section IV.A.

[55] Similarly, F Shirvani, 'Verfahrensgrundrechte in mehrstufigen, das EU-Recht vollziehenden Verwaltungsverfahren – Dargestellt am Beispiel des Arzneimittelzulassungs- und Gentechnikrechts' (2011) 126 *Deutsches Verwaltungsblatt* 674, 676.

[56] See L de Lucia, 'Conflict and Cooperation within European Composite Administration (Between Philia and Eris)' (2012), 55 *Review of European Administrative Law* 49–88.

[57] L Azoulai, *Les garanties procédurales en droit communautaire: recherches sur la procédure et le bon gouvernement*, EUI thesis, unpublished (2000), 148. Azoulai rightly noted that, in *France-Aviation*, n 42, the General Court demanded the respect of the rights of the defence in the course of national administrative stages, *as they are guaranteed at EU level*. Similarly, speaking in this regard of 'vertical convergence' of Union and national legal standards, is HP Nehl, n 11, 80–81.

[58] For an overview of the regime of 'dawn raids' in EU law and of the fundamental rights concerns they raise, see H Andersson, 'Dawn Raids under Challenge' (2014) 35 *European Competition Law Review* 135.

the General Court held that, like Union authorities, national authorities do not have to hear targeted individuals or organisations which would likely transfer their assets abroad if they became aware of an impending initial decision to seize assets or freeze their funds.[59]

(i) National Decisional Dominance

National authorities must observe the right to be heard when they exercise decisional dominance within a composite administrative procedure. Presumably, national authorities must provide a hearing where, according to the relevant legal provisions, they have the power to reject applications, eg for banking licences, and thereby terminate the administrative procedure before it even reaches the Union administration.[60] CJEU case law has not yet ruled on that specific scenario. However, it has made clear that the right to be heard applies when national authorities exercise decisional dominance (i) by adopting preparatory acts which are binding upon the Union administration in a subsequent stage; or (ii) by taking the final decision in a composite procedure where they have received non-binding recommendations from the Union administration.

The first category of situations has been the object of abundant case law regarding procedures for the EU-wide registration of protected designations of origin and protected geographical indications (PDOs and PGIs)[61] There is nonetheless at least one case which ought to be mentioned where the CJEU applied an identical line of reasoning to administrative procedures of the European Emissions Trading System. In that system, the Commission exercises no discretion – it merely checks whether national authorities have compiled the national lists of installations with free emissions quotas in accordance with the Union requirements as to how the allocation of such quotas is calculated. As decisional dominance falls to national authorities, the Commission is under no duty to hear affected private parties.[62]

However, most cases on the rule of primary contact and national decisional dominance concern the administrative procedure for the registration of products as PDOs or PGIs. The structure of the procedure was explained

[59] Case T-228/02 *Organisation des Modjahedines du Peuple d'Iran v European Council (OMPI I)*, ECLI:EU:T:2006:384, paras 127–30. The General Court rightly differentiated between the initial decisions to freeze the assets of groups and individuals, and subsequent decisions to keep them frozen. In regard to the latter, no element of surprise needs be ensured, since the targeted individuals are already aware of the freezing of their funds. Therefore, in procedures leading to subsequent decisions to freeze funds, EU courts have considered that the rights of the defence need to be fully respected.

[60] In this sense, F Shirvani, n 55, 679. These are the composite procedures where national authorities act as 'gatekeepers', as explained with several examples in Chapter 3, section III.B.(ii).

[61] Today, the procedures for the registration of PDOs and PGIs are found in Regulation No 1151/2012 of the European Parliament and the Council of 21 November 2012 on quality schemes for agricultural products and foodstuffs.

[62] See Case T-630/13 *DK Recycling and Roheisen GmbH v European Commission*, ECLI:EU:T:2014:833, paras 46 and 117.

in Chapter three.[63] The Commission is usually obliged to register a product as set out in applications endorsed by competent national authorities. Interested individuals or groups only have a right to participate in the administrative procedure at the stage before the Commission receives those applications.[64]

The absence of a right to be heard by the Commission came to the fore in a series of cases concerning the registration for EU-wide protection of certain types of cheese, honey and cider.[65] The CJEU denied that the Commission was obliged to hear affected parties. The defining argument was the decision-making structure of this composite procedure,[66] and more specifically that,

> under the scheme [of the procedure for the registration of PDOs and PGIs], the procedural safeguards expressly afforded to individuals fall *exclusively within the scope of responsibility of the Member States* and do *not involve* the exercise of *any power of assessment on the part of the Commission* (emphasis added).

Therefore, since 'the Commission is bound by [the competent national authority's] decision', it 'may not consider an objection communicated to it by any person other than a Member State'.[67] Indeed, the General Court implied that the Commission was not obliged to hear affected parties *because* it had no power to diverge from the assessment by national authorities[68] – ie because the latter exercised decisional dominance at the national preparatory stage. Given the lack of influence of the Commission over the content of the final decision that it is obliged to adopt, requiring hearings at the Union level would be rather futile.[69]

For the same reason, the CJEU has been right to require that, when the Union administration's role is limited to issuing non-binding recommendations, the observance of the right to be heard should fall to the national authorities. The recent *VodafoneZiggo* cases illustrate it well.

[63] See section III.B.(i).

[64] See Article 51(2) of Regulation No 1151/2012.

[65] See Cases T-114/99 *CSR Pampryl SA v European Commission*, ECLI:EU:T:1999:281, para 55; T-370/02 *Alpenhain-Camembert-Werk v European Commission*, ECLI:EU:T:2004:209, para 67; T-381/02 *Confédération générale des producteurs de lait de brebis et des industriels de Roquefort v European Commission*, ECLI:EU:T:2005:445, para 58; and T-35/06 *Honig-Verband eV v European Commission*, ECLI:EU:T:2007:250, para 53.

[66] It must be pointed out that the Grand Court made clear that even if the Commission enjoyed a power of appraisal, the composite procedure for the registration of PDOs and GIs is concluded with the adoption of measures of general application. For that reason, a right to be heard at the EU stage would have been ruled out unless explicitly provided for in the legislation (See *Pampryl*, n 65, paras 50–51). Where the Commission exercises decisional dominance by adopting acts of general application, it is not required to observe the right to be heard (see Case T-296/12 *Health Food Manufacturers' Association v European Commission*, ECLI:EU:T:2015:375, paras 98–100).

[67] See *Pampryl*, n 65, paras 52 and 58. See also Case T-215/00 *La Conqueste*, ECLI:EU:T:2001:23, paras 44, 49 and 50.

[68] *Pampryl*, n 65, paras 52–53.

[69] Indeed, the right to be heard should enable the adversely affected person to 'argue in favour of the adoption or non-adoption of the decision, or in favour of its having a specific content' (Case C-166/13 *Mukarubega v Préfet de police and Préfet de la Seine-Saint-Denis*, ECLI:EU:C:2014:2336, para 49).

The two cases concerned the consultation procedure enshrined in Directive 2002/21/EC (the 'Framework Directive').[70] According to the relevant procedure, national regulatory authorities (NRAs) in the domain of telecommunications may impose specific obligations on operators with significant market power. However, before doing so, the NRAs must carry out an open consultation on the draft measure they intend to take, in order to give interested parties the opportunity to comment on it. NRAs must also consult the NRAs of other Member States, the European Commission, and the Body of European Regulators for Electronic Communications (BEREC) in a European consultation stage. The Commission may then send its 'comments' on the draft measure, which the NRA must take into 'the utmost account', or in certain cases, the Commission may issue reservations and send non-binding recommendations for the measure to be amended or withdrawn. In other cases, the Commission may also exercise a right of veto and entirely block a draft measure which violates Union law, eg by erecting barriers within the single market.

VodafoneZiggo brought an action for annulment against the Commission after it had merely sent a letter with comments on a draft measure by the Dutch NRA. VodafoneZiggo argued that, by sending such comments instead of exercising its power of veto, the Commission had 'authorised' the Dutch decision. VodafoneZiggo claimed, among other things, that the Commission had failed to provide it with an opportunity to be heard, even though the Framework Directive did not contain any provision requiring the Commission to do so.

The General Court,[71] and subsequently the ECJ,[72] rejected this argument. It recalled that the European consultation procedure 'relates exclusively to the relations between the NRA concerned, on the one hand, and other NRAs, the Commission and BEREC on the other, since the Framework Directive is silent as regards possible involvement by interested parties at EU level'.[73] While this may be at first sight textually reminiscent of the purely inter-administrative approach to composite decision-making, the General Court *did* emphasise the need to observe procedural rights – but at the national level, where NRAs exercise significant discretion, rather than at the Union level, where the Commission's role is limited. In the General Court's reasoning,

> given that the measures referred to in the Framework Directive are in principle adopted at national level and not by the Commission, it is sufficient that interested parties be heard at national level, at least if the Commission confines itself to making comments.[74]

[70] Directive 2002/21/EC of the European Parliament and of the Council of 7 March 2002 on a common regulatory framework for electronic communications networks and services (Framework Directive) ([2002] OJ L 108/33) ('the Framework Directive').

[71] *VodafoneZiggo*, n 40.

[72] Case C-689/19 P *VodafoneZiggo*, ECLI:EU:C:2021:142, paras 126–27.

[73] *VodafoneZiggo*, n 40, para 68.

[74] *VodafoneZiggo*, n 40, para 82.

(ii) Union Decisional Dominance: Anticipating Hearings

Besides instances of decisional dominance at the national level, there is a second type of case where the rule of primary contact applies. These cases concern the more common scenario, where the Union administration exercises decisional dominance. National authorities must observe the right to be heard when they prepare the factual basis or make a proposal for the final decision that the Union administration will take.

This became clear as soon as the CJEU began its own shift away from the inter-administrative approach. In *TUM*, the CJEU unequivocally made the Commission responsible for the observance of the right to be heard. Four years later, in *France-Aviation*, the CJEU *appeared* to contradict itself.[75] *France-Aviation* concerned the composite procedure for the remission and repayment of customs debt. If minded to approve an application for remission or repayment, the national competent authority is obliged to forward that application, along with its own assessment of the case. The Commission then takes a decision on whether the requirements for remission or repayment are met, which must be implemented by the national authority when it takes the final decision of the administrative procedure.

France-Aviation imported aircraft components from outside the EU into France. It applied for repayment of customs duty that it had unnecessarily paid. Agreeing, the French customs administration sent a proposal to the Commission for a decision to grant repayment, along with the application and supporting documents. The Commission, however, decided that the requirements for repayment were not met. At no stage of the administrative procedure was France-Aviation given the opportunity to be heard.

Recalling the ruling in *TUM*, the General Court emphasised that the 'right on the part of a person concerned to be heard before the Commission' depends upon the latter holding a 'power of appraisal' (ie decisional dominance).[76] The General Court ultimately held that the right had been infringed upon in this case. The documents forwarded to the Commission had not included relevant written exchanges between France-Aviation and the French administration which could have led the Commission to decide differently. The Commission had therefore taken a decision based on an incomplete case-file.[77]

At this point, the *France-Aviation* ruling followed a line of argument that was new in comparison to *TUM*. It held that the 'right to be heard in a procedure such as that to which these proceedings relate must actually be secured in the first place in the relations between the person concerned and the national administration'.[78] The fact that the legislation did not provide for contact between

[75] *TUM*, n 29. France-*Aviation*, n 42.
[76] *France-Aviation*, n 42, paras 33–34.
[77] *France-Aviation*, n 42, para 35.
[78] *France-Aviation*, n 42, para 30.

that person and the Commission did not necessarily mean that the latter should uncritically follow the national administration's views. Indeed, insofar as it contemplated diverging from the national administration's proposal to approve the application, the Commission 'had a duty to arrange for the applicant to be heard by the [national] authorities'.[79]

Other cases followed suit, not only in customs law but also concerning procedures for freezing the assets of terrorist organisations or the management of the European Social Fund. The CJEU continued to require the right to be heard to be observed in national preparatory stages in composite procedures, even where the Union administration exercised decisional dominance. Interestingly, it began emphasising that, in such composite procedures, the right to be heard had to be observed not only in national procedural stages, but in Union procedural stages as well.[80]

The case law initiated in *France-Aviation* constitutes a clear derogation, in composite decision-making, from two aspects of CJEU's usual understanding of the right to be heard that were explained before.[81] First, it implies that national authorities must hear the person concerned before adopting a *purely preparatory* act.[82] Second, the case law implies that individuals do not simply have a right to be heard on the factual and legal basis of a decision, as usual, but a right to be heard on the *intended decision* itself. And third, while it generally only entitles persons *adversely affected* by a decision to be heard, the right to be heard must also be observed before the adoption of national preparatory acts which are, by definition, favourable to said persons. After all, in *France-Aviation* the French administration was required to hear the importer even though it had *supported* its application before the Commission.

However, these two are not the only reasons why the rule of primary contact may appear unusual. One other is that the CJEU recognises that, when it enjoys decisional dominance – usually expressed as the 'power of appraisal' or 'discretion' – the Union administration is under a duty to hear. And yet, the CJEU

[79] *France-Aviation*, n 42, para 36.

[80] See Cases *Mehibas*, n 42, para 45; *Kaufring*, n 35, paras 160–61; implicitly also *Lisrestal*, n 37, paras 49–50 and the ruling, on appeal, in Case C-32/95 P *European Commission v Lisrestal Organização Gestão de Restaurantes Colectivos Ld.a*, ECLI:EU:C:1996:402. On asset-freezing, see *OMPI I*, n 59, para 118 and G della Cananea, 'Return to the due process of law: the European Union and the fight against terrorism' (2007) 32 *European Law Review* 986.

[81] See Chapter 4, section II.A.

[82] Cases such as *OMPI*, further explained in the following subsections, illustrate that national authorities must hear the persons concerned when they adopt measures which are the final decision of a national administrative procedure, but are nevertheless treated as a preparatory act in a composite administrative procedure. *OMPI* concerned Union procedures for freezing the funds of terrorist organisations and supporters, where the Council adopts a regulation based on prior national decisions. Other national acts which qualify as final domestically, but preparatory in composite procedures, include national measures adopted pursuant to safeguard clauses – urgent and provisional national measures which require confirmation by the Commission to become definitive. See the analysis in Chapter 3, section III.C.(iii).

simultaneously requires national authorities to offer hearings when involved at a preparatory stage.

One could at first think the CJEU's reasoning contradictory. This is, however, not the case. The significance of the rule of primary contact in cases of Union decisional dominance only becomes apparent when one considers not only *which* level of administration is responsible for the observance of procedural rights, but *how* those rights may be observed in practice.

If, in cases where it exercises decisional dominance, the Union administration agrees with a national preparatory act, it does not need to ensure that individuals are heard multiple times. Instead, it may *choose* to observe their right to be heard by simply checking that a hearing has already been offered at the national preparatory stage. By requiring national authorities to offer hearings 'in the first place', the rule of primary contact ensures that the Union administration's observance of the duty to hear may be anticipated at that stage. Indeed, as will be explained below, this is one of the ways in which the Union administration may respect procedural rights by relying on the assistance of national authorities.

B. Direct Links and Mediated Hearings: The Right to be Heard and Union Decisional Dominance

Despite the Court's sudden shift in *TUM*, there was never a clean break from the inter-administrative approach. *France-Aviation* provides a good example of how, *semantically*, the language typical of that approach lingered in the case law, even if its solutions were in substance very different. When requiring hearings to be offered at the national preparatory stage, the General Court emphasised that the relevant procedure in customs law provided '*only* for contacts to take place between the person concerned and the administration, on the one hand, and between the administration and the Commission, on the other' (emphasis added).[83] Similarly, the CJEU characterised the procedures on financial assistance from the European Social Fund as creating 'a financial relationship between the Commission and the Member State on the one hand and between that Member State and the institution which is the recipient of the financial assistance on the other'.[84] Moreover, the case law began describing national administration as the 'sole' or 'privileged interlocutor' of the Commission.[85]

[83] *France-Aviation*, n 42, para 30.

[84] For many, T-53/11 *Associação de Empresas de Construção e Obras Públicas e Serviços (AECOPS) v European Commission*, para 52. This account of the ESF regime had been used already in Case 310/81 *Ente Italiano di Servizio Sociale (EISS) v European Commission*, ECLI:EU:C:1984:105, para 15.

[85] See Cases C-304/89 *Estabelecimentos Isidoro M Oliveira SA v European Commission*, ECLI:EU:C:1991:191; C-157/90 *Infortec – Projectos e Consultadoria Ldª v European Commission*, ECLI:EU:C:1992:243; C-291/89 *Interhotel v European Commission*, ECLI:EU:T:1997:117, para 16; *Innovation et Reconversion Industrielle*, n 37, para 24; *Primex*, n 42, para 58; *Eyckeler*, n 41, para 75;

Yet at the same time, the CJEU also began holding that the Union authorities were bound by a 'direct link' to individuals even in cases where national administration, according to the relevant legislation, constituted its 'sole interlocutor' and 'only contact'.[86] Such 'direct links' between the Commission and individuals necessarily meant that composite procedures could not be considered *only* to establish relations between authorities after all.

The coexistence of the two notions – 'direct links' and 'sole interlocutor' – appears inconsistent. However, upon closer inspection, the expression 'direct link' is a mere shorthand for the exercise, by Union administration, of the decisive discretionary power within a composite procedure.[87] In other words, 'direct links' with the Union administration exist when it exercises decisional dominance. The notion is a rhetorical device intended to emphasise that, *even if* the relevant legislation is intended to confine it to relations with national authorities, the Union administration may exercise powers which *immediately* affect the legal position of individuals. With decisional dominance comes a direct legal relationship between Union administration and individuals; with that legal relationship comes the Union administration's duty to hear.[88]

As it enjoys decisional dominance in most instances of composite decision-making, the Union administration usually bears ultimate responsibility for that duty. Indeed, the fact that national authorities have heard affected individuals will not exempt the Union administration from judicial scrutiny of whether it has ensured the right to be heard throughout the composite procedure.[89]

Much of the case law on unitary procedural protection revolves around a delicate balance. It strives to integrate the right to be heard in Union procedural stages of composite procedures, while preserving to the greatest degree possible their intended legislative design.

The key to this balance is perhaps the most conceptually innovative aspect of the case law. It is the implicit distinction between the administration with the duty to hear affected individuals and the administration which takes the concrete steps needed for that duty to be observed in practice. If dominant, the Union administration has the duty to hear. But if it so chooses, the Union administration may 'hear' affected parties by relying on the practical assistance

T-72/97 *Proderec – Formação e Desinvolvimento de Recursos Humanos, ACE v European Commission*, ECLI:EU:T:1998:179, para 72; and T-102/00 *Vlaams Fonds voor de Sociale Integratie van Personen met een Handicap v European Commission*, ECLI:EU:T:2003:192, para 60; T-159/07 *Cofac II*, n 45, para 34.

[86] *Lisrestal*, n 37, para 47.

[87] Case T-105/01 *Società Lavori Impianti Metano Sicilia (SLIM Sicilia) v European Commission*, ECLI:EU:T:2002:147, paras 56–57.

[88] See for instance Case T-23/03 *CAS*, ECLI:EU:T:2007:32, para 87 and T-329/00 *Bonn Fleisch Ex- und Import GmbH v European Commission*, ECLI:EU:T:2003:48, para 45 and Joined Cases T-180/96 and T-181/96 *Mediocurso – Estabelecimento de Ensino Particular Lda v European Commission (Mediocurso I)*, ECLI:EU:T:1998:208, para 52. Similarly, though in the specific area of European Structural Funds, see S Mento, 'I poteri amministrativi della Commissione europea in materia di fondi strutturali' (2007) *Rivista Trimestrale di Diritto Pubblico* 135, 163.

[89] See *FMC*, n 47, paras 177–95.

of national authorities – *through* hearings offered by national authorities in its stead. In the words of the General Court, an applicant's right to be heard before the Commission may be observed 'either directly in its dealings with the Commission or indirectly through the [national] authorities, or through the combination of those two administrative channels'.[90]

It is admittedly counterintuitive that one administration may fulfil the duty to hear *through* another administration. At any rate, the CJEU failed to explain that notion clearly. The result is that the case law could be interpreted as exempting Union administration from the duty to hear and as shifting that duty entirely to national authorities. Adopting that interpretation, Eckes and Mendes object that 'offering a possibility to be heard exclusively at the national level is not consistent with the rule according to which a direct link is established between the Commission and [affected parties]'.[91]

That the CJEU demands hearings 'exclusively at the national level' is not an implausible reading of the case law. That solution would indeed be inconsistent with the notion of 'direct links' between Union administration and individuals. More specifically, the interpretation made by Eckes and Mendes could find support in three elements of the case law:

(i) the notion that the right to be heard should be 'ensured in the first place' in the relations between individuals and national authorities;
(ii) the notion that the right to be heard is deemed to have been respected when the Union administration checks that national authorities have already provided a hearing;[92] and
(iii) the notion that the right to be heard is respected when the Union administration requests national authorities to provide a hearing.[93]

However, in the interpretation adopted here, only the first of those elements actually refers to hearings provided during national procedural stages – to the rule of primary contact, as explained above. The latter two elements concern the duty of the Union administration to hear – namely, the rule of confirmation (ii), according to which the Union administration may avail itself of hearings already offered by national authorities, and the rule of delegability (iii), according to which the Union administration may request national authorities to provide hearings on its behalf.

The difference between the three became clearer in *Mehibas*. Much like Eckes and Mendes, the Commission had interpreted *France-Aviation* as only requiring the right to be heard to be observed during national procedural stages. Accordingly, it reformed the procedures for repayment and remission of customs duty so as to

[90] See *Air Inter*, n 36, para 65.
[91] C Eckes and J Mendes, n 2, 657. See also G della Cananea, *Diritto amministrativo europeo: principi ed istituti*, 3rd edn (Giuffrè, 2011), 240–42 and HP Nehl, n 11, 78 ff.
[92] See for instance *Vlaams Fonds*, n 85, para 61.
[93] See *France-Aviation*, n 42, paras 30 and 36.

require applicants to sign a statement that they had already expressed all their views on the national authority's proposal for a decision.[94] In effect, this meant that applicants would waive any right to present their views in the ensuing procedural stage, where the Commission made its decision.

In *Mehibas*, the General Court found that this arrangement 'only partly' met the demands of *France-Aviation*. It held that the right to be heard had to be ensured not only at the national, but also at the Union procedural stages.[95] However, the General Court then proceeded to state that the Commission could observe that right by ensuring that the person concerned is 'heard by the national authorities'.[96] As the Commission exercised a decisive 'margin of assessment' in the procedure – ie decisional dominance –, it had a duty to hear applicants. It could do so while acknowledging that, in accordance with the legislation, it was also only required to interact directly with national authorities.[97]

C. The Rule of Confirmation

Under Union law, the administration is under no obligation to hear individuals twice on the same points of fact and law. As the CJEU puts it, 'that obligation does not apply to a mere restatement, redrafting or development of a point already made in respect of which the addressee of the decision at issue previously had the opportunity effectively to make known his views'.[98] This is a finding that the CJEU has extended to composite decision-making, in what will be termed the rule of confirmation.

The Union administration is not required to hear affected parties itself if it merely *confirms the findings of a national authority in their entirety*. Instead, it may observe the right to be heard simply by checking that individuals have already been heard by the national authority in question. The case law on financial corrections in the European Social Fund (ESF) illustrates this well.

The legal framework of the ESF used to provide that in cases of irregular uses of financial assistance, the Commission could take a final decision after considering a proposal for reduction or withdrawal of such assistance prepared by a national authority. The CJEU recognised that the Commission exercised decisional dominance (that it 'assumes legal liability') and was therefore under the duty to hear. However, the CJEU also held that a hearing already provided by national authorities at the preparatory stage – ie a hearing offered pursuant to the primary

[94] See Recital (12) of Commission Regulation (EC) No 12/97 of 18 December 1996.

[95] *Mehibas*, n 42, at paras 44–45.

[96] Ibid. The Court added that this was the position it had adopted both in *Eyckeler*, n 41 and *Primex*, n 42.

[97] Ibid, at para 46.

[98] See Case T-604/15 *European Road Transport Telematics Implementation Coordination Organisation – Intelligent Transport Systems & Services Europe (Ertico – ITS Europe v European Commission*, ECLI:EU:T:2019:348, para 46.

contact rule explained before – could suffice for the Commission to have properly discharged that duty.[99] In *Vlaams Fonds*, the General Court stated that

> the Commission, *which alone assumes legal liability* to the beneficiaries of the ESF assistance for the decision to reduce it, is not entitled to adopt such a decision without first giving those undertakings the possibility, or *ensuring that they have had the possibility*, of effectively setting forth their views on the proposed reduction in assistance (emphasis added).[100]

The Union administration may, as it were, 'ratify' hearings already provided by national authorities. Those hearings will retroactively count as if they had been offered by the Union administration itself. The case law indicated that confirmation may only apply if three requirements are met. The three requirements may be summarised as follows:

(i) According to the applicable provisions, a national authority prepares the factual basis or a makes a proposal for a final decision that is within the discretion of the Union administration (ie there is Union decisional dominance);
(ii) That national authority hears individuals on the collected facts and, if applicable, on the proposal for a final decision that it will send to the Union administration; (ie it follows the rule of primary contact); *and*
(iii) The Union administration adopts the definitive decision of the procedure based on *the exact same facts* and approving the *exact same* decisional outcome as proposed by the national authority.

Let us focus on the third requirement, which has proven rather important in cases involving customs law, the European Social Fund, or asset-freezing measures. In determining whether Union administration has respected the right to be heard, the CJEU will focus on whether it has made its decision based on the facts, or assessments of facts, that it received from national authorities.

In customs law, the CJEU holds that the Commission must provide a fresh hearing whenever it contemplates exercising its discretion by 'diverging from the position taken by the competent national authorities' (ie from their proposal to grant remission or repayment of customs debt).[101] In *Kaufring*, the CJEU clarified that the Commission cannot simply confirm hearings if it is minded to decide differently from that position, even if the facts on which the individual was heard are the same.[102]

Conversely, in *Cofac*, a ruling on the ESF, the General Court held that, because it had decided based on information and a proposal prepared by the Portuguese

[99] See Case *Proderec*, n 85, para 129.
[100] *Vlaams Fonds*, n 85, para 61. See also *Lisrestal*, n 37, para 49 and *Proderec*, n 85, para 127.
[101] See *France-Aviation*, n 42, para 36, *Hyper* n 39, para 49, *Eyckeler*, n 41, para 84, *Primex*, n 42, para 67, *Mehibas*, n 42, para 45, *Kaufring*, n 35, para 152.
[102] *Kaufring* n 35, para 161.

administration, and because the latter had heard the affected beneficiary on both, the Commission had respected the right to be heard.[103]

The aforementioned cases on confirmation of hearings in customs cases and the ESF concerned whether the Union administration agreed with national authorities' proposals for a final decision. In some case law on asset-freezing measures, by contrast, the CJEU examined whether, although agreeing with national authorities' proposals, the Union administration decided upon a distinct factual basis.

Common Position 2001/931/CFSP and Regulation (EC) No 2580/2001 establish a composite procedure for defining the lists of persons or groups suspected of supporting terrorist activities. In the presence of serious evidence of such support, national authorities may adopt a decision to freeze the funds owned by the targeted individuals or groups. In the following stage, the Council adopts a regulation listing the persons and groups whose assets are to be frozen across the Member States. Measures of this nature are intended to prevent the suspects' funds from being used to finance terrorist groups. This is why asset-freezing procedures in fact foresee two kinds of decisions: *initial* and *subsequent* decisions. The *initial decision* to freeze/seize assets is taken with a view to causing a certain 'surprise effect', without which the funds could be moved outside of the EU. However, those initial freezing orders regarding groups and individuals are re-examined periodically, every six months. Should the national authorities and the Council consider that maintaining the initial order is justified, then a *subsequent* decision is adopted.

In *Organisation des Modjahedines du Peuple d'Iran I* (*OMPI I*),[104] the applicant, OMPI, brought an action for annulment against a subsequent decision by the Council to freeze its funds. The General Court agreed with the applicant's argument that, despite the absence of legal provisions on the matter,[105] its right to be heard had to be observed. The Council's decision was annulled.

The General Court left detailed indications as to how the right to be heard was to be ensured. It held that that right was to be guaranteed, in principle, at both stages:[106] in the first place, before the competent national authority and, subsequently, before the Council.[107] The General Court ruled that the Council is obliged to offer a hearing if it adopts the final decision based on evidence brought to its attention *after* the national procedural stage – ie evidence on which the affected party could not have yet been heard.[108] If, however, the Council only uses evidence on which the affected person was already heard, then the observance of the right to be heard does not require 'that the party

[103] See Case T-158/07, *Cofac v European Commission (Cofac I)*, ECLI:EU:T:2009:489, paras 42 to 54 and *Cofac II*, n 45, paras 37–48. See also *Vlaams Fonds* n 85, para 83.

[104] *OMPI I*, n 59.

[105] *OMPI I*, n 59, para 160.

[106] *OMPI I*, n 59, para 118.

[107] *OMPI I*, n 59, paras 119–20.

[108] *OMPI I*, n 59, para 125. See also C Eckes and J Mendes, n 2, 657–58.

concerned *again* be afforded the opportunity to express his views'.[109] This reasoning had already been implied in *'Invest' Import und Export*, a ruling on a different blacklisting procedure. Because the Commission had taken a decision agreeing with facts and requests of the competent national authority on which the targeted company had already been heard, the General Court considered that the Commission was not required to hear the company again.[110]

D. The Rule of Delegability

The rule of confirmation allows the Union administration to observe the right to be heard by availing itself of hearings offered by national authorities at a prior preparatory stage. However, the confirmation of national hearings will not always be an option.

The Union administration will be under a duty to offer a second hearing if, despite there having been a prior hearing at national level, other requirements for confirmation are not met (eg, because the Union administration intends to decide differently from a national authority's proposal for a final decision). The Union administration will also be under a duty to hear if the national authority failed to observe its duty to offer a hearing under the rule of primary contact; or if the national authority was not under any duty to offer a hearing at all because that rule does not apply (eg, because, according to the relevant legislation, the national authority is neither involved at a prior preparatory stage, nor decisionally dominant).

CJEU case law reveals that, if required to offer a hearing, the Union administration has two options at its disposal. It may directly ask the interested party for her views, or require national authorities to conduct hearings on its behalf – ie *delegate* to national authorities the practical steps necessary for individuals to be heard. This will be termed the rule of delegability.

As Nehl and Sydow point out, the case law here admits of a 'peculiar' 'indirect right to be heard',[111] or, in the terminology proposed above, a kind of mediated hearing. The earliest example dates to *France-Aviation*. While holding that the national authorities involved in the first stage of the procedure should also be the first to offer a hearing to applicants for customs debt relief (ie, the rule of primary contact), the General Court also emphasised that applicants had a right to be heard during the subsequent procedural stage, by the Commission. However, the Commission's duty to hear does not equate with a duty to provide a hearing *itself*. Instead, the General Court held that it merely

[109] *OMPI I*, n 59, para 121. The quote omits the word 'usually' in the passage, which is employed in the judgment to pave the way for the two exceptions explained above.

[110] See Case T-189/00 R *'Invest' Import und Export GmbH v European Commission*, ECLI:EU:T:2000:203, para 40.

[111] HP Nehl, n 11, 79 and G Sydow, n 2, 272 ff.

'had a duty *to arrange* for the applicant to be heard *by the French authorities*' – '*to ensure* that the applicant's right to be heard was respected' (emphasis added).[112]

Other cases in customs followed suit.[113] In *Mehibas*, the General Court established that, though obliged to observe the right to be heard, the Commission 'need only deal with the Member State concerned' and is only 'under a duty to ensure that the person is heard by the national authorities'.[114] The Commission's pleadings in *Kaufring* are also revealing. The Commission argued that the observance of the right to be heard on its part 'does not necessarily require that a person who is likely to be adversely affected by the decision to be taken must be heard by the institution itself'.[115] It added that 'there are many procedures in which the interested party is heard only by the national authorities and not by Commission staff'.[116] Neither observation was denied by the General Court.

Support for delegable hearings can be found in some rulings concerning the European Social Fund.[117] *Mediocurso I* is a case in point. Beneficiaries have a right to be heard before Commission decisions reducing financial assistance – however, the right can be observed simply by making 'an invitation to the appellant *by or on behalf* of the Commission to submit its observations' (emphasis added).[118]

In short, the Union administration may fulfil its own duty to ensure the right to be heard by requiring national authorities to offer a hearing in its name. Upon being instructed to do so, national authorities do all the bureaucratic heavy-lifting – exchanges with the interested party, compiling its views, and reporting back to the Union administration – but it is to the Union administration that the observance of the right to be heard is attributed.

[112] *France-Aviation*, n 42, paras 36 and 30.

[113] In *Eyckeler*, n 41, para 84, and *Primex*, n 42, para 67, the General Court was somewhat less clear, as it omitted the reference to hearings *by national authorities* when quoting *France-Aviation*. Nevertheless, that the choice of words remained otherwise the same is telling: over the Commission hangs the 'duty to arrange for the applicant to be heard', rather than the duty *to hear the applicant*. This is corroborated by the judgment's version in French, which states that the Commission is under a duty to 'faire entendre'.

HP Nehl, n 11, 79 makes a different reading of these cases. He interprets the cases' reference to a right to be heard in the procedure 'before the Commission' as a demand that hearings take place directly before the Commission. The ambiguity of the wording is resolved by looking at other language versions. What is intended is that, *chronologically*, hearings are offered *during the procedural stage which takes place before the Commission*; not that affected parties have a right to be directly placed *before the Commission* in order to express their views on their case. This becomes clear from para 86 of the *Eyckeler* ruling, which refers to hearings being ensured by the Commission 'in the procedure before it' not least in the light of other language versions (such as the Portuguese, Spanish, German and French versions) which paraphrase this as the Commission giving the applicant an opportunity to express its views 'in the procedure unfolding before it'.

[114] *Mehibas*, n 42, paras 46 and 45.

[115] *Kaufring*, n 35, para 145.

[116] *Kaufring*, n 35, para 146.

[117] For an example in the domain of the European Regional Development Fund, see Case T-189/02 *Ente per le Ville vesuviane v European Commission*, ECLI:EU:T:2007:233, paras 93 ff.

[118] *Mediocurso I*, n 45, para 43.

This doctrinal construction is possible for two reasons. First, as there is no right to be heard orally,[119] that right can be satisfied by mere written exchanges; second, the transmission of the affected parties' views to the Union administration, according to the case law, finds a legal basis whenever legislation provides for a duty of national authorities to share information with the Union administration. Given the pervasiveness of duties to exchange information, it is fair to assume that delegated hearings may occur in practically all instances of composite decision-making.[120]

And yet, much of the literature has been critical of delegated hearings. Such hearings have been decried as 'baroque' (Cassese),[121] as an 'artificial mechanism' (Alonso de León),[122] and as an unnecessary 'bureaucratic detour' inconsistent with the CJEU's own view that the right to be heard must be observed even in the absence of specific legislative provisions (Nehl).[123]

However, at least in the reading supported here, the delegation of hearings *does* allow the Union administration to adequately observe the right to be heard. The implicit distinction between the *duty* to ensure the right to be heard and *the practical steps* needed to observe that right is crucial. It reflects a concern to respect both the right to be heard and the will of the Union legislature. If their intended role is merely to assist the Union administration, national authorities can rightly be expected to provide it with additional information obtained from interested parties. There is no reason why such information cannot include the points of law and fact that said parties may wish to raise regarding the decision that the Union administration intends to take. What is perhaps less consistent with the Union legislature's will is that the case law implies that the Union administration's duty to hear and national authorities' generic duties to exchange information, if combined, can be interpreted as a power of the Union administration to require – ie to *command* – the national authorities to offer hearings. The implications of this issue will be explained in due course.[124]

In any event, some of Nehl's concerns would be dispelled today. Whereas earlier rulings, such as *France-Aviation*, seemed to suggest that the Union administration was *obliged* to delegate hearings, other rulings, like *Mediocurso I*, suggest that it may simply *choose* to do so. This shift suggests a recognition that only the Union administration is well-placed to judge the merits of delegating hearings in each individual case.[125]

[119] Case T-256/07 *People's Mojahedin Organization of Iran v European Council (OMPI II)*, ECLI:EU:T:2008:461, para 93. The ruling applies analogically the judgment in Joined Cases T-134/03 and T-135/03 *Common Market Fertilizers SA v European Commission*, ECLI:EU:T:2005:339, where the General Court denied the right to an oral hearing in customs debt relief procedures. See also *Sgaravatti*, n 45, para 58.

[120] See Chapter 3, section IV.C.

[121] S Cassese, n 2, 31.

[122] S Alonso de León, n 50, 227.

[123] HP Nehl, n 11, 79.

[124] See the conclusions in Chapter 10.

[125] There may be sound policy reasons to delegate hearings. For example, it might be more practical for individuals to go to the same 'desk' at every stage of the procedure. In the domain of customs

IV. State Aid: The Last Stronghold of an Outdated Approach

Despite the advances for the right to be heard after the inter-administrative approach was abandoned, one composite procedure evaded the tide of change. In state aid review procedures, the inter-administrative approach is still applied.[126] Given the overall trajectory of the case law in other policy areas, the CJEU's fixation on he structure of state aid procedures, described as 'rather formalistic',[127] appears outdated and arbitrary.

The procedures in question have been summarised before.[128] After gathering evidence at a 'detailed investigation' stage, the Commission will rule on whether the particular aid is compatible with the internal market and, if not, abolish the aid and require its recovery by the Member State. What typically follows at the national level is that the beneficiary is ordered to return the aid it has received.[129]

In sharp contrast with the case law developing unitary procedural protection, and with the letter of Article 41(2)(a) of the Charter,[130] the CJEU denies that aid recipients have a right to be heard prior to a Commission decision abolishing aid. This is so despite the significant financial burden, sometimes even the risk of bankruptcy,[131] that such a decision inevitably imposes onto them.[132] Indeed, the case law only affords aid beneficiaries and their competitors a very thin form of participation – a right to submit comments once the Commission has taken the decision to *initiate* the detailed investigation procedure.[133]

procedures, it must be borne in mind that national customs officers are the 'human face' of the customs union – see T Lyons, *EC Customs Law* (Oxford University Press, 2008), 120. From the perspective of firms, it might even be preferable to have a hearing with the same national officials who assessed the initial application.

[126] This strand of case law seems to have originated in Case 323/82 *SA Intermills v European Commission*, ECLI:EU:C:1984:345, para 17 and has continued until as recently as Joined Cases T-427/04 and T-17/05 *French Republic and France Télecom SA v European Commission*, ECLI:EU:T:2009:474, paras 146 ff and Case T-362/10 *Vtesse Networks Ltd v European Commission*, ECLI:EU:T:2014:928, para 95.

[127] HP Nehl, n 11, 61.

[128] See Chapter 3, section III.B.(iii).

[129] See procedural provisions set out in Council Regulation 2015/1589 of 13 July 2015 laying down detailed rules for the application of Article 108 of the Treaty on the Functioning of the European Union.

[130] See HP Nehl, 'The Imperfect Procedural Status of Beneficiaries of Aid in EC State Aid Proceedings: Note on Case C-276/03 P, *Scott SA v. Commission*' (2006) 5 *European State Aid Law Quarterly* 57, 61 and H Hofmann and C Micheau, *State Aid Law of the European Union* (Oxford University Press, 2016), 345–47.

[131] This point was raised by the applicant in Case T-198/01 *Technische Glaswerke Ilmenau (TGI) GmbH v European Commission*, ECLI:EU:T:2004:222, para 178.

[132] M Maier and P Werner, 'Judgment of 30 November 2009 in Cases T-427/04 and T-1 7/05, France and France Telecom SA v Commission: Comments on Cases T-427/04 and T-1 7/05' (2011) 10 *European State Aid Law Quarterly* 715, 717 and 722.

[133] See for instance Joined Cases C-75/05 P and C-80/05 P *Federal Republic of Germany v Kronofrance SA*, ECLI:EU:C:2008:482, para 37, Case C-198/91 *William Cook plc v European Commission*,

The Court's view – its 'traditional dogma', as some have written[134] – is that the review of state aid constitutes a strictly inter partes procedure where Member States are the Commission's sole interlocutors and addressees of decisions on aid.[135] Based on the view that the procedure is initiated in respect of the Member State rather than of the aid recipients,[136] the Court holds the latter not to have any 'special role' 'by virtue of which it or they could rely on rights as extensive as the rights of the defence as such'.[137] The beneficiary's position, the CJEU states, is not that of a party to the procedure,[138] but rather that of a mere 'source of information for the Commission' which is only called upon if appropriate in the 'circumstances of the concrete case'.[139] Put differently, it is for the Commission to decide, on a *discretionary* basis, whether aid beneficiaries should be consulted in order to gather potentially useful information.[140] Counterintuitively, however, beneficiaries are considered to be individually and directly concerned by Commission decisions on state aid – which means that they are entitled to judicial protection before the CJEU – but not entitled to procedural protection before the Commission.[141]

The lack of a right in aid recipients to be heard by the Commission has not gone without the protest of legal scholarship.[142] It has often been argued that the Court's case law is inconsistent with the degree of protection it affords in other competition law processes.[143]

ECLI:EU:C:1993:197, para 22; C-225/91 *Matra SA v European Commission*, ECLI:EU:C:1993:239, para 16 and C-367/95 P *European Commission v Chambre syndicale nationale des entreprises de transport de fonds et valeurs (Sytraval)*, ECLI:EU:C:1998:154 para 38.

[134] A Bartosch, 'Procedural Rights Denied for Too Long: Is Legal Conservativism Finally Heading for Its "Götterdämmerung"?' (2011) 10 *European State Aid Law Quarterly* 580, 580.

[135] See Case C-276/03 P *Scott SA v European Commission*, ECLI:EU:C:2005:590, paras 33–34.

[136] See Joined Cases C-74/00 P and C-75/00 P *Falck*, ECLI:EU:C:2002:524, para 81; Joined Cases T-228/99 and T-233/99 *Westdeutsche Landesbank Girozentrale v European Commission*, ECLI:EU:T:2003:57, para 122; Cases T-68/03 *Olympiaki Aeroporia Ypiresies*, ECLI:EU:T:2007:253, para 43; and T-565/08 *Corsica Ferries France*, ECLI:EU:T:2012:415, para 50. The earliest judgment that EU courts quote to support this view seems to date back to Case 234/84 *Belgium v Commission*, ECLI:EU:C:1986:302, para 29.

[137] See Cases T-109/01 *Fleuren Compost*, ECLI:EU:T:2004:4, T-62/08 *ThyssenKrupp Acciai Speciali Terni SpA v European Commission*, ECLI:EU:T:2010:268, para 163; and T-354/05 *Télévision française*, para 101.

[138] *Scott*, n 135, para 34.

[139] See Cases T-266/94 *Foreningen af Jernskibs- og Maskinbyggerier i Danmark, Skibsvaerftsforeningen, Skibsværftsforeningen v European Commission*, ECLI:EU:T:1996:153 para 256; Joined Cases T-371/94 and T-394/94, *British Airways plc v European Commission*, ECLI:EU:T:1998:140, para 59; *TGI*, n 131, para 192 ff; *Scott*, n 135, para 34; *France Télecom*, n 126, para 147. Similarly, see Cases 70/72 *Commission v Germany*, ECLI:EU:C:1973:87, para 19 and *Westdeutsche Landesbank*, n 136, para 124.

[140] In this sense, H Hofmann and C Micheau, n 130, 342.

[141] See *Vtesse Networks* n 126, para 96.

[142] HP Nehl, n 11, 60; M Maier and P Werner, n 132; FC Laprévote, 'A Missed Opportunity? State aid Modernization and Effective Third Parties Rights in State aid Proceedings' (2014) 13 *European State Aid Law Quarterly* 426, 436 ff; and H Hofmann and C Micheau, n 130, 341 ff.

[143] See for instance Case *TGI*, n 131, para 179.

However, or so it is argued here, the real point of inconsistency is not in the fact that the case law has offered different solutions for substantively related policy fields. The real inconsistency is that, in every other policy area, the inter-administrative reading of composite procedures was abandoned 30 years ago as a plausible justification for denying procedural rights.[144] This is not to say that there might not be any potentially sound arguments to deny a right to be heard in state aid cases: that the diffuse effects of state aid in market relations may make it impossible to hear or even identify all interested parties; that it may be arbitrary only to hear beneficiaries and not competitors; or that the purely inter-administrative character of the procedure is constitutionally embedded into its regime in the Treaties.[145] However, that the state aid procedure is designed to function merely as a matter between the Commission and the Member States is, as such, simply not a convincing reason.

V. The Right to be Heard Beyond Executive Federalism

Some renowned scholars who have researched the right to be heard have lamented that composite procedures often 'fail to be considered as unitary procedures for purposes of procedural protection'.[146] As this chapter hopes to have made clear, the position taken here is quite the opposite. It argues that a transition can be observed in CJEU case law between two approaches to the right to be heard.

The first, clinging to old tenets of European Executive Federalism, was the inter-administrative approach. In this period of the case law, the CJEU did indeed fail to recognise composite procedures as unitary procedures, regarding their interdependent procedural stages rather as entirely separate administrative procedures. The second approach was unitary procedural protection. The unitary procedural protection principle aims to ensure that the division of decisional tasks between national and the Union authorities does not stand in the way of the rights of the defence. Unitary protection goes hand in hand with the test of decisional dominance. The test dissipates doubts as to which level of administration bears responsibility for the right to be heard by determining that it falls upon the one with the power to define the composite procedure's final outcome.

[144] *Cf* HP Nehl, n 11, 62 and H Hofmann and C Micheau, n 130, 346.

[145] See the Opinion of AG VerLoren van Themaat in Case 323/82 *Intermills*, ECLI:EU:C:1984:260. See also the Opinion of AG Jacobs in Case C-276/03 P *Scott SA v European Commission*, ECLI:EU:C:2005:229, para 74, advancing the view that the Treaty provisions on State aid procedure show no 'systematic concern to protect the interests of beneficiaries'.

[146] C Eckes and J Mendes, n 2, 652.

If national administration exercises decisional dominance, be it at the beginning or at the end of the procedure, it is under a duty to honour the right to be heard, pursuant to what was termed the rule of primary contact. In those cases where the Union administration exercises decisional dominance, the CJEU sought a compromise solution that required Union authorities to observe the rights of the defence but still respect the fact that the legislature intended to privilege the interactions between individuals and national administration.[147] That balance is achieved by

(i) demanding that national authorities provide a hearing if they are responsible for the preparatory stages of composite procedures (a second use of the rule of primary contact);
(ii) allowing the Union administration to refer back to a hearing already provided by a national authority if the Union agrees with that authority's opinion (the rule of confirmation); *and*
(iii) allowing the Union administration to request that hearings are offered to private parties on its behalf, at national level (the rule of delegability).

The rules of confirmation and delegability reveal perhaps the most radical change. They make clear that the case law on the right to be heard in composite decision-making is about far more than procedural protection. Under the guise of good administration rights, the CJEU redefined the relations between Union and state administration.

More specifically, the case law abandoned the separation principle. Two of that principle's historical postulates had been the notions that national and Union authorities are *exclusively* responsible for the observance of their own legal obligations, and that legal relations with individuals will fall *either* to national, *or* (exceptionally) to Union authorities.[148] The first notion was clearly abandoned by the rules of primary contact, confirmation and delegability, which allow the Union administration to share its own burden to fulfil the right to be heard with its national counterparts. The second notion was contradicted by the CJEU's 'determination to 'pierce the Member States' veil' and recognise *direct links* between individuals and the Union administration, even when national authorities are its sole intended interlocutors.[149]

[147] This is acknowledged by C Eckes and J Mendes, n 2, 656.
[148] See Chapter 2, section V.B.(i).
[149] E Barbier de la Serre, n 38, 240.

6

The Principle of Unitary Procedural Protection and the Right to a Reasoned Decision in Composite Decision-Making

I. Whose Reasons and for Whom?

Just like the right to be heard, the right to a reasoned decision is part of the fundamental right to a good administration.[1] While this requirement is sometimes explicitly enshrined in legislation instituting composite procedures,[2] Union law is generally quite clear about *when* national and Union authorities must state the reasons for the decisions that they adopt. As was explained in Chapter four, Union authorities must reason all their decisions. National authorities must reason all decisions that are potentially subject to judicial review. One could therefore expect the observance of the right to a reasoned decision to be less problematic in composite decision-making than the right to be heard has been.

And yet, as Mattarella suggests, the structure of composite procedures has occasionally led to doubts as to which administration is required to give reasons and how those reasons must be stated.[3] Indeed, given that the relative weight of decision-making power of national and Union administrations can vary significantly between different composite procedures, which of the two should be responsible for the statement of reasons? Moreover, the Union administration must clearly and unequivocally disclose the reasons for its decisions. But clear

[1] For just a few recent rulings, see Cases C-277/11 *M.M. v Minister for Justice, Equality and Law Reform*, ECLI:EU:C:2012:744, para 88; C-417/11 P *European Council v Bamba*, ECLI:EU:C:2012:718, para 49; T-383/11 *Makhlouf v European Council*, ECLI:EU:T:2013:431, para 60; C-249/13 *Boudjlida v Préfet des Pyrénées-Atlantiques*, ECLI:EU:C:2014:2431, para 38; T-593/11 *Al-Chihabi v European Council*, ECLI:EU:T:2015:249, para 61; and T-145/15 *Romania v Commission*, ECLI:EU:T:2017:86, para 43.

[2] See for example Article 6(6) of Regulation 1829/2003, which binds the European Food Safety Authority to a duty to substantiate the opinions it issues in the procedures for the authorisation of GMO food or feed. The European Medicines Agency is under the same duty when issuing opinions concerning the approval of pharmaceuticals (see Article 32(5) of Directive 2001/83).

[3] BG Mattarella, 'Procedimenti e Atti Amministrativi' in M Chiti (ed), *Diritto Amministrativo Europeo* (Giuffrè, 2013), 337.

and unequivocal *to whom*, given that those decisions are addressed to national administration, rather than to the individuals affected by them? And *whose reasons* should be stated, given that the final decision results from the joint exercise of national and Union decisional power?

The present chapter considers approaches that the CJEU has used to address such questions. The first, analysed in section II, is the purely inter-administrative approach to composite decision-making that was already set out before. According to that approach, and following the logic of strictly separate legal relations, the Union administration's decisions must be 'clear and unequivocal' primarily to the national authorities to which they are addressed, not to affected private parties.

Section III considers the second approach. It is the adoption by the CJEU of the principle of unitary procedural protection: the right to a reasoned decision should not suffer because of the involvement of multiple levels of administration. Just as in the case law on the right to be heard, this purpose is achieved by clearly assigning ultimate responsibility to the authority exercising decisional dominance. Just as with the right to be heard, when that responsibility falls to the Union administration, the latter may rely on the assistance of national authorities to observe the duty to give reasons.

Section IV concludes the present chapter. It summarises the main findings and stresses the importance of reasoned composite decision-making from the perspective of judicial review, which will be the focus of the book's Part III.

II. Intelligibility Beyond the Internal Administrative Sphere

A purely inter-administrative approach to procedural rights is not problematic if administrative procedures have no immediate impact on the legal position of individuals. In instances of what was termed *authentic* second-order administration – ie where the Union administration takes decisions which exclusively affect the Member States – it is understandable that the adequacy of given reasons is measured from the perspective of the national authorities concerned. In the context of clearance of accounts in the European Agricultural Funds, for instance, the CJEU rightly considers that Commission decisions are sufficiently reasoned 'if the Member State to which the decision is addressed was closely involved in the decision-making process'.[4]

What is problematic is if an inter-administrative approach is followed in instances of composite procedures that exist in *apparent* second-order administration, ie where, despite national authorities being its sole intended interlocutors, the Union administration takes decisions which also impact individuals. Just as with

[4] Case T-358/11 *Italy v Commission*, ECLI:EU:T:2015:394, para 93.

the case law concerning the right to be heard – albeit in fewer rulings – the inter-administrative approach was applied and subsequently replaced with the model of unitary procedural protection.

In *Universiteit Groningen* and *Nicolet I*, the Court was asked by national courts to review two distinct Commission decisions. Both decisions, adopted pursuant to the composite procedure for the duty-free importation of scientific instruments, had rejected the applicants' requests for exemption from customs duty. The applicants in both cases contended that the decisions were insufficiently reasoned and therefore invalid. The Court of Justice disagreed.

The Court began by restating its own standard formulation on the reasons-giving requirement. Statements of reasons, the Court recalled, must disclose 'in a *clear and unequivocal* fashion the reasoning followed by the Community authority … to make the *persons concerned* aware of the reasons for the measure and thus enable them to *defend their rights*' (emphasis added).[5] Such requirements would suggest that a statement of reasons must be 'clear and unequivocal' first and foremost to the 'persons concerned' and who may need to 'defend their rights'. And yet, the Court's approach was entirely different.

The Court recognised that the two decisions' statements of reasons were 'somewhat laconic', but nevertheless sufficient.[6] The two arguments used in this respect are telling. First, the decisions were addressed to the Member States, which had participated in the meetings of the group of experts which supported the Commission's decision, and which were therefore 'sufficiently familiar with the details of the case to be able to assess the scope of the decision'. Second, the decisions also contained 'the indispensable elements' for the applicants for customs duty exemptions to establish whether said decisions were 'vitiated by a manifest error of assessment'.[7]

If statements of reasons needed to be clear from the perspective of the 'person concerned' for said person to be able to defend their rights, then an inter-administrative approach cannot suffice. The sole relevant test of clarity of a decision's reasons should be their intelligibility to the persons who, being *directly affected* by that decision, may initiate judicial proceedings against it. And yet, the Court of Justice's findings not only considered it decisive that statements of reasons were clear from the perspective of national authorities; it considered that clarity from the perspective of affected parties simply did not matter.

Universiteit Groningen is illuminating in this regard, as the Court explicitly asserted that, since the Commission's decision was requested by, and addressed to, national administration, without any role being foreseen in the legislation for

[5] Cases 185/83 *Interfacultair Instituut Electronenmicroscopie of Universiteit Groningen v Inspecteur der Invoerrechten en Accijnzen, Groningen*, ECLI:EU:C:1984:331, para 38; and 203/85 *Nicolet Instrument GmbH v Hauptzollamt Frankfurt am Main-Flughafen (Nicolet I)*, ECLI:EU:C:1986:269, para 10.

[6] *Nicolet I*, n 5, para 11. See also *Universiteit Groningen*, n 5, para 39.

[7] Ibid.

individuals, the applicant 'does not have the right to demand information from the Commission regarding the basis for its decision'.[8]

Just as with the right to be heard, the Court of Justice took a radically different approach just a couple of years later, in *Technische Universität München* (*TUM*). In a similar administrative procedure, the Court considered that the Commission's decision was insufficiently reasoned, since it did not allow the person concerned to ascertain if it was vitiated by errors of appraisal.[9]

Despite the different outcome in *TUM* in comparison with the *Universiteit Groningen* and *Nicolet I* rulings, there was no significant difference in how the two decisions were reasoned. The statement of reasons in *Nicolet I* merely rephrased the applicable rules for the duty-free admission of scientific instruments into the common market.[10] 'Laconic', as the Court put it, was a gross understatement. The decision certainly did not meet the general requirement of 'clear and unequivocal' disclosure of reasons. But above all, it certainly did not meet that requirement to any lesser extent than the contested decision in *TUM* did.[11] What appears to have been the *fundamental* difference *in TUM* was that, unlike the previous two cases, the CJEU did not even consider whether the Commission's statement of reasons was 'clear and unequivocal' from the perspective of the addressee national authorities.[12]

Since *TUM*, the CJEU has largely abandoned the inter-administrative approach to the sufficiency of statements of reasons. Just as with the right to be heard, the only exception appears to be in the domain of state aid review. The *TGI* ruling provides good illustration. The General Court held that,

> When examining whether the obligation to state reasons was satisfied … it should be pointed out that the procedure for reviewing State aid is a *procedure initiated in respect of the Member State* responsible for granting the aid and that the parties concerned within the meaning of Article [108(3) TFEU], which include the recipient of the aid, cannot themselves seek to debate the issues with the Commission in the same way as may the abovementioned Member State (emphasis added).[13]

The problem, as Bierwagen has noted, is that the CJEU's position in this regard significantly diminishes the judicial protection of aid beneficiaries.[14] The case

[8] See *Universiteit Groningen*, n 5, paras 21–22.

[9] Case C-269/90 *Technische Universität München v Hauptzollamt München-Mitte (TUM)*, ECLI:EU:C:1991:438, para 27.

[10] Commission Decision of 6 August 1982 establishing that the apparatus described as 'Nicolet – High Speed Signal Averager, model 1174, with accessories' may not be imported free of Common Customs Tariff duties OJ L 243, 18.8.1982, 30–30.

[11] Commission Decision of 5 July 1983 establishing that the apparatus described as 'JEOL – Scanning Electron Microscope model JSM-35C' may not be imported free of Common Customs Tariff duties, OJ L 188, 13.7.1983, 22–22.

[12] *TUM*, n 9, para 27.

[13] Case T-198/01 *Technische Glaswerke Ilmenau (TGI) GmbH v European Commission*, ECLI:EU:T:2004:222, para 61. See also Case C-367/95 P *European Commission v Chambre syndicale nationale des entreprises de transport de fonds et valeurs (Sytraval)*, ECLI:EU:C:1998:154, para 59.

[14] R Bierwagen, 'Review of Judgment in Case T-198/01 Technische Glaswerke Ilmenau v. European Commission' (2004) 3 *European State Aid Law Quarterly* 699, 702.

law in state aid could benefit from greater consistency with the CJEU's shift away from the inter-administrative approach in every other policy sector. Such a shift, however, has not prevented the Union administration from attempting to evade the duty to give reasons. Those attempts – some recent – have been unsuccessful. Some cases emerging in the European Banking Union's Single Resolution Mechanism provide a good example of this.

The cases in question emerged from the procedures for the payment of ex ante contributions to the Single Resolution Fund (SRF). The SRF is an emergency fund which is used to finance bank resolutions and is funded by contributions from credit institutions. After national resolution authorities (NRAs) collect the requisite data, the Single Resolution Board calculates and takes a decision determining the exact amount of the annual contribution that each credit institution must pay. The decision is notified to the credit institutions by the NRAs.[15]

In *Hypo Vorarlberg Bank*, a credit institution (Hypo Vorarlberg) had brought an action for annulment against decisions of the SRB defining the ex ante contributions it needed to pay. The plaintiff argued that the SRB's decisions were insufficiently reasoned. The SRB claimed otherwise. It argued that there was no need for the credit institution to have access to a detailed statement of reasons because the contested SRB decisions were only addressed to the Austrian NRA. In the words of the ruling, 'since the addressee of the SRB's decisions [was] the Austrian NRA and not the applicant, the statement of reasons [needed to be] sufficient for that NRA to be able to understand the facts and legal considerations underpinning the calculation'.[16] Moreover, since the NRA had been involved in the procedure leading up to the adoption of the contested decisions, it had knowledge of how *Hypo Vorarlberg*'s contribution had been calculated.[17]

The General Court rejected this line of reasoning.[18] While it acknowledged that 'the decisions determining the *ex ante* contributions are addressed to the NRAs', the General Court found that 'the institutions which are liable to pay those contributions, including the applicant, are, contrary to the SRB's assertions, individually and directly concerned by those decisions'. Therefore, it concluded, 'the interest that those institutions may have in receiving explanations must also be taken into account when assessing the extent of the obligation to state the reasons for the decisions in question'.[19] Reasons, in short, must be intelligible to the persons affected by a decision – and not merely to the authorities who make it.[20]

[15] Article 70(1) and (2) of the Single Resolution Mechanism Regulation and Article 5 of Council Implementing Regulation (EU) 2015/81 of 19 December 2014 specifying uniform conditions of application of Regulation (EU) No 806/2014 of the European Parliament and of the Council with regard to ex ante contributions to the Single Resolution Fund.

[16] Joined Cases T-377/16, T-645/16 and T-809/16 *Hypo Vorarlberg Bank AG v Single Resolution Board (SRB)*, ECLI:EU:T:2019:823, paras 165–66.

[17] Ibid, para 168.

[18] For other similar rulings, see Case T-411/17 *Landesbank Baden-Württemberg v Single Resolution Board (SRB)* ECLI:EU:T:2020:435, paras 68, 88–89. Case T-365/16 *Portigon AG v Single Resolution Board (SRB)*, ECLI:EU:T:2019:824, paras 153, 163–64.

[19] *Hypo Vorarlberg*, n 16, paras 175–76.

[20] The Court of Justice set aside the General Court's ruling in *Portigon*, n 18, which it held not to have adequately balanced the requirements of clear reasons-giving and of respect for business secrecy.

III. Decisional Dominance and the Boundaries of National Administrative Assistance

The case law considered in the previous section showed that the CJEU has moved on from the inter-administrative approach to statements of reasons. It now requires the Union administration to disclose the reasons for its decisions in a manner that is clear and unequivocal to all affected parties.

A separate question, however, concerns how the burden of giving reasons should be distributed between national and Union administration. The case law provides three answers. First, the Union administration must include the reasons found in national preparatory acts in its statements of reasons. Second, it may do so by simply referring to said acts. Third, the Union administration cannot leave the fulfilment of the reasons-giving requirement entirely to the national authorities involved at the conclusion of a composite procedure.

As with the right to be heard, the CJEU's case law on reasons-giving is guided by a principle of unitary procedural protection – by an implicit overarching aim of ensuring that the division of tasks between national and Union authorities does not harm the procedural protection of individuals. To that end, both levels of administration must act as one.

The role of decisional dominance is, however, distinct from that which one could observe in the case law on the right to be heard. That role should be distinguished in respect of national and Union administrations.

As was noted before, the duty of national authorities to give reasons under Union law applies whenever they adopt decisions potentially subject to judicial review. This has two implications in composite decision-making. First, national authorities must give reasons when taking a final decision and, if relevant to that decision, must incorporate the reasons found in preparatory acts taken by the Union administration. Second, national authorities must give reasons if they perform binding preparatory acts in composite procedures – a requirement which does not apply in purely national decision-making. Indeed, as Chapter seven will show, decisional dominance is relevant not only to ascribe responsibility for the observance of procedural rights, but to determine which measures adopted within composite administrative procedures are subject to judicial review. For this reason, the duty to give reasons applies to all national acts which result from dominant national decisional power, *even if* those are formally not the final decision of the administrative procedure.

As for the Union administration, it was noted in Chapter four that it must give reasons for *all* binding measures it adopts. This flows from the general primary law provisions on the duty to give reasons, such as Article 296 TFEU and

However, one must not overlook that the Court of Justice, just like the General Court, held that the test to determine if a measure is sufficiently reasoned is whether it is understandable to the addressees *affected* by it (at para 82).

Article 41(2)(c) of the Charter. The implication is that the Union administration is legally required to give reasons for its final decisions *even* in composite procedures where there is national decisional dominance (ie even if it cannot diverge from binding national preparatory acts). Such would certainly justify the practice of the Commission, in composite procedures with national decisional dominance, of simply recording in the statement of reasons what the Union legislation applied was and what steps were followed in the course of the administrative procedure, and mentioning – *not justifying* – the prior position taken by national authorities. This is typically how the Commission gives reasons for implementing regulations registering protected designations of origin (PDOs) or geographic indications (PGIs).[21] The recent *Aquind* ruling gave the General Court the opportunity to confirm the legality of this reading in the field of energy. While acknowledging that the Commission was under a duty to give reasons for a delegated regulation that failed to give an infrastructural project for an interconnector the desired status of 'Project of Common Interest' (PCI), the General Court stressed the division of powers between the Union and the Member States in the sector. Under Regulation (EU) No 347/2013, as interpreted in conformity with Article 172(2) TFEU, the Member States enjoy a 'right of veto' over PCIs affecting their territory, exercised by stating their refusal to approve a PCI, and the Commission is 'not entitled to overrule that refusal'.[22] As the Commission cannot approve a PCI without the Member State's approval (ie because decisional dominance lies with the Member State rather than with the Commission), it will have satisfied the duty to give reasons if it chooses to simply refer to the Member State's refusal of a PCI, without any need to disclose the reasons behind it.[23]

However, if the Union administration must reason its own binding measures *anyway*, then what added value does the test of decisional dominance have when such dominance is exercised, not at the national, but at the Union level? The case law considered in the following three subsections illustrates that the CJEU tends to point out the Union administration's decisional dominance precisely in order to underline that the involvement of national authorities in the administrative procedure does not absolve it from bearing ultimate responsibility for the proper observance of the right to a reasoned decision. Indeed, the emphasis on such observance being *especially* important when the Union administration exercises decisional dominance is consistent with the CJEU's general requirement that all rights of the defence be respected in a particularly scrupulous

[21] For one of countless examples, see Commission Implementing Regulation (EU) 2021/2035 of 16 November 2021 entering a name in the register of protected designations of origin and protected geographical indications ('Alho da Graciosa' (PGI)). The recital of the implementing Regulation in question, which gives PGI status to a variety of garlic originating in the Azores, simply alludes to the application for PGI registration, supported by Portugal, that had previously been published in the EU's Official Journal, as stipulated in the PGI registration procedural rules.

[22] Case T-295/20 *Aquind Ltd v European Comission*, ECLI:EU:T:2023:52, paras 37–40.

[23] Ibid, para 43.

manner whenever Union authorities exercise discretion.[24] As will be shown, decisional dominance makes the Union administration ultimately responsible for the duty to give reasons, even if it merely reuses (subsection III.A.) or refers to (subsection III.B.) reasons contained in prior national preparatory acts, and is the reason why the Union administration cannot simply leave the fulfilment of that duty entirely to national authorities (subsection III.C).

A. The Rule of Replicability

The CJEU accepts that the Union administration may reason its decisions by simply replicating reasons set out in a previous national preparatory act. This becomes evident from judgments on the access to documents held by Union authorities, but which originate in the Member States.

The regime established in Regulation (EC) No 1049/2001 aims to ensure the transparency and openness of EU decision-making processes. The regime is built on the assumption that, in principle, all documents held by EU institutions should be accessible to the public.[25] However, it also allows those institutions to refuse access to documents based on a number of 'substantive exceptions' – that is, if their disclosure would undermine overriding interests such as public security or business secrets.[26] If requested documents originate from a Member State, the latter may oppose disclosure, provided that it justifies its position as falling under the 'substantive exceptions'.

What is termed here as the *rule of replicability* concerns the fact that the CJEU requires statements of reasons to reproduce the reasons contained in a national preparatory measure if those reasons were significant for the adoption of the Union administration's final decision. This notion has been present in the case law since *Sweden v Commission*.[27] Since then, the CJEU has insisted that,

> before refusing access to a document originating from a Member State, the institution concerned must examine whether that State has based its objection on the substantive exceptions in Article 4(1) to (3) of Regulation No 1049/2001 and has given proper reasons for its position. Therefore, when taking a decision to refuse access, the institution *must* make sure that those reasons exist and *refer to them in its decision refusing access at the end of the procedure* (emphasis added).[28]

[24] See Chapter 4, section II.

[25] See recital (11) of Regulation (EC) No 1049/2001 of 30 May 2001, regarding public access to European Parliament, Council and Commission documents.

[26] See Article 4(1) and (2).

[27] Case C-64/05 P *Sweden v European Commission*, ECLI:EU:C:2007:802, para 99.

[28] Case T-344/15, *French Republic v European Commission*, ECLI:EU:T:2017:250, para 41. See also Cases C-135/11 P, *IFAW Internationaler Tierschutz-Fonds gGmbH v European Commission*, ECLI:EU:C:2012:376, para 62; and T-669/11, *Spirlea v European Commission*, ECLI:EU:T:2014:814, para 53; T-545/11 RENV, *Stichting Greenpeace Nederland v European Commission*, ECLI:EU:T:2018:817 para 43; and T-74/16 *Pagkyprios organismos ageladotrofon (POA) Dimosia Ltd v European Commission*, ECLI:EU:T:2018:75, para 56.

In later case law, the CJEU clarified what 'referring to reasons' means. It is insufficient for the statement of reasons to 'merely record' that there has been an objection – it must specifically set out what those reasons were.[29]

The justification for the replicability of national reasons is the same as for unitary procedural protection in general. The point is that the right to a reasoned decision cannot be undermined by the division of tasks between national and Union administrations. The fact that decisional dominance lies with the Union administration also is significant. Indeed, while pointing out that the implementation of the Regulation on access to documents is 'entrusted jointly to the institution and the Member State',[30] the CJEU also highlights that national and Union authorities do not share decisional power equally. The Member State's opposition to disclosure of a document does not constitute 'a discretionary right of veto', but rather 'a form of assent'.[31] As only the Union authority may take a decision that an exception to disclosure applies, it must also give reasons for that decision. In the CJEU's own words, '*from the point of view of the person requesting access*, the Member State's intervention does not affect the nature of a European Union act of the decision subsequently addressed to him' (emphasis added).[32] The pivotal importance of the Union administration's decisional dominance vis-à-vis national authorities becomes explicit at the conclusion of the CJEU's line of reasoning: '*as the maker of a decision* to refuse access to documents, [the Union administration is] *responsible for the lawfulness of the decision*' (emphasis added).[33]

The CJEU will review the reasons given by the Union institution in question 'regardless of whether the refusal results from an assessment of those exceptions by the institution itself or by the relevant Member State'.[34]

B. The Rule of Referral

The Union administration may find the reasons contained in national preparatory acts so compelling that it decides to follow them in their entirety. When such is the case, the Union administration may well choose to replicate those reasons into its statement of reasons in the fashion described in the previous subsection. There is, however, another option. The Union administration has developed, at least in some policy fields, a practice of adopting statements of reasons that simply point to the contents of preparatory acts performed by national authorities. As an

[29] *French Republic v Commission*, n 28, para 42.
[30] *Sweden v Commission*, n 27, para 85.
[31] *Sweden v Commission*, n 27, paras 76 and 8; *Spirlea*, n 28, paras 49 and 51; and *Stichting Greenpeace Nederland*, n 28, para. 40.
[32] Case *IFAW*, n 28, para 60.
[33] *IFAW*, n 28, para 61; *Spirlea*, n 28, para 52.
[34] Cases *Stichting Greenpeace Nederland*, n 28, paras 40 and 103 and *POA*, n 28, para 73.

Advocate General explained, the practice prevents 'pointless duplication' of the work of national and Union authorities.[35]

The CJEU finds the practice admissible. It has developed an implicit rule that is akin to what was termed the rule of confirmation, in the case law on the right to be heard. As was explained, the Union administration is not required to give a second hearing if it simply agrees with a position taken by the national authority on which affected parties have already been heard.[36] Similarly, EU courts have developed a rule which will be termed here as the *rule of referral*. If the Union administration simply agrees with the reasons contained in a national preparatory act, it may fulfil the duty to state reasons by simply referring back to that act.

Reasoning decisions by referring to previous, often preparatory, acts is sometimes termed 'referential' or *per relationem* reasons-giving.[37] Referential reasons-giving does not *as such* constitute an innovation. It exists in many national administrative laws as well as under EU law, in administrative procedures which only involve Union authorities.[38] What is unique about referential statements of reasons in composite procedures is their composite structure – comprising both national and European elements – and the set of conditions to which they are subject.

Composite statements of reasons seem to have been used frequently when the Commission intended to withdraw or reduce financial assistance from the European Social Fund (ESF). The CJEU has accepted such statements of reasons since the *Branco I* ruling.[39] The formula used by the CJEU was later repeated in the case law with hardly any variations:

> *a decision of the Commission reducing financial assistance may be regarded as adequately reasoned if it* either clearly sets out itself the reasons which justify the reduction in assistance, or *refers with sufficient clarity to a measure of the competent national authorities* of the Member State concerned in which *those authorities set out clearly the reasons* for

[35] Case C-32/95 P *European Commission v Lisrestal Organização Gestão de Restaurantes Colectivos Ld.a*, ECLI:EU:C:1996:402, para 37.

[36] See Chapter 4, subsection IV.C.

[37] See S Alonso de León, *Composite Administrative Procedures in the European Union* (Iustel, 2017), 245, and the English language version of the ruling in Joined Cases T-180/96 and T-181/96 *Mediocurso – Estabelecimento de Ensino Particular Lda v European Commission (Mediocurso I)*, ECLI:EU:T:1998:208, para 97.

[38] See Case C-119/97 P *Union française de l'express (Ufex) v European Commission*, ECLI:EU:C:1999:116, para 57: 'the statement of reasons for an administrative act may refer to other acts and, in particular, take note of the content of an earlier act, especially if it is connected'. More recently, referential reasoning was accepted by the General Court as sufficient for the Commission to justify why it endorsed a resolution plan drafted by the Single Resolution Board. See Case T-510/17 *Del Valle Ruiz*, ECLI:EU:T:2022:312 para 557: 'where … the Commission endorses the resolution scheme, the statement of reasons for its decision may be limited to indicating that it agrees with the reasons contained in the scheme … the Commission must not repeat the SRB's analysis in its decision, but only endorse it'. Referential reasons-giving presents distinctive constitutional problems in administrative procedures involving Union agencies due to the *Meroni* doctrine – see F Brito Bastos, 'Referential reasons-giving and the limits of Union Agencies' power', *REALaw.blog*, available at; https://wp.me/pcQ0x2-tx.

[39] Case T-85/94 *Eugénio Branco, Ldª v European Commission (Branco I)*, ECLI:EU:T:1995:4, para 34.

> such a reduction, in so far as the undertaking in question has been *able to take cognisance of the measure* (emphasis added).[40]

This – rather complex – formula expresses the rule according to which Union administration *may choose* to give reasons *either* by setting out itself the motives for the final decision, *or* by referring to a national preparatory act.[41] However, the latter option is subject to four conditions:

1. The Union administration does no more than confirm the factual basis and solution contained in a national preparatory act;[42]
2. The reference made to the preparatory act in the Union authority's statement of reasons is sufficiently clear;[43]
3. The reasons contained in the national preparatory act referred to are themselves clearly set out;[44] *and*
4. The affected parties were able to take cognisance of said preparatory national act before it was forwarded to the Union administration.[45]

The four conditions must be jointly fulfilled by the national and Union administration. The first two are clearly a matter for the Union administration; the third and the fourth, a matter for the national authorities. The Union administration will, however, always be responsible for ensuring that, when put together, the distinct national and Union components of a referential statement of reasons meet the same requirements that apply to any single statement of reasons. Indeed, rulings

[40] Case T-199/99 *Sgaravatti Mediterranea Srl v European Commission*, ECLI:EU:T:2002:228, para 102. See also T-89/94 (122) *Eugénio Branco, Ldª v European Commission (Branco II)*, ECLI:EU:T:1998:156, para 36; T-551/93 and T-231/94 to T-234/94 *Industrias Pesqueras Campos SA v European Commission*, ECLI:EU:T:1996:54, paras 142–44; *Mediocurso I*, n 37, para 100; T-72/97 *Proderec – Formação e Desinvolvimento de Recursos Humanos, ACE v Commission of the European Communities*, ECLI:EU:T:1998:179, paras 104–105; T-126/97 *Sonasa*, ECLI:EU:T:1999:239, paras 68–69; T-182/96 *Partex Companhia Portuguesa de Serviços SA v European Commission*, ECLI:EU:T:1999:171, para 77; T-80/00 *Associação Comercial de Aveiro v European Commission*, ECLI:EU:T:2002:117, para 38; Joined Cases T-251/05 and T-425/05 *Mediocurso II*, ECLI:EU:T:2007:162, para 41; T-102/00 *Vlaams Fonds voor de Sociale Integratie van Personen met een Handicap v European Commission*, ECLI:EU:T:2003:192, paras 96 ff; T-51/11 *Associação de Empresas de Construção, Obras Públicas e Serviços v European Commission (AECOPS I)*, ECLI:EU:T:2013:203, para 81 ff, T-52/11 *AECOPS v European Commission (AECOPS II)*, ECLI:EU:T:2013:204 paras 84 and T-53/11 *AECOPS v European Commission (AECOPS III)*, ECLI:EU:T:2013:205, paras 80 ff.

[41] See for instance *Mediocurso I*, n 37, para 100.

[42] This is clearly stated in *Sgaravatti*, n 40, para 100, *AECOPS I*, n 40, para 81, *AECOPS II*, n 40, para 84 and *AECOPS III*, n 40, para 80.

[43] Case T-241/00 *Azienda Agricola 'Le Canne' v European Commission*, ECLI:EU:T:2002:57, paras 56–57 illustrates a situation in which the CJEU annulled a decision to reduce aid because the Commission had not been specific in referring to the aspects of the national preparatory acts it agreed with.

[44] Similarly, the case law of the Portuguese Supreme Administrative Court (*Supremo Tribunal Administrativo – STA*) only accepts reasons-giving *per relationem* if the addressee can understand the reasons of fact and law that are jointly contained in the statement of reasons and the measures to which it refers (See STA Ruling of 10 February 2010 (Rapporteur: Jorge de Sousa).

[45] For this latter requirement, see *Proderec*, n 40, para 105; *Partex*, n 40, para 77; *Sgaravatti*, n 40 para 102; *Associação Comercial de Aveiro*, n 40, paras 39–40.

such as *AECOPS III* indicate that, whenever the Union administration exercises decisional dominance – in this case, where it determined the reduction of an ESF beneficiary's funding[46] – it must make sure that the decision is sufficiently reasoned, even where it is assisted by national authorities.[47]

The fourth condition, the cognisance condition, requires some additional explanation.[48] It requires affected parties to have the opportunity to take due notice of the referenced national preparatory acts *before* they are forwarded to the Union administration.[49] Interestingly, the condition results in a level of protection of the right to a reasoned decision in composite decision-making that is comparatively high when considering purely Union or purely national administrative decision-making.

No similar condition exists when referential statements of reasons are made in administrative procedures taking place at Union level only.[50] Just to give the example of two Member States, the administrative law of both Italy and The Netherlands only requires public authorities to make preparatory acts available to interested parties after final decisions have been taken.[51] In contrast, the CJEU case law concerning the statement of reasons in composite decision-making seems closer to the standard of protection offered in Spanish administrative law, where statements of reasons may simply refer to acts adopted in the course of an administrative procedure, provided that the addressee of the final decision has had prior access to them.[52]

Requiring that the party affected by a Union decision in a composite procedure has previously had access to the national preparatory acts is fully justified from the perspective of judicial control, which is the main rationale of the reasons-giving requirement in Union law. The deadline to lodge actions for annulment under Article 263 TFEU only begins to run from the moment when the person concerned 'acquires precise knowledge of the content of the decision in question *and of the reasons on which it is based*' (emphasis added).[53] Only once such reasons

[46] *AECOPS III*, n 40, para 79.

[47] *AECOPS III*, n 40, para 81.

[48] On this condition, see G della Cananea, 'The European Union's Mixed Administrative Proceedings' (2004–2005) 68 *Law and Contemporary Problems* 197, 208–9.

[49] See *Proderec*, n 40, paras 39–47 and *AECOPS III*, n 40, para 83.

[50] Indeed, the condition is not mentioned, eg in the *Banco Popular* cases as a requirement for the admissibility of referential statements of reasons (see n 38).

[51] See the decision of the Italian Council of State, IV, 22 March 2013, Number 1632. In the ruling, the Consiglio di Stato considers that 'reasons-giving per relationem is legitimate under the condition that the acts referred to [in the statement of reasons] are indicated and made available'. However, this only requires that interested parties have the opportunity to 'to request and to obtain a copy of [said acts] based on the legal framework on the right of access to administrative documents'. Similarly, Section 3:49 of the Dutch General Administrative Law Act provides that '[to] state the reasons of an order or part of an order, it is sufficient to refer to an opinion drawn up in this connection if the opinion itself contains the reasons and communication of the opinion *has been or is given*' (emphasis added).

[52] See eg the Judgment of the Spanish Supreme Court of 9 July 2010 (Rapporteur: Teso Gamella) and case law cited there.

[53] Case T-185/05 *Italy v Commission*, ECLI:EU:T:2008:519, para 68.

are disclosed may that person make an informed choice on whether to bring an action at all.

The same logic justifies the demand that the parties concerned had access to the referenced national preparatory acts *prior* to the adoption of the final decision. If the statement of reasons for the final decision of a Union authority refers to national preparatory acts to which the persons concerned already had access during the administrative procedure, those persons will be able to know instantly whether the decision is sufficiently reasoned.

The case law on the right to be heard provides the answer as to *how* prior knowledge of a national preparatory act should be given. The answer lies in the rulings developing what were termed the rules of primary contact and of confirmation. The first requires national authorities to offer a hearing if they adopt preparatory acts in composite procedures where Union administration exercises decisional dominance. The rule of confirmation allows the Union administration to observe the right to be heard by referring back to a hearing already provided by a national authority, if the Union merely agrees with that authority's position.

Affected parties must take cognisance of the national administration's preparatory acts as part of the latter's duty to respect the right to be heard.[54] Indeed, that right means that national authorities must not only consider the comments of the parties affected by the procedure's final decision, but must also share with them something *upon which to comment* – the factual basis and assessments behind the preparatory acts that they will forward to the Union administration.

The *Proderec* case illustrates well how the rules of primary contact and confirmation relate to the rule of referral and the condition of cognisance.[55] The rules of primary contact and confirmation were applied. The affected beneficiary had the opportunity to comment on the national authorities' proposal for the reduction of ESF financial assistance, and the Commission, fully agreeing with that proposal, did not need to offer a second hearing in order to observe the beneficiary's right to be heard. However, the fact that the affected beneficiary had already been heard on the national preparatory acts was also key to establishing that it had taken cognisance of their content. The Commission's decision, which merely referred to those acts, was therefore sufficiently reasoned.

C. The Rule of Non-substitution

It should be clear by now that the CJEU allows the Union administration to fulfil its duty to give reasons by making use of reasons already contained in national preparatory acts. It was also highlighted, however, that, whenever it enjoys decisional dominance, the Union administration is responsible for the fulfilment of that duty (as well as any other procedural requirement flowing from good

[54] Similarly, see S Alonso de León, n 37, 248 and G della Cananea, n 48, 209.
[55] *Proderec*, n 40.

administration). This is why the Union administration may be *assisted*, but never *replaced* by national authorities. More specifically, the Union administration may not leave its own decisions unreasoned and expect the national authorities to compensate for this with a statement of reasons of their own at the conclusion of the composite procedure.

There are two important practical examples of this. The first one was *Branco II*.[56] The case concerned a Commission decision to reduce financial assistance from the European Social Fund. The Commission argued that, because the relevant legislation only established a relationship between itself and the national authorities, it was not required to give reasons for its own decisions. Instead, it claimed, the duty to give reasons fell to the national administration concerned, which formally took the final decision in respect of beneficiaries.[57]

The General Court fundamentally disagreed. It emphasised that, despite the national authority's involvement, 'it is the Commission – and *the Commission alone* – which had the *power to reduce* ESF financial assistance' (ie the Commission enjoyed decisional dominance). 'It follows', the General Court continued,

> that it is the Commission which assumes, vis-à-vis the recipient of ESF assistance, *the legal responsibility for the decision* by which its assistance is reduced, irrespective of whether that reduction was or was not proposed by the national authority concerned.

Consequently, the CJEU held that the Commission was under the duty to give reasons.[58]

A second, more recent example of this same line of reasoning can be found in the case law on ex ante contributions in the Single Resolution Mechanism. The basic structure of the composite procedures in question has already been set out before.[59]

In *Hypo Vorarlberg*, the SRB had determined the amounts of ex ante contributions but also left it at the discretion of the NRAs whether they communicated the SRB's method of calculation when notifying the credit institutions. The General Court strongly opposed this approach. Even though it acknowledged that the SRB's decisions 'are to be addressed to the NRAs alone', and that it falls to NRAs to communicate those decisions to the credit institutions, the General Court highlighted that 'the SRB is responsible for calculating and determining the ex ante contributions'. 'As a result', the ruling went on to state,

> it is for the SRB, *the author of those decisions, to state the reasons for those decisions. That obligation cannot be delegated to the NRAs, nor can the failure to fulfil that obligation be remedied by those NRAs*, without disregarding the role of the SRB as *the author of those decisions and its liability* in that respect (emphasis added).[60]

[56] *Branco II*, n 40.
[57] *Branco II*, n 40, paras 13–16. See the analysis of S Alonso de León, n 37, 246.
[58] *Branco II*, n 40, paras 23–24.
[59] See section II.
[60] *Hypo Vorarlberg* n 16, 204–6. See also *Portigon*, n 18, paras 179–81 and Case T-411/17 *Landesbank Baden-Württemberg*, n 18, paras 90–92.

In emphasising the SRB's substantive authorship of the decision, the CJEU made clear that its decisional dominance entails responsibility for procedural protection. Such responsibility meant that the SRB could not simply leave the duty to give reasons to be fulfilled by the NRAs at a later stage. Even though the NRAs' role was limited to notifying SRB decisions to interested parties, the same reasoning can be extended to a large number of composite procedures where national authorities formally take the final decision but without any ability to diverge from a prior Union act.[61]

Nevertheless, the CJEU's stance seems to raise a question when compared with the case law on the right to be heard. Why is the Union administration allowed to delegate to national authorities the observance of the right to be heard, but not of the right to a reasoned decision?

The answer can be inferred from the broader sense of the case law on unitary procedural protection and from the difference between where those two rights fit into the chronology of any administrative procedure. Unitary procedural protection, as stated many times before, requires that the procedural rights of individuals be effectively observed throughout a composite administrative procedure's national and Union stages. If the Union administration delegates the carrying out of hearings to national authorities, it will still be able to consider the viewpoints of the affected party, check if the hearing was properly given, and assess the need for additional hearings to be provided, all before the conclusion of the administrative procedure. This makes it possible for the Union administration to retain its responsibility for the right to be heard to be respected.

By contrast, the duty to give reasons must be fulfilled by the time that the Union administration has already taken its final decision. By the time a national authority is involved in a subsequent stage, the Union administration's role in the composite procedure is exhausted. It has already finished exercising its own decisional power and can no longer check that the reasons drafted by a national authority meet all the relevant requirements of the duty to give reasons.

It is immaterial if the national authority adopts a statement of reasons for the Union decision which incidentally meets those requirements.[62] It may, perhaps, *help prepare* a statement of reasons for the Union administration to adopt. But, if dominant in the composite procedure, the final say on the reasons given for a decision must belong to the Union administration alone.

IV. Reasons-giving Beyond Executive Federalism

The duty to give reasons has traditionally been neglected by general EU law scholarship.[63] This is perhaps reflected in the fact that very few have studied the

[61] See Chapter 3, subsection III.B.(ii).

[62] Implicitly, *Hypo Vorarlberg*, n 16, paras 202–3.

[63] J Mashaw, *Reasoned Administration: the European Union, the United States and the Project of Democratic Governance* (2007) 99 *George Washington Law Review* 101. See, however, a thoughtful

particularities of the CJEU's approaches to addressing that duty in composite decision-making.

The case law went through the same process as concerned the right to be heard. The CJEU was initially reluctant to abandon the doctrine of European Executive Federalism, most notably its principle of separation between national and Union administrations. It followed a purely inter-administrative approach which exempted the Union administration from any legal relations with individuals or duty to give reasons for decisions taken concerning them. From the early 1990s, this approach was superseded in the case law by an implicit principle of unitary procedural protection.

According to that principle, the right to a reasoned decision (like other procedural rights) may not be compromised because of the division of tasks between national and Union administrations that characterises composite decision-making. The CJEU achieves this purpose not only because it recognises the fundamental differences between composite decision-making and administrative decision-making under European Executive Federalism, but also because it recognises that, while decision-making power in composite procedures is always shared by both administrations, it is never shared equally. Accordingly, the responsibility to ensure procedural rights should not be equal, either. Ultimate and overall responsibility for the adequacy of statements of reasons is therefore ascribed to the level of administration which exercises decisional dominance.

In most composite procedures, such dominance lies with the Union administration. When such is the case, the CJEU case law allows it to rely on the cooperation of national authorities to fulfil the duty to give reasons. Decisional dominance imposes boundaries on such cooperation, namely in terms of what was called the rule of non-substitution – the Union administration may not simply abandon the burden of reasoning its own decisions to national authorities. However, provided that the Union administration retains the final say on the definitive reasons that will be given for its own decisions, it may avail itself of reasons contained in national authorities' preparatory acts. According to the rule of replicability, the Union administration may incorporate into its own statements of reasons the reasoning found in the preparatory measures brought to it by national authorities. According to the rule of referral, the Union administration may fulfil its duty to give reasons with a blanket reference to national preparatory measures, provided that some conditions are met. Those conditions require close coordination between the two levels: Union authorities must clearly indicate the relevant national preparatory acts; and national authorities must ensure that those acts are themselves clearly reasoned and that affected individuals have had the opportunity to be heard in respect of them.

analysis in A Cassatella, 'Il dovere di motivazione nello jus commune europeo' in G della Cananea and M Conticelli (eds), *I Procedimenti Amministrativi di Adjudication dell'Unione Europea: Principi Generali e Discipline Settoriali* (Giappichelli, 2017).

Like a sort of administrative Midas touch, the mere fact that the Union administration restates or refers to national preparatory measures converts them into 'part and parcel' of its own final decision and statement of reasons.[64] This is the conceptual step that allows the CJEU not to shy away from checking whether the European *and* the national parts of composite statements of reasons suffice for affected parties to understand why a decision was taken.[65] It reviews reasons contained in national preparatory acts just as if they had been drafted by the Union administration itself.

[64] The expression is found in *Sgaravatti*, n 40, para 103. See also Cases *Associação Comercial de Aveiro*, n 40, para 39; *Partex*, n 40, para 77; and *Proderec*, n 40, 105. A similar view, likely held in more legal systems, is followed in Portuguese administrative law: preparatory acts become 'absorbed and appropriated' by a decision which refers to them. See Ruling of the Portuguese Supreme Administrative Court 2 December 2010 (Rapporteur: Pais Borges).

[65] See *Mediocurso I*, n 40, para 100. See also *AECOPS I*, n 40, paras 82 ff and *AECOPS II*, n 40, paras 85 ff.

PART III

Judicial Review

7

Unitary Judicial Protection

I. Introduction: Interdependent Decision-Making in a Dual Judicial System

Judicial control represents perhaps the most well-known aspect of the European Union's conception of the rule of law.[1] Yet, the Union's judicial system, which is based on a strict separation between national and Union courts, and assumes a strict division between national and Union administration, is ill-equipped to ensure judicial control of composite decision-making. The system was not made with composite decision-making in mind.[2]

Part III of this book concerns the mismatch between composite decision-making and the principles of European Executive Federalism that underlie the Union's judicial system. It argues that the CJEU, in addressing that mismatch, has crafted novel principles to ensure judicial control which are unique to composite decision-making and derogate from well-established principles of European Executive Federalism that apply in any other instances of administrative decision-making.

Much as Chapter four did in respect of procedural rights, the present chapter develops a general theoretical and conceptual framework to fulfil a threefold aim. First, it aims to introduce greater analytical clarity to our understanding of the mismatch between composite decision-making and the Union's rule of law requirements of judicial control. The CJEU has been subject to criticism – as Part III will show, often unfounded – for supposed inconsistency and inability to ensure judicial protection. But the starting point, the precise nature of the dilemmas that the CJEU had to address, and its relative success in doing so, have often been overlooked. Second, the chapter maps the distinct doctrinal alternatives that the CJEU had at its disposal to address said mismatch. Third, it sets out the components of the approach that the CJEU adopted – the principle of unitary judicial protection, combined with a test of decisional dominance.

Section II offers a simple conceptualisation of the two key purposes of judicial control under EU constitutional law. One is subjective – safeguarding the

[1] Similarly, L Pech, 'A Union Founded on the Rule of Law: Meaning and Reality of the Rule of Law as a Constitutional Principle of EU Law' (2010) 6 *European Constitutional Law Review* 359, 372.

[2] F Brito Bastos, 'An Administrative Crack in the EU's Rule of Law: Composite Decision-making and Nonjusticiable National Law' (2020) 16 *European Constitutional Law Review* 63.

fundamental right of individuals to effective judicial protection. The other is objective – enforcing the legal constraints to public power.

Section III highlights two issues posed in any judicial review of administrative decisions. One is of a jurisdictional nature – how to determine whether a decision can form the subject of judicial review, which in Union law also determines which courts, the national courts or the CJEU, are competent for review. The other issue is of a substantive nature – it concerns the grounds for the invalidity of decisions under review. The section will offer a theoretical account of how, if applied to either issue, the principles of European Executive Federalism can compromise the ability of national and Union courts alike to fulfil both the subjective and the objective purposes of judicial control in composite decision-making. The basic components of the CJEU's approach to reconciling composite procedures and the need for judicial control will be set out. Those components are akin to the case law on unitary procedural protection analysed in Part II. The first is a principle of unitary judicial protection, according to which a single exercise of judicial review should suffice to review a decision taken pursuant to a composite administrative procedure. The second component is the test of decisional dominance, which is decisive to establish whether judicial review falls to national or Union courts and, in the latter case, whether Union courts may review national preparatory stages in composite procedures.

Section IV illustrates how the combination of unitary judicial protection, and the test of decisional dominance, applies in practice. After a general account of the case law, the complexity of unitary judicial protection will be shown to depend upon the structure of each composite administrative procedure. Because of that complexity, as Eliantonio rightly notes, 'it is inevitable that some challenges need to be directed against measures which are initial or intermediate in the decision making process'.[3] Judicial control of bottom-up composite procedures, where Union administration decides based on national preparatory acts, proves more convoluted than judicial control of top-down composite procedures, where it is the other way around. For that reason, the *Borelli* and the *Berlusconi* lines of case law, which represent two distinct doctrines for the review of bottom-up composite procedures, will be examined separately in Chapters eight and nine.

II. Judicial Control and the European Union's Rule of Law

Judicial control of public administration constitutes an indispensable component of the rule of law.[4] Indeed, the rule of law requires not only that public power

[3] M Eliantonio, 'Judicial Review in an Integrated Administration: the Case of 'Composite Procedures' (2014) 7 *Review of European Administrative Law* 65, 78.

[4] Y Marique, 'Rule of Law and Administrative Justice' in M Hertogh, R Kirkham, R Thomas, and J Tomlinson (eds), *The Oxford Handbook of Administrative Justice* (Oxford University Press, 2022).

be subject to legal constraints, but that such constraints, to be meaningful, be effectively enforceable by independent courts.[5]

Administrative law comparatists have traditionally distinguished between two models of judicial control. Whereas 'subjectivist' models, such as the German, aim primarily at the protection of individual rights, 'objectivist' models, such as the French, primarily aim at the judicial preservation of the principle of legality – ie at the enforcement of legal norms, whether or not they confer individual rights.[6] However, judicial protection of individual rights and judicial review of legality reinforce each other. Rather than distinguishing *models*, it appears more analytically apt to distinguish between two *purposes*, subjective and objective, of judicial control.[7]

Both purposes are 'inherent' requirements of the Union's rule of law.[8] This is evident from two early rulings, *Granaria* and *Les Verts*. The former stated that the 'principle of the rule of law within the community context' entails an individual right to judicial protection against illegal measures;[9] the latter became a landmark ruling, holding that, as a 'Community based on the rule of law', the Union must ensure (objective) judicial enforcement of Union law against the Institutions and the Member States alike.[10] However, the mismatch between composite decision-making and the Union's dual judicial system can undermine the subjective and objective purposes of judicial control alike. In order to pinpoint exactly why such a mismatch exists, and how it compromises judicial control, the two following subsections will first summarise what each of the two purposes entails under Union constitutional law.

A. The Subjective Purpose of EU Administrative Justice

Union law constitutionalises the subjective purpose of judicial control chiefly as a requirement of the fundamental right to effective judicial protection (or 'to an effective remedy').[11] The Court of Justice considers effective judicial protection

[5] J Raz, *The Authority of Law: Essays on Law and Morality* (Clarendon Press, 1979), 214–18; and B Tamanaha, 'A Concise Guide to the Rule of Law' in G Palombella and N Walker (eds), *Relocating the Rule of Law* (Hart Publishing, 2009), 3–6. See also K Lenaerts, 'New Horizons for the Rule of Law Within the EU' (2021) 21 *German Law Journal* 29.

[6] See E Schmidt-Aßmann and S Dagron, 'Deutsches und französisches Verwaltungsrecht im Vergleich ihrer Ordnungsideen. Zur Geschlossenheit, Offenheit und gegenseitigen Lernfähigkeit von Rechtssystemen' (2007) 67 *Zeitschrift für ausländisches öffentliches Recht und Völkerrecht* 395, 398.

[7] For a distinction between objective and subjective purposes of judicial control, see S Beljin, 'Rights in EU Law' in S Prechal and B van Roermund (eds), *The Coherence of EU Law: The Search for Unity in Divergent Concepts* (Oxford University Press, 2008).

[8] See Case C-14/19 P *European Union Satellite Centre v KF*, ECLI:EU:C:2020:492, para 58.

[9] Case 101/78 *Granaria BV v Hoofdproduktschap voor Akkerbouwprodukten*, ECLI:EU:C:1979:38, para 5.

[10] Case 294/83 *Parti écologiste 'Les Verts' v European Parliament*, ECLI:EU:C:1986:166, para 23.

[11] On the fundamental right to effective judicial protection, see for example A Arnull, 'The Principle of Effective Judicial Protection in EU law: An Unruly Horse?' (2011) 36 *European Law Review* 51 and

to be 'of the essence of the rule of law'.[12] Since the Treaty of Lisbon, effective judicial protection enjoys a firm constitutional basis in Articles 19 TEU and 47 of the Charter.[13] Nevertheless, the Court of Justice had long before held it to constitute a general principle of law derived from the common constitutional traditions of the Member States as well as from the European Convention on Human Rights (ECHR), eg in the *Johnston* and *Heylens* rulings.[14]

According to Article 52(3) and (4) of the Charter, this dual origin requires Article 47 of the Charter to be interpreted in harmony with national constitutional traditions and in a manner that offers no less protection of the right than the ECHR does.[15] Nevertheless, the fundamental right to effective judicial protection must be interpreted autonomously, within the specific context of EU constitutional law.[16] In comparison with the wording of Article 47 of the Charter, there are significant differences to how the right is enshrined in the ECHR For instance, whereas Articles 6(1) and 13(1) ECHR ensure the judicial protection only of the remaining rights contained in the ECHR, Article 47 of the Charter covers *any* right, regardless of the legal source where it is enshrined.

The core content of the fundamental right to effective judicial protection cannot be boiled down to one, single aspect, and rather consists of a cluster of multiple interrelated components.[17] Some components are nevertheless especially prominent. Access to the courts is certainly at the 'very core or essence' of effective judicial protection,[18] as is the right to obtain the retroactive annulment of harmful illegal measures.[19] Courts must be independent, in the sense of being insulated

M Bonelli, 'Effective Judicial Protection in EU Law: an Evolving Principle of a Constitutional Nature' (2019) 12 *Review of European Administrative Law* 35.

[12] Cases C-72/15 *R (on the application of PJSC Rosneft Oil Co) v HM Treasury*, ECLI:EU:C:2017:236, para 73 and C-216/18 PPU *LM* ECLI:EU:C:2018:586, para 51.

[13] The right's dual legal basis implies that its observance must be ensured even if Member States are not implementing Union law in the sense of Article 51(1) of the Charter and therefore acting outside its scope of application. See Cases C-64/16 *Associação Sindical dos Juízes Portugueses v Tribunal de Contas*, ECLI:EU:C:2018:117 and C-619/18 *Commission v Poland*, ECLI:EU:C:2019:531 and M Bonelli and M Claes, 'Judicial serendipity: how Portuguese judges came to the rescue of the Polish judiciary' (2018) 14 *European Constitutional Law Review*, 622.

[14] See Cases 222/86 *Union nationale des entraîneurs et cadres techniques professionnels du football (Unectef) v Heylens*, ECLI:EU:C:1987:442 and 222/84 *Johnston v Chief Constable of the Royal Ulster Constabulary*, ECLI:EU:C:1986:206. For more recent case law, see Cases C-467/01 *Ministero delle Finanze v Eribrand SpA*, ECLI:EU:C:2003:364, para 61; C-432/05 *Unibet (London) Ltd v Justitiekanslern*, ECLI:EU:C:2007:163, para 37; and C-279/09 *DEB Deutsche Energiehandels- und Beratungsgesellschaft mbH v Bundesrepublik Deutschland*, ECLI:EU:C:2010:811, para 29.

[15] See Article 52(3) of the Charter.

[16] M Safjan and D Düsterhaus, 'A Union of Effective Judicial Protection: Addressing a Multi-level Challenge through the Lens of Article 47 CFREU' (2014) 33 *Yearbook of European Law* 3, 31. See also the Opinion of Advocate General Cruz Villalón in Case C-69/10 *Samba Diouf v Ministre du Travail de l'Emploi et de l'Immigration*, ECLI:EU:C:2011:102, para 39.

[17] K Gutman, 'The Essence of the Fundamental Right to an Effective Remedy and to a Fair Trial in the Case-Law of the Court of Justice of the European Union: The Best is Yet to Come?' (2019) 20 *German Law Journal* 884, 888.

[18] See the Opinion of AG Bobek in Case C-403/16 *El Hassani v Minister Spraw Zagranicznych*, ECLI:EU:C:2017:659, para 110.

[19] Joined Cases C-584/10 P, C-593/10 P and C-595/10 P *European Commission v Kadi*, ECLI:EU:C:2013:518, para 134.

from external pressure,[20] and have the competence 'to consider all the issues of fact and of law that are relevant for resolving the case'.[21] The overall evolution of Union case law and academic commentary shows the components of effective judicial protection to reflect its 'double soul' as a fundamental right and, increasingly, as a tool of the Union's rule of law in shaping the institutional requirements of national judiciaries.[22]

As a fundamental right, effective judicial protection pulls judicial review towards its subjective purpose. It requires the rights of individuals to be protected with effective remedies *in each case*,[23] if necessary, by reinterpreting the rules of judicial process in their favour.[24] Given the difficulties of accommodating composite decision-making in the EU's system of judicial review, the EU's courts have often needed to resort to such reinterpretation.

B. The Objective Purpose of EU Administrative Justice

Effective judicial protection is, however, not the sole purpose, or indeed the dominant purpose, of judicial control in the EU. CJEU rulings tend to associate the rule of law with the imperative of judicial enforcement of the law against public authorities.[25] Judicial remedies available before Union courts display 'a rather strong orientation towards objective legality review'[26] – a characteristic resonating with their known origins in French administrative law.[27]

Indeed, it is striking how differently Article 19(1) TEU defines the tasks of the CJEU and of national courts. The CJEU's responsibility is to 'ensure that in the interpretation and application of the Treaties the law is observed'. National courts are required to 'provide remedies sufficient to ensure effective legal protection'.

[20] See Cases C-506/04 *Wilson v Ordre des avocats du barreau de Luxembourg*, ECLI:EU:C:2006:587, para 48 and C-685/15, *Online Games Handels GmbH v Landespolizeidirektion Oberösterreich*, ECLI:EU:C:2017:452, paras 60–61.

[21] Joined Cases C-245/19 and C-246/19 *B v État Luxembourgois*, ECLI:EU:C:2020:795, para 66.

[22] For an insightful and comprehensive literature review, see G Gentile, 'Effective Judicial Protection: Enforcement, Judicial Federalism and the Politics of EU Law' (2022) 2 *European Law Open* 1.

[23] See Cases 222/84 *Johnston*, n 14, para 19 and C-243/15 *Lesoochranárske zoskupenie VLK (LZ) v Obvodný úrad Trenčín*, ECLI:EU:C:2016:838, para 65.

[24] See Cases *Unibet*, n 14 and C-521/06 P *Athinaïki Techniki AE v European Commission*, ECLI:EU:C:2008:422, paras 44–45.

[25] Joined Cases T-222/99, T-327/99 and T-329/99 *Martínez v European Parliament*, ECLI:EU:T:2001:242 para 48 and Cases T-70/05 *Evropaïki Dynamiki – Proigmena Systimata Tilepikoinonion Pliroforikis kai Tilematikis AE v European Maritime Safety Agency (EMSA)*, ECLI:EU:T:2010:55, para 64 and C-335/09 P *Republic of Poland v Commission*, ECLI:EU:C:2012:385, para 48. See also K Lenaerts, 'The Basic Constitutional Charter of a Community Based on the Rule of Law' in M Poiares Maduro and L Azoulai (eds), *The Past and Future of EU Law: The Classics of EU Law Revisited on the 50th Anniversary of the Rome Treaty* (Hart Publishing, 2010), 303 ff.

[26] R Barents, 'EU Procedural Law and Effective Judicial Protection' (2014) 51 *Common Market Law Review* 1437.

[27] JL'Huillier, 'Une conquête du droit administratif français: Le contentieux de la Communauté européenne du charbon et de l'acier' (1953) 13 *Recueil Dalloz: Chronique* 63.

This distinction codifies longstanding case law holding that the Treaties establish a 'complete system of legal remedies and procedures designed to ensure *review of the legality* of acts of the institutions' and requiring the Member States 'to establish a system of legal remedies and procedures which ensure *respect for the right* to effective judicial protection' (emphasis added).[28]

In a nutshell, the principle of legality requires, in European administrative law, that the power of administrative authorities must be grounded in, and limited by, legal provisions.[29] Polities committed to the rule of law institute judicial review to enforce such legal constraints.

EU law adopts a holistic understanding of the principle of legality. Indeed, when interpreting and applying the Treaties the CJEU is required to observe 'the law', without distinction between implementing, delegated or basic legislation, general principles of law, or the Treaties.[30] Nevertheless, despite having a mandate to ensure that 'the law', broadly speaking, is observed, EU Courts do not have a mandate to ensure the observance of *national* law. This limitation to the CJEU's jurisdiction generally does not pose a rule of law problem in the review of acts adopted by EU authorities. However, as will be shown below, it does prove problematic in composite decision-making.

III. Judicial Control of Composite Decision-Making: Locating the Mismatch

As is almost unanimously agreed in the literature, composite administrative procedures fit poorly into the EU's judicial system.[31] Despite such broad agreement, the concrete reasons for that mismatch are not always articulated in an explicit or analytical fashion. The present section aims to fill that gap. The precise origins of the mismatch, and the exact nature of the legal issues it raises, must be thoroughly

[28] Case C-263/02 P *European Commission v Jégo-Quéré & Cie SA*, ECLI:EU:C:2004:210, paras 30–31.

[29] See Joined Cases 7/56, 3/57 to 7/57 *Algera v Common Assembly of the European Coal and Steel Community*, ECLI:EU:C:1957:7; C-90/95 P *De Compte v European Parliament*, ECLI:EU:C:1997:198; and Joined Cases 46/87 and 227/88, *Hoechst AG v European Commission*, ECLI:EU:C:1989:337. In the literature, see L Azoulai, 'Le Principe de Légalité' in JB Auby and J Dutheil de la Rochère (eds), *Droit Administratif Européen* (Bruylant, 2007).

[30] See G della Cananea, C Franchini and M Macchia, *I Principi dell'Amministrazione Europea*, 3rd edn (Giappichelli, 2017), 87 ff.

[31] See eg C Franchini, 'I principi applicabili ai procedimenti amministrativi europei' (2003) *Rivista Italiana di Diritto Pubblico Comunitario* 1037, 1055; E Nieto Garrido and I Martín Delgado, *European Administrative Law in the Constitutional Treaty* (Hart Publishing, 2007), 103; H Hofmann and A Türk, 'Legal Challenges in EU Administrative Law by the Move to an Integrated Administration' in H Hofmann and A Türk (eds), *Legal Challenges in EU Administrative Law: Towards an Integrated Administration* (Edward Elgar, 2009), 373; A Keessen, *European Administrative Decisions: how the EU regulates products on the internal market* (Europa Law Publishings, 2009), 228; HP Nehl, 'Legal Protection in the Field of EU Funds' (2011) 10 *European State Aid Law Quarterly* 629, 648; J Hofmann, 'Legal Protection and Liability in the European Composite Administration' in O Jansen and B Schöndorf-Haubold (eds), *The European Composite Administration* (Intersentia, 2011), 461; and M Eliantonio, n 3, 66 ff.

explained if one is to make sense of the sometimes counterintuitive ways in which they were addressed by the Court of Justice and the General Court.

It is submitted that the origins of that mismatch lie in the Court's principles of EU Executive Federalism which, as will be recalled,[32] the CJEU considered to be the Union's constitutional doctrine on the relations between national and Union administration. The principles in question are the principle of separation of *administrative power* between national and EU authorities, and the CJEU's old and rigidly dualistic understanding of the division of *judicial power* between national and EU courts. Both presuppose administrative power to be neatly divided between the authorities of the EU and those of the Member States, whereas composite decision-making is based on the interdependence between the two levels. This mismatch proves problematic from a rule of law perspective, for two reasons (though occasionally conflated in the literature as only one reason) which concern two key issues relevant to any judicial review. The first issue is of a jurisdictional nature – how to establish which courts, national or European, are competent to review a given decision. The second issue is substantive – on what grounds may one consider that such a decision is invalid at all.

A. Jurisdictional Issues: Reviewable Acts and Competent Courts

The first dimension of the mismatch between composite decision-making and the EU's judicial system is of a jurisdictional nature. It concerns a tension between the EU's system of judicial review, which is meant for instances where national and Union authorities decide independently, and composite decision-making, which is based on decisional interdependence between the two.

The early *Humblet* judgment represented a seminal step towards the development of the doctrine of European Executive Federalism. It was in that ruling that the Court for the first time referred to a principle of strict separation between national and Union *authorities*.

Beyond proclaiming a principle of 'strict separation' between the powers of national and Union authorities, the Court also proclaimed a principle of 'strict separation' between national and EU *judiciaries*.[33] From then onwards, the Court came to read into the division between the competences of national and European courts an ever more radically dualistic divide.[34] Indeed, the idea of a clear-cut

[32] See Chapter 2, section V.D.

[33] See Case 6/60 *Humblet v Belgian State*, ECLI:EU:C:1960:48, at 572.

[34] EU primary law provides for but one exception to that divide. Article 14(2) of the Statute of the European System of Central Banks and of the European Central Bank enshrines a 'special action for annulment' under which the CJEU may annul national decisions relieving governors of national central banks from office. See Joined Cases C-202/18 and C-238/18 *Rimšēvičs and European Central Bank v Republic of Latvia*, ECLI:EU:C:2019:139.

division of tasks between national and EU courts became so rooted in the Court's case law that it tends to be emphasised whenever the CJEU cites the constitutional necessity of judicial review and the rule of law.[35]

National courts have the *exclusive* competence to review decisions taken by national authorities;[36] and EU courts have the *exclusive* competence to review decisions taken by EU authorities.[37] This notion often appears labelled as the 'clear separation of functions' in preliminary rulings,[38] or 'strict separation of judiciaries' in liability cases.[39] This rigid division of judicial power has been aptly described by some scholars as the principle of 'double exclusivity'.[40]

Double exclusivity goes hand in hand with the separation principle. Just like the separation principle, the principle of double exclusivity is central to the doctrine of European Executive Federalism. For instance, the CJEU cites the *Deutsche Milchkontor* case law, the leading judgment on said doctrine, to emphasise that, just as administrative enforcement usually falls to national authorities, so must judicial review usually fall to national courts.[41] And, just like the separation principle, the principle of double exclusivity relies on an obvious implicit assumption. By requiring the powers of national and Union administration to be preserved as separate, and that their exercise is separately reviewed, both principles rest upon the assumption that national and Union authorities *do* exercise their respective powers independently from one another.[42]

However, that assumption does not hold in composite administrative procedures, which involve interdependent decision-making, rather than independent decision-making, by national and Union authorities. From this mismatch, the risk emerges of a serious gap in judicial control. Because neither the CJEU nor national courts are competent to review a composite administrative procedure in its entirety, the protection of individual rights and enforcement of objective

[35] *Les Verts*, n 10, para 23.

[36] See Cases 46/81 *Benvenuto*, ECLI:EU:C:1981:64 and 142/83 *Nevas v Social Welfare Fund for Lawyers, Athens*, ECLI:EU:C:1983:267; and C-467/12 *Gassiat v Ordre des avocats de Paris*, ECLI:EU:C:2013:104, para 8.

[37] Case 314/85 *Foto-Frost v Hauptzollamt Lübeck-Ost*, ECLI:EU:C:1987:452.

[38] See for instance Cases C-119/05 *Lucchini*, ECLI:EU:C:2007:434, para 43; C-220/05 *Auroux v Commune de Roanne*, ECLI:EU:C:2007:31, para 25; C-341/05 *Laval un Partneri Ltd v Svenska Byggnadsarbetareförbundet*, ECLI:EU:C:2007:809, para 45; C-373/08 *Hoesch Metals and Alloy*, ECLI:EU:C:2010:68, para 59; C-618/10 *Banco Español de Crédito*, ECLI:EU:C:2012:349, para 76; and C-62/14 *Gauweiler*, ECLI:EU:C:2015:400, para 15.

[39] See Case C-275/00 *First NV*, ECLI:EU:C:2002:711, para 33. Prior rulings had already suggested the same finding. See *Granaria* n 9.

[40] B Marchetti, 'Il Sistema Integrato di Tutela' in L de Lucia and B Marchetti (eds), *L'amministrazione europea e le sue regole* (Il Mulino, 2015), 198.

[41] Cases T-93/95 *Laga v European Commission*, ECLI:EU:T:1998:22, paras 33 ff and T-94/95 *Landuyt v European Commission*, ECLI:EU:T:1998:23, paras 33 ff.

[42] The Court's longstanding case law on the shared liability of national and Union authorities, which requires the successive lodging of actions for damages before national courts and the CJEU, has at times been justified as being 'in conformity with the division of powers between the Member States and the Community' (Opinion of AG Lenz in Case 62/83 *Eximo Molkereierzeugnisse Handelsgesellschaft mbH v European Commission*, ECLI:EU:C:1984:148).

legality – at the level of national administration, Union administration, or both – may fall between the cracks. In other words, the EU's dualistic judicial system could risk judicial impunity of public power and denial of justice, therefore putting into question the very rule of law in composite decision-making.[43]

In abstract, the CJEU could have chosen one of two approaches which guaranteed double exclusivity in one way or another. Quite remarkably, it never did. Indeed, and for all talk of strict separation between the jurisdiction of national and EU courts that it employs elsewhere, the CJEU *never* came to adopt in composite decision-making the same rigid understanding of double exclusivity that it still follows in contexts of either purely national or purely European administrative decision-making. Instead, it chose an approach which, despite the criticism from legal scholarship, succeeded in recognising the novel character of composite decision-making. It crafted a regime of judicial review that secures its conformity with the EU's rule of law based on two key notions – that composite procedures are unitary procedures, and that the decisional dominance of the administrations involved matters.

(i) Two Alternative Approaches: Authority and Act-based Tests

One approach would have been to direct judicial control separately against every administration engaged in a composite procedure. For instance, within the Single Supervisory Mechanism, credit institutions would need to successively sue national competent authorities, which propose the revocation of a banking licence to the ECB, and the ECB itself, which takes the final decision on revocation. National courts and the CJEU would both need to be seized in order for the administrative procedure to be reviewed in full. This approach would possibly be the one most bluntly consistent with the principle of double exclusivity. Indeed, by requiring the acts of national and Union administration to always be reviewed separately, this first approach preserves a strict separation between the competences of national and Union courts.

Nevertheless, this approach proves deeply unsatisfactory from the perspective of other requirements of the rule of law – most notably, those that concern the subjective purpose of judicial control. Many national administrative laws may oppose judicial challenges against purely preparatory, non-binding acts that may be reversed at a later stage of an administrative procedure – such as a national authority's proposal to revoke a banking licence. Moreover, the need to lodge actions for annulment in duplicate, against the national and Union authorities involved in what is the same administrative procedure, is difficult to reconcile with the requirements posed by the fundamental right to an effective judicial protection. At worst, a ruling on the first annulment proceedings could

[43] HC Röhl, 'Procedures in the European Composite Administration' in J Barnes (ed), *Transforming Administrative Procedure* (Global Law Press, 2008), 94–95.

be delivered after passage of the deadline for the second annulment proceedings to be brought.[44]

A second approach would have been to focus judicial review only on the end result of a composite procedure. This approach would arguably be in line with many national administrative laws, where administrative procedures are typically reviewed only once a final decision is taken.[45] It would also be fully in line with a conservative reading of double exclusivity. For judicial review purposes, the final decision is fictionalised as though it had been taken exclusively by national or Union administration. The reviewing court disregards the preparatory acts that lie beyond its competence.

Unlike the first approach, the second does not raise a problem of duplication of judicial review. Returning to the example of revocation of banking licences, only the ECB's final decision – and not the national authorities' non-binding proposals – would be subject to judicial review by the CJEU. However, an exclusive focus on the review of the final decision would only ever work well in composite procedures where decisional dominance and the power to take the final decision incidentally coincide. Yet, as was explained before, this is not always the case.[46] In some composite procedures, one administration exercises decisional dominance by adopting binding preparatory acts; the other administration, which takes the final decision, has no choice but to abide by them. If only the latter decision is judicially reviewed, the power of the dominant authority will simply remain unreviewed. One can hardly say that, in such cases, the objective function of judicial control, scrutinising illegal exercise of power, is effectively ensured.

Notwithstanding the shortcomings of both approaches, some authors, such as Keessen, suggest that the CJEU adopts the first; whereas others, like Nehl, suggest that it adopts the second. One key point of contention is the significance of the *Borelli* case law. *Borelli* requires judicial review to be directed against (some) national preparatory acts. For Keessen, *Borelli* demonstrates a preference for the first approach, that of separate judicial review of preparatory acts and final decisions.[47] For Nehl, *Borelli* constitutes but an artificial exception to the second approach, that of focusing judicial review only on final decisions.[48]

The view taken here differs from both Keessen's and Nehl's. *Borelli* constitutes neither the rule, nor the exception. Instead, it is argued that *Borelli* merely reflects how the CJEU's real approach to judicial review is applied in *one group* of

[44] Similar complications of coordinating lengthy parallel judicial proceedings in national and EU courts are known in cases involving shared liability of national authorities and the EU. See M Fink, 'EU liability for contributions to Member States' breaches of EU law' (2019) 56 *Common Market Law Review* 1227, 1261–62.

[45] M Eliantonio, n 3, 77.

[46] See Chapter 3, section III.B.

[47] A Keessen, n 31, 137.

[48] HP Nehl, *Europäisches Verwaltungsverfahren und Gemeinschaftsverfassung. Eine Studie gemeinschaftsrechtlicher Verfahrensgrundsätze unter besonderer Berücksichtigung „mehrstufiger" Verwaltungsverfahren* (Duncker & Humblot, 2002), 419 ff.

composite procedures. The approach is the same as for the observance of another rule of law requirement, the right to good administration, under what Part II of this book termed the principle of unitary procedural protection. The CJEU associates judicial review – *a single* exercise of judicial review – with decisional dominance, whatever the stage of the procedure or the level of administration by which it is exercised. *Borelli* concerns judicial review, by national courts, of national decisional dominance; whereas the other segment of the case law, represented by *Berlusconi*, concerns judicial review, by Union courts, of Union decisional dominance.

(ii) The CJEU's Approach: A Test of Decisional Dominance

The test of decisional dominance fits poorly with the rigid divide between national and EU administration, and national and EU judicial competences, that traditionally characterised EU Executive Federalism. This is because, by accepting that a composite administrative procedure is reviewed only at the level with the dominant decision-making power, that test allows one of the two levels of administration to be sued in the place of both – and therefore treats national and EU authorities in a unitary fashion. This is, nonetheless, the test that the CJEU has implicitly endorsed to this day.

A test of decisional dominance would fit best with the CJEU's general case law on the review of decision-making by the Union administration. The CJEU implicitly distinguishes between autonomous review – the possibility for a measure to be scrutinised in self-standing judicial proceedings – and indirect review – ie a review of a measure as a mere step in the review of another measure.[49] In order to establish whether an 'administrative act' of a Union authority can form the subject of an autonomous judicial review, the case law focuses on its 'substance'.[50] What is intended by 'substance' is that a decision must represent the 'material manifestation of the will of an authority',[51] expressed in the 'exercise, upon the conclusion of an internal procedure laid down by law, of a power provided for by law which is intended to produce legal effects'.[52] It must be a measure which 'definitively lays down the position of the institution on the conclusion of that procedure, and not a provisional measure intended to pave the way for the final decision'.[53]

Union preparatory acts that merely 'pave the way' for that decision – that are 'drawn up in a procedure involving several stages' – can *generally* not form the

[49] For a comparative overview of indirect judicial review of administrative action, see M Eliantonio and D Dragos (eds), *Indirect Judicial Review in Administrative Law Legality vs Legal Certainty in Europe* (Routledge, 2023).

[50] Cases T-95/10 *Cindu Chemicals BV v European Chemicals Agency (ECHA)*, ECLI:EU:T:2013:108, para 35 and T-309/10 *Klein v European Commission*, ECLI:EU:T:2014:19, para 79.

[51] Case T-673/13 *European Coalition to End Animal Experiments v European Chemicals Agency (ECHA)*, ECLI:EU:T:2015:167, para 23.

[52] Case 182/80 *HP Gauff Ingenieure GmbH & Co KG v European Commission*, ECLI:EU:C:1982:78, para 18.

[53] See eg Cases T-676/14 *Spain v Commission*, ECLI:EU:T:2015:602, para 13; and T-584/15 *Pagkyprios organismos ageladotrofon (POA) Dimosia Ltd v European Commission*, ECLI:EU:T:2016:510, para 33.

subject of an autonomous review.[54] Instead, such acts are checked indirectly, upon the challenge of the final decision.[55] As the CJEU puts it, 'any unlawful features vitiating … a preparatory act must be relied on in an action directed against the definitive act'.[56]

However, a closer look at the ruling and its later development shows that the *IBM* case law does not proscribe the autonomous review of *all* Union preparatory acts. In the ruling in *EPSU and Goudriaan*, the General Court clarified that, even though according to settled case law, 'it is in principle only those measures which definitively determine the position of the Commission upon the conclusion of an administrative procedure and which are intended to have legal effects, which are open to challenge', 'acts or decisions adopted in the course of preparatory proceedings' may be challenged if they constitute 'the culmination of a special procedure' and 'themselves produce binding legal effects'.[57]

Passages of the CJEU's case law such as these show that it recognises some preparatory acts to be more preparatory than others. It distinguishes between two kinds of preparatory acts.[58]

Some are purely internal and provisional, in the sense of only producing legal effects within the administrative procedure and reversible until the final decision has been made. Other preparatory acts, however, may be 'contested separately in so far as, by producing legal effects, they have a decisive influence on an issue in the main procedure'.[59] This will be the case when the acts in question bring about 'a distinct change in [the litigant's] legal position',[60] either because they constitute the final act in a distinct sub-procedure that is binding in its effects,[61] or because they already predetermine what the content of the final decision will be.[62] As Advocate General Slynn explained in *IBM*,

[54] Joined Cases T-10/92 to T-12/92 and T-15/92 *Cimenteries CBR SA v European Commission*, ECLI:EU:T:1992:123, para 28.

[55] Cases T-498/07 P *Krcova v Court of Justice of the European Union*, ECLI:EU:T:2009:178, paras 55–56; T-532/08 *Norilsk Norilsk Nickel Harjavalta Oy v European Commission*, ECLI:EU:T:2010:353, para 94; and T-23/12 *Mutuelle des architectes français assurances (MAF) v European Insurance and Occupational Pensions Authority (EIOPA)*, ECLI:EU:T:2013:632, para 33.

[56] See Cases 60/81 *International Business Machines Corporation (IBM) v European Commission*, ECLI:EU:C:1981:264, para 12; and T-404/08 *Fluorsid SpA v European Commission*, ECLI:EU:T:2013:321, para 133.

[57] Case T-310/18 *European Federation of Public Service Unions (EPSU) and Goudriaan v European Commission* ECLI:EU:T:2019:757, paras 22–23.

[58] J Schwarze, 'Judicial Review of European Administrative Procedure' (2004) 68 *Law and Contemporary Problems* 85, 89–90.

[59] See Joined Cases T-125/03 and T-253/03 *Akzo Nobel Chemicals Ltd v European Commission*, ECLI:EU:T:2007:58, paras 45–46. In the literature, see R Barents, *Remedies and Procedures before the EU Courts* (Wolters Kluwer, 2016), 165; A Türk, *Judicial Review in EU Law* (Edward Elgar, 2009), 21 and HC Röhl, 'Die Anfechtbare Entscheidung nach Art. 230 Abs. 4 EGV' in E Schmidt-Aßmann and B Schöndorf-Haubold (eds), *Der Europäische Verwaltungsverbund* (CH Beck, 2005), 330.

[60] *IBM*, n 56, para 9.

[61] Case 53/85 *Akzo Nobel Chemicals Ltd v* ECLI:EU:C:1986:256, paras 16 ff and Joined Cases T-213/01 and T-214/01 *Österreichische Postsparkasse AG v European Commission*, ECLI:EU:T:2006:151, paras 64–65.

[62] See Cases T-277/94 *Associazione Italiana Tecnico Economica del Cemento (AITEC) v European Commission*, ECLI:EU:T:1996:66, para 51 and T-37/92 *BEUC* ECLI:EU:T:1994:54, para 27.

> 'one should not examine too minutely whether a step marked the culmination of an administrative procedure … it is not the preliminary or definitive nature of the examination which matters … but only the question whether the concrete legal effects intended by the measures in question are provisional ones'.[63]

As a test for judicial review, decisional dominance follows the logic of the *IBM* case law – albeit in an adapted version. First, decisional dominance serves not only to identify autonomously reviewable acts, but also the courts that are competent to review a composite procedure. Second, whereas *IBM* merely *allows* the judicial review of binding preparatory acts, decisional dominance may *require* judicial review to be conducted *only* against such acts. Lastly, whereas the general *IBM* test applies to administrative procedures 'involving several stages', decisional dominance specifically applies to administrative procedures that are composite – namely, where the 'several stages' in question involve not just Union, but national administration as well.

B. Substantive Issues: Invalid Acts

The previous subsection discussed two issues that are always raised in the context of judicial control: whether a measure constitutes a reviewable act, and which court is competent to review it. A third issue, however, concerns whether that measure is indeed invalid. A measure is reviewable if it *intends* to produce legal effects. A measure is invalid if, because it violates legal norms, the measure is unable to produce its intended legal effects or at least unable to produce legal effects that will be safe from a decision removing them from the legal order.[64]

The distinction is not a technicality. Judicial review is not the sole way to annul illegal decisions. Illegal decisions may also be annulled by the authorities that adopted them,[65] as well as by a growing number of specialised boards of review.[66]

Different kinds of illegality can be distinguished. One can distinguish between substantive and procedural illegality. *Substantive* illegality refers to the violation of legal requirements that pertain to the content of a given decision. For example, a decision will be substantively invalid if it imposes an excessive financial penalty, in violation of the principle of proportionality. By contrast *procedural* illegality concerns the violation of requirements governing the formal process by which

[63] Opinion of AG Slynn in Case 60/81 *International Business Machines Corporation (IBM) v European Commission*, ECLI:EU:C:1981:213, quoting AG Roemer in Joined Cases 8/66 to 11/66 *Cimenteries v Commission* [1967] ECR 75, at 105.

[64] On the concept of invalidity, more generally, and identifying different reasons for invalidity, see R Guastini, 'Invalidity' (1994), 7 *Ratio Juris* 212.

[65] *Algera*, n 29 and Case T-727/16 *Repower AG v European Union Intellectual Property Office (EUIPO)*, ECLI:EU:T:2018:88, para 93.

[66] See eg M Chamon, A Volpato, and M Eliantonio, *Boards of Appeal of EU Agencies: Towards Judicialization of Administrative Review?* (Oxford University Press, 2022).

decisions are taken. Chapters five and six considered two such requirements: the right to be heard and the duty to give reasons. One could also name others which do not constitute rights, such as the duty of one authority to request an advisory opinion from another. However, to avoid excessive formalism, many legal systems do not allow *any* violation of procedural requirements to invalidate decisions, but only particularly serious ones.[67] Under Article 263(2) TFEU, the violation of 'essential procedural requirements' constitutes one of the grounds for review of Union acts. These are cases where failure to observe procedural requirements potentially impacts upon the substance of the final decision;[68] makes judicial review impossible (eg the absence of statements of reasons),[69] or subverts the balance of power between Union Institutions.[70]

A second relevant distinction in administrative law doctrine concerns whether a decision is invalid due to an illegality *of its own*, or due to *derivative illegality*. A decision is invalid due to a defect of its own when it is adopted in contravention of requirements of procedure, such as the right to be heard, or of substance, such as the principle of equal treatment.

By contrast, derivative illegality denotes the specific kind of illegality that results from a decision being based on another, illegal, decision. Metaphorically, one could describe this as a kind of 'contamination' of illegality from one measure to another – often from a preparatory act to a final decision. If a final administrative decision relies on a preparatory act, such as an advisory opinion, which was requested and received from the wrong body, that final decision is illegal because so too is the opinion on which it is based.

Derivative illegality, in instances such as these, is widely accepted in national laws.[71] The CJEU, too, regularly reviews Union acts based on reasoning of derivative illegality. The illegality of preparatory acts of the Union administration is reviewed indirectly, as part of the review of a final decision.[72] It is immaterial if the preparatory acts and final decision in question are adopted by different authorities.[73]

The final decisions adopted in composite procedures can be illegal due to a defect of their own. A final decision may violate procedural or substantive legal

[67] See for instance G della Cananea, *Due Process of Law beyond the State: Requirements of Administrative Procedure* (Oxford University Press, 2016), 167 ff.

[68] See eg Cases C-56/18 P *Miasto Gdynia*, ECLI:EU:C:2020:192 [80] and Case T-476/15 *European Food*, ECLI:EU:T:2016:568, para 67.

[69] See Case T-456/10 *Timab Industries v European Commission*, ECLI:EU:T:2015:296, para 132.

[70] See Case 138/79 *SA Roquette Frères v European Council*, ECLI:EU:C:1980:249, para 33. In general, on the notion of violation of essential procedural requirements, see K Lenaerts, I Maselis and K Gutman, *EU Procedural Law* (Oxford University Press, 2014), 371 ff.

[71] The concept of derivative illegality exists in the administrative law of Italy (R Millata and M Ramajoli, *Il Provvedimento Amministrativo*, 2nd edn (Giappichelli, 2017), 455 ff), Portugal (M Aroso de Almeida, *A Anulação de Actos Administrativos no Contexto das Relações Jurídico-Administrativas* (Almedina, 2021), 265 ff), Spain (Article 49(1) of the Spanish Law of Common Administrative Procedure of Public Administration) and Poland (Article 145, para 1 8) of the Polish Code of Administrative Procedure).

[72] See section III.A. above.

[73] See eg Cases T-570/17 *Algebris (UK) Ltd v European Commission*, ECLI:EU:T:2022:314 and C-445/00 *Austria v Council*, ECLI:EU:C:2003:445, para 33.

requirements even though the preparatory stages that preceded its adoption were carried out in full compliance with applicable laws.[74]

As for derivative illegality, it bears noting that while both national and EU administrative laws accept the derivative illegality of decisions taken at their respective levels of administration, composite procedures render the picture more complex. The competent courts for the review *of a decision* may not always be competent to review *all* irregularities in the procedure leading up to its adoption. An action for annulment brought against the final decision

> may not be able to cover errors which occurred at other levels than the one which took the final decision, while, at the same time, access to court is barred for all the steps which took place before the final measure was issued.[75]

This is not necessarily problematic in top-down phases of composite procedures. It is incontrovertible that a Union preparatory stage may 'contaminate' final decisions taken at national level.[76] Article 267 TFEU facilitates review by allowing national courts to refer to the ECJ for a preliminary ruling on the validity of the Union act at stake.

The opposite situation is far more complex. It concerns the question of whether irregularities occurring during national preparatory stages may provoke the illegality of final decisions taken by the Union administration. The question, once explored as 'imputation' of national irregularities,[77] has more recently originated a growing body of literature developing an explicit analysis through the lens of derivative illegality, be it from a general and constitutional,[78] or from a specialised and sectoral standpoint.[79]

Composite procedures raise two important questions from the point of view of derivative illegality, each with its own distinct problems. First, can Union administration *ever* be judicially accountable for illegalities that were actually committed by national authorities? Second, if so, may *all* such illegalities lead to the invalidity of final decisions of the Union administration? Whereas the traditional principles of European Executive Federalism would make it difficult to answer the first

[74] For instance, the CJEU considered in Case T-411/17 *Landesbank Baden-Württemberg v Single Resolution Board (SRB)*, ECLI:EU:T:2020:435, that a decision taken by the Single Resolution Board at the conclusion of a composite administrative procedure was invalid because it lacked an adequate statement of reasons.

[75] M Eliantonio, n 3, 78.

[76] See eg Cases 314/85 *Foto-Frost*, n 37 and C-6/99 *Association Greenpeace France v Ministère de l'Agriculture et de la Pêche*, ECLI:EU:C:2000:148, para 56.

[77] HP Nehl, n 48.

[78] See F Brito Bastos, 'Derivative illegality in European composite administrative procedures' (2018) 55 *Common Market Law Review* 101.

[79] Just to give the example of pharmaceutical regulation and banking supervision under the Single Supervisory Mechanism, see S Röttger-Wirtz and M Eliantonio, 'From Integration to Exclusion: EU Composite Administration and Gaps in Judicial Accountability in the Authorisation of Pharmaceuticals' (2019) 10 *European Journal of Risk Regulation* 393 and L Wissink, *Effective Legal Protection in Banking Supervision* (Europa Law Publishing, 2020), 110 ff.

question in the affirmative, the second question requires a nuanced answer due to several structural principles of EU constitutional law.

(i) Derivative Illegality in Composite Procedures and European Executive Federalism

To clarify the problems that European Executive Federalism may raise for derivative illegality, it may help to give an example. Under Union law,[80] the establishment of certain fish farms with cross-border environmental impacts requires a permit. The licensing procedure is composite. A national authority receives the application for the permit and, following a positive assessment, forwards a non-binding draft decision to the Commission for a final decision.

Supposing that the national draft decision is illegal, two principles of European Executive Federalism would oppose its indirect review as part of judicial control of the Commission's decision. Those are the principles of separation, on the one hand, and of double exclusivity, on the other.

The meaning of the separation principle was explained in Chapter two. The separation principle constitutes one of the key components of European Executive Federalism. It requires the powers of national and Union administration to be kept separate and that, as a consequence, the latter cannot be held responsible for the violation of the law by the former.

Early as well as recent rulings of the CJEU illustrate the implications for judicial control. In *FERAM*, a case about the High Authority of the European Coal and Steel Community's reliance upon certain national certificates, the Court held that if when those certificates 'are drawn up, a wrongful act is committed by a national official who acts … in the performance of purely national duties, the wrongful act cannot be imputed to the High Authority'.[81] Similarly, as recently as in *Pilatus*, a ruling about banking supervision, the CJEU pointed out that, when a national decision is taken 'within the competence' of a national competent authority, 'the ECB cannot be held liable for the consequences of such a decision'.[82]

The same line of reasoning permeates, albeit implicitly, the CJEU's longstanding case law on actions for damages. The CJEU holds that the Union administration cannot be liable for the unlawful behaviour of a national authority save in the rare instances where it has 'no discretion in the implementation of EU legislation', to the point that unlawful behaviour 'cannot be regarded, in reality, as attributable to the national authority at issue'.[83] It is worth pointing out that *Deutsche*

[80] Council Regulation No 708/2007 of 11 June 2007, concerning use of alien and locally absent species in aquaculture.

[81] Case 23/59 *Acciaieria Ferriera di Roma (FERAM) v High Authority of the European Coal and Steel Community*, ECLI:EU:C:1959:33.

[82] Case T-27/19 *Pilatus Bank plc v European Central Bank*, ECLI:EU:T:2022:46, para 244.

[83] See eg Cases T-786/14 *Bourdouvali v European Council*, ECLI:EU:T:2018:487, para 80; 175/84 *Krohn & Co. Import-Export (GmbH & Co. KG) v European Commission*, ECLI:EU:C:1986:85, para 19; and T-174/00 *Biret*, ECLI:EU:T:2002:2, para 33. For an insightful analysis of the CJEU's case law on the matter, see M Fink, n 44.

Milchkontor, the foundational ruling of European Executive Federalism, has often been cited to show this view's constitutional basis. Indeed, if national and Union administration exercise their powers separately, then making either liable exclusively for *their own* illegal conduct is consistent with the 'general principles on which the institutional system of the Community is based and which govern the relations between the Community and the Member States'.[84]

In this light, one may understand why the separation principle may oppose the idea of derivative illegality in composite decision-making. Returning to the example of aquaculture licensing, one could argue that holding the Commission's permit invalid simply because it relies on a national authority's illegal draft decision would amount to making the Commission accountable for illegalities resulting from actions of national authorities that it could not have prevented.

However, in addition to the separation principle, derivative illegality in composite decision-making may violate the principle of double exclusivity, another constituent requirement of European Executive Federalism. More specifically, it would run counter the CJEU's lack of competence to adjudicate on national decisions. Indeed, reviewing the derivative illegality of decisions taken by the Union administration (such as an aquaculture permit) necessarily involves an indirect review of national preparatory acts (such as a national authority's draft decision). If such an indirect judicial review is not admissible by the CJEU – the sole court that can review decisions of the Union administration – then derivative illegality cannot be reviewed by any court at all. Unless one wishes to make the Byzantine argument that a decision is still illegal even if its illegality is, according to its legal system, beyond the review of any court, one must concede that, in practice, the impossibility of such review is the same as to say that it is not illegal.

If confronted with an action for annulment against a purely national decision, the CJEU will typically dismiss that action as inadmissible. It will declare that it 'has no jurisdiction to take cognizance of applications seeking to have purely national laws or measures declared void' and that, instead, 'the review of the legality of acts or measures adopted by the national authorities of a Member State … comes within the jurisdiction of national courts or tribunals'.[85] Despite all *praeter legem* interpretations of the Treaty's system of remedies that have expanded its jurisdiction to review the acts of a growing number of EU bodies,[86] the prohibition

[84] Cases *Bourdouvali*, n 83, para 79; and Joined Cases 89 and 91/86 *L'Étoile commerciale and CNTA v European Commission*, ECLI:EU:C:1987:337, paras 11 and 17.

[85] See eg *Benvenuto*, n 36, para 3.

[86] See *Les Verts*, n 10; and T-411/06 *Sogelma – Societá generale lavori manutenzioni appalti Srl v European Agency for Reconstruction (EAR)*, ECLI:EU:T:2008:419. *Foto-Frost*, n 37, is often considered as an example of a *contra legem* interpretation of the Treaty. See for example V Constantinesco, 'The ECJ as a Law-Maker: *Praeter aut Contra Legem?*' in D O'Keefe and A Bavasso (eds), *Judicial Review in European Union Law: Liber Amicorum in Honour of Lord Slynn of Hadley*, I (Kluwer Law International, 2000), 77. The ruling *requires* national courts to refer to the Court of Justice whenever they are inclined to consider an act of EU law invalid, even though the wording of Article 267 TFEU suggests this to be a matter of their own *choice*.

on quashing measures of state authorities is one of the few sacred cows the CJEU has yet to slaughter. *Outside of composite decision-making*, that is.

Indeed, it is remarkable that the CJEU has never applied the principles of separation and double exclusivity to the review of composite decision-making and, in particular, to the review of derivative illegality. Recent case law has made explicit that the review of composite decision-making derogates from such principles. In *Pilatus*, the General Court distinguished between the review of a decision taken *only* by a national authority, on the one hand, and the review of national preparatory acts adopted within composite administrative procedures.[87] Similarly, an Opinion delivered by Advocate General Bobek notes that the purpose of actions for annulment under Article 263 TFEU 'is to verify the lawfulness of EU action' and that 'the Court has jurisdiction over *national* acts only in exceptional cases, where those acts are merely preparatory to the adoption of a final decision of an EU institution within a composite administrative procedure' (emphasis added).[88]

However, one additional distinction should be made. One question is whether, in the abstract, illegal national preparatory acts may invalidate final decisions taken by the Union administration. A different question is whether *any illegalities* affecting national preparatory acts may do so. As will be elaborated in the following section, there are good reasons why this should not be the case. Those reasons result not from European Executive Federalism, but from general constitutional principles of EU law.

(ii) Derivative Illegality in Composite Procedures: Constitutional Pitfalls

To illustrate the constitutional dilemma at stake, let us return to the example of the aquaculture permit procedure set out in the previous section and assume that an application is made to install a fish farm in Portuguese territorial waters. In such a case, Portuguese law would apply to the aspects of the administrative procedure which are not regulated by the relevant Union legislation. Under Portuguese administrative law, municipalities are entitled to be heard in any administrative procedure whenever certain public interests, including public health and the environment, may be affected within their territory.[89] Accordingly, if a national competent authority fails to hear a municipality where such interests are affected by a fish farm, the draft decision that the authority sends to the Commission is illegal.

If one were to accept the derivative illegality of Union decisions on grounds of national law breached at the national preparatory stages, that would mean in our

[87] *Pilatus*, n 82, paras 243–44.
[88] Opinion of AG Bobek in Joined Cases C-59/18 and C-182/1 *Italy v Council*, ECLI:EU:C:2021:812, para 48.
[89] Article 2(2), Law No 83/95, of 31 August.

concrete example that the Commission decision authorising the fish farm would be invalid. Yet EU constitutional law opposes this for three reasons.

First, one could say that derivative illegality of Union decisions on grounds of national law implies that such decisions can be reviewed by the CJEU against standards of national law. Such a review oversteps the limits of the CJEU's jurisdiction. Even if it were to claim jurisdiction to review national preparatory acts, the CJEU's own settled case law states that it may not apply national law.[90] Generally speaking, national law is a point of fact, not of law, in the CJEU's judicial proceedings.[91] As one Advocate General puts it, 'the adage juria novit curia does not extend to national law, of which the EU judicature is not deemed to be aware'.[92] Since its more cautious ruling in *Stork*, where the Court held that it was 'not normally required to rule on provisions of national law' in reviewing Union decisions,[93] the CJEU has rendered it crystal-clear that, in the review of Union decisions, 'the jurisdiction of the Court is *confined* to considering provisions of *EU law only*',[94] and that '*a national provision cannot be usefully relied upon*' (emphasis added).[95]

The second reason concerns the principle of uniformity. The administrative laws of the Member States may differ significantly. In fact, such differences have occasionally undermined effective cooperation and enforcement between national authorities even if they operate within the same policy area under Union law. The European Data Protection Board, for instance, has requested harmonisation of procedural rules, given the wildly different views that national data protection authorities take as to the timing of exercise of procedural rights within administrative procedures, the legal status of complainants as parties to procedures, or the meaning of concepts such as 'draft decision'.[96]

[90] See for instance Case C-50/00 P *Unión de Pequeños Agricultores v European Council*, ECLI:EU:C:2002:462, para 43.

[91] For a critical and more nuanced analysis, see M Prek and S Lefèvre, 'The EU Courts as "National" Courts: National Law in the EU Judicial Process' (2017) 54 *Common Market Law Review* 369. The authors admit, however, that only one provision of the Treaties suggests that national law may serve as a point of law and not of fact. This is Article 272 TFEU, which extends the CJEU's jurisdiction by virtue of arbitration clauses contained in contracts concluded by or on behalf of the Union, regardless of whether said contracts are governed by (national or European) public or private law. Prek and Lefèvre also consider that *renvoi* to national law contained in Union legislation renders that national law applicable by the CJEU.

[92] See the Opinion of AG Bot in Case C-530/12 P *National Lottery Commission* ECLI:EU:C:2013:782, para 71.

[93] Case 1/58 *Friedrich Stork & Cie v High Authority of the European Coal and Steel Commmunity*, ECLI:EU:C:1959:4.

[94] See eg Cases C-457/09 *Chartry v Belgian State*, ECLI:EU:C:2011:101, para 21 and C-361/07 *Polier v Najar EURL*, ECLI:EU:C:2008:16, para 9.

[95] Case T-187/11 *Trabelsi v European Council*, ECLI:EU:T:2011:384, para 61.

[96] EDPB Letter of 10 October 2022, available at https://edpb.europa.eu/system/files/2022-10/edpb_letter_out2022-0069_to_the_eu_commission_on_procedural_aspects_en_0.pdf. See also Giulia Gentile and Orla Lynskey, 'Deficient by design? The transnational enforcement of the GDPR' (2022) 71 *International and Comparative Law Quarterly* 799, 806–8.

If the legality of final Union decisions depends on conformity of their preparatory acts with national laws, then the legality of those decisions would depend upon the administrative laws of the Member States where said preparatory acts were adopted even if all factual circumstances remained the same. The uniform application of the legislative instruments establishing composite procedures would therefore be compromised – despite the fact that the invariability of EU law across the Member States is essential to the authority and unity of the EU's legal order.[97] Historically, the CJEU's powers – indeed, the CJEU itself[98] – exist to ensure such uniformity.[99] It would be entirely inconsistent with that constitutional function to require the CJEU to be the guardian of national administrative law idiosyncrasies when reviewing composite decision-making.

The third reason is probably the most constitutionally significant. It touches upon a principle that is of no less than *existential* importance to the EU legal order[100] – the principle of the autonomy of EU law. The remote origins of the principle lie in the *Bosch* ruling, where the Court of Justice first acknowledged that the 'law of any Member State … and Community law constitute two separate and distinct legal orders'.[101] Shortly thereafter, the Court delivered the *Van Gend en Loos* and *Costa v ENEL* rulings,[102] where it famously anointed the EU as a 'a new legal order', gifted with 'its own legal system'. By claiming its own normative autonomy, the EU legal order asserts itself as a self-referential legal system, in the sense that the 'creation, validity, application and interpretation of a legal rule depend exclusively on the order of which that rule constitutes a part'.[103] Accordingly, autonomy requires that the validity of Union acts only be assessed against Union law – not national law.[104] As the CJEU puts it,

> the law stemming from the EU Treaty and the FEU Treaty, an independent source of law, cannot because of its very nature be overridden by rules of national law, however framed, without the legal basis of the European Union itself being called into question.[105]

[97] Case 55-77 *Maris v Rijksdienst voor Werknemerspensioenen*, ECLI:EU:C:1977:203, para 27. The concern with preserving the unity of the Union's legal order has famously pervaded the CJEU's case law relating to conflicting fundamental rights standards in Union and national constitutional law. For many, see Case 44/79 *Hauer v Land Rheinland-Pfalz*, ECLI:EU:C:1979:290, para 14 and, more recently, Joined Cases C-357/19, C-379/19, C-547/19, C-811/19 and C-840/19 *Criminal proceedings against PM*, ECLI:EU:C:2021:1034, para 211.

[98] See for instance A Donner, 'National Law and the Case Law of the Court of Justice of the European Communities' (1963) 1 *Common Market Law Review* 8, 11–12.

[99] Joined Cases C-188/10 and C-189/10 *Melki and Abdeli*, ECLI:EU:C:2010:363, para 64.

[100] See N Nic Shuibhne, 'What is the Autonomy of EU Law, and Why Does that Matter?' (2019) 88 *Nordic Journal of International Law* 9.

[101] Case 13/61 *Kledingverkoopbedrijf de Geus en Uitdenbogerd v Robert Bosch GmbH*, ECLI:EU:C:1962:11.

[102] See Cases 26/62 *NV Algemene Transport- en Expeditie Onderneming van Gend en Loos v Netherlands Inland Revenue Administration*, ECLI:EU:C:1963:1 and 6/64 *Costa v ENEL*, ECLI:EU:C:1964:66.

[103] R Barents, *The Autonomy of Community Law* (Kluwer Law International 2004), 239 ff; R Barents, 'The Precedence of EU Law from the Perspective of Constitutional Pluralism' (2009) 5 *European Constitutional Law Review* 421, 426; and K Tuori, *European Constitutionalism* (Cambridge University Press, 2015), 54.

[104] K Tuori, n 103, 57.

[105] *Trabelsi*, n 95, para 61. See also Case 11/70 *Internationale Handelsgesellschaft mbH v Einfuhr- und Vorratsstelle für Getreide und Futtermitte*, ECLI:EU:C:1970:114, para 3.

In this light, it becomes apparent why the principle of autonomy opposes derivative illegality on grounds of national law. Such illegality would undermine the requirement that the acts of Union bodies be immune to national law. Like a sort of administrative Trojan horse, a tainted national preparatory act would carry the violation of national law into Union administration, render its decisions invalid on grounds of national law, and thus break the autonomy of the EU legal order from within.

(iii) Derivative Illegality, the Rule of Law, and Decisional Dominance

The two preceding subsections illustrated that there are two categories of objections to derivative illegality within composite procedures. The first category concerns the specific principles of European Executive Federalism, which oppose making the EU administration responsible for the actions of national authorities (principle of separation) or reviewing acts taken by those national authorities before the CJEU (principle of double exclusivity).

The second category concerns general requirements of EU constitutional law which would specifically oppose derivative illegality of Union decisions on grounds of national law. A review of Union decisions just because they are based on preparatory acts that violate purely national law is effectively a review of Union decisions for their compatibility with a variety of national laws. Such would violate the limits of the CJEU's jurisdiction and undermine the uniformity and autonomy of EU law.

The problem of treating these objections too strictly, however, is that they would lead to the illegal preparatory acts of national authorities becoming unreviewable. If a preparatory act may only be reviewed indirectly, upon the review of the final decision to which it leads, and if the competent court to review that final decision (the CJEU) cannot consider the illegality of the preparatory act, then no judicial control whatsoever is possible over the preparatory act.

Rejecting derivative illegality *altogether* would hence be incompatible with the objective purpose of judicial control – enforcing the legal constraints to public power. Such a rejection would also be incompatible with the subjective purpose – judicially protecting the individual. If the CJEU were unable to enforce all applicable legal requirements throughout a composite procedure – including at national preparatory stages – then the fundamental right to effective judicial protection would be violated. Indeed, the right requires any court to have the jurisdiction to examine all relevant questions of fact *and law*.[106]

Such a complete failure to ensure judicial control could have represented a failure of the rule of law itself. And yet, it is striking that the CJEU never allowed that to happen. Instead, it developed a body of case law that addresses most of the objections to derivative illegality set out above.

[106] See section II.A. above.

The most important aspect of that case law is that it derogates from the CJEU's old principles of separation and double exclusivity. The CJEU implicitly recognised that, in composite decision-making, national and Union administration do not exercise their respective powers separately, but in an interdependent manner. In particular, it understood the implications of the fact that the Union administration often takes decisions which require the prior adoption of national preparatory acts.

The CJEU resolved the substantive issue of derivative illegality with the same test as it used to resolve the jurisdictional issue explained in subsection III.A., that of determining whether judicial review of composite decision-making should fall to national or Union courts. The test is one of decisional dominance. If the relevant legislation requires the Union administration to decide in conformity with a binding national preparatory act (ie if national administration enjoys decisional dominance), its final decision cannot be affected by derivative illegality. If, however, the Union administration does enjoy the discretion to make its own decision (ie if it enjoys decisional dominance), that decision may be derivatively illegal if the EU administration *chooses* to adhere to national preparatory acts which are illegal. In the latter case, the CJEU found ways to ensure respect for its own jurisdictional boundaries and for the principles of autonomy and uniformity of Union law (as Chapter nine will explain).

By employing the test of decisional dominance, the CJEU succeeded in ensuring that judicial control of composite procedures is effective with regard to both national and Union stages and despite the division of labour between the two levels. Indeed, it requires that judicial protection be afforded in a unitary fashion that treats any composite administrative procedure as a single decision-making process.

IV. Decisional Dominance and Unitary Judicial Protection: A Practical Overview

The previous sections have sought to illustrate two problems that composite procedures raise for effective judicial control. First, what court, if any, may review a measure adopted by composite procedure and second, whether the decisions of EU administration may be voidable in cases where they rely on illegal national preparatory acts.

The approach of the CJEU to solving these problems has remained consistent over time and across cases involving composite procedures in quite different policy areas and of many different eras. In composite decision-making, the CJEU's approach is to abandon the dualistic logic of European Executive Federalism. Rather than treating national and Union authorities as strictly separate, the CJEU requires their review as a single, integrated administration. The CJEU requires every composite procedure to be reviewed as a unified decision-making process so that judicial control is not compromised by the existence of distinct stages at national and EU levels. Indeed, since the *Berlusconi* ruling in 2018, the CJEU has made repeated reference to the need to ensure a 'single judicial review' in composite decision-making.[107] This requirement constitutes what will be termed as the *principle of unitary judicial protection*.

The key to operationalising such a 'single judicial review' lies in a simple test, which relates to the structure of each composite administrative procedure or, put differently, to how it allocates decision-making power between national and Union authorities. As with the distribution of the burden to observe good administration rights, that test is the location of *decisional dominance*.

When using the test of decisional dominance, the CJEU has occasionally phrased it as one level of administration enjoying an 'exclusive decision-making power' or 'exclusive authority'.[108] This characterisation is not entirely accurate. By definition, decisions adopted in a composite procedure require the exercise of decision-making powers by national *and* Union administration. As neither level of administration can decide without the other, decision-making power is shared. What can be said is that this power is not shared equally, as one of the two will always exercise decisional dominance, be it by adopting a binding opinion in a preparatory procedural stage that predetermines the final decision, or by exercising discretionary power at the procedure's conclusion.

The two following subsections briefly illustrate how decisional dominance applies in top-down composite procedures, where Union decision-making is followed by national decision-making, and in bottom-up procedures, where it is the other way around. As noted before, many composite procedures follow a 'back-and-forth' structure, ie involve top-down as well as bottom-up elements.[109] In such procedures, analysis of top-down and bottom-up composite decision-making should be seen as complementary rather than mutually exclusive.

A. Decisional Dominance in Top-down Procedures

Top-down procedures display national decisional dominance when national authorities are *not* obliged to take final decisions that implement prior preparatory acts of the Union administration. Top-down procedures display Union decisional dominance when they are. In the former, judicial control should be exercised by national courts and directed against the national authority's final decision. In the

[107] See Cases C-219/17 *Berlusconi and Finanziaria d'investimento Fininvest SpA (Fininvest) v Banca d'Italia*, ECLI:EU:C:2018:1023, para 49; C-414/18 *Iccrea Banca SpA Istituto Centrale del Credito Cooperativo v Banca d'Italia*, ECLI:EU:C:2019:1036, paras 42 and 53; and T-660/18 *VodafoneZiggo Group BV v European Commission*, ECLI:EU:T:2019:546, para 112.

[108] Case T-205/99 *Hyper Srl v European Commission*, ECLI:EU:T:2002:189.

[109] See Chapter 3, section III.C.(i).

latter, judicial control should be exercised by the Union courts against the Union administration's binding preparatory acts.

The *van Parys* and, more recently, the *VodafoneZiggo* case, illustrate well how judicial review should be exercised in instances of top-down composite decision-making. *Van Parys* concerned a procedure on the allocation of tariff quotas where the Commission's role was rather limited. National authorities forwarded the lists of traders applying for a licence to import certain quantities of bananas under the tariff quota; the Commission then distributed a 'worksheet' to national administrations indicating whether it had found any irregularities. The trader Van Parys sought annulment of one such 'worksheet', but the General Court denied that it constituted a reviewable decision, as decisional dominance in determining the quantities covered by the allocated import licences was a matter for national authorities.[110]

VodafoneZiggo concerned a composite procedure for the regulation of electronic communications services.[111] Under the applicable Union legislation, national regulatory authorities may impose specific regulatory obligations on operators with significant market power. However, such measures may only be adopted only after a procedural stage is initiated at European level, where the European Commission is consulted on the intended national measures, and issues recommendations if they are found to harm consistency in the enforcement of Union law.[112] VodafoneZiggo lodged actions to annul a binding decision that it alleged was contained in a Commission letter addressed to the Dutch regulatory authority concerning the measures the latter intended to adopt. The General Court held that the Commission 'plays more of a coordinating role in [the European consultation] procedure than one of decision-making';[113] its recommendations to the national regulatory authorities are mere *preparatory acts*, adopted in the exercise of a 'power to exhort and to persuade, as distinct from the power to adopt powers having binding force'.[114] The General Court stated that 'when it assigned tasks to the national regulatory authorities and the Commission, the EU legislature wished to assign a central role to the national regulatory authorities',[115] and that said authorities exercise, 'alone, the final decision-making power without being bound by the preparatory acts adopted by [the Union] bodies'.[116] Accordingly, the General Court concluded that only the final decision taken by the Dutch authority was reviewable, while the Commission's recommendations were not. Given the

[110] See Case T-160/98 *Firma Léon Van Parys NV v European Commission*, ECLI:EU:T:2002:18, para 64.

[111] *VodafoneZiggo*, n 107. The General Court's ruling was confirmed by the Court in Case C-689/19 P *VodafoneZiggo*, ECLI:EU:C:2021:142.

[112] See Article 32(4) of Directive 2018/1972 of the European Parliament and of the Council of 11 December 2018 establishing the European Electronic Communications Code.

[113] *VodafoneZiggo*, n 107, para 35.

[114] *VodafoneZiggo*, n 107, para 43.

[115] *VodafoneZiggo*, n 107, para 32.

[116] *VodafoneZiggo*, n 107, paras 110–111.

need for a 'single judicial review' it was for the Dutch courts to review the Dutch regulatory administrative measures.[117]

The CJEU considers that composite procedures must be judicially reviewed at Union level whenever, unlike in *Van Parys* and *VodafoneZiggo*, it is the Union administration and not the national that enjoys decisional dominance. There are countless examples of this. The case law on the European Social Fund provides plenty. According to the old legal framework of the ESF, no longer in force, the Commission took decisions, which were binding for the competent national authorities, on whether an irregularity justified reducing or withdrawing financial assistance. Given that they predetermined the final national decision taken in respect of the ESF beneficiary, the CJEU reviewed such decisions without hesitation.[118]

It is incontrovertible today that, in cases of Union decisional dominance, the CJEU must review Union acts even if they are followed by a final national decision. It is nonetheless striking how Union authorities have tried to evade judicial challenges in composite procedures by pleading that their measures were of a purely preparatory kind. They have often done so by advocating the 'inter-administrative' approach to composite procedures seen in cases on procedural rights.[119]

In *Control Data*, for instance, a case concerning composite procedures on customs duty relief,[120] the Commission initially claimed that its decision could not be challenged on the basis that it represented an act 'internal to the Community and the Member States: the final act is that of the [national] authorities who implement the decision'. Tacitly agreeing with the Advocate General that national administration was obliged to 'automatically apply' the Commission's decision, the Court reviewed and annulled it.[121]

In the *Hypo Vorarlberg* ruling,[122] an action for annulment was lodged against certain Single Resolution Board (SBR) decisions determining the ex-ante contributions that Hypo Vorarlberg Bank would need to pay into the Banking Union's Single Resolution Fund. Just like the Commission in *Control Data*, the SRB claimed that its decisions were purely preparatory acts in an administrative procedure

[117] *VodafoneZiggo*, n 107, para 112.

[118] See for instance Cases C-291/89 *Interhotel Sociedade Internacional de Hoteis SARL v European Commission*, ECLI:EU:C:1991:189, para 13; C-32/95 P *European Commission v Lisrestal Organização Gestão de Restaurantes Colectivos Ld.a*, ECLI:EU:C:1996:402, para 46; T-72/97 *Proderec – Formação e Desinvolvimento de Recursos Humanos, ACE v Commission of the European Communities*, ECLI:EU:T:1998:179, para 34; T-102/00 *Vlaams Fonds voor de Sociale Integratie van Personen met een Handicap v European Commission*, ECLI:EU:T:2003:192, para 60; and T-53/11 Case T-53/11 *Associação de Empresas de Construção e Obras Públicas e Serviços v European Commission (AECOPS I)*, ECLI:EU:T:2013:205 Case T-53/11 *Associação de Empresas de Construção e Obras Públicas e Serviços v European Commission (AECOPS I)*, ECLI:EU:T:2013:205, para 52.

[119] See Chapter 4, section III.

[120] Case 294/81 *Control Data Belgium NV SA v European Commission*, ECLI:EU:C:1983:84.

[121] Opinion of AG Slynn in Case 294/81 *Control Data Belgium NV SA v European Commission*, ECLI:EU:C:1983:24.

[122] Joined Cases T-377/16, T-645/16 and T-809/16 *Hypo Vorarlberg AG v Single Resolution Board (SRB)*, ECLI:EU:T:2019:823.

where national resolution authorities take the final decision (ie the national act requesting the ex-ante contributions from credit institutions).[123] The General Court rejected the Single Resolution Board's argument. It held that the SRB's decisions were reviewable because they definitively fixed the amounts owed by credit institutions, while national resolution authorities lacked any discretion in charging those amounts.[124]

Even though the Union administration's decisions in *Control Data* and *Hypo Vorarlberg* were addressed to national administration, the latter in fact lacked any discretion at the conclusion of the procedure. Plaintiffs were individually and directly concerned in the sense of Article 263(4) TFEU and therefore had the standing to bring actions for annulment before the CJEU. Except where they obviously had such standing and failed to lodge actions within the prescribed deadline,[125] plaintiffs may also choose to challenge the final national decision and then request the national court to refer to the CJEU for a preliminary ruling on the validity of the preceding Union act. Indeed, according to the Court of Justice's ruling in *Foto-Frost*, a historic judgment for Union law which concerned in fact a composite procedure in customs law, the national court will be *obliged* to make a reference if inclined to consider that a Union decision is invalid.[126] For this reason, it is right to argue, as Marchetti does, that the judicial challenge of the final national decision will be no more than a formality – a 'prelude' to a preliminary reference where, in practice, the Union judge will rule as the real judge of the case.[127]

B. Decisional Dominance in Bottom-up Procedures

The case law on the judicial control of bottom-up composite procedures is significantly more complex than that on the top-down variant. The CJEU has to rely on a 'reverse preliminary reference' to national courts to inquire on the lawfulness of national preparatory acts preceding a Union-level decision.

Even so, the basic test of judicial review remains the same. Decisional dominance has been implicitly used by EU courts for decades as a test to ensure judicial control of bottom-up composite procedures. However, only recently has the CJEU made explicit that its case law has long followed a two-track model. In *Berlusconi & Fininvest* (henceforth, *Berlusconi*) Advocate General Campos Sánchez-Bordona

[123] *Hypo Vorarlberg*, n 122, para 50–51.

[124] *Hypo Vorarlberg*, n 122, paras 68–70.

[125] In such cases, the CJEU will hold that the preliminary reference fraudulently circumvents time-limits for annulment and cannot be admissible. See Cases C-188/92 *TWD Textilwerke Deggendorf GmbH v Bundesrepublik Deutschland*, ECLI:EU:C:1994:90; and C-72/15 *R (on the application of PJSC Rosneft Oil Company) v HM Treasury*, ECLI:EU:C:2017:23, para 128.

[126] *Foto-Frost*, n 37.

[127] B Marchetti, 'Fondi Strutturali e tutela giurisdizionale: Variazione degli schemi regolatori e conseguenze sull'architettura giudiziaria dell'EU' (2012) *Rivista Italiana di Diritto Pubblico Comunitario* 1105, 1120–21.

correctly held that there are two lines of case law that can apply to the review of a composite procedure. Which line of case law applies depends upon 'how the decision-making power is distributed within that procedure' between national and EU authorities,[128] and more specifically 'who has the *real* decision-making power in the composite administrative procedure'.[129]

As it currently stands, the case law can be divided into the *Borelli* and the *Berlusconi* doctrines. Both comprise jurisdictional elements (on the allocation of judicial jurisdiction) and substantive elements (on derivative illegality of final EU decisions).

Borelli applies to (bottom-up) composite procedures where national administration exercises decisional dominance. *Borelli* requires judicial control to be exercised by national courts and proscribes derivative illegality. *Berlusconi* applies to (bottom-up) composite procedures where the Union administration exercises decisional dominance. *Berlusconi* requires judicial control to be exercised by Union courts and, subject to conditions, accepts derivative illegality. Because of their special complexity and theoretical and practical importance, both doctrines will be explored in depth in two separate chapters (Chapters eight and nine).

The most important thing to note at this point is that these principles are *unique* to composite decision-making, as they lack any equivalent in – and in fact, derogate significantly from – the EU law requirements for exclusively national or exclusively Union administrative decision-making. The key differences lie in the judicial review of national preparatory acts and the implications of their illegality for decisions of the Union administration. Under EU law, the right to effective judicial protection does not *require* the judicial review of preparatory acts that national authorities adopt in purely domestic administrative procedures.[130] By contrast, in composite decision-making, the CJEU either *requires* national courts to review national preparatory acts if they are binding on the EU administration (*Borelli*) or *prohibits* national courts from doing so if they are not (*Berlusconi*).

V. Mending the Mismatch

This chapter has sought to illustrate why composite decision-making fits poorly with the principles of European Executive Federalism. The mismatch risks weakening the rule of law requirements associated with judicial control in the European Union. The different alternative approaches that the CJEU could have chosen to address said mismatch, their underlying constitutional dilemmas and inherent weaknesses, tend not to be explicitly discussed in the literature. Indeed, the case

[128] Opinion of AG Campos Sánchez-Bordona in Case C-219/17 *Berlusconi and Finanziaria d'investimento Fininvest SpA (Fininvest) v Banca d'Italia*, ECLI:EU:C:2018:502, para 63.

[129] Ibid, para 60.

[130] See Cases *Heylens*, n 14, *Diouf*, n 16, paras 55–56 and, implicitly, *B v État Luxembourgois*, n 21, paras 81–84.

law of the CJEU on the review of composite procedures tends to be analysed almost exclusively from the perspective of effective judicial protection. That perspective rarely acknowledges how other purposes of judicial control are safeguarded. The key point made here, however, is that an exclusive focus on judicial protection obscures the institutional limitations of the CJEU emerging from its historical adoption of European Executive Federalism and, above all, the lengths to which it went in overcoming those limitations.

Crucially, the approach of the CJEU to the review of composite decision-making derogates from two key tenets of European Executive Federalism. Those are the principle of separation, according to which one level of administration cannot be held responsible for the behaviour of the other; and the principle of double exclusivity, according to which only national courts may review national acts and only Union courts may review Union acts.

In the view taken here, it is therefore inaccurate to suggest that the CJEU argues 'in terms of division of powers', in terms, that is, of 'a legal fiction', and 'ignores the reality of an integrated administration'.[131] Indeed, the CJEU developed, though until recently in a mostly implicit manner, a principle of unitary judicial protection and a test of decisional dominance. According to the principle of unitary judicial protection, a single exercise of judicial control should suffice for the judicial review of a composite administrative procedure. The test of decisional dominance serves a twofold purpose: determining whether national or Union administration holds the decisive powers in the procedure in order to solve the jurisdictional issue of locating the court competent for judicial review and, in bottom-up composite procedures, the substantive issue of whether illegal national preparatory acts may contaminate final Union decisions.

Combined, the test of decisional dominance and the principle of unitary judicial protection imply that national and Union stages of a composite procedure must be considered together, as parts of a single whole, and their relative weight in the decision-making process compared.[132] The profound implications of this for the most common instances of composite procedures – bottom-up procedures – will be analysed in depth in the two following chapters.

[131] S Alonso de León, *Composite Administrative Procedures in the European Union* (Iustel, 2017), 320.

[132] From a different perspective, but also noting that the CJEU's approach, over time, has also tended to review composite administrative procedures as unitary decision-making processes, see J Fernández Gaztea, *Cooperación Procedimental en la Unión Europea* (Tirant lo Blanch, 2020), 262.

8

The *Borelli* Doctrine

I. Introduction: Oil Mills, Halloumi, and Constitutional Geometry

The *Borelli* ruling represented a watershed moment in the history of European administrative law. It provided the CJEU with a first opportunity to explicitly address the unique challenges that composite decision-making raises from the point of view of judicial control.[1] In doing so, the CJEU crafted a doctrine unique to composite decision-making.

Section II begins by offering a summary of the facts and ruling in *Borelli*. The judgment established a doctrine which specifically applies to procedures where national administration exercises decisional dominance during preparatory stages – eg by adopting binding opinions which oblige the Union administration to take a specific final decision. The scenario where Union administration enjoys decisional dominance at the conclusion of a composite procedure is the domain of the *Berlusconi* doctrine, which will be considered in Chapter nine.

The case was the first to explicitly address both of the jurisdictional and substantive questions conceptualised in Chapter seven: first, which courts are competent to review a composite administrative procedure; and second, whether final decisions taken by Union authorities may be 'contaminated' by illegal national preparatory acts. As section III will explain, the CJEU's answer to the first question – the jurisdictional *Borelli* principle – is that judicial review falls solely to national courts. Serious doctrinal objections have been raised against this point. As section IV will explain, the CJEU's answer to the second question – the substantive *Borelli* principle – is that such contamination, ie derivative illegality, may never occur.

Section V analyses later development of *Borelli*. A triad of rulings concerning protected designations of origin (PDOs), *POA*, *CRM*, and *Jeanningros*, introduced a novel procedural right, drawn from the right to good administration, according to which the Union administration is indirectly bound by national courts'

[1] Case C-97/91 *Oleificio Borelli SpA v European Commission*, ECLI:EU:C:1992:491. On this case, see R Caranta, 'Sull'impugnabilità degli atti endoprocedimentali adottati dalle autorità nazionali nelle ipotesi di coamministrazione' (1994) 1 *Foro Amministrativo* 752 and L Maeso Seco, 'I Procedimenti Composti Comunitari: Riflessioni Intorno alla Problematica della Impossibilità a Difendersi ed Eventuali Alternative' in G della Cananea and M Gnes (eds), *I Procedimenti Amministrativi dell'Unione Europea. Un'Indagine* (Giappichelli, 2004).

judgments. The crucial implication of that procedural right is that, in most cases, the need to review final Union decisions is entirely obviated. This represented a drastic departure from the principle of double exclusivity that is so central to European Executive Federalism. Instead of demanding separate judicial review of national and Union decision-making, the CJEU's *Borelli* doctrine provides that a single exercise of judicial review, carried out by national courts in respect of national stages, must suffice to control the entire composite procedure. It thus reflects an overarching pattern in the case law of combining an implicit principle of unitary judicial protection with the application of a test of decisional dominance to locate the court competent for such protection.

II. The *Borelli* Ruling: Facts and Findings

Borelli was an Italian undertaking that planned to build an olive oil mill and had applied for agricultural aid from the Guidance Section of the European Agricultural Guidance and Guarantee Fund (EAGGF). Under the applicable legislation, each project had to be co-funded by the Union and by the relevant Member State. The granting of aid by the Commission depended on a positive opinion issued by national authorities on whether the project met all necessary requirements.[2] In *Borelli*, the competent authority, the Region of Liguria, had issued a negative opinion. The Commission, accordingly, decided to refuse aid.

Borelli lodged actions for annulment. Because Italian law classified Liguria's opinion as a mere preparatory act, which was therefore unreviewable, Borelli argued that it should be possible for the CJEU to review the Commission's final decision. Because the opinion had made an erroneous assessment of the application for aid, and was therefore illegal, the Commission's decision, which 'encapsulated' the illegal opinion, Borelli claimed, had to be annulled.[3]

The CJEU's ruling in response 'birthed' the first doctrine specific to composite procedures. *Borelli* and subsequent case law further clarified that doctrine's scope of application and fleshed out its two constituent principles. *Borelli*'s scope of application depends upon two conditions:

(i) a national authority adopts a preparatory act which, according to the relevant Union legislation, '*forms part* of a Union decision-making procedure' (ie the national act is issued within a composite administrative procedure); *and*
(ii) that act '*is binding* on the Union decision-taking authority *and therefore determines the terms* of the Union decision to be adopted' (ie the national authority exercises decisional dominance).[4]

[2] Articles 17 and 13(3) of Regulation No 355/77.
[3] See the Report of the Hearing in the *Borelli* case, [1992] ECR I-6313.
[4] *Borelli*, n 1, para 10. See also Cases T-114/99 *CSR Pampryl SA v European Commission*, ECLI:EU:T:1999:281, para 57; C-269/99 *Carl Kühne GmbH & Co KG and Others v Jütro Konservenfabrik*

If both conditions are met, then the principles of the *Borelli* doctrine apply.[5] The two principles, which are sometimes conflated, concern the two distinct issues which, as mentioned before,[6] composite decision-making raises for judicial review. One is a *jurisdictional* issue: how to locate the competent judiciary to review a composite procedure. The other is a *substantive* issue: whether a final Union decision can be derivatively invalid due to illegal national preparatory acts. The two principles will be examined in greater detail in the remainder of the chapter, but can be summarised as follows.

The first will be termed the *jurisdictional Borelli principle*. After stressing that it lacked the jurisdiction to review national decisions, the CJEU declared that

> it is for the national courts … to rule on the lawfulness of the national measure at issue on the same terms on which they review any definitive measure adopted by the same national authority which is capable of adversely affecting third parties.[7]

The second aspect of *Borelli*, here termed the *substantive Borelli principle*, goes much further. The CJEU not only declined the jurisdiction to indirectly review Liguria's binding opinion – it held that 'any irregularity that might affect the opinion cannot affect the validity of the decision by which the Commission refused the aid applied for'.[8] Put differently, under the substantive *Borelli* principle, derivative illegality cannot occur.

III. The Jurisdictional *Borelli* Principle

The first principle of the *Borelli* case law, the *jurisdictional Borelli* principle, defines which measures may be reviewed in composite procedures with national decisional dominance, and which judicial jurisdiction may do so. To that end, the jurisdictional *Borelli* principle simultaneously entails a prohibition and a command.

The CJEU *may not* review Union decisions if that necessarily involves reviewing binding preparatory acts taken by national authorities. National courts, in contrast, *must* agree to review such acts. As they necessarily predetermine what

GmbH & Co KG, ECLI:EU:C:2001:659, para 57; C-64/05 P *Kingdom of Sweden v Commission*, ECLI:EU:C:2007:802, para 92; C-343/07 *Bavaria NV v Bayerische Brauerbund eV*, ECLI:EU:C:2009:415, paras 55–57 and 64–67; and C-785/18 *GAEC Jeanningros v Institut national de l'origine et de la qualité (INAO)*, ECLI:EU:C:2020:46, para 27.

[5] For a more detailed account of the *Borelli* ruling, see F Brito Bastos, 'The Borelli Doctrine Revisited: Three Issues of Coherence in a Landmark Ruling for EU Administrative Justice' (2015) 8 *Review of European Administrative Law* 269. Other scholars, such as Aperio Bella, appear to have supported the conceptualisation of the *Borelli* case law as a discrete doctrine (F Aperio Bella, 'Composite Procedures and Procedural Guarantees: the 'Borelli Doctrine' in the Light of ReNEUAL Model Rules' (2020) 2 *Roma Tre Law Review* 7.

[6] See Chapter 7, section III.

[7] *Borelli*, n 1, para 13. This had also been the view proposed by the Advocate General. See the Opinion of AG Darmon in Case C-97/91 *Oleificio Borelli SpA v European Commission*, ECLI:EU:C:1992:254, paras 32–34.

[8] *Borelli*, n 1, para 12.

decisions the Union administration may take, binding national preparatory acts are 'capable of adversely affecting third parties' and must be reviewed by national courts 'on the same terms on which they review any definitive measure adopted by the same national authority'.[9] Because the CJEU will not review binding national preparatory acts, the right to effective judicial protection requires national courts to do so – *even if* judicial challenges against preparatory acts are generally not allowed under national law.[10]

A. Subsequent Development

Shortly after the *Borelli* ruling was delivered, the CJEU reached similar conclusions in *Emerald Meats*.[11] The case involved an administrative procedure intended to distribute a limited number of licences under an import quota for frozen beef originating from third countries. National authorities received and decided on applications for licences. The Commission's role was limited to

> checking that a given applicant does not appear on more than one list and to determining, having regard to the quantities indicated in the various national lists and to the total quota to be allocated, in what proportion the national authorities can accept the applications admitted by them.[12]

Therefore, the Court held, importers should seek judicial protection before national courts, against the competent national authorities.

However, the most visible application of the jurisdictional *Borelli* principle has been in the field of protected designations of origin (PDOs) and geographic indications (PGIs). The structure of the relevant composite procedure for the registration of PDOs and PGIs has already been explained.[13] The procedure accords decisional dominance to national authorities, which define the scope of the protected designation or indication. The Commission is legally obliged to implement the applications supported by national authorities, and to register designations of origin and geographic indications so as to give them EU-wide protection. The CJEU may not review the Commission's final decision to register where such would necessarily involve reviewing the national binding preparatory act adopted to support an application.[14] Instead, and precisely as in *Borelli*, such acts must be reviewed by national courts just as they would review any final administrative

[9] *Borelli*, n 1, paras 10 and 13.

[10] *Borelli*, n 1, para 13.

[11] Joined Cases C-106/90, C-317/90 and C-129/91 *Emerald Meats Ltd v European Commission*, ECLI:EU:C:1993:19. On this case, see A Türk, 'Judicial Review of Integrated Administration in the EU' in H Hofmann and A Türk (eds), *Legal Challenges in EU Administrative Law: towards an integrated administration* (Edward Elgar, 2009), 224.

[12] *Emerald Meats*, n 11, paras 38, 40 and 50.

[13] See Chapter 4, section IV.B.(i).

[14] *Pampryl*, n 4, para 57.

act.[15] In *Pampryl*, the General Court even went as far as to state that a refusal by a national court to do so would constitute a breach of EU law sufficiently serious to warrant institution of infringement proceedings against a Member State.[16]

The jurisdictional *Borelli* principle was also applied in *Association Greenpeace France*.[17] The case related to the general authorisation procedure for the placing of genetically modified organism (GMO) products on the market. The procedure neatly fits into the category of 'arbitral' composite procedures examined in Chapter three,[18] and can be summarised as follows. Following an application by the interested undertaking, the competent authority of the Member State where the product is to be first placed on the market carries out an assessment of public health and environmental risks. If the rapporteur authority's assessment is positive, but other Member State authorities object to its intention to authorise the GMO, the Commission takes a binding decision to settle the disagreement. If the Commission decides that the GMO should be authorised, the rapporteur national authority is obliged to take a final decision giving its 'consent in writing' to the marketing of the GMO.[19]

In *Association Greenpeace France*, the CJEU held that a national preparatory measure such as the positive assessment report could be autonomously challenged before national courts. This could be seen as an unexpected use of the jurisdictional *Borelli* principle. The national act in question was technically not binding upon the Union administration – and could not, therefore, fit in any literal sense into the *Borelli* doctrine's scope of application.

However, as the CJEU recognised, the 'decision of the competent authority is the prerequisite for the Community procedure and, *in the absence of any indication to the contrary* from another Member State', the positive assessment report adopted in the first national stage of a composite procedure '*may even determine its outcome*' (emphasis added).[20] One could compare it to what typically happens at an auction: just as the highest bidder's offer will be the final offer unless another bidder makes an even higher offer before the auctioneer's hammer comes down on a lot, the rapporteur national authority's draft decision will be the final decision, as is, unless another authority raises an objection. And much as it is out of the bidder's hands whether her bid will be the 'hammer price', it is beyond the national rapporteur authority's control whether other authorities will refrain from

[15] *Carl Kühne*, n 4, paras 57–58 and *Bavaria NV*, n 4, para 57.

[16] *Pampryl*, n 4, paras 57–59.

[17] See Case C-6/99 *Association Greenpeace France v Ministère de l'Agriculture et de la Pêche*, ECLI:EU:C:2000:148.

[18] See Chapter 3, section IV.B.

[19] The composite administrative procedure for the authorisation for GMO products to enter the market was originally established in Directive 90/220, and remains essentially the same under Directive 2001/18. On the difficulties in ensuring judicial control that arise from the administrative procedure's complex structure, see R Tavares Lanceiro and M Eliantonio, 'The Genetically Modified Organisms' Regime: A Playground for Multi-Level Administration and a Nightmare for Effective Judicial Protection?' (2021) 22 *German Law Journal* 371.

[20] See *Association Greenpeace France*, n 17, para 51.

objecting and the draft decision will therefore become final. Since, as far as the national authority is concerned, its preparatory act will become the final decision, it makes sense to allow that act to be judicially challenged under *Borelli*.

From *Association Greenpeace France*, one may infer that the jurisdictional *Borelli* principle may be extended to other arbitral procedures, eg in biocides or medicines, where a national authority's draft decisions *will become* final decisions unless another authority objects.[21] One may however also infer, a fortiori, that the same principle applies where a national authority adopts decisions which *already are* final within the Member State even if they may constitute preparatory acts within a composite procedure. This is the case with composite procedures emerging from safeguard clauses. National safeguard decisions are already final decisions of a national administrative procedure. Yet such decisions only remain temporarily in force, until the Union administration has taken a definitive view on whether they are justified. National safeguard decisions may therefore be challenged in national courts.[22]

B. Doctrinal Objections: Effective Judicial Protection, Double Standards, and National Institutional Autonomy

Borelli was received by the literature with overwhelming disapproval. Some commentators considered that the CJEU had unexpectedly risked effective judicial protection by leaving individuals stranded in a 'no-man's-land' between national and Union courts.[23] One author explicitly describes *Borelli* as a 'paradigmatic example of the lack of protection' of individuals in composite decision-making.[24]

Given such sustained criticism, it may appear puzzling that the CJEU often cites *Borelli* as an important judgment on effective judicial protection.[25] Though admittedly 'harsh', as one Advocate General conceded, the jurisdictional *Borelli* principle is intended to ensure that the CJEU does not overstep the limits of its

[21] Similarly, see M Eliantonio, 'Judicial Review in an Integrated Administration: the Case of 'Composite Procedures' (2014) 7 *Review of European Administrative Law* 65 and S Röttger-Wirtz and M Eliantonio, 'From Integration to Exclusion: EU Composite Administration and Gaps in Judicial Accountability in the Authorisation of Pharmaceuticals' (2019) 10 *European Journal of Risk Regulation* 393.

[22] See Joined Cases C-58/10 to C-68/10 *Monsanto SAS v Ministre de l'Agriculture et de la Pêche*, ECLI:EU:C:2011:553, para 79.

[23] See G della Cananea, 'The European Union's Mixed Administrative Proceedings' (2004–2005), 68 *Law and Contemporary Problems* 197, 198 and L Maeso Seco, n 1, 12 and 29. Similarly, BG Mattarella, 'Procedimenti e Atti Amministrativi' in M Chiti (ed), *Diritto Amministrativo Europeo* (Giuffrè, 2013), 338.

[24] F Aperio Bella, n 5.

[25] See for instance Cases C-459/99 *Mouvement contre le racisme, l'antisémitisme et la xénophobie ASBL (MRAX) v Belgian State*, ECLI:EU:C:2002:461, para 101; T-315/01 *Kadi v European Council*, ECLI:EU:T:2005:332, para 210; and Joined Cases C-924/19 PPU and C-925/19 PPU *FMS v Országos Idegenrendészeti Főigazgatóság Dél-alföldi Regionális Igazgatóság*, ECLI:EU:C:2020:367, para 144.

powers, as such would 'be most unwise and would do nothing to promote the cause of respect for the rule of law'.[26]

Hypothetically, the Court could have simply dismissed Borelli's action as inadmissible, much as it does in any case where it is requested to review a national decision. Instead, it recognised such would lead to a kind of 'catch 22' where no court would be competent to review a composite procedure in its entirety.[27] The CJEU, though solely competent to review Union decisions, cannot review national acts preparatory to them. National courts, though solely competent to review national acts, cannot usually review preparatory acts except when reviewing a final decision.

This would have been irreconcilable with the CJEU's commitment to the right to effective judicial protection. That is precisely why, rather than simply refusing to review binding national preparatory acts, the CJEU requires that national courts review such acts 'on the same terms on which they review any definitive measure'.[28] Effective judicial protection is best ensured by national courts. Not only do national courts compensate for the CJEU's lack of jurisdiction;[29] they are simply better placed for judicial review in administrative procedures which are 'predominantly national' – ie where national authorities exercise decisional dominance.

A second point of criticism raised against *Borelli* concerns its consistency with the Court's own standards for the review of *Union* preparatory acts. Herwig Hofmann criticises the CJEU for tending 'to refer cases to Member States' courts and oblige them to offer legal protection in much more lenient conditions than it itself is ready to give'.[30] In Hofmann's view, the jurisdictional *Borelli* principle is inconsistent with the CJEU's own case law – which, in the author's view, proscribes judicial review of preparatory acts.

The view proposed here begs to differ. If examined closely, CJEU case law actually allows the review of any measure, preparatory or final, provided that it is intended by the administration to produce binding legal effects. The jurisdictional *Borelli* principle adapts that case law by *requiring* of national courts what the CJEU's case law merely *allows* in respect of binding preparatory acts of Union bodies.

[26] Opinion of AG Mischo in C-6/99 *Association Greenpeace France v Ministère de l'Agriculture et de la Pêche*, ECLI:EU:C:1999:587, para 99.

[27] R Caranta, 'Judicial Protection Against Member States: a New *Jus Commune* Takes Shape' (1995) 32 *Common Market Law Review* 703, 716.

[28] *Borelli*, n 1, paras 10 and 13.

[29] Given this compensatory function, one could describe the jurisdictional *Borelli* principle as an instance of 'remedial complementarity'. See M Safjan and D Düsterhaus, 'A Union of Effective Judicial Protection: Addressing a Multi-level Challenge through the Lens of Article 47 CFREU' (2014) 33 *Yearbook of European Law* 3, 6.

[30] H Hofmann, 'Composite decision making procedures in EU administrative law' in H Hofmann and A Türk (eds), *Legal Challenges in EU Administrative Law: towards an integrated administration* (Edward Elgar, 2009), 154.

A third objection, raised by García de Enterría, is that *Borelli* interferes with national procedural autonomy by imposing a new remedy, a right to challenge preparatory acts.[31] Even disregarding the fact that Italian law probably allowed Borelli to challenge the preparatory act after all,[32] national procedural autonomy may occasionally be limited by a need to ensure uniform enforcement of Union law.[33] One may doubt whether such uniformity could be minimally satisfied if judicial protection against composite procedures, which involve a plurality of national and Union administrations, depended on parochial tests, rather than a Union test, as to what constitutes a reviewable national act. Lastly, while the jurisdictional *Borelli* principle does indeed constitute a new remedy, García de Enterría overestimates its scope. *Borelli* does not apply to national preparatory acts *in general*. Neither does it apply to *any* national preparatory act adopted in a composite procedure. *Borelli* applies only to the preparatory acts of national administration, and only when it exercises decisional dominance.

IV. The Substantive *Borelli* Principle

The previous section addressed the first part of the answer that the Court of Justice gave to Borelli's case. It articulated a jurisdictional principle whereby the Union Courts refrain from reviewing, even indirectly, binding national preparatory acts, and require said acts to be reviewed instead by national courts. The second part of the answer was to articulate what can be termed the substantive *Borelli* principle.[34] That principle concerns the validity of the final Union decision as such and *regardless of whether it forms the subject of a judicial challenge or not*.

Borelli's key argument was that the Commission's decision was unlawful 'on the ground that the unfavourable opinion of the region of Liguria on the basis of which that decision was adopted was itself unlawful'.[35] As 'any illegality affecting intermediate acts is reflected in the final act',[36] Borelli argued, the errors of appraisal contained in the opinion rendered the Commission's decision invalid.

[31] E García de Enterría, 'La ampliación de la competencia de las jurisdicciones contencioso-administrativas nacionales por obra del Derecho Comunitario. Sentencia Borelli de 3 de diciembre de 1992 del Tribunal de Justicia y el artículo 5 CEE' (1993) 77 *Revista Española de Derecho Administrativo* 297, 311. For the notion of national procedural autonomy, see Chapter 2, section V.D.(i).

[32] See M Eliantonio, *Europeanisation of administrative justice?: The influence of the ECJ's case law in Italy, Germany and England* (Europa Law Publishing, 2009), 36 and 42 and P Virga, *La Tutela Gurisdizionale nei confronti della Pubblica Amministrazione*, 3rd edn (Giuffrè, 1982), 249.

[33] DU Galetta, *Procedural Autonomy of EU Member States: Paradise Lost?* (Springer, 2010), 79–80 and A Adinolfi, 'The "Procedural Autonomy" of Member States and the Constraints Stemming from the ECJ's Case Law: Is Judicial Activism Still Necessary?' in HW Micklitz and B de Witte, *The European Court of Justice and the Autonomy of the Member States* (Intersentia, 2012), 294–96.

[34] Ibid. See also F Aperio Bella, 'Procedimenti composti in materia di implementazione della politica agricola comune e garanzie procedimentali: il caso Oleificio Borelli "riletto" alla luce delle model rules in materia di decisioni individuali' in G della Cananea and M Conticelli (eds), *I Procedimenti amministrativi di adjudication dell'Unione Europea: principi generali e discipline settoriali* (Giappichelli, 2017), 314.

[35] *Borelli*, n 1, para 7.

[36] Report of the Hearing, [1992] ECR I-6313, at 6318.

The Court held that, besides being beyond the remit of its jurisdiction, '[an] irregularity that might affect the [national] opinion cannot affect the validity of the decision by which the Commission refused the aid applied for'.[37] This passage gave birth to the substantive *Borelli* principle: whenever national administration exercises decisional dominance, the illegality of its preparatory acts cannot lead to the derivative illegality of final decisions taken by the Union administration. This is a principle which the CJEU has preserved to this day, as is plain not only from its rulings on DPO decisions, but from the recent *Di Taranto* case.[38]

Di Taranto sued the European Public Prosecutor's Office (EPPO) before the General Court. The plaintiff requested the annulment of an EPPO decision that appointed a number of delegated prosecutors in Italy. Said decision did not appoint Mr di Taranto, as he had not been one of the prosecutors nominated by the Italian Superior Council of the Judiciary, the body responsible for selecting candidates at the national stage of the appointment procedure. According to the rules governing the appointment procedure, the delegated prosecutors nominated by the Member States *shall* be appointed to the position, save in a few rather unlikely and limited cases.[39] The General Court interpreted the provisions in question as determining that the EPPO *must* designate delegated prosecutors nominated by the competent national authorities (ie as conferring decisional dominance upon the latter). Consequently, the General Court dismissed the action. The plaintiff had not claimed the EPPO decision to be tainted by an illegality of its own. He rather relied solely upon an argument that it was affected by derivative illegality from the Italian body's decision. Such derivative illegality would not be possible, given that the Union authority, the EPPO, only had a very limited margin of discretion.[40]

The substantive *Borelli* principle may at first appear as a counterintuitive solution. One could expect that the illegality of preparatory acts should matter for the legality of final decisions *especially* when the latter must conform with such preparatory acts. It is therefore understandable that *Borelli* was received with some perplexity and much criticism by EU administrative law scholarship.[41] Many have found it 'less persuasive',[42] or even 'embarrassing',[43] that the Court rejected derivative illegality.[44]

[37] *Borelli*, n 1, para 12.

[38] Case T-368/21 *Di Taranto v European Public Prosecutor's Office*, ECLI:EU:T:2022:162.

[39] See Article 17 of Council Regulation 2017/1939 of 12 October 2017 implementing enhanced cooperation on the establishment of the European Public Prosecutor's Office.

[40] *Di Taranto*, n 38, paras 28–30.

[41] R Caranta n 1, 760 and HP Nehl, 'Legal Protection in the Field of EU Funds' (2011) 10 *European State Aid Law Quarterly* 629, 650.

[42] G Gaja, 'Case C-6/99, Association Greenpeace France and Others v. Ministère de l'Agriculture et de la Pêche and Others. Judgment of the Full Court of 21 March 2000' (2000) 37 *Common Market Law Review* 1427, 1431.

[43] R Caranta, 'Coordinamento e divisione dei compiti tra Corte di giustizia delle comunità europee e giudizi nazionali nelle ipotesi di coamministrazione: il caso dei prodotti modificati geneticamente' (2000) *Rivista Italiana di Diritto Pubblico Comunitario* 1133, 1141.

[44] See for instance M Veronelli, 'Procedimenti composti e problemi di tutela giurisdizionale' in G della Cananea and M Gnes (eds), *I Procedimenti Amministrativi dell'Unione Europea. Un'Indagine* (Giappichelli, 2004).

However, there are powerful constitutional arguments against derivative illegality in composite procedures. Those arguments have already been explained in Chapter seven, and apply particularly forcefully to composite administrative procedures where, as in *Borelli*, the Union administration *has no choice* but to incorporate national preparatory acts into its final decision.

Two arguments flow from the constitutional principles of uniformity and autonomy of EU law. According to said principles, the validity of Union acts must be equal throughout the Member States and can only be judged against rules of Union law. Gaja, one critic of *Borelli*, contends that the CJEU should 'in principle' be able to examine whether national preparatory acts are in conformity with Union *as well as national* law.[45] Yet doing so would mean that final Union decisions would be vulnerable to the violation of rules found in a multitude of distinct national legal systems. While only hinted at in the *Borelli* ruling – where the Commission argued that its decision had been 'drawn up in the context of two distinct legal systems',[46] this concern was later spelled out in Advocates General's Opinions.[47]

A second argument concerns the lack of jurisdiction of the CJEU to review national decisions. Some authors hold that the CJEU should be able to review the derivative illegality of final Union decisions if based on national preparatory acts adopted in violation of Union law,[48] whether it be general principles of EU law or relevant sectoral legislation. Yet even in such cases, national decisional dominance determines that the Union administration *has no choice* but to incorporate national preparatory acts into the final decision. Just as the final Union decision is the result of national decision-making in all but form, so too would review of that final decision by Union courts necessarily require reviewing national decision-making under the formal guise of reviewing Union decision-making.

While sensitive to the need to protect the autonomy of the EU legal order and to respect the jurisdictional limits of EU courts, *Borelli* could still raise concerns from the perspective of effective judicial protection, a key rule of law requirement. Indeed, such protection would seem to be curtailed by the refusal of the Union courts to hear cases concerning Union acts that are based on illegal binding national preparatory acts.

One may, however, also doubt whether the rule of law would actually be served if the CJEU were responsible for reviewing composite procedures characterised by national decisional dominance. Lacking the jurisdiction to apply national law or to review national decision-making, the CJEU would necessarily focus on the Union administration, which is legally obliged to rubber-stamp a national authority's acts. The national authority, which exercises the dominant powers, would be spared from any judicial control, and this would undermine the objective purpose of judicial control.

[45] G Gaja, n 42.

[46] *Borelli*, n 1, Report of the Hearing, [1992] ECR I-6313, at I-6321.

[47] See Chapter 9, section IV.B.

[48] H Hofmann and A Türk, 'Legal challenges in EU administrative law by the move to an integrated administration' in H Hofmann and A Türk (eds), *Legal Challenges in EU Administrative Law: Towards an Integrated Administration* (Edward Elgar, 2009), 375.

Borelli, in the view supported here, actually does *promote* the rule of law. It denies judicial review by Union courts only to redirect it to those courts, the national courts, which are best suited to enforcing all legal requirements, national and European, that the dominant administration, national administration, ought to respect. Union Courts *rightly* cite *Borelli* as a landmark on effective judicial protection in Union law. The ruling illustrates how inventive they are willing to be to ensure such protection without undermining their own jurisdictional boundaries.

One could be excused for thinking that *Borelli* merely continues the traditional view, according to which jurisdiction over national and Union authorities is divided between national and Union courts. However, later rulings have showed that this is not the case. In order to prevent any gaps in judicial protection, the CJEU now finds the Union administration to be legally bound by national judgments delivered under the *Borelli* doctrine which annul preparatory acts.

V. *Borelli*: National Judicial Protection as a Question of Good Union Administration

From the outset, the *Borelli* doctrine offered a deceptively simple approach to the judicial review of national decisional dominance. National preparatory acts must be reviewed by national courts – not the CJEU – as if they were final decisions. Yet the question remained open as to what the implications would be for a final Union decision if its preceding preparatory acts were reviewed – and annulled – by national courts.

It was only after 2015 that a string of three landmark cases, emerging from the field of protected designations of origins, addressed the issue. The first, *Pagkyprios organismos ageladotrofon Dimosia* (*POA*), addresses what should happen when a national preparatory act is judicially challenged *before* the final decision at EU level is adopted, but is only annulled by the national court *after* that final decision is taken. The second, *CRM*, addresses what should happen when the national preparatory act is both judicially challenged *and* annulled *before* the EU administration has had the opportunity to take the final decision of the procedure. The third case, *Jeanningros*, addresses what should happen when the national preparatory act is both judicially challenged and annulled *after* the final decision has already been taken at EU level.

A. *POA*: Judicial Challenges to a National Preparatory Act before the EU Administration Takes the Final Decision

The *POA* case resulted from judicial proceedings brought to the General Court by POA, an organisation of cow's milk producers in Cyprus. POA was negatively affected by the Cypriot authorities' application for the registration of halloumi cheese as a protected designation of origin, in particular by the requirements for a cheese to be marketed as halloumi. POA judicially challenged the Cypriot authorities' application in a national court. It also brought an action for annulment and an application for interim relief against the Commission's measure of publishing the Cypriot application, enabling interested parties across the Union to be able to object before the Commission took a final registration decision.

POA's request for interim relief was dismissed by the CJEU – as was the main action for annulment, a year later.[49] POA had failed to show that the Commission's decision would cause it irreversible harm.[50] However, and just as importantly, the judicial proceedings that POA had launched against the Cypriot authorities were still pending in the national court.

Much like previous rulings of the *Borelli* line of case law, *POA* is worded in a legalistic style, as though it only concerned the enforcement of specific sectoral legislation. Its basic findings may nevertheless apply whenever national authorities exercise decisional dominance. What was innovative in *POA* was that the CJEU for the first time explicitly addressed what the Commission must do if the national court annuls a binding preparatory act. If the national court annuls the national preparatory act (ie the application for the protection of a designation of origin) *before* the Commission takes the final decision, then the Commission should refrain from taking that decision; if the national ruling is delivered *after* the Commission takes the final decision, then Commission should amend or withdraw the decision it has already taken.[51]

The CJEU's reasoning in *POA* largely followed the technical language of the legislative text. It refrained from providing any constitutional justification for its findings in the case. Such constitutional justification, however, was ultimately given in later rulings – explicitly so, in *CRM*, and implicitly so, in *Jeanningros*.

B. *CRM*: Judicial Challenge *and* Annulment of a National Preparatory Act *before* the EU Administration Takes the Final Decision

In the *CRM* case, an application had been submitted to register piadina romagnola, a type of flatbread, with a PGI. The application was approved by a decree of the competent Italian authority. However, after an action for annulment was filed, an Italian lower administrative court judged the application illegal in so far as the definition of piadina romagnola included *industrially produced* varieties.

[49] Given that the contested measure was purely preparatory to the final decision to register the PDO for halloumi, and had no binding legal effects of its own, it could not be considered a reviewable act under Article 263 TFEU. See Case T-584/15 *Pagkyprios organismos ageladotrofon (POA) Dimosia Ltd v European Commission*, ECLI:EU:T:2016:510.

[50] Case T-584/15 R *Pagkyprios organismos ageladotrofon (POA) Dimosia Ltd v European Commission*, ECLI:EU:T:2015:946.

[51] *POA*, n 50, para 36.

Following the advice of the competent Italian authority, which had appealed from the lower court to the *Consiglio di Stato*, the Commission finalised the administrative procedure and registered piadina romagnola with PGI, with EU-wide effects, in the definition approved by the decree. To add to the confusion, after the Commission adopted the final decision, the *Consiglio di Stato* overturned the lower court's ruling.

The key issue that the General Court had to address in *CRM* was what should happen to a Commission decision taken after a national judgment has already annulled the national preparatory acts on which it was supposed to be based.[52] The General Court addressed that issue by framing it as a matter pertaining to two fundamental rights: the right to good administration (including the EU administration's duty of care) and the right to effective judicial protection.

In the General Court's view, the Commission had 'committed a procedural irregularity' by failing to perform a formal check on the preparatory act, as provided by the applicable sectoral legislation. Moreover, the Commission had failed to assess the consequences of the Italian lower administrative court's ruling partly annulling the national preparatory act – namely, by considering that act formally incomplete. The General Court therefore held the Commission to have violated the duty of care.[53] It went on to conclude that

> the fact that the Commission held it was not for it to assess autonomously the consequences of the annulment … by a national court … and that it registered the challenged PGI despite that annulment must be considered as meaning that it irregularly adopted the [national] application for registration and that it ignored its duty to investigate and the principle of good administration.[54]

The General Court highlighted that national courts ought to review binding national preparatory acts *before* they are forwarded to the EU administration.[55] It also acknowledged that it is *primarily* for national administration to draw consequences from a national ruling annulling those acts.[56] However, the General Court also concluded that because such a ruling had already been delivered, 'the Commission could not have considered itself obliged to proceed, despite the wishes expressed in that regard by the national authorities, with the registration procedure'. The Commission adopting the composite procedure's final decision would bear the risk of '*depriving of effectiveness the judicial control at national level* of the national acts forming part of the procedure for the registration of a PGI' (emphasis added).[57] In other words, the fundamental right to effective judicial protection entails an obligation for the Commission to ensure that the national

[52] Case T-43/15 *CRM Srl v European Commission*, ECLI:EU:T:2018:208.
[53] *CRM*, n 52, paras 71 ff.
[54] *CRM*, n 52 para 75.
[55] To make that point, the General Court cites *Bavaria NV*, n 4, para 93.
[56] *CRM*, n 52, para 85.
[57] *CRM*, n 52, para 87.

judicial control of binding national preparatory acts remains fully effective. It must therefore refrain from adopting a final decision based on those preparatory acts.

Despite asserting good administration and effective judicial protection, the CJEU did not annul the Commission's decision. It held that the violation of the rules on formal checks, and of the principles of good administration and effective judicial protection constituted an illegality of a formal nature.[58] The Court applied its usual reasoning according to which the annulment of decisions is only justified if the violation of procedural requirements could affect the substance of the decision.[59] Since in the specific situation of CRM the *Consiglio di Stato* had ultimately overturned the lower court's judgment, the formal illegalities caused by the Commission had no bearing on the validity of its final decision.

C. *Jeanningros*: Judicial Challenge *and* Annulment of a National Preparatory Act *after* the EU Administration Takes the Final Decision

The *Jeanningros* case concerned a minor amendment to the PDO 'Comté', a type of French cheese.[60] The French administration adopted a decree aimed at altering the product specification for Comté so as to ban its production with milk drawn with the help of robotic milkers. Just as in *POA* and *CRM*, the national act – the decree – constituted a step in the composite procedure for registration of a PDO/PGI, where national authorities exercise decisional dominance and the Commission, though taking the final decision, has only 'limited, if any, discretion'.[61]

GAEC Jeanningros, an agricultural cooperative, challenged the French Ministers' decree. However, while the judicial proceedings were still pending before the *Conseil d'État*, the Commission took the final decision, and approved the French decree's amendments to the EU-wide registered PDO 'Comté'. The *Conseil d'État* submitted a preliminary reference to the European Court of Justice. It inquired whether, with the Commission's decision concluding the administrative procedure, the judicial challenge brought against the national preparatory act had now become devoid of purpose or was required by the right to an effective judicial protection to be allowed to proceed. The *Conseil d'État*'s case law had hitherto taken the first view.

Following the *Borelli* case law, and agreeing with the Advocate General, the Court considered that *only* France's courts – not the CJEU – could rule on the legality of binding preparatory acts of the French administration.[62] The Court then concluded that the right to effective judicial protection would be compromised if,

[58] *CRM*, n 52, para 91.
[59] See Chapter 7, section III.B.
[60] Case C-785/18 *Jeanningros*, n 4.
[61] *Jeanningros* n 4, paras 24–25.
[62] *Jeanningros* n 4, paras 28 and 35.

once the Commission had taken the final decision, a national court found there to be no longer any need to adjudicate on an action for annulment against the national preparatory decision.[63] The reason that the Court gave for this was that, because the EU courts cannot review that national preparatory decision, an action before national courts 'is the *only opportunity* for natural or legal persons affected by such a decision to oppose it' (emphasis added).[64]

At this stage, the ECJ had already answered the *Conseil d'État*'s specific preliminary question. However, and much as had occurred in the original *Borelli* ruling almost 30 years earlier, the Advocate General and the ECJ went much further in providing extensive additional guidance for future cases.

As will be recalled, *Borelli* did not merely deny that the CJEU was competent to review binding national preparatory acts adopted in composite procedures – the case requires national courts to review such acts just like any final administrative decisions. *Jeanningros* gave the Court an opportunity to settle an important doubt which had in fact lingered ever since *Borelli*. The doubt concerned what should happen to a final decision *already taken* by the Union administration if the national preparatory act that preceded it is *subsequently* annulled by a national court.

In a previous writing, I took the view that the final decision of the Union administration would have to be considered invalid if its prior national preparatory acts are quashed by a national court. Because in composite procedures the *existence* of a national preparatory act constitutes a 'factual presupposition' without which the final Union decision cannot be legally adopted, the annulment of that national act 'will leave the subsequent EU legal act without an essential presupposition for its valid enactment'.[65] Put differently, it is not the invalidity of the national preparatory act as such, but its *elimination* by a national ruling, that entails the invalidity of the Union administration's final decision. That decision is not invalid due to derivative illegality from the national act (which the substantive *Borelli* principle forbids), but due to a defectiveness of its own. The decision *becomes* invalid because it is retroactively robbed of one of its essential legal requirements once a national court annuls its requisite preparatory acts.

This seems also to have been the view taken by the Court in *Jeanningros*. The Court agreed with the Advocate General,[66] who had proposed that the national court's judgment annulling the national preparatory act generated 'a chain reaction in the form of depriving the Commission's decision of a legal basis'.[67] It is telling that, in this respect, the Court did not rely on its jurisprudence relating to derivative illegality. Rather, the Court of Justice relied on its past case law concerning re-examination of decisions already taken, and that have already become

[63] *Jeanningros* n 4, paras 32–36.
[64] *Jeanningros* n 4, paras 37–38.
[65] F Brito Bastos, n 5, 297.
[66] *Jeanningros*, n 4, para 39.
[67] See the Opinion of AG Campos Sánchez-Bordona in Case 785/18 *GAEC Jeanningros v Institut national de l'origine et de la qualité (INAO)*, ECLI:EU:C:2019:789, para 65.

definitive, due to substantial changes of fact.[68] The implicit argument in the *Jeanningros* ruling, in this respect, is that the illegality and annulment of national binding preparatory acts do not constitute a *question of law* leading to the illegality of final decisions taken by Union administration, but a question of *fact* and more specifically of material changes in factual circumstances that justify withdrawing a previous decision.

Nevertheless, the Court's and the Advocate General's view, that a final EU decision becomes illegal once its binding national preparatory act is annulled by a national court, still left open the question of *how* that illegality could be reviewed. Like von Danwitz and Keessen before me,[69] I had assumed until *Jeanningros* that individuals would need to lodge actions for annulment, first, against the national preparatory act and subsequently, if that action was successful, against the final decision taken at Union level. In fact, I criticised this unfortunate duplication of annulment proceedings as the weakest aspect of the *Borelli* doctrine from the point of view of effective judicial protection.[70] Separating judicial review of national and of Union contributions to a composite procedure would, however, be in line with double exclusivity, ie the principle according to which only national courts may review national acts, and only Union courts may review Union acts.[71]

However, it would have been impossible to anticipate the Court's surprising and innovative solution to this issue in *Jeanningros*. The Court held that the annulment of the national preparatory act by a national court must entail 'a review of the case by the Commission'.[72] While not as detailed in its reasoning, the Court of Justice agreed with the conclusion supported in the Opinion delivered by Advocate General Campos Sánchez-Bordona. Just as in the General Court's *CRM* ruling, the Commission had to be obliged to give full effect to the national judgment by virtue of the fundamental rights to effective judicial protection and to good administration.[73] There was, however, a crucial difference from *CRM*. Under *CRM*, giving full effect to a national judgment annulling a preparatory act meant

[68] The Court cites Joined Cases C-454/16 P to C-456/16 P and C-458/16 P *Global Steel Wire SA v European Commission*, ECLI:EU:C:2017:818, para 31. That ruling makes reference to the *Inpesca* case law, which in essence repeats 'settled case law that the existence of substantial new facts may justify the submission of a request for reconsideration of a previous decision which has become definitive' (see Case T-186/98 *Compañía Internacional de Pesca y Derivados (Inpesca) v European Commission*, ECLI:EU:T:2001:42, paras 47–48 and judgments cited there).

[69] See A Keessen, *European Administrative Decisions: how the EU regulates products on the internal market* (Europa Law Publishing, 2009), 137 and T von Danwitz, *Europäisches Verwaltungsrecht* (Springer, 2008), 644.

[70] F Brito Bastos, n 5, 297.

[71] This was noted in Chapter 7, section III.A.

[72] *Jeanningros*, n 4, para 39.

[73] See the Opinion of AG Campos Sánchez-Bordona, n 67, paras 66–67. The Advocate General also suggested (at para 68) that these two fundamental rights should also be interpreted to mean that *national authorities* must not forward their binding preparatory acts in PDO procedures to the Commission in the first place if those acts are under pending judicial scrutiny and, a fortiori, if a national court has already annulled them. The Court of Justice's ruling, however, did not address these scenarios.

that the Commission must *refrain from taking* a decision. Under *Jeanningros*, giving such full effect means that the Commission must review a decision that it has *already taken*.[74]

D. The Discreet Demise of 'Strict Separation' and the Birth of a New Procedural Right

The original *Borelli* ruling left many questions open. One of them was the implications of national courts' judicial review of national preparatory acts for the final decision taken at Union level. Together, *POA*, *CRM* and *Jeanningros* finally provide an answer to that question. The answer depends on the exact moments in time when the national ruling is delivered, and when the final Union decision is adopted. The answer heavily relies on deploying the fundamental right to good administration, as enshrined in Article 41 of the Charter, as a constitutional justification for binding the Union administration to observe national rulings. In so doing, the recent completion of the *Borelli* doctrine shows how willing the CJEU is to abandon old dogma so that judicial protection in composite decision-making is ensured.

Before the triad of cases, one could have interpreted *Borelli* very differently. The ruling could have suggested that the CJEU was unwilling to abandon the view of a strict jurisdictional divide between national and Union courts. Indeed, one renowned commentator even wrote in this regard that *Borelli* 'amounts to an artificial splitting up of a unitary procedure solely for the purpose of judicial protection before the national courts'.[75]

In my doctoral dissertation, in fact, my reading was that the jurisdictional *Borelli* principle represented a rare instance where, in the domain of composite decision-making, the CJEU had not distanced itself significantly from European Executive Federalism. My reading was that *Borelli* merely reflected an interpretive choice favouring a rigid jurisdictional divide and requiring actions for annulment to be brought successively against national and Union authorities.[76] The CJEU's inventiveness since then has proved that reading – one also shared by others – wrong.

[74] While it did clarify the implications of national review under *Borelli* for Union decisions already taken, *Jeanningros* also left open new, important questions. One concerns how to reconcile the relatively short, two-month deadline for bringing actions for annulment against Union decisions with the host of different deadlines found in national laws for lodging actions for annulment (which, depending on the severity of the illegalities affecting the national acts, may even be indefinite). In this regard, see F Brito Bastos, 'Judicial Annulment of National Preparatory Acts and the Effects on Final Union Administrative Decisions: Comments on the Judgment of 29 January 2020, Case C-785/18 *Jeanningros*, ECLI:EU:C:2020:46' (2021) 14 *Review of European Administrative Law* 109.

[75] HP Nehl, *Principles of Administrative Procedure in EC Law* (Hart Publishing, 1999), 90.

[76] It will be recalled that such a duplication of proceedings, which would be in line with a rigid understanding of double exclusivity, already exists in cases of shared liability between national and Union administration. See Chapter 7, section III.A.(i).

Even semantically, the *Borelli* doctrine seemed to reflect a view of the strict separation between national and Union administrative power so central to European Executive Federalism. On multiple occasions, the CJEU has stated that *Borelli* was meant for cases where Union legislation aims 'to establish a division between two powers, one national and the other of the Community'.[77] One should, however, also note that other language versions, for instance French, prefer terms closer to 'distribution' ('*repartition*') or 'sharing' ('*partage*') of competences, rather than terms which, like 'division', suggest some separation.

Most importantly, however, for all the talk of 'divided powers', the CJEU's *Borelli* doctrine does not *treat* national and Union decision-making as though they were wholly separate and detached from one another. Rather, composite procedures must be handled as a unified whole – as a single decision-making process where national and Union administration decide interdependently even if one of the two will always be dominant.

Whenever it enjoys such dominance, the *Borelli* doctrine requires judicial review to be conducted against the national administration. Indeed, in predominantly national administrative procedures – procedures where national bodies play a critical role and where, whenever Union legislation is silent, national laws apply – national courts are, comparatively, best placed to ensure judicial control. That is the ingenuity of *Borelli*. *Borelli* mobilises the jurisdiction of national courts so that they offer much more extensive judicial protection than the Union courts, constitutionally barred from enforcing national law and reviewing national acts, ever could. *Borelli*, in its current form, abandons the rigidity and formalism of double exclusivity by subjecting the entirety of the composite procedure – both national and Union stages – to a single exercise of judicial review by national courts.

The use that the CJEU recently found for the fundamental right to good administration was the missing link in *Borelli*. It is now the key to ensuring that judicial national judicial control is effective throughout the composite procedure's national and Union-level stages.

When the Charter became binding law after the Treaty of Lisbon, legal scholars debated whether Article 41, the provision which enshrined the right to good administration, merely listed pre-existing rights or whether it its open-ended texture made the development of new such rights possible.[78] The *CRM* and *Jeanningros* rulings now illustrate how the latter reading has proved more accurate. Both rulings have provided the Court of Justice with an opportunity to discover a novel, unwritten requirement which, by definition, can only apply within composite decision-making. That requirement can be termed as (the Union administration's) 'duty to observe national judgments'.

The Union administration is under an obligation to implement national judgments annulling national preparatory acts regardless of whether such judgments are delivered *before* (*CRM*) or *after* (*Jeanningros*) the final decision. If the national

[77] Case C-64/05 P *Sweden v Commission*, ECLI:EU:C:2007:802, para 93.
[78] For this discussion, see Chapter 4, section II.

judgment on the national preparatory act is delivered *before* the final Union decision, the Union administration is required under *CRM* to *refrain* from adopting the final decision; if that judgment is delivered *after* the final Union decision has been taken, the Union administration must revoke that decision under *Jeanningros*.

By introducing a duty of the Union administration to respect national judgments, the CJEU ensured the effectiveness of judicial control at the national level. On the one hand, this ensures the subjective purpose of judicial control, ie, respect for the fundamental right to effective judicial protection – the same right that had already justified, decades earlier, the in itself novel *Borelli* requirement of self-standing review of national preparatory acts. On the other hand, the objective purpose of judicial control is also safeguarded. Given that there is no derivative illegality under *Borelli*, if it were not obliged to review its final decisions as a result of national judgments, the Commission would render an illegal preparatory act binding 'throughout the Union despite its annulment in the legal order from whence it came'.[79]

Crucially, the case law fine-tuning the *Borelli* doctrine since 2015 also implies that, even though it is not subject to the jurisdiction of national courts, the EU administration is indirectly bound by their judgments, by virtue of the fundamental right to good administration. It is also required to assist the national administration in respecting national judgments. In combination, these developments imply that, under *Borelli*, the CJEU no longer clings to the old dogmas of strict separation between national and Union judicial review, and of strict separation between national and Union administration.

VI. National Dominance and Union Duties in Administrative Procedure

Perhaps because *Borelli* lacks any equivalent in other instances of administrative decision-making under Union law, academic commentary has largely remained critical.[80] The ruling tends to be depicted as symptomatic of the Court of Justice's inability to ensure adequate judicial protection in composite decision-making. It is hoped that this chapter made a sufficiently clear case for the opposite reading.

The *Borelli* case law in fact represented two waves of significant innovation in EU administrative law. First, according to the original *Borelli* ruling, the CJEU must refrain from reviewing binding national preparatory acts and refer such review to the national courts (the jurisdictional *Borelli* principle). The illegality of said preparatory acts is irrelevant for the final Union decision (the substantive

[79] *CRM*, n 52, para 60. The applicant in *CRM* was right to imply this risk – a risk that is also valid in the *Jeanningros* scenario.

[80] See eg S Alonso de León, *Composite Administrative Procedures in the European Union* (Iustel, 2017), 275–76.

Borelli principle). Second, the period of 2015–20 saw a triad of judgments (*POA*, *CRM*, and *Jeanningros*) that addressed one of the critical loose ends of the *Borelli* doctrine, namely the chronological relation between the final Union decision and the requirement of national courts to review binding preparatory acts. There is no doubt that difficult open questions remain, such as issues concerning deadlines for the annulment of national preparatory acts when the final Union decision has already been taken.[81]

It will be conceded that the *Borelli* doctrine may appear counter-intuitive and perhaps even far-fetched. Administrative procedures are typically reviewed only once a final decision is taken, as that is the moment when the administration's final will on a case is declared. However, *Borelli* illustrates how the CJEU recognised composite decision-making to differ profoundly from any traditional dual divide between national and Union administrative decision-making, and that that difference required novel principles upon judicial review. In crafting those principles, the CJEU had to reconcile the limits of its own jurisdiction and the autonomy of Union law, on the one hand, and rule of law requirements of judicial control, on the other.

In fact, both the original *Borelli* ruling and its subsequent developments show that the CJEU was willing to go much further than addressing only those issues that were directly raised in each of the specific cases that were brought to it. The CJEU did not merely dismiss Borelli's actions for annulment. It left clear instructions for national courts as to how to proceed in cases involving similar composite procedures. The CJEU did not merely reply to the French *Conseil d'État* in *Jeanningros* that its practice of rejecting annulment claims against binding national preparatory acts after final Union-level decisions violated the right to effective judicial protection. It explained in detail how the Commission should respond to national annulment rulings and why.

Even though *Borelli* could prima facie suggest an artificial 'severing in half' of composite procedures, more recent developments show that it actually relies on an implicit principle of unitary judicial protection. Indeed, in order to fully prevent gaps in judicial protection that could result from the multilevel structure of the administrative procedure, the CJEU also extracted a new procedural right from the fundamental right to good administration. According to that right, the Union administration must give full effect to national courts' judgments annulling national preparatory acts. Such a right is irreconcilable with the core doctrinal tenets of European Executive Federalism, which regards national and Union administration as forming strictly separate spheres.

[81] See F Brito Bastos, n 74.

9

The *Berlusconi* Doctrine

I. Introduction: *Berlusconi*, Culmination and Codification

Chapter eight considered the judicial development of the *Borelli* doctrine. The twin principles of *Borelli*, jurisdictional and substantive, apply in composite procedures where national administration exercises decisional dominance. Decision-making powers, however, tend to be overwhelmingly distributed in the inverse manner, with decisional dominance pertaining to the Union administration.

And yet, the CJEU took almost three decades after *Borelli* to finally develop an explicit doctrine for cases of Union decisional dominance. That doctrine finally emerged in December 2018, with the *Berlusconi* ruling.[1]

Borelli marked the *beginning* of a line of case law on the review of composite procedures with national decisional dominance. *Berlusconi*, by contrast, largely consolidated the essential aspects of the approach that the CJEU had been gradually developing for decades, albeit in an extremely fragmented fashion.[2] Decisional dominance determines which courts are responsible for judicial review. Much as in *Borelli* national decisional dominance means judicial review by national courts, in *Berlusconi* Union decisional dominance means judicial review by Union courts.

Despite its continuity with previous rulings, it is hard to disagree with the characterisation of *Berlusconi* as a 'milestone' in the case law on composite decision-making.[3] Besides consolidating such case law, *Berlusconi* partly innovated in one, fundamental respect. It confirmed the view of some of the literature that, outside of the scope of *Borelli*, national courts are not only not required to review, but are forbidden from reviewing, national preparatory stages of composite procedures.[4]

[1] Case C-97/91 *Oleificio Borelli SpA v European Commission*, ECLI:EU:C:1992:491; Case C-219/17 *Berlusconi and Finanziaria d'investimento Fininvest SpA (Fininvest) v Banca d'Italia*, ECLI:EU:C:2018:1023.

[2] Similarly, M Eliantonio and P Dermine, 'Case Note: CJEU (Grand Chamber), Judgment of 19 December 2018, C-219/17, Silvio Berlusconi and Finanziaria d'investimento Fininvest SpA (Fininvest) v Banca d'Italia and Istituto per la Vigilanza Sulle Assicurazioni' (2019) 12 *Review of European Administrative Law* 237, 245.

[3] Opinion of AG Campos Sánchez-Bordona in Case C-219/17 *Berlusconi and Finanziaria d'investimento Fininvest SpA (Fininvest) v Banca d'Italia*, ECLI:EU:C:2018:502, para 59.

[4] F Brito Bastos, 'Derivative illegality in European composite administrative procedures' (2018) 55 *Common Market Law Review* 101, 134.

The present chapter will begin by considering the facts and findings of the *Berlusconi* judgment in section II. Like *Borelli*, *Berlusconi* can be described as a doctrine entailing both a jurisdictional principle – on the allocation of competence for judicial review – and a substantive principle – on the admissible reasons for the invalidity of final Union decisions. Both are implicitly based on the same overarching principle as *Borelli*, the principle of unitary judicial protection – ie of a single judicial review for national and Union decision-making – albeit with the opposite implications. Section III examines the jurisdictional *Berlusconi* principle, according to which a composite procedure in which Union administration exercises decisional dominance may only be reviewed by Union courts. Section IV examines the substantive *Berlusconi* principle. The principle accepts derivative illegality, though the case law preceding *Berlusconi* suggests that this is subject to multiple constitutional limits. Section V highlights the major weakness of the *Berlusconi* doctrine – a sort of rule of law blind-spot. The doctrine makes it possible for the violation of national law in composite decision-making to go without any kind of judicial control. Section VI concludes by summarising the chapter's findings and considering the broader implications of the *Berlusconi* doctrine.

II. The *Berlusconi* Ruling: Facts and Findings

The *Berlusconi* ruling (also called the *Berlusconi & Fininvest* ruling) concerned a qualifying holding held by Silvio Berlusconi. A qualifying holding comprises 'a direct or indirect holding in an undertaking which represents 10% or more of the capital or of the voting rights or which makes it possible to exercise a significant influence over the management of that undertaking'.[5] Such 'significant influence' makes it highly desirable for holders to fulfil essential requirements of financial expertise, experience, and good repute. To ensure ex ante control of such requirements, the acquisition and increase of qualifying holdings presupposes the granting of a prior authorisation by the competent banking supervision authority.[6]

After he was convicted for tax fraud, the Italian banking supervision administration held that Silvio Berlusconi no longer fulfilled the good reputation

[5] See Articles 2(8) of Council Regulation (EU) No 1024/2013 of 15 October 2013 conferring specific tasks on the European Central Bank concerning policies relating to the prudential supervision of credit institutions (Single Supervisory Mechanism Regulation, henceforth SSMR) and 4(1) of Regulation (EU) No 468/2014 of the European Central Bank of 16 April 2014 establishing the framework for cooperation within the Single Supervisory Mechanism between the European Central Bank and national competent authorities and with national designated authorities (SSM Framework Regulation, henceforth SSMFR).

[6] See Article 23 of Directive of the European Parliament and of the Council of 26 June 2013 on access to the activity of credit institutions and the prudential supervision of credit institutions and investment firms, also known as the Capital Requirements Directive IV (CRD IV).

requirement. This led to a number of procedures examining whether Fininvest, a bank controlled by Berlusconi, could own qualifying holdings credit institutions, namely in Banca Mediolanum.

In 2015, the Bank of Italy (Banca d'Italia) initiated the procedure established in Article 15 SSMR and further elaborated by the ECB itself in Articles 85 to 87 SSMFR. The provisions establish a composite, two-step administrative procedure. First, a national banking supervision authority assesses whether the acquisition of a particular qualifying holding meets the applicable substantive requirements. The national banking supervision authority then proposes to the ECB, as the case may be, that the latter should adopt the final decision of the procedure by opposing or not opposing the qualifying holding. The ECB exercises decisional dominance: it is entirely free to make its own independent assessment of the case, and legally empowered to decide differently from the national supervision authority's proposal.

Having considered that Mr Berlusconi and Fininvest lacked the requisite good reputation, the Bank of Italy drafted a preparatory act proposing to the ECB that it oppose the acquisition of that qualifying holding. The ECB agreed with the Bank of Italy, and took the final decision accordingly.

Besides bringing actions for annulment against the ECB's decision before the General Court,[7] Mr Berlusconi and Fininvest lodged actions against the preparatory acts of the Bank of Italy in national courts. Ultimately, the *Consiglio di Stato*, deciding in last instance, referred the case to the Court for a preliminary ruling to clarify which courts, the Union's or Italy's, were competent to review the preparatory acts adopted by the national banking supervision authorities.

In its reply, the Court of Justice broadly followed the Advocate General's views. Campos Sánchez-Bordona explicitly characterised the review of qualifying holdings as a composite procedure – the first time that the term had appeared in an Advocate General's Opinion. He further noted that such procedures 'are not new in EU law', but instead had long existed in areas 'such as structural funds, agriculture, and the appointment of members of the European parliament'.[8]

The Advocate General held that the CJEU should answer the preliminary reference by considering previous rulings which, though on a rather fragmentary, 'case-by-case and non-exhaustive basis', addressed the difficulties of judicial review in composite decision-making.[9] The Advocate General therefore considered that the answer to the main issue raised by the *Consiglio di Stato* could only be given after considering the case law on composite procedures *and* analysing the legal

[7] The action for annulment led to the General Court's ruling in Case T-913/16 *Finanziaria d'investimento Fininvest SpA (Fininvest) and Silvio Berlusconi v European Central Bank*, ECLI:EU:T:2022:279, which upheld the ECB's decision.

[8] See the Opinion of AG Campos Sánchez-Bordona in *Berlusconi*, n 3, paras 3 and 57–58.

[9] Opinion of AG Campos Sánchez-Bordona in *Berlusconi*, n 3, paras 56–59.

provisions governing the concrete administrative procedure that the Bank of Italy and the ECB had followed in the case.

The ECJ's Grand Chamber agreed that past case law since *Borelli* had differentiated between two kinds of situations. Some administrative procedures, the Court of Justice recalled, involve a division of power between national and Union authorities, whereby the former adopt preparatory acts that leave the latter with no discretion when making the final decision. In other administrative procedures, however, national authorities adopt preparatory acts, but it is the Union administration which enjoys 'an exclusive decision-making power' when making the final decision.[10] The Court of Justice held that the ECB's decisions on qualifying holdings are adopted pursuant to such a procedure.[11] In such administrative procedures, judicial review had to be carried out in fundamentally differently terms from those of *Borelli*.

Borelli had established a jurisdictional principle for cases of national decisional dominance. The jurisdictional *Borelli* principle requires national courts to review – and forbids the CJEU from reviewing – binding national preparatory acts. *Berlusconi* establishes the opposite jurisdictional principle for cases of Union decisional dominance. The jurisdictional *Berlusconi* principle accords the CJEU *exclusive* jurisdiction to review not only the final Union decision, but the non-binding national preparatory acts which preceded it. National courts are forbidden from reviewing said preparatory acts.

Borelli also established a substantive principle concerning not the division of judicial competence as such, but the validity of final Union decisions. According to the substantive *Borelli* principle, Union decisions are categorically immune to derivative illegality: their validity is *never* affected by the illegality of binding national preparatory acts. Again, *Berlusconi* establishes the opposite substantive principle. Final Union decisions *can* be invalid on grounds of derivative illegality, that is, if the non-binding national preparatory acts which precede them are illegal themselves.

Neither the jurisdictional nor the substantive *Berlusconi* principle emerged overnight. Except for its explicit prohibition on national courts reviewing preparatory acts, which was truly innovative and required a novel justification under EU constitutional law, *Berlusconi* largely restates previously implicit case law. It must be read in the context of that case law. The table below outlines the *Borelli* and *Berlusconi* doctrines and the following sections illustrate the antecedents and constitutional basis for the *Berlusconi* doctrine's two principles.

[10] *Berlusconi*, n 1, para 44.
[11] *Berlusconi*, n 1, para 57.

	National courts	**CJEU**	**Validity of final decision of EU administration**
Borelli doctrine Applies if a national preparatory act (a) is part of an EU administrative procedure (b) is binding on the EU decision-taking authority and therefore determines the terms of the EU-level decision to be adopted (ie national decisional dominance)	National courts *must* accept the review of the national preparatory act, 'on the same terms on which they review any definitive measure adopted by the same national authority' *specific to composite procedures*	CJEU *must not* review the preparatory act as part of the review of the final decision taken by an EU authority. *specific to composite procedures*	The illegality of the national preparatory act is irrelevant for the validity of the final EU-level decision. (ie no derivative illegality) *specific to composite procedures*
	Jurisdictional *Borelli* principle		Substantive *Borelli* principle
Berlusconi doctrine Applies if a national preparatory act (a) is part of an EU administrative procedure (b) is *not* binding on the EU decision-taking authority, and *does not* determine the terms of the EU-level decision to be adopted (ie Union decisional dominance)	National courts *must not* review the national preparatory act (implicit in previous case law, but only made explicit in *Berlusconi & Fininvest*) *specific to composite procedures*	CJEU *may* review the preparatory act as part of the review of the final decision taken by an EU authority. *specific to composite procedures* (implicit in previous case law, such as *Sweden v Commission* and *Association Greenpeace France*)	The illegality of the national preparatory act may lead to the invalidity of the final EU-level decision. (ie derivative illegality is possible) *specific to composite procedures*
	Jurisdictional *Berlusconi* principle		Substantive *Berlusconi* principle

III. The Jurisdictional *Berlusconi* Principle

Long before *Berlusconi* the EU courts had reviewed decisions taken by the Union administration in composite procedures where it enjoyed decisional dominance. *Branco*, *Sweden v Commission*, and *Acino* are just three examples from among many.

In *Branco*, the Commission had adopted a decision reducing financial support from the European Social Fund, on the grounds that some of Branco Ltª's expenditure was ineligible for funding. According to the relevant procedure, such decisions are taken based on non-binding preparatory acts by which national authorities propose reduction, withdrawal, or suspension of funding. Once the Commission decides, the national authority is obliged to implement that decision. As it exercised decisional dominance, the Commission was wrong to claim that Branco should only have enjoyed judicial protection against flawed decisions of the national Portuguese authority.[12] In the case law of the CJEU – and of Portuguese courts – only the Commission's decisions reducing funding – and not the national authority's proposals – are considered amenable to judicial review.[13]

In *Sweden v Commission*, the CJEU grappled with similar doubts on judicial review. The case concerned an administrative procedure governing requests for access to documents that are in the possession of a Union body, but which originate in a Member State.

The structure of the procedure has already been explained in Chapter six, in regard to what was described as the rule of replicability of reasons. The rather confusing wording of Article 4(5) of Regulation No 1049/2001 states that the Member State may 'request' that a document is not released without its 'prior agreement'. Due to its equivocal formulation, the provision is subject to different interpretations. The General Court in *Sweden* v *Commission* originally interpreted the provision as enshrining national decisional dominance. It concluded that the Member States' acts of opposition constituted a binding 'instruction' which vetoed disclosure of documents by a Union body.[14] Advocate General Maduro, by contrast, interpreted the provision as enshrining the decisional dominance of the Union administration. Following this view, the ECJ came to consider that it is ultimately for the EU body in possession of the document to decide whether the legal conditions for withholding information are satisfied and reconsider the position taken by the national authorities.[15] Accordingly, it was for Union courts

[12] Case T-85/94 *Eugénio Branco, Ldª v European Commission (Branco I)*, ECLI:EU:T:1995:4, para 18.

[13] Portuguese administrative courts have considered national preparatory acts certifying expenses as merely 'instrumental' acts which do not 'bind or pre-empt the final decision that is exclusively enacted by the Commission'. See the Judgments of the Portuguese Supremo Tribunal Administrativo (Supreme Administrative Court) STA 26 September 2002 (Rapporteur: Isabel Jovita), 7 May 2003 (Rapporteur: Isabel Jovita), 29 June 2004 (Rapporteur: António Madureira), and 12 March 2009 (Rapporteur: Pais Borges).

[14] Case T-168/02 *IFAW Internationaler Tierschutz-Fonds gGmbH (IFAW I) v European Commission*, ECLI:EU:T:2004:346, para 58.

[15] See the Opinion of AG Poiares Maduro in Case C-64/05 P *Sweden v Commission*, ECLI:EU:C:2007:433 and Case C-64/05 P *Sweden v Commission*, ECLI:EU:C:2007:802. See also Cases T-250/08 *Batchelor v European Commission*, ECLI:EU:T:2011:236, para 45; C-135/11 P *IFAW Internationaler Tierschutz-Fonds v European Commission (IFAW III)*, ECLI:EU:C:2012:376, paras 57–58; T-603/11 *Ecologistas en Acción-CODA v European Commission*, ECLI:EU:T:2014:182, para 36; T-669/11 *Spirlea v European Commission*, ECLI:EU:T:2014:814, para 53.

to review both a Union decision denying access to documents *and* the national act of objection to disclosure which led to that decision. Indeed, the raising of such an objection could not call into question the CJEU's jurisdiction since,

> from the point of view of the person concerned, the Member State's intervention does not affect the [Union] nature of the decision that is subsequently addressed to him by the institution in reply to the request he has made for access to a document in its possession.[16]

In *Acino*, the CJEU was requested to review a Commission decision, taken after a national authority's report and in consultation with the European Medicines Agency, that prohibited the marketing of a several drugs containing an antiplatelet active substance, Clopidogrel, manufactured in India.[17] The relevant administrative procedure makes it possible for national pharmaceutical regulation authorities to propose the adoption of certain measures to the Commission, in liaison with the European Medicines Agency, if they consider that a manufacturer no longer fulfils regulatory requirements.[18] As decisional dominance lay with the Commission – and not with the national authority – the CJEU seems to have considered its own jurisdiction to review the decision to be too self-evident to discuss.[19]

In short, by the time the Court of Justice was requested to rule on the preliminary reference of the *Consiglio di Stato* in *Berlusconi*, it could already draw on decades of accumulated case law. While it could have modelled a solution for the review of the qualifying holdings approval procedure on many previous judgments, the Court, like the Advocate General, chose *Sweden v Commission* as the leading case.

The Court recalled the assertion in *Sweden v Commission* according to which the prior involvement of national authorities does not change the Union nature of final decisions taken by the Union administration. Hence, it concluded, the acts adopted by national authorities within the administrative procedure in *Berlusconi* 'constitute a stage of a procedure in which an EU institution exercises, alone, the final decision-making power without being bound by the preparatory acts or the proposals of the national authorities'.[20] In procedures where a Union authority holds 'exclusive decision-making power', it is for EU courts, 'by virtue of their exclusive jurisdiction to review the legality of EU acts on the basis of Article 263 TFEU', to rule on the legality of that authority's final decision.[21]

[16] *Sweden v Commission*, n 15, para 94.

[17] Case C-269/13 P *Acino AG v European Commission*, ECLI:EU:C:2014:255. See also Case C-361/14 P *European Commission v McBride*, ECLI:EU:C:2016:434.

[18] Article 20 of Regulation (EC) No 726/2004 of the European Parliament and of the Council of 31 March 2004 laying down Community procedures for the authorisation and supervision of medicinal products for human and veterinary use and establishing a European Medicines Agency.

[19] Recent case law similarly shows that the CJEU's jurisdiction is not even questioned in cases involving composite procedures where the Union administration, exercising decisional dominance, has the power to designate national authorities as rapporteurs of the final decision it will take, eg in area of pesticides regulation. See Case T-629/20 *Delifruit SA v European Commission*, ECLI:EU:T:2022:448.

[20] *Berlusconi*, n 1, para 43.

[21] *Berlusconi*, n 1, para 44.

The key passage of the ruling then follows: the CJEU's jurisdiction in such cases extends to examining 'any defects vitiating the preparatory acts or the proposals of the national authorities that would be such as to affect the validity of that final decision'.[22] The need for Union courts to review such national preparatory acts, the Court found, resulted from the fundamental right of the persons concerned to effective judicial protection.[23]

However, the Court of Justice went further than merely ascribing the Union Courts jurisdiction to review non-binding national preparatory acts. It also explained why such acts *should not* be reviewed by domestic courts. On this point, the Court arrived at the same conclusion as the Advocate General, but based on a different line of reasoning. The Advocate General had argued that the ECJ's case law refusing judicial review of *acts of EU authorities* that are purely preparatory, without external legal effects of their own, could be 'extrapolated' – ie extended – to decision-making procedures where the preparatory acts are taken by *national authorities*. In other words, Advocate General Campos Sánchez-Bordona argued that the (non-binding) preparatory acts of national authorities should be subject to the same line of reasoning as that found in the *IBM* case law.[24] CJEU case law opposes judicial challenges to preparatory acts which merely pave the way for a final decision because such challenges would anticipate review of a procedural stage where the administration has not yet even had the opportunity to form an opinion as to how it will decide.

If pre-emptively reviewing an administrative procedure's purely preparatory acts constitutes an inadmissible interference by the Union courts in the sphere of the Union administration, then it makes no difference if such acts are adopted by Union bodies (the situation considered in the *IBM* case law) or by the national administration. This had also been my own view on the issue before the *Berlusconi* judgment.[25]

By contrast, the Court's reasoning did not rely on the *IBM* case law or its possible adaptations. Rather, it relied on two distinct arguments.

First, the Court held that Article 263 TFEU had to be interpreted in light of the general principle of loyal cooperation enshrined in Article 4(3) TEU. It considered that where the EU legislature decides to create 'an administrative procedure under which the national authorities adopt acts that are preparatory to a final decision of an EU institution', it 'seeks to establish between the EU institution and the national authorities a specific cooperation mechanism which is based on the exclusive decision-making power of the EU institution'.[26] Anticipating the judicial

[22] *Berlusconi*, n 1, para 44.

[23] *Berlusconi*, n 1, para 44.

[24] Besides Case 60/81 *International Business Machines Corporation (IBM) v European Commission*, ECLI:EU:C:1981:264, see Cases T-64/89 *Automec Srl v European Commission*, ECLI:EU:T:1990:42, para 46 and T-41/16 *Cyprus Turkish Chamber of Industry v European Commission*, ECLI:EU:T:2016:613, para 42.

[25] F Brito Bastos (n 4), 110 and 134.

[26] *Berlusconi*, n 1, para 47–48.

review of the composite procedure at national level would deprive the Court of the chance to exercise its exclusive jurisdiction to review the final decision of the ECB – or any other EU authority – in particular when it follows the advice in national preparatory acts.[27]

Second, the Court of Justice reasoned that for an administrative procedure of this kind to be effective, 'there must necessarily be a single judicial review'.[28] If it were possible to challenge judicially the preparatory acts or proposals of Member State authorities before national courts, alongside judicial challenges against the final decision by the EU authority,

> the risk of divergent assessments in *one and the same procedure* would not be ruled out and, therefore, the Court's exclusive jurisdiction to rule on the legality of that final decision could be compromised, in particular where the EU institution's decision follows the analysis and the proposal of those authorities (emphasis added).[29]

For the Court, two issues are clearly of significant importance: first, the unity of the administrative procedure, despite its division into national and Union stages, which requires it to be subject to a unitary judicial review; and second, the location of decisional dominance at the Union level, which requires, in contrast to *Borelli*, that such unitary judicial review be conducted by Union, not national courts.[30]

In December 2019, just a year after *Berlusconi*, the Court of Justice delivered its ruling in *Iccrea*.[31] The ruling proved to be an opportunity for the Court of Justice to apply the *Berlusconi* doctrine, and to restate it more forcefully in a case outside the scope of the Single Supervisory Mechanism.[32] *Iccrea* concerned the judicial review of decisions of the Single Resolution Board (SRB) that define annual the ex ante contributions which credit institutions must pay into the Single Resolution Fund. Said contributions are calculated by the SRB based on the data collected by national resolution authorities, which provide it with preparatory and operational support. Once the SRB has made the decision on the levies due from each credit institution, the national resolution authorities notify those institutions.

Iccrea Banca brought an action against the notification it received from the Italian resolution authority, the Bank of Italy, of the SRB decisions determining Iccrea's ex-ante contributions owed to the SRF for the year of 2016. The Italian

[27] *Berlusconi*, n 1, para 50.

[28] *Berlusconi*, n 1, para 49.

[29] *Berlusconi*, n 1, para 50.

[30] *Berlusconi*, n 1, para 45–46.

[31] Case C-414/18 *Iccrea Banca SpA Istituto Centrale del Credito Cooperativo v Banca d'Italia*, ECLI:EU:C:2019:1036. For an insightful case note on the implications of *Iccrea* and its continuity with *Berlusconi*, see M Markakis, 'Composite Procedures and Judicial Review in the Single Resolution Mechanism: Iccrea Banca' (2021) 13 *Review of European Administrative Law* 109.

[32] It should be stressed, however, that the CJEU delivered further judgments within the domain of the Single Supervisory Mechanism where it restated the jurisdictional and substantive aspects of the *Berlusconi* doctrine. See eg Cases T-351/18 and T-584/18 *Ukrselhosprom PCF LLC v European Central Bank*, ECLI:EU:T:2021:669, para 223; T-230/20 *PNB Banka AS v European Central Bank*, ECLI:EU:T:2022:782, para 73; and T-72/20 *Satabank plc v European Central Bank*, ECLI:EU:T:2023:149, paras 71–72.

court referred the case for a preliminary ruling on the validity of the SRB's decisions. Even though the Court of Justice held the reference to be inadmissible, it unequivocally reaffirmed the *Berlusconi* case law.

The Court of Justice considered Union courts to have exclusive jurisdiction to review the *entirety* of the administrative procedure, *including* the national preparatory measures collecting the relevant data for the SRB's calculations. Making abundant references to what it had previously decided in *Berlusconi*, the Court of Justice again emphasised the implications of Union decisional dominance, the unity of the administrative procedure, and the concomitant need for unitary judicial control.

In the key passages of the judgment, the Court of Justice began by recognising that 'the Board exclusively exercises the final decision-making power'.[33] As 'the role of the national resolution authorities is confined … to providing operational support to the Board' – the preparatory findings that those authorities may make 'cannot in any way be binding on the Board'.[34] The Court had therefore established that decisional dominance was located at the Union level.

'Consequently', the ruling continued,

> the EU Courts alone have jurisdiction to determine, when reviewing the legality of a decision of the Board setting the amount of the individual ex ante contribution to the SRF of an institution, whether an act adopted by a national resolution authority that is preparatory of such a decision is vitiated by defects capable of affecting that decision of the Board, and no national court can review that national act.[35]

The Court, in short, applied the jurisdictional *Berlusconi* principle. In extending that principle to the domain of the Single Resolution Mechanism, the Court of Justice relied on the same reasoning as in *Berlusconi*. Given that ex ante contributions were defined within a unitary composite procedure – 'in one and the same procedure' – the requirement of unitary judicial protection – 'the concept of a single judicial review' – could not be undermined.[36]

IV. The Substantive *Berlusconi* Principle: Conditional Derivative Illegality

When recognising that it could indirectly review national preparatory acts as part of a challenge to final Union decisions, the CJEU did not only address a question of jurisdiction. Rather than simply clarifying which court had the jurisdiction to review such acts, *Berlusconi* also entails a substantive dimension. It implies, as the

[33] *Iccrea*, n 31, para 47.
[34] Ibid.
[35] Ibid, para 48.
[36] Ibid, para 53.

Advocate General put it, that the defectiveness of national preparatory acts may 'contaminate the entire procedure'.[37]

The *Berlusconi* doctrine holds that the CJEU has jurisdiction

> to examine, in order to ensure effective judicial protection of the persons concerned, *any defects vitiating the preparatory acts or the proposals of the national authorities that would be such as to affect the validity of that final decision* (emphasis added).[38]

The statement explicitly recognises that Union decisions may be invalid on grounds of *derivative illegality*, ie invalid because they are based on illegal national preparatory acts.

The Union courts had implicitly accepted that such illegality could occur in composite administrative procedures, either in abstract or in specific cases, for many decades before *Berlusconi*. Crucially, derivative illegality was always reserved for instances where – unlike the *Borelli* scenario – the Union administration enjoyed decisional dominance and could therefore decide differently from the preparatory acts received from national authorities.

The *Association Greenpeace France* case had already provided the CJEU with an opportunity to differentiate between *Borelli* and the approach that would be concretised almost 20 years later in *Berlusconi*. Advocate General Mischo correctly held that the *Borelli* ruling's finding, that the validity of final Union decisions cannot be affected by illegal national preparatory acts, cannot apply to just any composite procedure. In his own words,

> the fact that an irregularity in the national procedure does not affect the validity of the subsequent Community act must not be misunderstood, particularly in a case such as the present one where, *unlike the situation that obtained in Oleificio Borelli* [a national act] *did not automatically* entail a favourable decision by the Community but did *make it possible* (emphasis added).[39]

Association Greenpeace France is an important ruling for another reason. It shows that some composite administrative procedures may be subject not only to the jurisdictional *Borelli* principle – that some non-final national decisions must in principle be reviewed by national courts – but also to the substantive *Berlusconi* principle as well – that the illegality of those decisions may be relied upon when reviewing the final Union decision to which they led. Arbitral composite procedures, like the GMO regulation procedure at stake in *Association Greenpeace France*, as well as safeguard procedures, provide good examples.

Both types of composite procedure lead a sort of double life: within the legal order of the relevant Member State, the national acts in question already produce binding effects. In arbitral procedures, national authorities' drafts decisions will in principle become final unless an objection from another national authority

[37] Opinion of AG Campos Sánchez-Bordona in *Berlusconi*, n 3, para 112.
[38] *Berlusconi*, n 1, paras 44 and 57; *Iccrea*, n 31, para 48; and *Ukrselhosprom*, n 32, para 223.
[39] Opinion of AG Mischo in C-6/99 *Association Greenpeace France v Ministère de l'Agriculture et de la Pêche*, ECLI:EU:C:1999:587, para 100.

causes the Union administration to intervene. As the Court said in *Association Greenpeace France*, the 'decision of the competent authority is the *prerequisite for the Community procedure* and, in the absence of any indication to the contrary from another Member State … may even determine its outcome' (emphasis added).[40] In safeguard procedures, the urgent decisions taken by national authorities already produce legal effects, such as bans on a category of allegedly contaminated food items, but will only remain in force indefinitely, or be repealed, once confirmed or rejected by the Union administration.

However, once the composite procedure reaches the Union level, both kinds of national measure serve as preparatory acts paving the way for the exercise of decisional dominance by the Union administration. In such cases, the national draft decision, or safeguard measure can be reviewed indirectly as part of a judicial control of the final Union decision.[41]

The *Pfizer* case provides a good example of a composite procedure resulting from such a safeguard clause.[42] Yet it also illustrates what is perhaps the most important point in derivative illegality in composite decision-making. *Pfizer* shows that, even in instances of Union decisional dominance, illegalities that occur during national procedural stages never mean that the final Union decision is *automatically* illegal itself.

The company Pfizer contended before the General Court that a Danish decision banning an antibiotic used in animal feed, on grounds of public health, was illegal. It argued too that 'the fact that the safeguard measure is unlawful means that the contested regulation is also unlawful, given that it was adopted on the basis of that measure'.[43] The General Court emphasised that the Commission enjoyed a power to assess risks independently from the assessment by national authorities (ie that it held decisional dominance). Accordingly,

> Only the lawfulness of the Community-level risk assessment is subject to judicial review by the Court in this case. It follows that, *even if the safeguard measure taken by the Danish authorities were unlawful*, notably because the scientific evidence provided by the authorities was inadequate, *that would still not prove that the contested regulation was unlawful* (emphasis added).[44]

In other words, *Pfizer* illustrates one important aspect of the case law on derivative illegality in composite decision-making up to and since *Berlusconi*. Irregularities of national preparatory acts do not *necessarily* make the final Union decision illegal *ipso facto*. In order for its implications to be fully understood, the *Berlusconi* doctrine needs to be read in the context of that case law.

Besides only applying in cases where the Union administration enjoys decisional dominance, derivative illegality may only occur if several conditions are met.

[40] Ibid, para 51.
[41] See eg Case T-168/16 *Grizzly Tools GmbH & Co.KG v European Commission*, ECLI:EU:T:2018:246.
[42] Case T-13/99 *Pfizer Animal Health SA v European Council*, ECLI:EU:T:2002:209.
[43] Ibid, para 175.
[44] Ibid, para 184.

Reconstructing the CJEU's rulings, it becomes apparent that the case law requires an illegality committed at national level:

(i) to be or become imputable to the Union authority;
(ii) to result from the violation of EU law; *and*
(iii) in cases of procedural illegality, to qualify as a breach of an 'essential procedural requirement' in the sense of Article 263 TFEU.

These conditions are unique to the law of composite decision-making. They do not apply in instances of derivative illegality within administrative procedures where *only* Union authorities, or *only* national authorities, decide. In comparison to such instances, there is a significant restriction in the kind of illegalities which may affect the final decision's validity.

Indeed, illegalities that are either not imputable to Union authorities, which result from the violation of national law, or which do not have an impact on the substance of the final decision are beyond judicial control by Union courts. Given that the *Berlusconi* doctrine forbids national courts from reviewing non-binding preparatory acts, these illegalities will not be reviewable by national courts either. The rule of law implications of this are sensitive and will be examined in greater depth below.

Nevertheless, the three conditions above are intended to preserve the key concerns already set out in Chapter seven, and which were also decisive in the development of the *Borelli* doctrine. Whereas the first condition aims to ensure that Union courts respect as far as possible the jurisdictional limits forbidding the review of national acts, the latter two preserve the autonomy and uniformity of EU law. These are all important constitutional concerns to which, CJEU case law implies, certain concessions on the side of the rule of law must be made.

A. Condition 1: Imputability

The CJEU's lack of jurisdiction to review national decisions was one of the key reasons why no derivative illegality was possible under *Borelli*. Indeed, if national authorities enjoy decisional dominance, it would be impossible for the CJEU to review the Union administration's final decision without primarily reviewing their preparatory acts. The national authorities decide what the Union administration will decide. As the CJEU stated in *Emerald Meats*, the Union administration 'does not have the power to substitute itself for the national authorities' and is 'neither under a duty nor indeed empowered to check the correctness' of the preparatory acts taken by those authorities, which it has *no choice* but to adopt.[45]

[45] For a case in which the Court refused to find derivative illegality in a composite procedure because the Commission *was not* empowered to correct an irregularity caused by national authorities, see Joined Cases C-106/90, C-317/90 and C-129/91 *Emerald Meats Ltd v Commission*, ECLI:EU:C:1993:19, paras 36 and 38.

In contrast, under *Berlusconi*, the decisional dominance of the Union administration means that it can choose whether, and to what extent, its final decisions will be based on national preparatory acts. When conducting a review of derivative illegality, the CJEU's review will therefore not focus primarily on the illegal preparatory act as such, but on what the Union body decided to do with it. It will indeed scrutinise illegalities that occurred *during national procedural stages*, but solely on the ground that they later became *imputable* to the Union administration.

The basic criterion of imputability may be summarised as follows. National preparatory acts that are voluntarily adopted in the final decision, and which are tainted by illegalities that the Union administration fails to correct, become imputable to the Union administration itself.

It appears that the Union administration must correct illegalities that affect national preparatory acts if they result from the violation of legal requirements that apply both at the national and at the Union stages of the administrative procedure. By contrast, there is no duty to correct of illegalities occurring at the national stage when the national and the Union administration are responsible for *entirely separate* issues.

Schenker, a ruling emerging in the field of customs law, provides a case in point. Despite their composite structure,[46] administrative procedures for remission or repayment of customs debt are based on a 'division of powers between national and [Union] authorities'.[47] Given that both fulfil different tasks, and that 'the Commission *has no power* to review the lawfulness of decisions taken by national customs authorities', the unlawfulness of such decisions may not be ascribed to the Commission itself.[48]

However, the Court does accept pleas in law relating to whether the Commission, in a given case, correctly applied the conditions upon which its decisions regarding remission or repayment of the customs debt depend.[49] Such Commission decisions are preceded by a preliminary assessment by national customs authorities on whether those same conditions are met. Both levels of administration make assessments on the same subject-matter. For this reason, while the CJEU does not consider the Union administration to be under a duty to correct national-level illegalities in the procedure for *payment* of customs duty as such (as in *Schenker*), such a duty exists in the procedure for the *remission* and *repayment* of customs debt. For instance, in *France-Aviation* the national authority had proposed to the Commission that a market actor should benefit from the repayment of customs debt. The proposal was, however, based on an incomplete case file and therefore illegal. Having failed to give the applicant the opportunity to provide additional

[46] The structure of such procedures has already been explained before. See Chapter 3, section III.C.(i).

[47] See Case T-205/99 *Hyper Srl v European Commission*, ECLI:EU:T:2002:189, para 100.

[48] Case T-576/11 *Schenker Customs Agency BV v European Commission*, ECLI:EU:T:2015:206, paras 50–51.

[49] *Schenker*, n 48, para 50.

information, the Commission had neglected to correct the illegality affecting the national preparatory act, and its decision was annulled.[50]

Besides *France-Aviation*, many other cases have shown the kind of instances where the CJEU holds illegalities caused by national authorities to be imputable to the Union administration. The ample case law on safeguard measure procedures offers numerous examples.[51]

The General Court's *CSF* ruling illustrates that case law well.[52] Even though national authorities may take measures to eg suspend the marketing of certain machinery, 'it is still for the Commission to review whether those measures are justified, by satisfying itself in particular of the merits of the legal and factual grounds for the adoption of the measures'. Thus, the CJEU may ascertain whether a decision confirming national safeguard measures 'is decision is based on a misinterpretation of [the relevant legislation] made by the competent national authorities and then upheld by the Commission'. In such a case, the CJEU will review whether the Commission's error is 'capable of invalidating the decision in which the Commission found the national measures at issue to be justified'.[53]

Lastly, the violation of procedural rights in national procedural stages provides an interesting example of the Union administration's duty of correction. As was explained in Part II, where the Union administration enjoys decisional dominance, it is responsible for ensuring that the procedural rights of affected parties are observed throughout the composite procedure. It will have an obligation to ensure that those parties are afforded an opportunity to be heard and that the decisions concerning them are duly reasoned. In doing so, the Union administration is allowed – not obliged – to rely on the assistance of national authorities. Pursuant to the rules of confirmation and delegability, national administrations may even fulfil a Union authority's procedural obligations by anticipating the hearings that it is obliged to offer to affected parties, or by offering a hearing on its behalf.[54]

The reverse side of the coin, however, is that the Union administration relies on the assistance of national bodies at its own peril. The violation of procedural rights which are in principle for the Union administration to fulfil is imputable to the Union administration alone. A decision of the Union administration *may* be reasoned by simply restating reasons contained in a prior national preparatory act – such as a national objection to disclosing a document – but will also be invalid if such reasons are inadequate.[55] If national administrations offer a flawed hearing, or no hearing at all, or if they fail to transmit the affected party's observations to the Union authority deciding in the subsequent stage of the composite procedure, that authority must rectify this procedural irregularity. If it does not,

[50] Case T-346/94 *France-Aviation v European Commission*, ECLI:EU:T:1995:187, paras 35–36.
[51] For the structure of safeguard clause procedures, see Chapter 3, section III.C.(iii).
[52] Case T-337/13 *CSF Srl v European Commission*, ECLI:EU:T:2015:502.
[53] Ibid, paras 46–47.
[54] See Chapter 5, sections III.B. to III.D.
[55] See *Sweden v Commision*, n 15, para 88;, para 79; *Ecologistas en Acción*, n 15, para 40; *Spirlea*, n 15, para 52; paras 40 and 58; *Batchelor*, n 15, para 67 and T-74/16 *PAO* ECLI:EU:T:2018:75, para 73.

the Union courts will annul the final Union decision. In *Lisrestal*, for instance, the CJEU annulled a Commission decision withdrawing financial support for a vocational training programme from the European Social Fund after the Commission failed to remedy the fact that the beneficiary had not been heard by the competent national authority.[56]

B. Condition 2: Breach of EU Rules

The second condition of derivative illegality is that the national preparatory act must be illegal *on grounds of Union law*. The purpose of this condition is twofold: first, to ensure that the assessment of the legality of final EU measures is based exclusively on rules of Union law, as the principle of the autonomy of the EU legal order dictates; and second, to preserve the limits of the jurisdiction of the CJEU, which is only competent to interpret and apply EU law.

An early indication of this condition was *Toepfer*, an early case concerning safeguard measures in the common market in cereal crops.[57] Toepfer, a company, challenged a Commission decision confirming a national measure, a decision which it argued had been adopted in breach of essential procedural requirements. During the national preparatory stage that preceded the Commission's decision, the national authority had disregarded its procedural rights under German administrative law. However, while Advocate General Roemer considered this a matter for the national courts, the Court simply avoided responding to the question. The Court ultimately annulled the decision on different grounds.[58]

The Opinions of Advocates General in more recent landmark judgments make clear that the CJEU is not only aware, but determined to avoid the risk of judging a final Union decision against standards of national law. As Campos Sánchez-Bordona wrote in *Berlusconi*, the rather restrictive approach to derivative illegality that the CJEU had already taken in cases such as *Borelli* 'was justified by the need to ensure that administrative acts of the European Union cannot be rendered invalid where the national courts annul national administrative acts on the ground of breach of national rules'.[59] Similarly and even before, in *Association Greenpeace France*, Advocate General Mischo had held that it was 'impossible to see how the [Union] Court, which has sole jurisdiction to declare a [Union] act invalid, could form an opinion as to the existence of an irregularity with respect to national law'.[60]

[56] Case T-450/93 *Lisrestal – Organização Gestão de Restaurantes Colectivos Ld^a v Commission*, ECLI:EU:T:1994:290, paras 40 and 49–51. See also the ECJ's ruling on appeal from the latter judgment, C-32/95 P *European Commission v Lisrestal – Organização Gestão de Restaurantes Colectivos Ld^a*, ECLI:EU:C:1996:402.

[57] See Joined Cases 106/63 and 107/63 *Alfred Toepfer and Getreide-Import Gesellschaft v Commission*, ECLI:EU:C:1965:65.

[58] Opinion of AG Roemer in Joined Cases 106 and 107-63 *Alfred Toepfer and Getreide-Import Gesellschaft v Commission*, ECLI:EU:C:1965:49.

[59] Opinion of AG Campos Sánchez-Bordona in *Berlusconi*, n 3, para 66.

[60] Opinion of AG Mischo in *Association Greenpeace France*, n 39, para 98.

In contrast, Union courts show little reluctance in accepting derivative illegality if EU authorities follow preparatory national acts that are illegal on grounds of *Union law*. Indeed, the case law shows the possible relevant violations of Union law to be quite broad.[61] Derivative illegality of a Union decision is possible when its preceding national preparatory acts breach procedural requirements, such as the right to be heard. Yet while it is true that the violation of procedural rights is one of the most common causes of derivative illegality,[62] it would be inaccurate to suggest that derivative illegality is but a technical device to protect rights.[63]

First, substantive illegalities in national preparatory acts may affect the validity of final Union decisions. *Infront* provides a good example. The case related to a composite procedure regulating the granting of exclusive broadcasting rights for events of major importance for society. In the procedure, the Commission checks whether national measures granting those rights are in conformity with the relevant Union law requirements. The General Court found that the review it was invited to carry out in *Infront* 'concern[ed] solely the legality of the Commission's finding that [national] measures are compatible with [Union] law'.[64] This reasoning implies that the correct assessment by the Commission of whether national measures are compatible with EU law is a prerequisite for the validity of the final decision. Thus, and even though the Commission decision was annulled for different reasons, the General Court held it had the jurisdiction to review the legality of that decision on the grounds that it approved allegedly illegal national measures.

Second, there may only be derivative illegality if procedural requirements that *are recognised in Union law* are breached. For instance, in *Pampryl*, a case on the registration of protected designations of origin, the applicants claimed that, because they had not been heard by the national administration, the final Commission regulation registering the PDO was illegal.[65] The argument was rejected, as according to settled Union case law, there is generally no right to be heard in procedures leading to the adoption of regulations.[66]

Lastly, not all violations of procedural requirements leading to derivative illegality concern procedural rights. *Association Greenpeace France* is a case in point. Before the French courts, a group of organisations challenged an administrative decree authorising the placing on the market of a type of herbicide-resistant

[61] F Brito Bastos, n 4.

[62] See H Hofmann and A Türk, 'The Development of Integrated Administration in the EU and its Consequences' (2007) 13 *European Law Journal* 253, 268.

[63] HP Nehl, 'Legal Protection in the Field of EU Funds' (2011) 10 *European State Aid Law Quarterly* 629, 644.

[64] See Case T-33/01 *Infront WM AG v European Commission*, ECLI:EU:T:2005:461, para 109.

[65] Case T-114/99 *CSR Pampryl SA v European Commission*, ECLI:EU:T:1999:281, paras 50–51. It must be noted that the case concerned a composite procedure falling under the scope of the *Borelli* doctrine, so that derivative illegality would have been inadmissible anyway.

[66] For the most developed analysis of the constitutional and administrative implications of this case law, see J Mendes, *Participation in EU Rule-Making: A Rights-Based Approach* (Oxford University Press, 2011).

GMO maize.[67] That decree constituted the final decision of a complex composite procedure.[68] It transposed into French law a prior Commission decision which, in turn, authorised the GMO based on a risk assessment made by the same French authority. The plaintiffs claimed that the first stage of the procedure was irregular because the application for an authorisation did not include sufficient data upon which to assess the public health risks of GMO maize. The Commission decision authorising the GMO was invalid, so went the argument, because it was based on a risk assessment by the French administration which, contrary to the relevant Union legislation, did not rely on sufficient information. In this regard, the Court of Justice considered that it was for the national court to assess whether, 'owing to irregularities in the conduct of the examination of the notification by the competent national authority', 'those irregularities are such as to affect the validity of the Commission's … decision'.[69]

C. Condition 3: The Union's Test of Essential Procedural Requirements

Association Greenpeace France also showcases a third condition for derivative illegality. Besides only being possible where procedural requirements are enshrined in Union law – be it in general legal principles or in legislative provisions – derivative illegality can only result from the violation of an 'essential procedural requirement' in the specific sense of Article 263 TFEU. According to the interpretation of the concept by the Union courts, a Union measure is invalid on procedural grounds 'where, if the rule had not been breached, the outcome of the procedure or the content of the adopted act could have been substantially different'.[70]

EU law's general test of what constitutes an essential breach of a procedural requirement has always been meant for the judicial review of decision-making processes *of the Union administration*. However, the CJEU's case law began to extend that test to national procedural stages of composite administrative procedures.[71] A Union decision will be invalid if its national preparatory acts are tainted by procedural illegalities that could have a *decisive* influence on its content. This may occur when procedural illegalities are consciously maintained or not corrected, or when they induce the Union administration into error when

[67] At the time, the administrative procedure in force was found in Directive 90/220, which was later repealed by Directive 2001/18.

[68] The authorisation procedure for GMOs falls within the category of 'arbitral procedures' set out in Chapter 3, section III.C.(ii).

[69] Case C-6/99 *Association Greenpeace France v Ministère de l'Agriculture et de la Pêche*, ECLI:EU:C:2000:148, para 55.

[70] For many, see Cases 30/78 *Distillers Company Ltd v European Commission*, ECLI:EU:C:1980:186, para 26 and T-240/10, *Hungary v European Commission*, ECLI:EU:T:2013:645, para 84.

[71] R Caranta, 'Coordinamento e divisione dei compiti tra Corte di giustizia delle comunità europee e giudizi nazionali nelle ipotesi di coamministrazione: il caso dei prodotti modificati geneticamente' (2000) *Rivista Italiana di Diritto Pubblico Comunitario* 1133.

it makes a final decision. Most cases concern the former situation. *Association Greenpeace France*, by contrast, provides an interesting example of the latter.

Part II of this book showed that Union administration may be aided by national authorities in fulfilling its obligation to ensure respect for procedural rights. The violation by national authorities of such rights will typically constitute an infringement of an essential procedural requirement which may render the final Union decision invalid. *Branco*, *Partex* and *Mediocurso* represent cases where the Commission had adopted decisions withdrawing or reducing European Social Fund assistance. Those decisions were reasoned by simply alluding to insufficiently reasoned national preparatory acts. The CJEU held the Commission's decision in each case to be invalid due to a breach of the duty to give reasons, an essential procedural requirement.[72] The *August Wolff* ruling, which concerned a restriction on a medicine, held that a Union decision violated the procedural requirement of impartiality because it was based on a report made by a national regulatory agency without sufficient assurances of prevention of bias.[73] In *Cheminova*, the General Court examined whether a breach of the right to be heard and of the duty of care by national authorities in the preparatory stages of an administrative procedure had any impact on the final Union decision banning a plant protection product containing an organophosphate insecticide.[74]

Association Greenpeace France, in contrast, did not concern the violation of procedural rights by national authorities. Rather, the ruling concerned a national preparatory act based on defective fact-finding. As the Advocate General acknowledged, such an irregularity in a preparatory act may not be visible to the Union administration and may mislead it into making an erroneous decision.[75] The Court recognised that the incompleteness of the risk assessment report prepared by the French administration could have eventually induced the Commission to overlook the risks that the GMO posed to the environment or human health.[76] The CJEU considered that, in such a case, the irregularity of the national preparatory act could render the Commission's decision invalid.

V. A Rule of Law Blind-Spot?

The *Berlusconi* doctrine, and the case law which it codifies, illustrate the efforts of the CJEU to ensure that composite administrative decision-making is subject to

[72] *Branco I*, n 12, paras 36–37; Case T-182/96 *Partex – Companhia Portuguesa de Serviços SA v European Commission*, ECLI:EU:T:1999:171, para 172 and Joined Cases T-251/05 and T-425/05 *Mediocurso – Estabelecimento de Ensino Particular, SA v Commission (Mediocurso II)*, ECLI:EU:T:2007:162, paras 35 ff. See also Case T-53/11 *Associação de Empresas de Construção e Obras Públicas e Serviços v European Commission (AECOPS I)*, ECLI:EU:T:2013:205, para 80.

[73] Case C-680/16 P *Dr August Wolff GmbH & Co KG Arzneimittel v European Commission*, ECLI:EU:C:2019:257, para 41.

[74] Case T-326/07 *Cheminova A/S v European Commission*, ECLI:EU:T:2009:299, para 249.

[75] Opinion of AG Mischo in *Association Greenpeace France*, n 39, paras 110–12.

[76] Case C-6/99, *Association Greenpeace France*, n 69, para 55.

judicial control. However, it is also evident that the case law is modelled around the need to reconcile judicial control with other EU constitutional requirements. As was observed before, such requirements concern, among other things, the limits of the CJEU's jurisdiction, loyal cooperation between national and Union courts, and the autonomy and uniformity of Union law. Indeed, one may legitimately wonder if the case law goes too far in compromising judicial control for the sake of those requirements.

In particular, the CJEU, the only court competent to review national preparatory acts, cannot annul a final decision of the Union administration on the grounds that such acts violated purely national law.[77] As de Pretis has pointed out, composite administrative procedures are by definition incomplete procedures, in that the Union legislation that establishes them never does so exhaustively.[78] Member States may, in the exercise of their national procedural autonomy,[79] adopt all rules deemed appropriate to fully regulate national procedural stages. This means that Member States may also add procedural requirements to the national phases of composite procedures beyond those foreseen in Union legislation.[80] Member States may do so either by instituting new administrative law provisions specifically for the composite procedure, or by resorting to pre-existing general provisions of administrative law.

And yet, given that under *Berlusconi* only Union courts may review the composite administrative procedure, national courts may not review preparatory acts in order to scrutinise the violation of the law by the national administration. On the other hand, from the three conditions placed by the case law on derivative illegality, it becomes apparent that not all illegalities committed by national administration may be reviewed by the Union courts. The net result is that judicial review in composite administrative decision-making leaves out many irregularities committed at national level. More specifically, it has a 'blind-spot' for illegalities that either result from a breach of national law, or have little influence upon the final decision at the Union level.[81]

That blind-spot concerns the fact that it is impossible to review legal requirements which are only established in national law and have no equivalent in sectoral Union legislation or in the general principles of Union law, such as rules on quorum, conflict of interests, or the consultation of other authorities. This enforcement gap proves problematic from a rule of law standpoint. The case law

[77] This issue was already briefly implied by R Caranta, n 71 (at 1145, 1148 and 1151). Caranta notes that, by extending the EU test of what constitutes the violation of an essential procedural requirement, the CJEU may have rendered the violation of (at least some) national procedural rules irrelevant.

[78] D de Pretis, 'Procedimenti amministrativi nazionali e procedimenti amministrativi europei' in G Falcon (ed), *Il procedimento amministrativo nei diritti europei e nel diritto comunitario* (CEDAM, 2008), 68.

[79] See eg Case C-161/15 *Bensada Benallal v État belge*, ECLI:EU:C:2016:175, para 24.

[80] See L de Lucia, *Amministrazione Transnazionale e Ordinamento Europeo: saggio sul pluralismo amministrativo* (Giappichelli, 2009), 135.

[81] F Brito Bastos, 'An Administrative Crack in the EU's Rule of Law: Composite Decision-making and Nonjusticiable National Law' (2020) 16 *European Constitutional Law Review* 63.

insufficiently ensures that composite decision-making is subject to judicial control, in regard to both its subjective and objective purposes (ie those of protection of individuals and preservation of legality).

The right of individuals to effective judicial protection requires the reviewing court to have the 'jurisdiction to examine all questions of fact and law relevant to the dispute before it'.[82] Given that the CJEU has the exclusive jurisdiction to review the final decision taken by the Union administration, as well as the national preparatory acts leading to it, a violation of national law governing the national procedural phases of composite procedures is undoubtedly a question of law that is relevant to a dispute on the review of the final decision. And yet, the impossibility for the CJEU to conduct an indirect review of the national preparatory measures in light of both EU *and national* law compromises the ability of affected parties to challenge the *entirety* of the decision-making process.

The non-reviewability of violations of national law also fails to ensure the objective purpose of judicial control. It fails to ensure adequate enforcement of the binding legal standards to which national authorities owe their obedience (whether or not such standards confer individuals' rights). Despite assertions that the Treaties establish 'a complete system of legal remedies and procedures designed to ensure judicial review of the legality of European Union acts',[83] that system is unable to ensure that, in composite administrative procedures, legal requirements of national law are just as justiciable as legal requirements of EU law.

Even so, one can perhaps identify a few *potential* exceptions to the non-reviewability of national law violations in composite procedures. One first exception could exist within the Single Supervisory Mechanism, where the *Berlusconi* judgment originated. The SSM confers on the ECB an unprecedented mandate not only to apply all relevant Union law but, 'where this Union law is composed of Directives, *the national legislation transposing those Directives*'.[84] The Advocate General in *Berlusconi* confidently asserted that the ECB's new mandate implies an 'extension of jurisdiction' of the Court of Justice to apply said national legislation.[85] In *Cornelli*, the General Court supported that view.[86] However, as some prominent scholars have pointed out, the ECB's mandate to apply national law may extend to the national rules on administrative procedure that national banking supervision authorities must usually follow,[87] which could even include those found in general administrative law codes. It is not entirely obvious that

[82] Joined Cases C-245/19 and C-246/19 *B v État Luxembourgois*, ECLI:EU:C:2020:795, para 66.

[83] See eg Case C-583/11 P *Inuit Tapiriit Kanatami v European Parliament*, ECLI:EU:C:2013:625, para 92.

[84] Article 4(3) SSMR. See also F Coman Kund and F Amtenbrink, 'On the Scope and Limits of the Application of National Law by the European Central Bank within the Single Supervisory Mechanism' (2018) 33 *Banking and Finance Law Review* 133.

[85] See the Opinion of AG Campos Sánchez-Bordona in *Berlusconi*, n 3, para 114.

[86] Case T-502/19 *Corneli v European Central Bank*, ECLI:EU:T:2022:627.

[87] L Wissink, 'Challenges to an Efficient European Centralised Banking Supervision (SSM): Single Rulebook, Joint Supervisory Teams and Split Supervisory Tasks' (2017) 18 *European Business Organisation Law Review* 431, 454.

just any provision of general administrative law, which national authorities must observe *in any* policy field, constitutes 'national law transposing Directives' in banking supervision. At least *some* such provisions will not. That means that, even within the mandate of the ECB under Article 4(3) SSMR to apply national law – which at any rate does not exist in any other area of Union law – many provisions of national public law may be violated by national supervisory authorities without any repercussion for judicial review of the final ECB decisions.

A second exception to the non-reviewability of national law concerns principles of administrative law which are common to both European and national administrative law. One could in this respect think of a variety of procedural rights,[88] such as the right to be heard. *Berlusconi* offers yet another interesting example. Mr Berlusconi and Fininvest claimed that the contested ECB decision was based on a national preparatory act which allegedly disregarded a final judicial decision of the Italian Court of Cassation and therefore violated the principle of res judicata. The Advocate General conceded that the violation of res judicata could be assessed by EU courts – but in light of the CJEU's own case law on that principle.[89] Nevertheless, the Member States' laws can have more demanding and generous standards of protection that those offered by the version of the principles of administrative law that has been developed by EU courts. For instance, unlike Union law, Portuguese administrative law recognises the right to be heard not only in administrative procedures leading to individual decisions, but also in procedures leading to 'administrative regulations', ie measures of general application.[90] The application of the principle of protection of legitimate expectations, as understood by the CJEU, is subject to much more stringent requirements than it is in many national laws.[91] Given principles such as the uniformity and autonomy of Union law, is difficult to see how the CJEU could enforce diverging national variations of the same legal requirements when reviewing the Union administration's decisions.

There is a third category of violations of national law that may possibly be reviewable: the manifest incompetence of the authority involved in the national stage of the composite administrative procedure. Some judgments on Council measures blacklisting terrorist organisations,[92] as well as on Commission decisions

[88] C Franchini, 'European Principles Covering National Administrative Proceedings' (2004–2005), 68 *Law and Contemporary Problems* 183.

[89] See the Opinion of AG Campos Sánchez-Bordona in *Berlusconi*, n 3, paras 20 ff. The General Court followed a different view in the annulment proceedings brought by Berlusconi and Fininvest against the ECB, as it held that res judicata at national level could not affect the exercise of the ECB's exclusive competences. See Case T-913/16 *Berlusconi*, n 7, paras 102–8.

[90] Article 100 of the Portuguese Code of Administrative Procedure.

[91] See for example Case C-383/06 *Vereniging Nationaal Overlegorgaan Sociale Werkvoorziening v Minister van Sociale Zaken en Werkgelegenheid*, ECLI:EU:C:2008:165, paras 44–53. On this topic, see M Weisbrot, 'Application of the Principle of Protection of Legitimate Expectations in Recovery of Unduly Paid Subsidies in the Context of Judicial Coherence in the European Union' (2015) 8 *Review of European Administrative Law* 347.

[92] Case T-256/07 *People's Mojahedin Organization of Iran v European Council (OMPI II)*, ECLI:EU:T:2008:461, paras 144–45. See also Case T-348/07 *Stichting Al-Aqsa v European Council*,

refusing access to documents,[93] show that the CJEU is willing to search if the Union administration based a decision on preparatory acts adopted by the *competent* national authority.

In spite of the three exceptions the violation of national law in composite procedures remains largely unreviewable. They may eventually attenuate the damage caused to the rule of law at national level, but not in any meaningful way. The first exception, because it applies *exclusively* to one among countless composite administrative procedures. The second exception, because it in fact only allows the review of the violation of national procedural standards *to the extent* that they offer *the same* degree of protection – not more, not less – as the equivalent procedural standard in EU administrative law. The third exception, because of its scope being limited to probably quite rare instances of manifest incompetence of the national authority that authored the preparatory acts in a composite procedure.

VI. Union Decisional Dominance and the CJEU's Expanded Jurisdiction

Berlusconi's recognition of the ECJ's jurisdiction to review national preparatory acts constitutes the symmetric opposite of the case law in *Borelli*. More specifically, the *Berlusconi* judgment represents the contrary position to *Borelli's* prohibition for Union courts to review *binding* national preparatory acts (ie the prohibition dictated by the jurisdictional *Borelli* principle) and to the assertion that the validity of final decisions taken at EU level cannot be contaminated by the illegality of preceding national preparatory measures (ie the substantive *Borelli* principle).

However, and despite these structural differences, the *Borelli* and *Berlusconi* doctrines share the same conceptual foundations and the same basic principle. Both rely on an implicit concept of decisional dominance – the location of the decisive decision-making powers within a composite procedure – as the key test to determine the appropriate judicial jurisdiction and grounds of review for judicial review. Moreover, *Borelli* and *Berlusconi* both rely on what the Court of Justice refers to as a 'concept' of 'single judicial review' – a notion which could be more accurately described as a *principle* of single judicial review or, in the terminology proposed in this book, as a principle of unitary judicial protection. Indeed, the need for a 'single judicial review', more than constituting a mere legal concept, a linguistic shortcut to describe features of a legal regime, is a normative standard that the Union courts apply to justify findings. According to that standard, only national or Union courts should be competent to review the entirety of a composite

ECLI:EU:T:2010:373, para 89 and Joined Cases T-208/11 and T-508/11 *Liberation Tigers of Tamil Eelam (LTTE) v European Council*, ECLI:EU:T:2014:885, para 106. For an explanation of the procedure, see Chapter 3, section III.B.(iii).

[93] Case T-76/02 *Messina v European Commission*, ECLI:EU:T:2003:235, paras 46 and 48.

administrative procedure, depending on whether decisional dominance lies at the national or Union level. Whereas the *Borelli* doctrine, according to its developments since 2015, ensures the unity of judicial review by indirectly binding the Union administration to the rulings of national courts as part of its duty to ensure good administration, the *Berlusconi* doctrine is much more straightforward. It ensures that there is a 'single judicial review' by giving the Union courts the jurisdiction to review both the final Union decision and the national preparatory acts on which it is based.

Like the *Borelli* doctrine, the *Berlusconi* doctrine represents an important shift away from the postulates of the doctrine of European Executive Federalism. This is so both in regard to said doctrine's dualistic understanding of the relations between national and Union courts, on the one hand, and of the relations between national and Union administration, on the other.

First, the adoption of unitary judicial protection is incompatible with the principle of double exclusivity. This is certainly the case in the *Borelli* doctrine, as Chapter eight illustrated, but the CJEU's reasoning since *Berlusconi* is especially clear. In *Iccrea*, when acknowledging that only the Union courts could review national preparatory acts, the Court of Justice contrasted the notion of 'single judicial review' with the general principle according to which national courts are exclusively competent to review national decisions (including decisions taken solely by national resolution authorities).[94] For the Union courts not only to claim jurisdiction to review national (preparatory) acts, but to deprive national courts of the jurisdiction to do so, is a world of difference from the assertion made outside of composite decision-making that the Union's judicial system is based on a 'strict' division of exclusive judicial competences. Indeed, as an Advocate General has noted, composite administrative procedures within the scope of the *Berlusconi* case law constitute an exception to that division, and more specifically to the lack of CJEU jurisdiction to review national acts.[95]

Second, it will be recalled that the Union courts generally hold that the Union administration cannot be held responsible for the illegalities practised by national authorities. This notion can be traced to a broader principle of separation between the powers of national and Union authorities. The separation principle requires both levels to be treated as exclusively responsible for their own actions. That such a notion does *not* apply in composite decision-making is evident from *Berlusconi* and the case law which preceded it. It is, however, even more evident in the 2022 *Pilatus* ruling, yet another case on banking supervision under the SSM.[96] The ability of a national measure to render a final ECB decision unlawful depends on whether it constitutes 'an act, adopted by a national competent authority, that is an initiating act, preparatory act or non-binding proposal'.[97]

[94] *Iccrea*, n 31, paras 49–52.

[95] Opinion of AG Bobek in Joined Cases C-59/18 and C-182/18 *Italy v European Council*, ECLI:EU:C:2021:812, para 48.

[96] Case T-27/19 *Pilatus Bank plc v European Central Bank*, ECLI:EU:T:2022:46.

[97] Ibid, para 243.

By contrast, if the national measure in question constitutes a decision falling within the competence of a national authority, 'the ECB [read: any Union authority] cannot be held liable for the consequences of such a decision'.[98] In settings of decisional independence, the separation principle applies – and Union administrative decision-making is invulnerable to illegal national decision-making. In settings of decisional interdependence – ie in composite administrative procedures – and where Union administration exercises decisional dominance – ie within the scope of *Berlusconi* – Union decision-making can be illegal due to illegal national decision-making.

Berlusconi was a landmark ruling. It rationalised a fragmented case law on judicial review that had piled up over the preceding decades. It stated, expressly, what had just been suspected by some, until then – that only the CJEU is competent to review non-binding preparatory acts adopted by national administration. Lastly, it initiated a fresh seam of case law that leaves unequivocal the distinctiveness of judicial review in composite decision-making. Indeed, one of the rulings of that seam, *Satabank*, builds on *Berlusconi* to state that the judgment's findings are specific to 'composite administrative procedures' – the very first time that the concept was openly used, in black and white, in the reasoning of the CJEU.[99] To this extent, *Satabank* is an explicit culmination of a process that began over 30 years earlier, with *Borelli*. That is the process by which the CJEU crafted a unique doctrinal framework specifically for the review of composite decision-making. A doctrinal framework that goes beyond even the most basic tenets of the historical doctrine of European Executive Federalism.

[98] Ibid, para 244.
[99] *Satabank*, n 32, paras 70–73.

Conclusion

10

Beyond Executive Federalism

'And no man putteth new wine into old wineskins, else the new wine doth burst the skins, and the wine is spilled and the skins will be marred. But new wine must be put into new wineskins.'

(Mark 2:22 KJ21)

I. The Bigger Picture

Up until now, the argument has remained doctrinal in nature. Part I of the book offered a contextualised analysis of the principles of European Executive Federalism and showed why such principles are not well-suited to governing composite decision-making. Parts II and III proposed a reconstruction of the implicit principles that the CJEU gradually developed to preserve rule of law requirements in composite decision-making. The present chapter takes stock of the CJEU's doctrinal shift away from Executive Federalism and into a novel model of administrative law which specifically governs composite procedures.

Section II offers a summary of the Unitary Protection doctrine. Section III explains why the Unitary Protection doctrine represents a rejection of European Executive Federalism. Section IV argues that the principles of that doctrine treat national and Union administration as a single, integrated whole. In what follows, section V of the chapter sets out a myriad of far-reaching constitutional, political, and conceptual implications of the rise of the Unitary Protection doctrine. Unitary Protection denotes a judicial choice for the rule of law over jurisdictional boundaries. It lays the administrative federalism of the EU's founding years to rest. It represents a shift from the age-old 'touch of stateness' in European administrative law. It suggests an EU competence to partly harmonise national administrative procedure. It confirms empirical findings of an ongoing merging between national and Union administration. Lastly, it generates a *tertium genus* of administration that is neither purely national, nor purely European. In short, as section VI concludes, the rise of Unitary Protection represents, legally if maybe not in practice, a process of unification of national and Union administration specifically within the scope of composite decision-making.

II. Unitary Protection in a Nutshell

Doctrinal theories aim to systematise legal sources into coherent clusters of concepts and principles. This book has proposed one possible doctrinal reconstruction of the CJEU's intricate case law on composite decision-making, which spans across decades and extremely different policy areas. A brief summary of that reconstruction will be sketched out in the present section.

The CJEU's case law encapsulates what was termed as a doctrine of Unitary Protection, composed of two principles of unitary procedural and judicial protection. The overall purpose of that doctrine is to safeguard respect for key requirements of the Union's rule of law despite the complex structure and allocation of power within composite decision-making. That purpose is primarily pursued through a test of decisional dominance. Locating decisional dominance – ie the power to decide the composite procedure's final outcome – is essential to determine whether the duty to ensure respect for procedural rights and judicial accountability fall to national or Union administration. The two principles of Unitary Protection, jointly with the test of decisional dominance, began emerging in the case law from the early 1990s.

The principle of unitary procedural protection first appeared in case law concerning composite procedures in customs law, aviation, the European Social Fund, access to documents, and asset-freezing measures. The principle demands that the procedural rights of individuals – which are part of the fundamental right to good administration, a rule of law requirement – are fully respected throughout composite procedures and despite their multilevel structure. The duty to ensure this aim will fall to national or Union administration, depending on which exercises decisional dominance. If it exercises decisional dominance, national administration is under a duty to hear affected parties (the primary contact rule) and must give reasons for binding preparatory acts because such acts, under unitary judicial protection, may be judicially challenged. Decisional dominance of the Union administration has two special implications. First, the Union administration is bound by direct legal relations to individuals – including a duty to preserve their procedural rights – even if applicable legislation foresees no interaction between them. For instance, the Union administration is required to hear affected parties and to reason its decisions in a manner intelligible to them and not only to national authorities. Second, the Union administration may observe procedural rights by relying on the assistance of national authorities. CJEU case law implies at least six specific rules on such assistance.

National authorities must hear affected individuals before sending preparatory acts to the Union administration (the rule of primary contact). This is because the Union administration will not need to offer an additional hearing if it intends to decide in conformity with such acts (the rule of confirmation). The Union administration may request that national authorities offer hearings on its behalf (the rule of delegability). The Union administration may reason its own decisions by restating (the rule of replication) or merely alluding to (the rule of referral) the reasons contained in a prior national preparatory act. What it may not do is to abdicate its final responsibility to give reasoned decisions entirely to national authorities (the rule of non-substitution).

The principle of unitary judicial protection has permeated the case law of the CJEU for three decades, but has recently been referred to in more explicit terms. In fact, the very first time that the CJEU openly used the concept of 'composite administrative procedures' in its reasoning was precisely to stress that such administrative procedures follow their own rules in terms of judicial review and to set out how jurisdiction is allocated between national and Union courts.[1] As a composite administrative procedure constitutes a single administrative procedure, and not a 'combination of two separate procedures, one taking place at national level and the other at EU level', judicial control must be exercised by a single court – there must, in the CJEU's words, be a 'single judicial review'.[2] This will be undertaken by a national or Union court, depending on whether decisional dominance falls to a nation or to a Union authority. The case law has been especially complex with regard to bottom-up composite procedures – ie administrative procedures where national authorities are involved at a preparatory stage and where the Union administration takes the final decision. Bottom-up procedures will be subject to what were termed the *Borelli* and the *Berlusconi* doctrines if they involve, respectively, national or Union decisional dominance.

If national authorities adopt binding preparatory acts, thus exercising decisional dominance, then such acts must be reviewable by national courts (and only by national courts). If illegal, binding national preparatory acts will not contaminate the validity of the final decision taken at Union level – ie derivative illegality *is not* possible. These two findings were termed the jurisdictional and the substantive *Borelli* principles. They have been complemented, in recent years, by fresh case law clarifying what the Union administration must do if confronted with judicial proceedings in Member States' courts against binding national preparatory acts. If the national judgment on the national preparatory act is delivered before the final Union decision, the Union administration is required under *POA* and *CRM* to refrain from adopting the final decision; if that judgment is delivered after the final Union decision has been taken, the Union administration must review that decision under *Jeanningros*.[3]

If national authorities adopt non-binding preparatory acts, and decisional dominance therefore falls to the Union administration, then such acts must be reviewed by the CJEU (and only the CJEU) as part of the review of the final decision taken at Union level. If illegal, non-binding national preparatory acts may

[1] Case T-72/20 *Satabank plv v European Central Bank*, ECLI:EU:T:2023:149, paras 70–73.

[2] Case T-660/18 *VodafoneZiggo Group BV v European Commission*, ECLI:EU:T:2019:546, paras 76 and 89.

[3] Cases T-584/15 *Pagkyprios organismos ageladotrofon (POA) Dimosia Ltd v European Commission*, ECLI:EU:T:2016:510; T-43/15 *CRM Srl v European Commission*, ECLI:EU:T:2018:208; C-785/18 *GAEC Jeanningros v Institut national de l'origine et de la qualité (INAO)*, ECLI:EU:C:2020:46.

contaminate the validity of that decision – ie, derivative illegality *is* possible. While both could perhaps be inferred from previous case law, the two findings were systematised in the 2018 *Berlusconi* ruling, which is why they are termed the jurisdictional and the substantive *Berlusconi* principles, respectively. Prior case law also indicates, however, that certain conditions must be met for derivative illegality to occur. The illegalities of national preparatory acts must have become imputable to the Union administration, must result from the violation of Union law and, in the case of procedural illegalities, national authorities must have violated an 'essential procedural requirement' in the sense of Article 263 TFEU.

III. Abandoning the Dual Administration

The principles of unitary procedural and judicial protection, as well as their ramifications in the case law, represent a stark departure from the principles of European Executive Federalism. In crafting the Unitary Protection doctrine, the CJEU recognised that, unlike most other forms of administrative cooperation in the EU, composite decision-making does not obey a model of a dual divide in administrative power. Old principles that assumed such a divide to exist could simply no longer apply.

The principle of unitary procedural protection deviates from the separation principle completely. The separation principle requires the powers of national and Union administration to be preserved as distinct from one another, without mutual interference. Unitary procedural protection, in contrast, turns respect for good administration rights *throughout* the procedure into the responsibility of only one administration – the administration which exercises decisional dominance.

The separation principle holds either level of administration to be exclusively responsible for the observance of the law in the exercise of its own powers. In composite decision-making, this is contradicted by the fact that the Union administration may have recourse to the assistance of national authorities to take the practical steps needed to hear individuals or give reasoned decisions. As it may share the practical burden of respect for procedural rights (and is accountable for mistakes of national authorities if it does so) the Union administration is no longer *exclusively* responsible for the observance of such rights. It is only *ultimately* responsible, as it remains accountable if national authorities violate procedural rights.

Lastly, if applicable legislation does not provide for the exercise of Union power over individuals, the separation principle often translates into a notion of separate legal relations between individuals and national authorities, on the one hand, and between national authorities and the Union administration, on the other. This view may have been reinforced by a historical conception of the Union administration primarily intended to relate to national technocrats rather than individuals, as well as by the CJEU's view of cooperation between national and Union administration as internal to the two. The principle of unitary procedural protection does not follow this logic of separate legal relations. Indeed, the CJEU's notion of 'direct links' emphasises that Union authorities are connected by legal relations to individuals, even if a screen of national bureaucracies exists between them. Even if ordinary Union legislation only regulates, or presumes, individuals' legal relations to national authorities, the Union administration may exploit those relations when asking national authorities for assistance in respecting procedural rights. Above all, said legislation does not prevent the Union administration from choosing to deal directly with individuals and to bypass national authorities entirely.

Just like the principle of unitary procedural protection, the principle of unitary judicial protection derogates from the doctrinal tenets of European Executive Federalism. More specifically, unitary judicial protection derogates from the principles of double exclusivity and separation.

The principle of double exclusivity holds that national authorities are only subject to judicial control by national courts, and that the Union administration is only subject to judicial control by the CJEU. This view is contradicted by the CJEU's notion of a 'single judicial review' – the notion that a composite administrative procedure may be subject, in its entirety, to judicial control by national or Union courts.[4] It is further contradicted by specific aspects of the *Borelli* doctrine – eg the novel requirement in *Jeanningros* that obliges the Union administration to give effect to national judgments – as well as of the *Berlusconi* doctrine – eg the CJEU's expanded jurisdiction to review national preparatory acts.

Unitary judicial protection also represents a departure from the separation principle. The substantive *Berlusconi* principle – ie the acceptance of derivative illegality from national preparatory acts to final Union decisions – contradicts the notion according to which the Union administration may not be liable for illegalities committed by national authorities. That is a notion that remains valid, to this day, when national and Union authorities make decisions outside the scope of a composite administrative procedure.[5]

IV. Embracing a Unitary Composite Administration

The CJEU's case law has been rightly noted to treat composite procedures as single decision-making processes.[6] It ensures that judicial control and procedural rights

[4] Indeed, AG Bobek has noted that the CJEU's review of national preparatory acts in composite administrative procedures represents an exception to the absence of CJEU jurisdiction to control national decision-making. See the Opinion of AG Bobek in Joined Cases C-59/18 and C-182/18 *Italy v European Council*, ECLI:EU:C:2021:812, para 48.

[5] Case T-27/19 *Pilatus Bank plc v European Central Bank*, ECLI:EU:T:2022:46, paras 243 and 244.

[6] This view has also been supported HP Nehl, *Principles of Administrative Procedure in EC Law* (Hart Publishing, 1999), 93–94; S Cassese, 'European Administrative Proceedings' (2004–2005) 68 *Law and Contemporary Problems* 21, 31–32; and G della Cananea, *Diritto amministrativo europeo: principi ed istituti*, 3rd edn (Giuffrè, 2011), 243.

remain effective by subjecting all procedural stages, at national or Union level, to consistent legal standards. Nevertheless, it is submitted that the argument must go further.

The principles of Unitary Protection do not only deviate from the principles of European Executive Federalism; indeed, they represent a shift away from the Court of Justice's very understanding of the relations between national and Union administration. It is not only that the actions of national and Union authorities are treated as parts of a unified decision-making process. More importantly, national and Union authorities are simply no longer treated as separable from one another. Instead, they are treated as one, integrated, administration, which exercises power jointly rather than separately. The principles of Unitary Protection presuppose national and Union authorities to function as a unitary, albeit composite, administration – as an integrated administration, one could also say, in the sense of consisting of distinct parts that are combined into a single whole.[7]

This is visible in two ways. First, the CJEU has systematically placed national administration under the same legal standards that it first developed for Union administration, and which presuppose continuity between the two. Second, the CJEU's test of decisional dominance, in particular when dominance falls to Union authorities, tends to place one administration in a supporting, or even subordinate role vis-à-vis the other.

A. Legal Continuity

The principles of Unitary Protection extend to national authorities the same pre-existing legal standards that the CJEU would usually apply to administrative procedures that only involve the Union administration. From the perspective of procedural protection, one may give three simple examples.

First, in general, ie in administrative procedures which are not composite, the Union administration is not required to hear an affected individual more than once on the same issues of fact and law. Specifically in composite procedures, the rule of confirmation implies that, if already heard by a national authority, it is as if an individual has been heard by the Union administration itself.

Second, according to the principle of impartiality, if 'a number of EU institutions or bodies are given separate responsibilities of their own in the context of a procedure', they must all contribute to preventing the appearance of bias. The final decision will be invalid 'even where only one of them has breached that requirement'. The *August Wolff* ruling implies that the impartiality of the Union administration may depend upon the lack of bias of a national authority, just as

[7] D Curtin, *Executive Power in the European Union: Law, Practices, and the Living Constitution* (Oxford University Press, 2009), 34.

if both were 'EU institutions or bodies' exercising 'separate responsibilities of their own in the context of a procedure'.[8]

Third, CJEU case law implies that the violation of rules of procedure by national authorities may qualify as the breach of an 'essential procedural requirement' – one of the grounds of review for Union decisions under Article 263 TFEU. As a result, the final decision of a composite procedure, if taken by the Union administration, will be illegal regardless of whether such a requirement has been violated by national or Union authorities.

From the perspective of judicial control, one need only consider the CJEU's adaptation of the *IBM* test. The *IBM* test serves to determine which measures taken within a Union administrative procedure are subject to judicial review. It holds that, in a 'procedure involving several stages', the CJEU may review 'only those measures which definitively determine the position of the Commission or the Council', and not 'intermediate measures whose purpose is to prepare for the final decision'.[9] *Borelli* as well as *Berlusconi* recognise composite procedures as 'procedures involving several stages'. Both rulings extend the *IBM* test to national procedural stages as well. In *Berlusconi*, 'intermediate measures', taken by national authorities, may not be judicially reviewed except as part of an action against the final Union decision that they are meant to prepare. *Borelli*, perhaps more impressively, adapts the *IBM* test to make binding national preparatory acts reviewable as measures 'which definitively determine the position' adopted by the Union administration.

B. Institutional Continuity

The expansion of the legal standards of Union administration to national authorities is not the only way in which both become integrated. The same effect results from the novel principles that the CJEU made specifically for composite decision-making. Essentially, Unitary Protection and the test of decisional dominance have led to one administration taking on a secondary supportive role and to the other being responsible for the behaviour of both.

Unitary procedural protection tasks the dominant administration with ensuring that the authorities involved coordinate to take all steps for procedural rights to be fully observed. In cases of national decisional dominance, this is straightforward. It will fall to the national authority, not to the Union administration, to carry out hearings and adopt adequate statements of reasons.

When, however, decisional dominance falls to the Union administration, then the latter has more tools at its disposal. It may fulfil procedural rights *through*

[8] Case C-680/16 P *Dr August Wolff GmbH & Co KG Arzneimittel v European Commission*, ECLI:EU:C:2019:257, para 28.

[9] Case T-470/11 *Total SA v European Commission*, ECLI:EU:T:2015:241, para 82.

the administrations of the Member States, even at the national preparatory stages of composite procedures.

The Union administration may not evade the duty to give reasons, but it may adopt statements of reasons which either reproduce the reasons suggested in national preparatory acts or simply allude to said acts. In the latter case, the Union administration must first check that national authorities have indeed performed certain tasks – like making preparatory acts clear and hearing affected parties regarding those acts. The case law on the right to a reasoned decision, in short, treats the reasons found in national preparatory acts as an integral part of the reasoning behind the decisions of the Union administration.

Turning to the right to be heard, some have noted that the primary contact rule requires national and Union administration to honour the same standards of procedural protection.[10] While there are other instances of such 'vertical convergence' in EU law,[11] the expectation that national authorities will observe the right to be heard *as the Union administration would* is particularly important in composite decision-making. This is because, under the rules of confirmation and delegability, hearings offered by national authorities may count as if they had been offered the Union administration itself. The rule of confirmation allows the Union administration to fulfil the duty to hear by 'ratifying' hearings already offered by national authorities. Accordingly, the latter should be no less scrupulous than the Union administration is required to be when observing the right to be heard. The rule of delegability, in contrast, allows the Union administration to essentially deputise national authorities. The former may, according to *France-Aviation*,[12] 'ensure' the right to be heard by 'requesting' national authorities to conduct hearings on its behalf as though they were its representatives, or indeed, an extension of itself. As one scholar briefly noted, such implies 'a unitary conception of [the] public authorities' involved.[13]

The principle of unitary judicial protection implies, through and through, that national and Union administration exercise power jointly. This becomes apparent if one confronts that principle with the way in which the review of Union-level decision-making is normally conceptualised by the CJEU. As noted above, the CJEU adapts the *IBM* test to establish which measures adopted within composite procedures are subject to judicial review. Yet the use of *IBM* suggests far more.

First, the *IBM* case law states that judicial challenges may only be brought against the 'material manifestation of the will of an authority'[14] – ie its definitive

[10] L Azoulai, *Les Garanties Procédurales en Droit Communautaire: recherches sur la procédure et le bon gouvernement* (unpublished EUI doctoral thesis), 148.

[11] Eg the requirement that national courts must offer interim relief against national measures in breach of Union law (see Case C-213/89 *R v Secretary of State for Transport, ex parte Factortame Ltd*, ECLI:EU:C:1990:257). See G Greco, 'Il potere amministrativo nella (più recente) giurisprudenza del giudice comunitario' (2009) *Rivista Italiana di Diritto Pubblico Comunitario* 819, 859.

[12] Case T-346/94 *France-Aviation European Commission*, ECLI:EU:T:1995:187, para 30.

[13] T Tridimas, *The General Principles of EU law*, 2nd edn (Oxford University Press, 2006), 388.

[14] Case T-673/13 *European Coalition to End Animal Experiments v European Chemicals Agency (ECHA)*, ECLI:EU:T:2015:167, para 23.

position on a case. With the 'concept of a single judicial review', as the CJEU puts it, judicial proceedings may only be brought once and against the dominant administration. The decisions taken by the dominant administration – which, it will be recalled, can be binding preparatory acts – express 'the will of an authority' which is composite, and consists of the national and Union administrations combined. Unitary judicial control implies that national and Union administration express a joint, unitary will and that one of the two – the dominant – will be judicially answerable in the place of both. Under the *Berlusconi* doctrine, Union administration answers for the action of national authorities. Under the *Borelli* doctrine, only national authorities are defendants, but the Union administration will be indirectly bound by the same national judgment as binds them.

Second, the *IBM* case law considers that purely preparatory acts do not externalise the will of an authority. Instead, such acts are only 'internal to the administration' and adopted pursuant to an 'internal procedure'.[15] The implication is that, just as in administrative procedures involving only Union administration, the purely preparatory acts adopted by national or Union authorities are 'internal' to the administration – the composite, unitary administration that is composed of both.

V. Constitutional, Political, and Conceptual Implications of Unitary Protection

The argument in this book is one of contextualised doctrinal analysis. It is an argument of doctrinal analysis because it has reconstructed the basic legal implicit principles of the CJEU's case law on composite decision-making and the conception that said principles assume of their object – the relations between national and Union administration. The argument is one of contextualised doctrinal analysis because it situates composite decision-making, and the competing doctrine of European Executive Federalism, in the political, historical and institutional setting by which they were shaped.

However, the argument must still take one step further. Indeed, the CJEU's implicit principles of Unitary Protection are not only passively *shaped* by a broader context. They also have the potential actively to *shape* broader fundamental questions on the distinctive trajectory of the Union, on a political and constitutional level. The six following subsections outline some of the most important, higher-level implications of the Unitary Protection doctrine in that regard.

[15] For many, see Cases T-320/09 *Planet AE Anonymi Etaireia Parochis Symvouleftikon Ypiresion v European Commission*, ECLI:EU:T:2011:172, paras 37–39 and T-29/15 *International Management Group v European Commission*, ECLI:EU:T:2017:56, para 35.

A. Beyond Jurisdictional Boundaries

In crafting the doctrine of Unitary Protection, the CJEU succeeded in ensuring the rule of law in composite decision-making. Nevertheless, the rise of Unitary Protection was not inevitable, and it should not be taken for granted. As litigation increased, the CJEU was faced with a constitutional choice so fundamental that it transcends composite decision-making as such. The choice was one between preserving the Union's balance of power and preserving the Union's rule of law.

Indeed, the principles of European Executive Federalism reflected a historical commitment to reconcile the power of the Member States and the power of the Union. The principles of separation and double exclusivity ensure that national administrations – and consequently, the Member States to which they belong – enjoy a sphere of untouched autonomy free from Union interference; and that Union administration – and consequently, the Union as such – can exercise its powers independently from the Member States.[16] Unlike its German blueprint, the CJEU's doctrine of European Executive Federalism never drew a constitutional boundary between the domains of national and Union administrative power. But it did result from the CJEU's view that the Treaties immediately establish constitutional requirements intended to guarantee that such boundaries, which have always been for the Union legislator to define, were fully respected.

Confronted with composite decision-making, the CJEU could have insisted on artificially enforcing a separation between national and Union administrative powers which simply did not exist. While consistent with its supposed constitutional pedigree, sustaining the separation principle would have come at the expense of the Union's rule of law requirements. The CJEU's earlier inter-administrative approach to procedural rights illustrated well the consequences of that choice.

A second possible choice was the opposite. The choice was to recognise that the principles of European Executive Federalism were developed with an administrative system in mind wherein national and Union authorities exercised independent powers. The choice was to recognise that composite procedures, which are instead based on decisional interdependence, required novel principles. Such principles could make it possible for the Union's rule of law to be preserved, but only at the expense of the constitutional protection that the CJEU once gave to the divide between national and Union power.

Since the 1990s, the CJEU has made the latter choice. While it served the Union's rule of law, the CJEU's Unitary Protection doctrine also fundamentally redefined the relations between national and Union administrative power. Within composite decision-making, the CJEU abandoned European Executive Federalism and, with it, the federal conception of the European administrative system so dear to many historic 'Eurolawyers'.

[16] I have made this point before. See F Brito Bastos, 'Luxembourg v B: How Far Should Jurisdictional Limits be Eroded in the Name of Effective Judicial Protection' (2020) 41 *EU Law Live* 10.

Unitary Protection dismantled the separation between the administrative power of the Member States and of the Union. But not because the CJEU intended to engage in 'judicial activism' to compromise the autonomy of the former and expand the powers of the latter. Rather, the CJEU took the principled stance that the rule of law ought to take precedence over constitutional divides that attend the balance of power between the Union and the Member States.

While overwhelmingly successful, it will not be denied that Unitary Protection is imperfect in sustaining the rule of law. On the one hand, the CJEU fails to apply the principle of unitary procedural protection in state aid review. This is inconsistent with its own case law and undermines the procedural rights of undertakings. On the other hand, the principle of unitary judicial protection may be effective in enforcing Union law, but also enables the violation of national law to fall through the cracks and thus remain immune to judicial review. The principle also weakens the vertical safeguards against intrusion of the Union in Member States' institutions, another aspect of the EU rule of law, namely by removing national courts' jurisdiction to review certain aspects of national administrative decision-making. Some have proposed that Treaty change could mend this gap by instituting 'inverse preliminary references', allowing the CJEU to ask national Supreme Courts for rulings on the validity of national authorities' measures, or on the interpretation of national law, when reviewing composite decision-making.[17] Such creative solutions could indeed be helpful, but would unquestionably alter the longstanding balance of the preliminary reference and the relative functions of the national and Union courts. It would also be a Treaty change that could be politically difficult to obtain.

Yet without far-reaching change in the current state of Union law, only time will tell how damaging the CJEU's case law may become to the rule of law specifically *of the Member States*. Only time will tell if such damage will ever be prevented by a Treaty change enabling the CJEU to submit 'inverse preliminary rulings'.

B. Beyond Federalism

As the book has sought to emphasise from the outset, the transition away from European Executive Federalism did not occur in other forms of multilevel administration. Most consist of instances where national and Union administration can exercise their own independent powers but do so in a cooperative manner. Accordingly, there is no reason why the principles of separation and double exclusivity should not continue to apply.

The implication, however, is that two models of relations between individuals, national administration, and Union administration, have emerged over time.

[17] For many, see T Ellerbrok, 'Das umgekehrte Vorabentscheidungsverfahren als Schlussstein im europäischen Rechtsschutzverbund' (2022) 113 *Verwaltungsarchiv* 302 and S Alonso de León, *Composite Administrative Procedures in the European Union* (Iustel, 2017), 351.

One model, the first to appear, is the doctrine of European Executive Federalism. The other model, emerging since the 1990s, is the doctrine of Unitary Protection.

The first, as Chapter two suggested, was largely a product of the CJEU's own creativity. The bold assertion that its principles derived immediately from the Treaties never sat easily with the Treaties' silence on relations between national and Union administration. The notions that Union administration only exceptionally exercises powers directly over individuals, and that the Union's administrative law must anticipate an inescapable federal destiny, would strike most EU lawyers today as unrealistic and quaint. In fact, such notions would appear questionable even to some of the leading scholars of the Union's foundational period. Ipsen, for example, implied that the federalist interpretation of overlapping independent sovereign powers, followed by influential actors like Hallstein, Ophüls or Wohlfahrt, was skewed by preconceptions drawn from German federalism.[18] The Treaties have always allowed for far more flexibility than many of the early neofunctionalists and federalists seem to have believed.

In developing the principles of Unitary Protection, the CJEU did not simply acknowledge that the Treaties do not contain a single, constitutionally entrenched model of administrative law.[19] The CJEU also abandoned the German federal blueprint by which European Executive Federalism, as a supposed constitutional doctrine, had been inspired.

Indeed, German Executive Federalism entails a constitutional ban on composite decision-making between federal and *Land* administrations, known in Germany as *Mischverwaltung* ('mixed administration'), unless 'explicitly authorised' by the German Basic Law (henceforth, *Grundgesetz* or GG).[20]

Like European Executive Federalism, German Executive Federalism entails that the States' authorities implement federal law in their own right.[21] The latter, however, also entails the 'separation of the administrative spheres' of the *Bund* (the Federation) and the *Länder* (the States),[22] which derives from separation of federal and *Land* sovereignty itself.[23]

Under German Executive Federalism, cooperation between the federal and the *Land* administrations, in itself, is not problematic.[24] Similarly, as noted in Chapter three, the dualistic principles of European Executive Federalism can easily accommodate most forms of administrative cooperation in the European Union.

[18] See HP Ipsen, 'The Relationship between the Law of the European Communities and National Law' (1966) 3 *Common Market Law Review* 379, 394 and 'Deutsche Verwaltung und europäische Wirtschaftsintegration' (1968) 21 *Die öffentliche Verwaltung* 441, 441–45.

[19] See similarly S Cassese (n 5), 35.

[20] BVerfGE 32, 145 (156) and BVerfGE 39, 96 (119).

[21] Article 83 GG.

[22] BVerfGE 63, 1, (37).

[23] J Oebbecke, 'Verwaltungszuständigkeit' in J Isensee and P Kirchhof (eds), *Handbuch des Staatsrechts der Bundesrepublik Deutschland*, Vol VI, (Müller, 2008), 747.

[24] Cf B Küchenhoff, *Die verfassungsrechtlichen Grenzen der Mischverwaltung* (Nomos, 2010), 116 ff.

What represents unconstitutional *Mischverwaltung* under German Executive Federalism, at least according to the current state of the German Federal Constitutional Court's case law, is something different. What is unconstitutional is the equivalent of what, throughout this book, has been termed decisional interdependence – the defining characteristic of composite decision-making. As neither federal nor State administration may be forced by legislators to abdicate from its own decisional autonomy,[25] it is unconstitutional to make the exercise of the competences of either conditional upon the exercise of competences by the other.[26]

Ironically, composite procedures may well have been protected by the relative flexibility of the Treaties when compared to the *Grundgesetz*. This is because the constitutional ban on *Mischverwaltung* concerns instances of decisional interdependence between the federal and State administrations in subjects which, under the *Grundgesetz*, are the competence of one of the two.[27] Unlike the *Grundgesetz*, however, the Treaties never established any rigid division between matters that are necessarily the competence of Union or Member State administration.[28]

Nothing in the Treaties has ever opposed or imposed hybrid forms of administration. In fact, this was even explicitly pointed out by Ophüls, one of the drafters of the European Economic Community Treaty. Even though he held that the Treaty enshrined the German constitutional model, Ophüls specifically pointed noted that it 'stepped back from the question of the Community's own administration as well as from the possibility of mixed forms of administration'.[29] Constitutional openness to composite decision-making was built into the EU Treaties all along.

Exploiting the Treaties' silence, the CJEU gradually accommodated composite decision-making under the Union's constitutional order. It did so by crafting

[25] This was explicitly referenced as the German Federal Constitutional Court's underlying criterion in BVerfGE 41, 291 (311) and BVerfGE 106, 1 (26).

[26] This view was defended explicitly by the German Federal Constitutional Court already in 1960 (BVerfGE 11, 105 (124)). In the same vein, J Pietzcker, 'Zuständigkeitsordnug und Kollisionsrecht im Bundesstaat' in J Isensee and P Kirchhof (eds), *Handbuch des Staatsrechts der Bundesrepublik Deutschland*, Vol. VI (Müller, 2008), 535 and D Ehlers, 'Verwaltung und Verwaltungsrecht im demokratischen und sozialen Rechtsstaat' in H-U Erichsen and D Ehlers (eds), *Allgemeines Verwaltungsrecht*, 14th edn (De Gruyter, 2010), 245.

[27] J Isensee, 'Idee und Gestalt des Föderalismus im Grundgesetz' in J Isensee and P Kirchhof (eds), *Handbuch des Staatsrechts der Bundesrepublik Deutschland*, Vol VI (Müller, 2008), 111–12, notes that the Federal Constitutional Court's case law seemed to have been reversed for a period beginning in 1983. In that year, the FCC stated that a form of 'administrative organisation is not unconstitutional simply because it is to be characterised as mixed administration, but only when it is opposed by mandatory norms of competence or organisation or other provisions of constitutional law' (BVerfGE 63, 1 (38)). Another possible reading would be, however, that the FCC had simply developed a concept of mixed administration that encompassed instances of administrative organisation with and without decisional interdependence, and considered only the former to be incompatible with the Basic Law.

[28] See R Schütze, 'From Rome to Lisbon: "Executive Federalism" in the (New) European Union' (2010) 47 *Common Market Law Review* 1385.

[29] C-F Ophüls, 'Zur ideengeschichtlichen Herkunft der Gemeinschaftsverfassung' in E von Caemmerer, HJ Schlochauer and E Steindorff, *Probleme des europäischen Rechts. Festschrift Walter Hallstein zu seinem 65. Geburtstag* (Klostermann, 1966), 405.

Unitary Protection, a doctrine which not only goes beyond Executive Federalism, German or European, but indeed beyond federalism itself.

It is worth, at this point, engaging with the leading scholar embracing a federal interpretation of EU constitutional law. The author in question, Robert Schütze, has argued that the European Union's constitutional model of administration remains that of European Executive Federalism. He contends, unlike most European administrative law scholars, that one cannot speak of an integrated, unitary administration in the EU in the sense of an administration 'juxtaposed to executive federalism', but rather of a plurality of integrated administrations ie of 'organizationally autonomous entities that cooperate in a *federal* relationship'.[30]

Indeed, as Chapter three explained, most instances of multilevel (or 'integrated') administration are entirely compatible with the duplication of autonomous levels of administrative power enshrined in European Executive Federalism. To this extent, the argument made in this book largely shares Schütze's views. Where the argument differs, however, is in his characterisation of European *Mischverwaltung* – in which he rightly included composite decision-making – as a form of 'cooperative federalism'.[31]

Cooperative federalism, in Schütze's work, signifies the coexistence of dual government, including of the administrative branch, where federal and State governments are mutually complementary and, by working together in the same areas, share power.[32] It stands in opposition to dual federalism, a system where federal and State governments 'are co-equal and operate independently in their separate spheres'.[33] Schütze argues that the EU has transitioned, over time, from a dual to a cooperative model of federalism. Given the increasing extent of cooperation between national and Union administration, that shift would include the EU's administrative system.[34] This very same shift (from dual to cooperative federalism) is what many European administrative law scholars have in mind when they argue, using a different terminology, that the dual divide of European Executive Federalism, between national and Union administration, is now obsolete.

As Schütze himself recognises, however, *any* form of federalism implies dual government – a dual set of branches of government. There is certainly a federal, yet cooperative duality of the administrative branch in European Executive Federalism, as a legal doctrine, and in most European multilevel administration as a living system. However, *no such dual order of power* exists in composite decision-making. As demonstrated above, national and Union administration do not exercise independent powers at all. The principles of unitary procedural and judicial protection require national and Union authorities to function as a single,

[30] R Schütze, n 28, 1420.

[31] Ibid, n 28, 1420–21.

[32] R Schütze, *From Dual to Cooperative Federalism: The Changing Structure of European Law* (Oxford University Press, 2013), 5.

[33] Ibid, 5.

[34] Ibid, 6.

composite, and indeed unitary administration. This is precisely why Schütze's characterisation of composite (in his terms, 'joint') decision-making as a manifestation of cooperative federalism, does not hold in the view supported in this book.[35] One cannot speak of federalism, cooperative or otherwise, where no duality of authority exists.

German federalism constitutes the uncontested source of inspiration for European Executive Federalism and therefore remains its most relevant comparator. Yet one may also draw the conclusion that composite decision-making is a form of administration too integrated to qualify as an instance of cooperative federalism by considering the archetype of federal constitutional systems – the American system.

Much like Schütze, in respect of the Union system, so has much of US legal literature contended that a duality of State and federal spheres of authority constitutes a defining aspect of federalism, be it dual or cooperative.[36] For this reason, a third, albeit very rare, scenario of federalism has been considered constitutionally problematic. That scenario, 'coequal federalism', represents 'joint governance' by the federal administration and by States' authorities. This is a kind of governance where both levels engage in 'a single, joint decision-making process',[37] and is, thus, unlike dual or cooperative federalism, where no duality of power exists at all.[38] To this extent, 'coequal federalism' in US law would be the kind of administrative arrangement which would resemble European composite decision-making the most. Indeed, even the institutional advantages offered to justify joint federal-State governance resemble those that underlie the rise of composite decision-making.[39] However, there are also important differences. The decisional involvement of federal and State governments occurs by the creation, by the US Congress, of a joint agency, where both levels of government are represented. It is thus closer to what in EU administrative law is known as 'institutional cooperation' than to composite decision-making, where joint decision-making by national and Union authorities does not occur by convening said authorities within a single body, but by requiring their successive involvement at different stages of a single administrative procedure. Crucially, 'joint governance' in so-called 'coequal federalism' is purely voluntary – US States participate only if they so wish and may exit the joint decision-making processes at any time. This makes it possible to evade the anticommandeering principle – ie the constitutional principle according to which the federal government cannot compel States to enforce federal laws.[40]

[35] R Schütze, *European Constitutional Law*, 3rd edn (Oxford University Press, 2021), 352–53.

[36] For many, see P Weiser, 'Towards a Constitutional Architecture for Cooperative Federalism (2001) 79 *North Carolina Law Review* 663.

[37] D Owen and H Wiseman, 'Coequal Federalism and Federal-State Agencies' (2020) 55 *Georgia Law Review* 287, 320.

[38] Ibid, 298.

[39] See ibid, 307 ff and 320 ff.

[40] On the principle, see generally W Campbell, 'Commandeering and Constitutional Change' (2012–2013) 112 *Yale Law Journal* 1104 and A Johnstone, 'Commandeering Information – and Informing the Commandeered' (2012) 161 *University of Pennsylvania Law Review* 205.

As the US Supreme Court puts it, any attempt by Congress to 'conscript state [agencies] into the national bureaucratic army' would be 'fundamentally incompatible with [the American] constitutional system of dual sovereignty'.[41] Anticommandeering and, generally, a concern with compromising State sovereignty, represent the key reasons why, except for the management of a few airports, most attempts at establishing joint administration in the US have been thwarted.[42] Decisions taken by joint agencies would necessarily demand enforcement by both the federal and the State governments.

Under Union law, by contrast, the lawfulness of joint (ie composite) decision-making does not require voluntary participation of Member States. National and Union administration are locked together, required to operate interdependently, by mandate of the Union legislator, rather than independently, as is the case in dual as well as cooperative federalism. The CJEU's principles of Unitary Protection are intended for an administration that tore down the dual divide of power that, alongside cooperation, had remained central to European Executive Federalism. The principles of Unitary Protection are principles of and for a form of administration evolving beyond federalism altogether – for a post-federal administration.

C. Beyond the 'Touch of Stateness'

From the very earliest of days of the functioning of the European Court of Justice, insights from national administrative law pervaded and shaped the trajectory of Union (not only administrative) law. Indeed, as then President of the Court, Andreas Donner, put it in 1963, while the formal sources of Community law were the Treaties and secondary legislation, it was clear that 'the real sources of law are mainly the national laws of the states'.[43] Within the Court of Justice – which, in Donner's own words, could best be described as the 'administrative, and sometimes constitutional court of the Communities'[44] – the influence of national administrative laws was especially powerful.

Nevertheless, it was one thing to incorporate into the Community law of the time individual principles, such as the power of an authority to revoke its own illegal decisions, or legal concepts such as 'abuse of power' (or *détournement de pouvoir*). Afterall, such instances of legal transplants from national law were examples of principles and concepts widely shared in national systems of administrative law. It was an altogether different thing to gaze into the Treaties' nebulous textual silence, searching for clues on how national and Union authorities were to relate, and to divine that the Treaties had adopted the constitutional system of

[41] See *Printz v United States*, 521 US 898, 935 (1997).

[42] D Owen and H Wiseman, n 37, 331–32.

[43] A Donner, 'National Law and the Case Law of the Court of Justice of the European Communities' (1963) 1 *Common Market Law Review* 8, 8.

[44] Ibid, 11.

one, specific Member State. Indeed, it is no coincidence that it was mostly German federalist lawyers (but not exclusively) who advanced the notion that European Executive Federalism was embedded in the Treaties. For the German *Eurolawyers*, the fate of the Communities was federal – indeed, Hallstein insisted political unification would occur *within a generation*[45] – and the legal edifice of its administrative system happened to mirror their own national constitutional model of *Vollzugsföderalismus*.

In short, the rise of European Executive Federalism in the ranks of the Commission and, gradually, in the Court of Justice's case law may have been one of the earliest instances of the 'touch of stateness' – of the interpretation of Union law being distorted by national legal preconceptions. Nevertheless, and whatever its remote historical origins, the fact is that European Executive Federalism, for the most part, remains good law to this day. Its principles remain valid in the countless situations where national and Union administration are legally conferred powers to make decisions without the interference of the other. Yet we should also acknowledge that the principles of European Executive Federalism are not twin siblings, but, better, perhaps, cousins, of similar principles in German Executive Federalism. The doctrine of European Executive Federalism has always differed from its German blueprint. The former, unlike the latter, is a model for *interpreting* the Treaties and the legislative allocation of powers between the Union and its Member States, rather than an a model that *constrains* the choices of the Union legislator in deciding about such allocation.

The principles of European Executive Federalism can still be applied in practice without even giving any thought to the federalist assumptions behind their rise. In fact, by ensuring separate judicial review and preventing unwarranted mutual interference, said principles can actually promote clearer accountability of national and Union administrative authorities. European Executive Federalism does find support in many Treaty provisions (such as Articles 4(3) TEU and 291 TFEU). What is crucial to bear in mind, however, is that the interpretation of Treaty provisions can change as the European integration advances. Accordingly, so can the constitutional framework of European administrative law. That framework is not chained to the ideals of the Union's half-mythical founding fathers of a neofunctionalist and federalist persuasion (or of the less well-known jurists who supported them).

The judicial making of the Unitary Protection doctrine shows just that. It represents a coming of age of European administrative law beyond the touch of stateness (beyond the 'touch of federal stateness', one could say), and towards an administrative law with an identity of its own. Unitary Protection brought novel principles of administrative law that did not previously exist in national laws. These are distinctively *European* principles on relations between national authorities, Union authorities, and the individual. And while the case law is still very

[45] W Hallstein, *Die Europäische Gemeinschaft* (ECON, 1979), 396.

limited – mostly confined to exchanges of tax information – we may yet see a rise of similarly sophisticated doctrines for horizontal decision-making in the relations between authorities of different Member States.

D. Beyond Textual Limits to Codification

The Unitary Protection doctrine treats national administration as being integrated with – or, in some cases, as an extension of – the Union administration. It does so with the aim of preserving the Union's rule of law. That aim is of a constitutional importance that is at least equal to one of the most important provisions on administrative law found in EU primary law – Article 298 TFEU. The CJEU's understanding of the rule of law in composite decision-making requires that provision to be interpreted extensively.

Article 298(1) TFEU states that, '[in] carrying out their missions, the institutions, bodies, offices and agencies of the Union shall have the support of an open, efficient and independent European administration'. While it is considered to constitute a legal basis for a general codification of administrative procedure, the provision's scope is debated.[46] As Article 298 TFEU only refers to the 'European administration' supporting the Union's own authorities, there is a consensus that the scope of a codifying Regulation could only govern administrative procedures of the Union's own administration but *not* of the administrations of the Member States.[47]

Nevertheless, the CJEU's rulings show that it would be pointless to interpret Article 298 TFEU so as to exclude the adoption of general Union law legislation to regulate *some* aspects of national administrative decision-making. The provision does not allow the harmonisation of *national administrative procedures*;[48] yet, if interpreted in harmony with CJEU case law Article 298 is certainly sufficient to harmonise specifically the *national stages of composite administrative procedures*.

Such harmonisation could but formalise a law of composite decision-making that already exists, albeit only in implicit principles that have remained scattered in fragmentary and convoluted case law. In that law, and regardless of how decisional dominance is allocated, the CJEU unequivocally considers that, in composite decision-making, national authorities act within an administrative procedure of the Union administration. A national preparatory act, as the CJEU

[46] See for instance G della Cananea, 'The European Administration: *Imperium* and *Dominium*' in C Harlow, P Leino and G della Cananea (eds), *Research Handbook on EU administrative Law* (Edward Elgar, 2017), 62.

[47] See, for many, J Schwarze, 'European Administrative Law in the Light of the Treaty of Lisbon' (2012) 18 *European Public Law* 285.

[48] Article 197(2) TFEU corroborates this reading, as it explicitly rules out harmonisation of national laws to promote effective implementation and administrative cooperation by the Member States.

explicitly states, 'forms part of a Union decision-making procedure';[49] it 'is part of a decision-making process of the European Union'.[50]

For that reason, it is logical that national and Union administration are subject to the same set of legal standards – the standards that would typically apply to the Union administration itself and which presuppose continuity between the distinct stages of the same procedure. In this regard, the *August Wolff* ruling may represent the most remarkable though discreet development in recent years. It will be recalled that the CJEU insists that Article 41 of the Charter of Fundamental Rights, per se, only enshrines a fundamental right of individuals to good administration vis-à-vis the Union administration.[51] While individuals do also enjoy that right vis-à-vis national authorities, this is not by virtue of the Charter but because it constitutes a general principle of law. In *August Wolff*, however, the CJEU required a national regulatory agency involved in a composite procedure to observe the good administration duty of impartiality – not by invoking good administration as a general principle of law, but by explicitly applying Article 41 of the Charter *directly*.[52]

Harmonisation of national procedural stages could go beyond merely codifying the CJEU's principles of Unitary Protection. It could extend, to national authorities, other procedural standards that generally apply to the Union administration. This could be especially valuable to compensate one unfortunate implication of the case law. That is the fact that national preparatory stages in most composite procedures (those where Union decisional dominance exists) cannot be reviewed for violations of national law and are therefore de facto only subject to Union law.[53]

E. Beyond Law in the Books

Lawyers will be excused for some scepticism as to whether the principles of Unitary Protection find any grounding in institutional reality. Requiring national and Union administration to act as a single, integrated administration will sound like naïve wishful thinking to many. The notion may perhaps push too far the already excessive expectations that Union law has been said to place upon the loyalties of national officials – paid and empowered by their Member State – towards the Union administration.[54]

[49] Case C-785/18 *GAEC Jeanningros*, n 3 above, para 27.

[50] Case C-219/17 *Berlusconi and Finanziaria d'investimento Fininvest SpA (Fininvest) v Banca d'Italia*, ECLI:EU:C:2018:1023, para 45.

[51] See Chapter 4, sII.

[52] *August Wolff*, n 8, 39–41.

[53] See Chapter 9, section V.

[54] See S Kadelbach, 'European Administrative Law and the Law of a Europeanized Administration' in C Joerges and R Dehousse, *Good Governance in Europe's Integrated Market* (Oxford University Press, 2002), 176 ff and AJ Menéndez, 'Is European Union law a pluralist legal order?' in AJ Menéndez and JE Fossum, *The Post-Sovereign Constellation: Law and Democracy in Neil D. MacCormick's Legal and Political Theory* (Arena, 2008), 249.

And yet, many findings in empirical political science suggest that the CJEU's Unitary Protection doctrine may not be as detached from administrative and political practice as one may assume. Indeed, the findings in question may even reflect how adaptive European administrative law can be to the constant evolution of such practices.

Though referring to practices of comitology rather than composite decision-making, Wessels argues that national and EU administration are undergoing a process of *fusion*.[55] Describing the administrative integration in some policy sectors, Heidbreder maintains that 'national public administrations take the role of executing bodies under the authority of the European Commission'.[56] Europe's administrative system, Genschel and Jachtenfuchs write, 'absorbs parts of the national administrations of the member states into an integrated European framework, and puts them at the disposal of EU institutions'; so that 'the EU's administrative power is larger than the low numbers of Commission staff suggest'.[57]

The same claim, that national authorities have been incorporated into the Union administration, has been made especially forcefully with regard to national agencies. While noting that 'in formal terms it is usually quite clear which bodies belong to national governments and which belong to the European Union', Egeberg has argued that 'national administrations, or more correctly, *parts* of national administrations, have over the past couple of decades to some extent also become parts of a kind of EU administration'.[58] This is a point that Egeberg has also made in work co-penned with Trondal – that national agencies are already 'becoming parts of a multilevel Union administration in which the Commission in particular forms the new executive centre'.[59] The latter author, with Peters, has proposed a 'centralisation hypothesis' in the European administrative system. Trondal and Peters contend that administrative integration increases the Union's 'ability to co-opt administrative subcentres by stealth' – in particular, the Commission's ability to co-opt domestic agencies.[60]

The CJEU's case law on composite decision-making may offer important interdisciplinary insights. First, political science may well find that Union law confirms the pertinence of findings that national authorities are now extensively integrated into the Union administration. Second, however, the CJEU's rulings

[55] W Wessels, 'Comitology: Fusion in Action. Politico-administrative Trends in the EU System' (1998) 5 *Journal of European Public Policy* 209.

[56] E Heidbreder, 'Structuring the European Administrative space: Policy Instruments of Multi-level Administration' (2011) 18 *Journal of European Public Policy* 709, 713.

[57] P Genschel and M Jachtenfuchs, 'Introduction: Beyond Market Regulation. Analysing the European Integration of Core State Powers' in P Genschel and M Jachtenfuchs (eds), *Beyond the Regulatory Polity? The European Integration of Core State Powers* (Oxford University Press, 2014), 7.

[58] M Egeberg, 'EU Administration: Center Formation and Multilevelness' in M Bauer and J Trondal (eds), *The Palgrave Handbook of the European Administrative System* (Palgrave Macmillan, 2015), 66.

[59] M Egeberg and J Trondal, 'National Agencies in the European Administrative Space: Government Driven, Commission Driven, or Networked?' (2009) 87 *Public Administration* 779, 781.

[60] J Trondal and G Peters, 'A Conceptual Account of the European Administrative Space' in M Bauer and J Trondal (eds), *The Palgrave Handbook of the European Administrative System* (Palgrave Macmillan, 2015), 88.

also indicate the need for two additional focal points for empirical analysis. One is that incorporation of national administration has – legally, at least – transcended the bureaucratic relations specifically between Union administration and national *agencies*, which has been a key research focus. Indeed, not all judgments concerned composite procedures involving independent agencies. Some involved regional governments (like *Borelli*), national ministries (like *Association Greenpeace France*) or general directorates within ministries (like *Lisrestal*). Lastly, the unique legal status of composite decision-making when compared to other forms of multilevel administration may justify new empirical focal points. Further research is needed to determine whether relations between administrations within composite procedures, or in policy areas where composite decision-making exists, also function in a distinctively more integrated manner than in other instances of multilevel administration.

F. Beyond Direct or Indirect Administration

The development of the Unitary Protection doctrine corroborates, at the judicial level, what many scholars have suggested for years. Curtin and Egeberg, among many others, have pointed out that the 'distinction of direct and indirect administration has become blurred, with the levels being interwoven to form a more *unitary pattern of "integrated administration"*'.[61] Hofmann and Türk similarly describe the emergence of composite decision-making as a key development of European integrated administration.[62]

It is nevertheless hoped that the argument made in the book thus far has sufficiently demonstrated that composite decision-making – unlike other forms of multilevel administration – does indeed blur the divide between national/indirect and Union/direct administration. Composite decision-making operates neither in a scheme of direct, nor of indirect administration, and not even in one of mere coordination between the two. Combined, the authorities that act interdependently in composite decision-making represent a legal hybrid escaping the division between the two categories.[63]

Indeed, direct and indirect administration have never been characterised merely as consisting of authorities created by the Union or the Member States. Under Union law, national and Union administration are incorporated into the institutional framework of either the Member States or the Union and, under

[61] D Curtin and M Egeberg, 'Tradition and innovation: Europe's accumulated executive order' (2008) 31 *West European Politics* 639, 649.

[62] H Hofmann and A Türk, 'The Development of Integrated Administration in the EU and its Consequences' (2007) 13 *European Law Journal* 253.

[63] Legal hybrids can be defined as 'legal phenomena that our inherited conceptual framework is unable to capture and imprison in a determinate conceptual box' – see K Tuori, 'Transnational Law: on Legal Hybrids and Perspectivism' in M Poiares Maduro, K Tuori and S Sankari (eds), *Transnational Law: Rethinking European Law and Legal Thinking* (Cambridge University Press, 2014), 14.

the supervision of the respective courts, exercise their own independent powers subject to the applicable Union law requirements. Some requirements may apply both to national and Union administration – like sectoral legislation and general principles of law – or only to one – like national procedural autonomy and its limiting principles, for the former; and institutional balance and the *Meroni* doctrine, for the latter.

The integrated administration that exists in composite decision-making is similar in one respect, but differs in two. Composite decision-making continues to rely on the *organisational separation* between national and Union administration. National and Union authorities never cease to be incorporated into the Member States' and the Union's own political and constitutional systems. However, composite decision-making does not establish separate and independent, but rather joint and interdependent powers. Moreover, rather than merely recognising such interdependence, the doctrine of unitary protection provides it with an appropriate legal framing. Indeed, in order to account for decisional interdependence, the principles of Unitary Protection apply *specifically* to the national *and* Union authorities involved composite decision-making. Under the unique test of decisional dominance, those principles derogate from the law that governs purely national or European administration by determining that one court is competent to supervise the two and that general principles of law – including good administration rights – must apply according to special rules.

Given these two differences, it is fair to conclude that composite decision-making represents a *tertium genus* of administration, distinct from direct and indirect administration. It consists of national and Union administrations which, though organisationally separate, are legally governed and judicially controlled as one.

<table>
<tr><td rowspan="2">National administration</td><td colspan="2">Composite decision-making</td><td rowspan="2">Union administration</td></tr>
<tr><td colspan="2">Unitary procedural protection
Unitary judicial protection
Decisional dominance determines competence of national or Union courts and how burden to observe procedural rights is shared</td></tr>
<tr><td colspan="2">National courts
Specific principles – eg national procedural autonomy and its limits, effectiveness and equivalence</td><td colspan="2">Union courts
Specific principles – eg institutional balance and the Meroni doctrine
(+ legal basis for codification under Article 298 TFEU)</td></tr>
<tr><td colspan="4">Sectoral Union legislation
General principles of EU administrative law</td></tr>
</table>

VI. Europe's Administrative *Sonderweg*

At practically all of its major turns, Union constitutional law involved litigation against public administrative authorities. From *van Gend en Loos* to *Hauer*,[64] and from *Foto-Frost* to *N.S.* and *Schrems*,[65] such litigation pushed the CJEU to some of its most momentous innovations. Rulings such as *Berlusconi* – making the CJEU exclusively competent to review certain actions of national authorities – or *Jeanningros* – requiring the Commission to enforce national courts' judgments – are of no less constitutional significance. Yet these are but two rulings in a decades-long, slow-motion transformation of Union administrative law. That transformation was the process by which composite administrative procedures emerged and, guided by the hand of CJEU case law, were fitted with a legal framework of their own.

Such principles were needed because composite decision-making blurred the divide between national and Union administrative power beyond recognition. From the perspective of European political dynamics, this is somewhat ironic. After all, as Chapter three noted, one of the key reasons for the ubiquity of composite decision-making is its promise to strike an adequate balance of power between national and Union administration – specifically in terms of not granting the Union administration too much power to interfere with national administration. Yet for all their historical concern with keeping their administrations independent from the Union, the Member States advanced a form of administration that even federal states consider to unconstitutionally subvert the division of power between the States and the federation. It was the Member States, not the CJEU, which undermined that division. The CJEU's principles, inventive though they are, merely respond to the need to accommodate highly integrated administration by setting European Executive Federalism aside. New wineskins for new wine, where the old wineskins would undoubtedly crack.

The contrast between the political aim to preserve Member States' power and the implications of composite decision-making is particularly ironic in composite procedures where Union administration exercises decisional dominance – that is, in the overwhelming majority of composite procedures. Indeed, if that is what it takes to fully preserve rule of law requirements, the CJEU's case law allows national authorities to be treated as an extension of the Union administration. This is much like the sort of 'merger and acquisition' of national bureaucracies into the Union's own administration that the European Political Community Treaty would have allowed in 1954 – had it not been rejected for being too great a leap in the integration process.

[64] Cases 26/62 *NV Algemene Transport- en Expeditie Onderneming van Gend en Loos v Netherlands Inland Revenue Administration*, ECLI:EU:C:1963:1 and 44/79 *Hauer v Land Rheinland-Pfalz*, ECLI:EU:C:1979:290.

[65] Case 314/85 *Foto-Frost v Hauptzollamt Lübeck-Ost*, ECLI:EU:C:1987:452, Joined Cases C-411 and C-493 *N.S.*, ECLI:EU:C:2011:865, and Case C-362/14 *Schrems v Data Protection Commissioner*, ECLI:EU:C:2015:650.

However, the argument made here is *not* that actual administrative practice reflects such extensive cooperation. The point is doctrinal, not empirical. The point is merely that the CJEU's case law on composite decision-making generates the framework for an administrative system which could ultimately function in a far more integrated fashion than it does today – in a manner that tips from administrative integration into vertical administrative unification. Certain aspects of the CJEU's case law clearly imply that a 'shadow of hierarchy', legally at least, has already crept into the relations between national and Union administration. For instance, if the latter is required to scrutinise and, if need be, rectify the illegal contribution of national bodies to the administrative procedure, or answer judicially for said contribution in Union courts, then it is assumed *already* to be able to exercise some kind of supervisory control over national administration.

As throughout the course of European integration, Member States today may still wish to ultimately prevent national administration from dissolving into a joint, Union-led administration, or Union law from making such a scenario possible. If so, Member States must consider other options for the Union's administrative governance that they have hitherto found unattractive. The surest way to exploit the virtues of Union administration in the enforcement of Union law, without conscripting national authorities, is not to involve national authorities at all. Paradoxically, a strictly divided, dual order of power and a large, centralised Union administration may be what best serves the two conflicting aims of the Member States – to reap the benefits of sharing sovereignty while still preserving what remains of their own. If that is the case, it is perhaps to the American blueprint of a federal administrative system, rather than to the German, that the Union could look to next.

One well-known account holds that the European Union has followed a *constitutional Sonderweg* – a 'special path'.[66] The argument goes as follows. The Union's distinctive strand of constitutional law, a constitutional federalism without a federal *demos*, has been able to secure the Union's delicate balance of power, and hence its stability, by virtue of a set of unique constitutional principles and dynamics.

Inconspicuous in comparison to its more celebrated constitutional sibling, the Union's administrative law has followed a *Sonderweg* of its own. The administrative *Sonderweg* is complex, cooperative, and strives to uphold the Union's rule of law and, when possible, its jurisdictional divides. And in it, old principles forged from belief in Europe's federal destiny coexist with new principles that may yet pave the way for post-federal administration.

[66] See J Weiler, 'In Defence of the Status Quo: Europe's Constitutional *Sonderweg*' in J Weiler and M Wind (eds), *European Constitutionalism Beyond the State* (Cambridge University Press, 2003).

BIBLIOGRAPHY

Aarnio, A, *Essays on the Doctrinal Study of Law* (Springer, 2011).

Adinolfi, A, 'The "Procedural Autonomy" of Member States and the Constraints Stemming from the ECJ's Case Law: Is Judicial Activism Still Necessary?' in HW Micklitz and B de Witte, *The European Court of Justice and the Autonomy of the Member States* (Intersentia, 2012), 294.

Alexy, R, 'On the Structure of Legal Principles' (2000) 13 *Ratio Juris* 294.

Alonso de León, S, *Composite Administrative Procedures in the European Union* (Iustel, 2017).

Andersson, H, 'Dawn Raids under Challenge' (2014) 35 *European Competition Law Review* 135.

Aperio Bella, F, 'Procedimenti composti in materia di implementazione della politica agricola comune e garanzie procedimentali: il caso Oleificio Borelli "riletto" alla luce delle model rules in materia di decisioni individuali' in G della Cananea and M Conticelli (eds), *I Procedimenti amministrativi di adjudication dell'Unione Europea: principi generali e discipline settoriali* (Giappichelli, 2017), 314.

—— 'Composite Procedures and Procedural Guarantees: the 'Borelli Doctrine' in the Light of ReNEUAL Model Rules' (2020) 2 *Roma Tre Law Review* 7.

Arnull, A, 'The Principle of Effective Judicial Protection in EU law: An Unruly Horse?' (2011) 36 *European Law Review* 51.

Aroso de Almeida, M, *A Anulação de Actos Administrativos no Contexto das Relações Jurídico-Administrativas* (Almedina, 2021).

Arroyo Jiménez, L, 'Introduction: Quelle Théorie pour le Droit Administratif Européen?' in JB Auby and J Dutheil de la Rochère, *Traité de Droit Administratif Européen*, 3rd edn (Bruylant, 2022).

Avbelj, M, *The European Union under Transnational Law: A Pluralist Appraisal* (Hart Publishing, 2018).

Azoulai, L, 'Le Principe de Légalité' in JB Auby and J Dutheil de la Rochère (eds), *Droit Administratif Européen* (Bruylant, 2007).

—— *Les Garanties Procédurales en Droit Communautaire: recherches sur la procédure et le bon gouvernement* (unpublished EUI doctoral thesis).

Bach, T and Ruffing, E, 'The Transformative Effects of Transnational Administrative Coordination in the European Multi-level System' in E Ongaro and S van Thiel (eds), *The Palgrave Handbook of Public Administration and Management in Europe* (Palgrave Macmillan, 2017), 748.

Barbier de la Serre, E, 'Procedural Justice in the European Community Case-law concerning the Rights of the Defence: Essentialist and Instrumental Trends' (2006) 12 *European Public Law* 225.

Barents, R, *The Autonomy of Community Law* (Kluwer Law International, 2004).

—— 'The Precedence of EU Law from the Perspective of Constitutional Pluralism' (2009) 5 *European Constitutional Law Review* 421.

—— 'EU Procedural Law and Effective Judicial Protection' (2014) 51 *Common Market Law Review* 1437.

—— *Remedies and Procedures before the EU Courts* (Wolters Kluwer, 2016).

Barnes, J, 'Sobre el Procedimiento Administrativo: Evolución y Perspectivas' in J Barnes (ed), *Innovación y Reforma en el Derecho Administrativo* (Global Law Press, 2006), 261.

Bartosch, A, 'Procedural Rights Denied for Too Long: Is Legal Conservativism Finally Heading for Its "Götterdämmerung"?' (2011) 10 *European State Aid Law Quarterly* 580.

Beljin, S, 'Rights in EU Law' in S Prechal and B van Roermund (eds), *The Coherence of EU Law: The Search for Unity in Divergent Concepts* (Oxford University Press, 2008).

Benz, A., 'European Public Administration as Multilevel Administration: A conceptual Framework' in M Bauer and J Trondal (eds), *The Palgrave Handbook of the European Administrative System* (Palgrave Macmillan, 2015), 35.

Benz, A, Corcaci, A and Doser, JW, 'Unravelling multilevel administration. Patterns and dynamics of administrative co-ordination in European governance' (2016) 23 *Journal of European Public Policy* 999.

Bernard, N, *Multilevel Governance in the European Union* (Kluwer Law International, 2002).

Bhousta, R, 'Who Said There is a "Right to Good Administration"? A Critical Analysis of Article 41 of the Charter of Fundamental Rights of the European Union' (2013) 19 *European Public Law* 481.

Bierwagen, R, 'Review of Judgment in Case T-198/01 Technische Glaswerke Ilmenau v. European Commission' (2004) 3 *European State Aid Law Quarterly* 699.

Blauberger, M and Rittberger, B, 'Orchestrating Policy Implementation: EU Governance Through Regulatory Networks' in K Abbott, P Genschel, D Snidal and B Zangl (eds), *International Organizations as Orchestrators* (Cambridge University Press, 2015), 44.

Bobek, M, 'Thou shalt have two Masters: The Application of European Law by Administrative Authorities in the New Member States' (2008) 1 *Review of European Administrative Law* 51.

Bonelli, M, 'Effective Judicial Protection in EU Law: an Evolving Principle of a Constitutional Nature' (2019) 12 *Review of European Administrative Law* 35.

Bonelli, M and Claes, M, 'Judicial serendipity: how Portuguese judges came to the rescue of the Polish judiciary' (2018) 14 *European Constitutional Law Review*, 622.

Brito Bastos, F, 'The Borelli Doctrine Revisited: Three Issues of Coherence in a Landmark Ruling for EU Administrative Justice' (2015) 8 *Review of European Administrative Law* 269.

—— 'Derivative illegality in European composite administrative procedures' (2018) 55 *Common Market Law Review* 101.

—— 'An Administrative Crack in the EU's Rule of Law: Composite Decision-making and Nonjusticiable National Law' (2020) 16 *European Constitutional Law Review* 63.

—— 'Luxembourg v B: How Far Should Jurisdictional Limits Be Eroded in the Name of Effective Judicial Protection?' (2020) 41 *EU Law Live* 10.

—— 'Composite Procedures in the SSM and SRM – an Analytical Overview' in C Zilioli and KP Wojcik (eds), *Judicial Review in the European Banking Union* (Edward Elgar, 2021).

—— 'Doctrinal Methodology in EU Administrative Law: Confronting the "Touch of Stateness"' (2021) 22 *German Law Journal* 593.

—— 'Judicial Annulment of National Preparatory Acts and the Effects on Final Union Administrative Decisions: Comments on the Judgment of 29 January 2020, Case C-785/18 *Jeanningros*, ECLI:EU:C:2020:46' (2021) 14 *Review of European Administrative Law* 109.

—— 'Referential reasons-giving and the limits of Union Agencies' power', *REALaw.blog*, 2022 (https://wp.me/pcQ0x2-tx).

—— 'Repurposing Administrative Procedures to Meet Novel Challenges in EU Competition Law' in C Colombo and M Eliantonio (eds), The Evolving Governance of EU Competition Law in a Time of Disruptions: a Constitutional Perspective (Hart Publishing, 2023).

Brito Bastos, F and Curtin, D, 'Interoperable Information Sharing and the Five Novel Frontiers of EU Governance: A Special Issue' (2020) 26 *European Public Law* 59.

Brito Bastos, F and de Ruijter, A, 'Break or Bend in Case of Emergency? Rule of Law and State of Emergency in European Public Health Administration' (2020) 10 *European Journal of Risk Regulation* 611.

Britz, G, 'Vom Europäischen Verwaltungsverbund zum Regulierungsverbund? Europäische Verwaltungsentwicklung am Beispiel der Netzzugangsregulierung bei Telekommunikation, Energie und Bahn' (2006) *Europarecht* 46.

Brosset, E, 'The Prior Authorisation Procedure Adopted for the Deliberate Release into the Environment of Genetically Modified Organisms: the Complexities of Balancing Community and National Competences' (2004) 10 *European Law Journal* 555.

Brouwer, O and Curtin D, 'Why? The Giving Reasons Requirement of EU Administration' in M Bulterman, L Hancher, A McDonnell and H Sevenster (eds), *Views of European Law from the Mountain – Liber Amicorum Piet Jan Slot* (Kluwer Law International, 2009), 135.

Campbell, W, 'Commandeering and Constitutional Change' (2012–2013) 112 *Yale Law Journal* 1104.

Caranta, R, 'Sull'impugnabilità degli atti endoprocedimentali adottati dalle autorità nazionali nelle ipotesi di coamministrazione' (1994) 1 *Foro Amministrativo* 752.
—— 'Judicial Protection Against Member States: a New *Jus Commune* Takes Shape' (1995) 32 *Common Market Law Review* 703.
—— 'Coordinamento e divisione dei compiti tra Corte di giustizia delle comunità europee e giudizi nazionali nelle ipotesi di coamministrazione: il caso dei prodotti modificati geneticamente' (2000) *Rivista Italiana di Diritto Pubblico Comunitario* 1133.
Casetta, E, *Manuale di Diritto Amministrativo*, 11th edn (Giuffrè, 2009).
Casini, L, Cassese, S and Napolitano, G, 'The New Italian Public Law Scholarship' (2011) 9 *International Journal of Constitutional Law* 301.
Cassatella, A, 'Il dovere di motivazione nello *jus commune* europeo' in G della Cananea and M Conticelli (eds), *I Procedimenti Amministrativi di Adjudication dell'Unione Europea: Principi Generali e Discipline Settoriali* (Giappichelli, 2017), 17.
Cassese, S, *Le Basi del Diritto Amministrativo* (Garzanti, 2000).
—— 'European Administrative Proceedings' (2004–2005) 68 *Law and Contemporary Problems* 21.
Chalmers, D, 'Risk, anxiety and the European mediation of the politics of life' (2005) 30 *European Law Review* 649.
Chalmers, D and Barroso, L, 'What *van Gend en Loos* stands for' (2014) 12 *International Journal of Constitutional Law* 105.
Chamon, M, Volpato, A and Eliantonio, M, *Boards of Appeal of EU Agencies: Towards Judicialization of Administrative Review?* (Oxford University Press, 2022).
Chirulli, P, 'Amministrazioni Nazionali ed Esecuzione del Diritto Europeo' in L de Lucia and B Marchetti (eds), *L'Amministrazione Europea e le sue Regole* (Il Mulino, 2015) 167.
Chiti, E, 'An important part of the EU's institutional machinery: features, problems and perspectives of European agencies' (2009) 46 *Common Market Law Review* 1395.
—— 'The Administrative Implementation of European Union law: a Taxonomy and its Implications' in H Hofmann and A Türk (eds), *Legal Challenges in EU Administrative Law* (Edward Elgar, 2009) 9.
Chiti, M, 'I Procedimenti Composti nel Diritto Comunitario e nel Diritto Interno' in *Quaterni del Consiglio di Stato: Attività amministrativa e tutela degli interessati. L'influenza del diritto comunitario* (Centro studi e documentazione del Consiglio di Stato, 1997).
Classen, KD, *Gute Verwaltung im Recht der Europäischen Union* (Duncker & Humblot, 2006).
Coman Kund, F and Amtenbrink, F, 'On the Scope and Limits of the Application of National Law by the European Central Bank within the Single Supervisory Mechanism' (2018) 33 *Banking and Finance Law Review* 133.
Constantinesco, V, 'The ECJ as a Law-Maker: *Praeter aut Contra Legem?*' in D O'Keefe and A Bavasso (eds), *Judicial Review in European Union Law: Liber Amicorum in Honour of Lord Slynn of Hadley*, I (Kluwer Law International, 2000), 77.
Craig, P, *EU Administrative Law*, 2nd edn (Oxford University Press, 2012).
—— *EU Administrative Law*, 3rd edn (Oxford University Press, 2018).
Curtin, D, 'Constitutionalism in the European Community. The Right to Fair Procedures in Administrative Law' in B Walsh and J O'Reilly, *Human Rights and Constitutional Law. Essays in Honour of Brian Walsh* (Round Hall Press, 1992).
—— *Executive Power in the European Union: Law, Practices, and the Living Constitution* (Oxford University Press, 2009).
Curtin, D and Egeberg, M, 'Tradition and innovation: Europe's accumulated executive order' (2008) 31 *West European Politics* 639.
Da Cruz Vilaça, 'Effective Judicial Protection with Regard to Community Funds – May One be Directly Concerned by a Decision Addressed to a Member State?' in JL da Cruz Vilaça, *EU Law and Integration: Twenty Years of Judicial Application of EU Law* (Hart Publishing, 2014), 178.
De Lucia, L, *Amministrazione Transnazionale e Ordinamento Europeo: saggio sul pluralismo amministrativo* (Giappichelli, 2009).
—— 'Conflict and Cooperation within European Composite Administration (Between Philia and Eris)' (2012) 5 *Review of European Administrative Law* 49.

De Pretis, D, 'Procedimenti amministrativi nazionali e procedimenti amministrativi europei' in G Falcon (ed), *Il procedimento amministrativo nei diritti europei e nel diritto comunitario* (CEDAM, 2008), 68.

Della Cananea, G, 'The European Union's Mixed Administrative Proceedings' (2003–2004) 68 *Law and Contemporary Problems* 197.

—— 'Return to the due process of law: the European Union and the fight against terrorism' (2007) 32 *European Law Review* 986.

—— *Diritto amministrativo europeo: principi ed istituti*, 3rd edn (Giuffrè, 2011).

—— *Due Process of Law beyond the State: Requirements of Administrative Procedure* (Oxford University Press, 2016).

—— 'The European Administration: *Imperium* and *Dominium*' in C Harlow, P Leino and G della Cananea (eds), *Research Handbook on EU administrative Law* (Edward Elgar, 2017), 62.

Della Cananea, G, Franchini, C and Macchia, M, *I Principi dell'Amministrazione Europea*, 3rd edn (Giappichelli, 2017).

Detterbeck, S, *Allgemeines Verwaltungsrecht mit Verwaltungsprozessrecht*, 18th edn (CH Beck, 2020).

Donner, A, 'National Law and the Case Law of the Court of Justice of the European Communities' (1963) 1 *Common Market Law Review* 8.

—— *The Role of the Lawyer in the European Communities* (Northwestern University Press, 1968), 14.

Due, O, 'Le respect des droits de la défense dans le droit administratif communautaire' (1987) *Cahiers de Droit Européen* 383.

—— 'Article 5 du traité CEE. Une disposition de caractère fédéral?' in F Emmert (ed), *Collected Courses of the Academy of European Law* (Martinus Nijhoff, 1991), 23.

Duijkersloot, T, 'Consequences of the Violation by Administrative Authorities of the Right to be heard under EU Law: the Case M.G. and N.R.' (2014) 7 *Review of European Administrative Law* 81.

Eckes, C and Mendes, J, 'The right to be heard in composite administrative procedures: Lost in between Protection?' (2011) 36 *European Law Review* 665.

Egeberg, M, 'EU Administration: Center Formation and Multilevelness' in M Bauer and J Trondal (eds), *The Palgrave Handbook of the European Administrative System* (Palgrave Macmillan, 2015), 66.

Egeberg, M and Trondal, J, 'National Agencies in the European Administrative Space: Government Driven, Commission Driven, or Networked?' (2009) 87 *Public Administration* 779, 781.

Ehlers, D, 'Verwaltung und Verwaltungsrecht im demokratischen und sozialen Rechtsstaat' in H-U Erichsen and D Ehlers (eds), *Allgemeines Verwaltungsrecht*, 14th edn (De Gruyter, 2010), 245.

Eliantonio, M, *Europeanisation of Administrative Justice?: The influence of the ECJ's case law in Italy, Germany and England* (Europa Law Publishing, 2009).

—— 'Judicial Review in an Integrated Administration: the Case of "Composite Procedures"' (2014) 7 *Review of European Administrative Law* 65.

—— 'Information Exchange in European Administrative Law: A Threat to Effective Judicial Protection?' (2016) 23 *Maastricht Journal of European and Comparative Law* 531.

Eliantonio, M and Dermine, P, 'Case Note: CJEU (Grand Chamber), Judgment of 19 December 2018, C-219/17, *Silvio Berlusconi and Finanziaria d'investimento Fininvest SpA (Fininvest) v Banca d'Italia and Istituto per la Vigilanza Sulle Assicurazioni*' (2019) 12 *Review of European Administrative Law* 237.

Eliantonio, M and Dragos, D, *Indirect Judicial Review in Administrative Law Legality vs Legal Certainty in Europe* (Routledge, 2023).

Ellerbrok, T, 'Das umgekehrte Vorabentscheidungsverfahren als Schlussstein im europäischen Rechtsschutzverbund' (2022) 113 *Verwaltungsarchiv* 302.

Everling, U, 'Zur föderalen Struktur der Europäischen Gemeinschaft' in K Heibronner, G Ress and T Stein (eds), *Staat und Volkerrechtsordnung. Festschrift für Karl Doehring* (Springer, 1989).

—— 'Die Europäische Union als föderaler Zusammenschluss von Staaten und Bürgern' in A von Bogdandy and J Bast, *Europäisches Verfassungsrecht: theoretische und dogmatische Grundzüge* (Springer, 2009).

Fernández Gaztea, J, *Cooperación Procedimental en la Unión Europea* (Tirant lo Blanch, 2020).

Fink, M, 'EU liability for contributions to Member States' breaches of EU law' (2019) 56 *Common Market Law Review* 1227.

Franchini, C, *Amministrazione Italiana e Amministrazione Comunitaria*, 2nd edn (CEDAM, 1993).

—— 'I principi applicabili ai procedimenti amministrativi europei' (2003) *Rivista Italiana di Diritto Pubblico Comunitario* 1037.

—— 'European Principles Covering National Administrative Proceedings' (2004–2005) 68 *Law and Contemporary Problems* 183.

Friant-Perrot, M, 'The European Union Regulatory Regime for Genetically Modified Organisms and its Integration into Community Food Law and Policy' in L Bodiguel and M Cardwell (eds), *The Regulation of Genetically Modified Organisms: Comparative Approaches* (Oxford University Press, 2010), 90.

Fritz, V, 'Activism on and Off the Bench: Pierre Pescatore and the Law of Integration' (2020), 57 *Common Market Law Review* 475.

Gaja, G, 'Case C-6/99, *Association Greenpeace France and Others v. Ministère de l'Agriculture et de la Pêche and Others*. Judgment of the Full Court of 21 March 2000' (2000) 37 *Common Market Law Review* 1427.

Galetta, DU, 'Coamministrazione, reti di amministrazioni, *Verwaltungsverbund*: modelli organizzativi nuovi o alternative semantiche alla nozione di «cooperazione amministrativa» dell'art 10 TCE, per definire il fenomeno dell'amministrazione intrecciata?' (2009) *Rivista Italiana di Diritto Pubblico Comunitario* 1689.

—— *Procedural Autonomy of EU Member States: Paradise Lost?* (Springer, 2010).

—— 'Informal Information Processing in Dispute Resolution Networks: Informality Versus the Protection of Individual's Rights?' (2014) 20 *European Public Law* 71.

Galetta, DU, Hofmann, H and Schneider, JP, 'Information Exchange in the European Administrative Union: An Introduction' (2014) 20 *European Public Law* 65.

Gambardella, M, Rovetta, D and van Cutsem, S, *Remission and Repayment of customs duties in the EU* (Wolters Kluwer, 2014).

García de Enterría, E, 'La ampliación de la competencia de las jurisdicciones contencioso-administrativas nacionales por obra del Derecho Comunitario. Sentencia Borelli de 3 de diciembre de 1992 del Tribunal de Justicia y el artículo 5 CEE' (1993) 77 *Revista Española de Derecho Administrativo* 297.

Genschel, P and Jachtenfuchs, M, 'Introduction: Beyond Market Regulation. Analysing the European Integration of Core State Powers' in P Genschel and M Jachtenfuchs (eds), *Beyond the Regulatory Polity? The European Integration of Core State Powers* (Oxford University Press, 2014), 7.

Gentile, G, 'Effective Judicial Protection: Enforcement, Judicial Federalism and the Politics of EU Law' (2022) 2 *European Law Open* 1.

Gentile, G and Lynskey, O, 'Deficient by Design? The Transnational Enforcement of the GDPR' (2022) 71 *International and Comparative Law Quarterly* 799.

Giannini, MS, 'Profili di un diritto amministrativo delle Communità europee' (1967), published posthumously in (2003) 53(4) *Rivista Trimestrale di Diritto Pubblico* 979.

Giorgio Mattarella, B, 'Procedimenti e Atti Amministrativi' in M Chiti (ed), *Diritto Amministrativo Europeo* (Giuffrè, 2013) 338.

Grande, E, and McCowan, M, 'The Two Logics of Multilevel Administration in the EU' in M Bauer and J Trondal (eds), *The Palgrave Handbook of the European Administrative System* (Palgrave Macmillan, 2015).

Greco, G, 'Il potere amministrativo nella (più recente) giurisprudenza del giudice comunitario' (2009) *Rivista Italiana di Diritto Pubblico Comunitario* 819.

Guastini, R, 'Invalidity' (1994) 7 *Ratio Juris* 212.

Gutman, K, 'The Essence of the Fundamental Right to an Effective Remedy and to a Fair Trial in the Case-Law of the Court of Justice of the European Union: The Best is Yet to Come?' (2019) 20 *German Law Journal* 884.

Hallstein, W, *Die Europäische Gemeinschaft* (ECON, 1979).

—— 'Zu den Grundlagen und Verfassungsprinzipien der Europäischen Gemeinschaften' in W Hallstein and H-J Schlochauer (eds), *Zur Integration Europas. Festschrift für Carl Friedrich Ophüls FS Ophüls* (Müller, 1965).

Halpin, A, 'The Concept of a Legal Power' (1996) 16 *Oxford Journal of Legal Studies* 129.

Harlow, C, *Accountability in the European Union* (Oxford University Press, 2002).

—— 'Three Phases in the Evolution of EU Administrative Law' in P Craig and G de Búrca (eds), *The Evolution of EU Law* (Oxford University Press, 2011), 450.

Harlow, C and Rawlings, R, *Law and Administration*, 4th edn (Cambridge University Press, 2021).

Heidbreder, E, 'Structuring the European Administrative Space: Policy Instruments of Multi-level Administration' (2011) 18 *Journal of European Public Policy* 709.

Hofmann, H, 'Composite decision making procedures in EU administrative law' in H Hofmann and A Türk (eds), *Legal Challenges in EU Administrative Law: Towards an integrated administration* (Edward Elgar, 2009), 137.

—— 'Decision-Making in EU Administrative Law – The Problem of Composite Procedures' (2009) 61 *Administrative Law Review* 199.

—— 'Seven Challenges for EU Administrative Law' in K de Graaf, J Jans, A Prechal and R Widdershoven (eds), *European Administrative Law: Top-Down and Bottom-up: Proceedings of the First REALaw Research Forum* (Europa Law Publishing, 2010).

Hofmann, H and Micheau, C, *State Aid Law of the European Union* (Oxford University Press, 2016).

Hofmann, H and Mihaescu, B, 'The Relation between the Charter's Fundamental Rights and the Unwritten General Principles of EU Law: Good Administration as the Test Case' (2013) 9 *European Constitutional Law Review* 73.

Hofmann, H, Rowe, G, and Türk, A, *Administrative Law and Policy of the European Union* (Oxford University Press, 2011).

Hofmann, H and Tidghi, M, 'Rights and Remedies in Implementation of EU Policies by Multi-Jurisdictional Networks' (2014) 20 *European Public Law* 147.

Hofmann, H and Türk, A, 'The Development of Integrated Administration in the EU and its Consequences' (2007) 13 *European Law Journal* 253.

—— 'Legal Challenges in EU administrative Law by the Move to an Integrated Administration' in H Hofmann and A Türk (eds), *Legal Challenges in EU Administrative Law: Towards an Integrated Administration* (Edward Elgar, 2009).

Hofmann, J, 'Legal Protection and Liability in the European Composite Administration' in O Jansen and B Schöndorf-Haubold (eds), *The European Composite Administration* (Intersentia, 2011), 461.

Hooghe, L and Marks, G, *Multi-Level Governance and European Integration* (Rowman & Littlefield, 2002).

Ipsen, HP, 'The Relationship between the Law of the European Communities and National Law' (1966) 3 *Common Market Law Review* 379.

—— 'Deutsche Verwaltung und europäische Wirtschaftsintegration' (1968) 21 *Die Öffentliche Verwaltung* 441.

Isensee, J, 'Idee und Gestalt des Föderalismus im Grundgesetz' in J Isensee and P Kirchhof (eds), *Handbuch des Staatsrechts der Bundesrepublik Deutschland*, vol VI (Müller, 2008), 111.

Johnstone, A, 'Commandeering Information – and Informing the Commandeered' (2012) 161 *University of Pennsylvania Law Review* 205.

Kadelbach, S, 'European Administrative Law and the Law of a Europeanized Administration' in C Joerges and R Dehousse, *Good Governance in Europe's Integrated Market* (Oxford University Press, 2002), 176.

Kahl, W, *Wissenschaft, Praxis und Dogmatik im Verwaltungsrecht* (Mohr Siebeck, 2020).

Kańska, K, 'Towards Administrative Human Rights in the EU. Impact of the Charter of Fundamental Rights' (2004) 10 *European Law Journal* 296.

Keessen, A, *European Administrative Decisions: how the EU regulates products on the internal market* (Europa Law Publishing, 2009).

Koivisto, I, 'From Moral Rules to Individual Rights – and Beyond? The Institutionalization of Good Administration in Finland and in Europe' (2018) 1 *Förvaltningsrättslig Tidskrift* 71.

Komesar, N, *Imperfect Alternatives: Choosing Institutions in Law, Economics, and Public Policy* (University of Chicago Press, 1997).
Küchenhoff, B, *Die verfassungsrechtlichen Grenzen der Mischverwaltung* (Nomos, 2010).
L'Huillier, J, 'Une conquête du droit administratif français: Le contentieux de la Communauté européenne du charbon et de l'acier' (1953) 13 *Recueil Dalloz: Chronique* 63.
Laprévote, FC, 'A Missed Opportunity? State aid Modernization and Effective Third Parties Rights in State aid Proceedings' (2014) 13 *European State Aid Law Quarterly* 426.
Lauwaars, R, 'Rights of Defence in Competition Cases' in D Curtin and T Heukels (eds), *Institutional Dynamics of European Integration: Essays in Honour of Henry G. Schermers*, vol II (Martinus Nijhoff, 1994).
Leino, P, 'Efficiency, Citizens and Administrative Culture. The Politics of Good Administration in the EU' (2014) 20 *European Public Law* 681.
Lenaerts, K, 'The Basic Constitutional Charter of a Community Based on the Rule of Law' in M Poiares Maduro and L Azoulai (eds), *The Past and Future of EU Law: The Classics of EU Law Revisited on the 50th Anniversary of the Rome Treaty* (Hart Publishing, 2010), 303.
—— 'The Court's Outer and Inner Selves: Exploring the External and Internal Legitimacy of the European Court of Justice' in M Adams, H de Waele, J Meeusen and G Straetmans (eds), *Judging Europe's Judges: The Legitimacy of the Case Law of the European Court of Justice* (Hart Publishing, 2013).
—— 'New Horizons for the Rule of Law in the EU' (2020) 21 *German Law Journal* 29.
Lenaerts, K, Maselis, I and Gutman, K, *EU Procedural Law* (Oxford University Press, 2014).
Limbach, K, *Uniformity of Customs Administration in the European Union* (Hart, 2015).
Lottini, M, 'From 'Administrative Cooperation' in the Application of European Union Law to 'Administrative Cooperation' in the Protection of European Rights and Liberties' (2012) 18 *European Public Law* 127.
Loughlin, M, *The Foundations of Public Law* (Oxford University Press, 2010).
Lupo, N, 'The Advantage of Having the First Word in the Composite European Constitution' (2018) 10 *Italian Journal of Public Law* 186.
Lyons, T, *EC Customs Law* (Oxford University Press, 2008).
Maeso Seco, L, 'I Procedimenti Composti Comunitari: Riflessioni Intorno alla Problematica della Impossibilità a Difendersi ed Eventuali Alternative' in G della Cananea and M Gnes (eds), *I Procedimenti Amministrativi dell'Unione Europea. Un'Indagine* (Giappichelli, 2004), 12.
Maier, M and Werner, P, 'Judgment of 30 November 2009 in Cases T-427/04 and T-1 7/05, *France and France Telecom SA v Commission*: Comments on Cases T-427/04 and T-1 7/05' (2011) 10 *European State Aid Law Quarterly* 715.
Majone, G, 'From the Positive to the Regulatory State: Causes and Consequences of Changes in the Mode of Governance' (1997) 17 *Journal of Public Policy* 139.
Marchetti, B, 'Fondi Strutturali e tutela giurisdizionale: Variazione degli schemi regolatori e conseguenze sull'architettura giudiziaria dell'EU' (2012) *Rivista Italiana di Diritto Pubblico Comunitario* 1105.
—— 'Il Sistema Integrato di Tutela' in L de Lucia and B Marchetti (eds), *L'amministrazione europea e le sue regole* (Il Mulino, 2015), 198.
Marique, Y, 'Rule of Law and Administrative Justice' in M Hertogh, R Kirkham, R Thomas, and J Tomlinson (eds), *The Oxford Handbook of Administrative Justice* (Oxford University Press, 2022).
Markakis, M, 'Composite Procedures and Judicial Review in the Single Resolution Mechanism: *Iccrea Banca*' (2021) 13 *Review of European Administrative Law* 109.
Martinière, JM, *Collaboration entre l'ordre juridique communautaire et les ordres juridiques nationaux dans le secteur de l'agriculture: rapport français présenté à la Commission I (Agriculture) du Vième congrès international de droit européen* (Fédération Internationale pour le Droit Européen (FIDE), 1970), 10.
Mashaw, J, 'Reasoned Administration: the European Union, the United States and the Project of Democratic Governance' (2007) 76 *George Washington Law Review* 99.
Massaro, M, 'Between Integration and Protection of National Sovereignty in the European Union's Radio Spectrum Policy' (2019) 9 *Journal of Information Policy* 174.

Mastenbroek, E and Martinsen, D, 'Filling the gap in the European Administrative Space: the Role of Administrative Networks in EU Implementation and Enforcement' (2018) 25 *Journal of European Public Policy* 422.
Mattarella, BG, 'Procedimenti e Atti Amministrativi' in M Chiti (ed), *Diritto Amministrativo Europeo* (Giuffrè, 2013), 337.
—— 'Indeterminacy and Legal Uncertainty in EU Law' in J Mendes (ed), *EU Executive Discretion and the Limits of Law* (Oxford University Press, 2019).
Mazzotti, P, and Eliantonio, M, 'Transnational Judicial Review in Horizontal Composite Procedures: Berlioz, Donnellan, and the Constitutional Law of the Union' (2020) 5 *European Papers* 41.
Mendes, J, *Participation in EU Rule-Making: A Rights-Based Approach* (Oxford University Press, 2011).
—— 'Discretion, Care and Public Interests in the EU Administration: Probing the Limits of Law' (2016) 53 *Common Market Law Review* 421.
—— 'The Foundations of the Duty to Give Reasons and a Normative Reconstruction' in E Fisher, J King and A Young (eds), *The Foundations and Future of Public Law: Essays in Honour of Paul Craig* (Oxford University Press, 2020), 299.
—— 'The Foundations of EU Administrative Law as a Scholarly Field: Functional Comparison, Normativism and Integration' (2022) 18 *European Constitutional Law Review* 706.
Menéndez, AJ, 'Is European Union law a pluralist legal order?' in AJ Menéndez and JE Fossum, *The Post-Sovereign Constellation: Law and Democracy in Neil D. MacCormick's Legal and Political theory* (Arena, 2008), 249.
Mento, S, 'I poteri amministrativi della Commissione europea in materia di fondi strutturali' (2007) *Rivista Trimestrale di Diritto Pubblico* 135.
Mihaescu Evans, B, *The Right to Good administration at the Crossroads of the Various Sources of Fundamental Rights in the EU Integrated Administrative System* (Nomos, 2015).
Millata, R and Ramajoli, M, *Il Provvedimento Amministrativo*, 2nd edn (Giappichelli, 2017).
Nehl, HP, *Principles of Administrative Procedure in EC Law* (Hart Publishing, 1999).
—— *Europäisches Verwaltungsverfahren und Gemeinschaftsverfassung. Eine Studie gemeinschaftsrechtlicher Verfahrensgrundsätze unter besonderer Berücksichtigung 'mehrstufiger' Verwaltungsverfahren* (Duncker & Humblot, 2002).
—— 'The Imperfect Procedural Status of Beneficiaries of Aid in EC State Aid Proceedings: Note on Case C-276/03 P, *Scott SA v. Commission*' (2006) 5 *European State Aid Law Quarterly* 57.
—— 'Legal Protection in the Field of EU Funds' (2011) 10 *European State Aid Law Quarterly* 629.
Nic Shuibhne, N, 'What is the Autonomy of EU Law, and Why Does that Matter?' (2019) 88 *Nordic Journal of International Law* 9.
Nieto Garrido, E and Martín Delgado, I, *European Administrative Law in the Constitutional Treaty* (Hart Publishing, 2007), 103.
Oebbecke, J, 'Verwaltungszuständigkeit' in J Isensee and P Kirchhof (eds), *Handbuch des Staatsrechts der Bundesrepublik Deutschland*, vol VI (Müller, 2008).
Oliveira, FP and Figueiredo Dias, JE, *Noções Fundamentais de Direito Administrativo*, 5th edn (Almedina, 2022).
Ophüls, C-F, 'Zur ideengeschichtlichen Herkunft der Gemeinschaftsverfassung' in E von Caemmerer et al (eds), *Probleme des europäischen Rechts. Festschrift für Walter Hallstein zu seinem 65. Geburtstag* (Vittorio Klostermann, 1966), 405.
Owen, D and Wiseman, H, 'Coequal Federalism and Federal-State Agencies' (2020) 55 *Georgia Law Review* 287.
Pagoulatos, G and Tsoukalis, L, 'Multilevel Governance' in E Jones, A Menon and S Weatherill (eds), *The Oxford Handbook of the European Union* (Oxford University Press, 2012), 62.
Pech, L, 'A Union Founded on the Rule of Law: Meaning and Reality of the Rule of Law as a Constitutional Principle of EU Law' (2010) 6 *European Constitutional Law Review* 359.
—— 'The Rule of Law as a Well-Established and Well-Defined Principle of EU Law' (2022) 14 *Hague Journal on the Rule of Law* 107.
Perfetti, L, 'Diritto ad una buona amministrazione, determinazione dell'interesse pubblico ed equità' (2010) 3 *Rivista Italiana di Diritto Pubblico Comunitario* 789.

Pescatore, P, 'Distribución de competencias y de poderes entre los estados miembros y las comunidades europeas' (1967) 1 *Derecho de la Integración* 108.

—— *The Law of Integration: emergence of a new phenomenon in international relations, based on the experience of the European Communities* (AW Sijthoff, 1974).

Pietzcker, J, 'Zuständigkeitsordnug und Kollisionsrecht im Bundesstaat' in J Isensee and P Kirchhof (eds), *Handbuch des Staatsrechts der Bundesrepublik Deutschland*, vol VI (Müller, 2008), 535.

Pöyhönen, J, 'On the Role of Theories in Legal Dogmatics' (1981) 2 *Rechtstheorie* 127.

Prek, M and Lefèvre, S, 'The EU Courts as "National" Courts: National Law in the EU Judicial Process' (2017) 54 *Common Market Law Review* 369.

Pünder, H, 'Administrative procedure – mere facilitator of material law versus cooperative realisation of commonwelfare' in H Pünder and C Waldhoff (eds), *Debates in German Public Law* (Hart Publishing, 2014) 240.

Rabinovici, I, 'The Right to Be Heard in the Charter of Fundamental Rights of the European Union' (2012) 18 *European Public Law* 149.

Raitio, J, 'Does the concept of rule of law have any material content? A Nordic point of view' (2017) 24 *Maastricht Journal of European and Comparative Law* 774.

Rasmussen, M, 'The Origins of a Legal Revolution: The Early History of the European Court of Justice' (2008) *14 Journal of European Integration History* 77.

Raz, J, *The Authority of Law: Essays on Law and Morality* (Clarendon Press, 1979).

—— 'Authority, Law and Morality' (1985) 68 *The Monist* 295.

Reichel, J, 'Communicating with the European Composite Administration' (2014) 15 *German Law Journal* 883.

Rengeling, HW, *Rechtsgrundsätze beim Verwaltungsvollzug des Europäischen Gemeinschaftsrechts* (Carl Heymanns, 1977).

Reuter, E, 'L'engagement général de coopération des Etats Membres avec la Haute Autorité et les nécessités de contrôle dans le domaine des prix' (1966) *Cahiers de Droit Européen* 52.

Röhl, HC, 'Die Anfechtbare Entscheidung nach Art. 230 Abs. 4 EGV' in E Schmidt-Aßmann and B Schöndorf-Haubold (eds), *Der Europäische Verwaltungsverbund* (CH Beck, 2005), 330.

—— 'Procedures in the European Composite Administration' in J Barnes, *Transforming Administrative Procedure* (Global Law Press, 2008).

Röttger-Wirtz, S, 'Fine-tuning the Impartiality of EMA Procedures: Case C-680/16 P *Dr. August Wolff GmbH vs European Commission*' (2019) 3 *European Pharmaceutical Law Review* 192.

Röttger-Wirtz, S and Eliantonio, M, 'From Integration to Exclusion: EU Composite Administration and Gaps in Judicial Accountability in the Authorisation of Pharmaceuticals' (2019) 10 *European Journal of Risk Regulation* 393.

Sacchi Morsiani, *Il potere amministrativo delle Comunità europee e le posizioni giuridiche dei privati* (Giuffrè, 1965).

Sajfan, M and Düsterhaus, D, 'A Union of Effective Judicial Protection: Addressing a Multi-level Challenge through the Lens of Article 47 CFREU' (2014) 33 *Yearbook of European Law* 3.

Sandulli, A, 'The Double Face of the Rule of Law in the European Legal Order: an Administrative Law Perspective' (2020) 5 *European Papers* 237.

Schmidt-Aßmann, E, 'Strukturen des Europäischen Verwaltungsrechts: Einleitende Problemskizze' in E Schmidt-Aßmann and W Hoffmann-Riem (eds), *Strukturen des Europäischen Verwaltungsrechts* (Nomos, 1999) 9.

—— 'Cuestiones Fundamentales Sobre la Reforma de la Teoría General del Derecho Administrativo. Necesidad de la Innovación y Presupuestos Metodológicos' in J Barnes (ed), *Innovación y Reforma en el Derecho Administrativo* (Global Law Press, 2006).

—— 'Introduction: European Composite Administration and the Role of European Administrative Law' in O Jansen and B Schöndorf-Haubold (eds), *The European Composite Administration* (Intersentia, 2011), 1.

Schmidt-Aßmann, E and Dagron, S, 'Deutsches und französisches Verwaltungsrecht im Vergleich ihrer Ordnungsideen. Zur Geschlossenheit, Offenheit und gegenseitigen Lernfähigkeit von Rechtssystemen' (2007) 67 *Zeitschrift für ausländisches öffentliches Recht und Völkerrecht* 395.

Schneider, JP, 'Basic Structures of Information Management in the European Administrative Union' (2014) 20 *European Public Law* 89.
—— *Verwaltungsrechtliche Dogmatik* (Mohr Siebeck, 2013).
Scholten, M, 'Mind the trend! Enforcement of EU law has been moving to "Brussels"' (2017) 24 *Journal of European Public Policy* 1348.
—— 'Shared Tasks, but Separated Controls: Building the System of Control for Shared Administration in an EU Multi-Jurisdictional Setting' (2019) 10 *European Journal of Risk Regulation* 538.
Schöndorf-Haubold, B, *Die Strukturfonds der Europäischen Gemeinschaft: Rechtsformen und Verfahren europäischer Verbundverwaltung* (CH Beck, 2005).
Schütze, R, *From Dual to Cooperative Federalism: The Changing Structure of European Law* (Oxford University Press, 2009).
—— 'From Rome to Lisbon: "Executive Federalism" in the (New) European Union' (2010), 47 *Common Market Law Review* 1385.
—— *From Dual to Cooperative Federalism: The Changing Structure Of European Law* (Oxford University Press, 2013).
—— *European Constitutional Law*, 3rd edn (Oxford University Press, 2021).
Schwarze, J, *Europäisches Verwaltungsrecht: Entstehung und Entwicklung im Rahmen der Europäischen Gemeinschaft* (Nomos, 1988).
—— 'Developing principles of European administrative law' (1993) *Public Law* 229.
—— 'The Procedural Guarantees in the Recent Case-law of the European Court of Justice' in D Curtin and T Heukels (eds), *Institutional Dynamics of European Integration: Essays in Honour of Henry G. Schermers*, vol II (Martinus Nijhoff, 1994).
—— 'Judicial Review of European Administrative Procedure' (2004) 68 *Law and Contemporary Problems* 85.
—— *Europäisches Verwaltungsrecht: Entstehung und Entwicklung im Rahmen der Europäischen Gemeinschaft*, 2nd edn (Nomos, 2005).
—— 'European Administrative Law in the Light of the Treaty of Lisbon' (2012) 18 *European Public Law* 285.
Shapiro, M, 'The Giving Reasons Requirement' (1992) 92 *University of Chicago Legal Forum* 179.
Shaw, J, and Wiener, A, 'The Paradox of the "European Polity"' in M Green Cowles and M Smith (eds), *Risks, Reform, Resistance, and Revival* (Oxford University Press, 2000).
Shirvani, F, 'Verfahrensgrundrechte in mehrstufigen, das EU-Recht vollziehenden Verwaltungsverfahren – Dargestellt am Beispiel des Arzneimittelzulassungs- und Gentechnikrechts' (2011), 126 *Deutsches Verwaltungsblatt* 674.
Simoncini, M, *Administrative Regulation beyond the Non-Delegation Doctrine: A study on EU Agencies* (Hart Publishing, 2018).
—— 'Challenges of Justice in the European Banking Union: Administrative Integration and Mismatches in Jurisdiction' (2021) 40 *Yearbook of European Law* 310.
Somek, A, *Individualism* (Oxford University Press, 2008).
Sydow, G, *Verwaltungskooperation in der Europäischen Union* (Mohr Siebeck, 2004).
Tamanaha, B, *On the Rule of Law: History, Politics, Theory* (Cambridge University Press, 2004).
—— 'A Concise Guide to the Rule of Law' in G Palombella and N Walker (eds), *Relocating the Rule of Law* (Hart Publishing, 2009).
Tarrant, A and Keleman, D, 'Reconceptualising European Union Regulatory Networks: A response to Blauberger and Rittberger' (2017) 11 *Regulation & Governance* 213.
Tavares Lanceiro, R and Eliantonio, M, 'The Genetically Modified Organisms' Regime: A Playground for Multi-Level Administration and a Nightmare for Effective Judicial Protection?' (2021) 22 *German Law Journal* 371.
Thomas, R, 'Reasons-giving in English and European Community Administrative Law' (1997) 3 *European Public Law* 213.
Tridimas, T, *The General Principles of EU law*, 2nd edn (Oxford University Press, 2006).

Trondal, J, 'National Agencies in the European Administrative Space: Government Driven, Commission Driven or Networked?' (2009) 87 *Public Administration* 779.
Trondal, J and Bauer, M, 'Conceptualizing the European multilevel administrative order: capturing variation in the European administrative system' (2017) 9 *European Political Science Review* 73.
Trondal, J and Peters, G, 'A Conceptual Account of the European Administrative Space' in M Bauer and J Trondal (eds), *The Palgrave Handbook of the European Administrative System* (Palgrave Macmillan, 2015), 88.
Tuori, K, *Ratio and Voluntas* (Ashgate, 2011).
—— 'Transnational Law: on Legal Hybrids and Perspectivism' in M Poiares Maduro, K Tuori and S Sankari (eds), *Transnational Law: Rethinking European Law and Legal Thinking* (Cambridge University Press, 2014), 14.
—— *European Constitutionalism* (Cambridge University Press, 2015).
Türk, A, *Judicial Review in EU Law* (Edward Elgar, 2009).
—— 'Judicial Review of Integrated Administration in the EU' in H Hofmann and A Türk (eds), *Legal Challenges in EU Administrative Law: towards an integrated administration* (Edward Elgar, 2009), 224.
Van Bael, I, 'The EEC Anti-dumping Rules – A practical approach' (1978) 12 *International Lawyer* 523.
Van Dam, C, 'Guidance documents of the European Commission: a typology to trace the effects in the national legal order' (2017) 10 *Review of European Administrative Law* 75.
Veronelli, M, 'Procedimenti composti e problemi di tutela giurisdizionale' in G della Cananea and M Gnes (eds), *I Procedimenti Amministrativi dell'Unione Europea. Un'Indagine* (Giappichelli, 2004).
Virga, P, *La Tutela Gurisdizionale nei confronti della Pubblica Amministrazione*, 3rd edn (Giuffrè, 1982).
Von Bogdandy, A, 'Ways to Frame the European Rule of Law: Rechtsgemeinschaft, Trust, Revolution, and Kantian Peace' (2018) 14 *European Constitutional Law Review* 675.
Von Bogdandy, A and Dann, P, 'International Composite Administration: Conceptualizing Multi-Level and Network Aspects in the Exercise of International Public Authority' (2008) 9 *German Law Journal* 2013.
Von Danwitz, T, *Europäisches Verwaltungsrecht* (Springer, 2008).
—— 'The Rule of Law in the Recent Jurisprudence of the ECJ' (2014) 37 *Fordham International Law Journal* 1311.
Von der Pfordten, D, 'About concepts in law' in J Hage and D von der Pfordten (eds), *Concepts in Law* (Springer, 2009).
Voßkuhle, A, 'Neue Verwaltungsrechtswissenschaft' in W Hoffmann-Riem, E Schmidt-Aßmann and A Voßkuhle (eds), *Grundlagen des Verwaltungsrechts*, 2nd edn, vol I (CH Beck, 2012).
Weiler, J, 'In Defence of the Status Quo: Europe's Constitutional *Sonderweg*' in J Weiler and M Wind (eds), *European Constitutionalism Beyond the State* (Cambridge University Press, 2003).
Weisbrot, M, 'Application of the Principle of Protection of Legitimate Expectations in Recovery of Unduly Paid Subsidies in the Context of Judicial Coherence in the European Union' (2015) 8 *Review of European Administrative Law* 347.
Weiser, P, 'Towards a Constitutional Architecture for Cooperative Federalism (2001) 79 *North Carolina Law Review* 663.
Werner, F, 'Verwaltungsrecht als konkretisiertes Verfassungsrecht' in F Werner, KA Betterman, and CH Ule, *Recht und Gericht unserer Zeit* (Carl Heymanns, 1971).
Wessels, W, 'Comitology: Fusion in Action. Politico-administrative Trends in the EU System' (1998) 5 *Journal of European Public Policy* 209.
Widdershoven, R, 'European Administrative Law' in R Seerden (ed), *Administrative Law of the European Union, its Member States and the United States* (Intersentia, 2012), 245.
Wils, W, 'The Oral Hearing in Competition Proceedings before the European Commission' (2012) 35 *World Competition* 397.
Wissink, L, 'Challenges to an Efficient European Centralised Banking Supervision (SSM): Single Rulebook, Joint Supervisory Teams and Split Supervisory Tasks' (2017) 18 *European Business Organisation Law Review* 431.

—— *Effective Legal Protection in Banking Supervision* (Europa Law Publishing, 2020).

Wockelberg, H, 'Why "Multi-Level" and "Governance" are Concepts of Relevance for our Understanding of Member State Implementation of EU Law' in AS Lind and J Reichel (eds), *Administrative law beyond the State: Nordic perspectives* (Martinus Nijhoff, 2013).

Wohlfahrt, E, Everling, U, Glaesner, HJ and Sprung, S (eds), *Die Europäische Wirtschaftsgemeinschaft, Kommentar zum Vertrag* (Vahlen, 1960).

Wymeersch, E, 'The European Banking Union, a First Analysis', *Financial Law Institute Working Paper Series* WP 2012-07 (https://ssrn.com/abstract=2171785).

Xanthoulis, N, 'Administrative factual conduct: Legal effects and judicial control in EU law' (2019) 12 *Review of European Administrative Law* 39.

Zglinski, J, *Europe's Passive Virtues: Deference to National Authorities in EU Free Movement Law* (Oxford University Press, 2020).

Ziller, J, 'Introduction: les concepts d'administration directe, d'administration indirecte et de co-administration et les fondements du droit administrative européen' in JB Auby and J Dutheil de la Rochère (eds), *Droit Administratif Européen* (Bruylant, 2007), 243.

—— 'Multilevel Governance and Executive Federalism: Comparing Germany and the European Union' in P Birkinshaw and M Varney (eds), *The European Union Legal Order after Lisbon* (Wolters Kluwer, 2010), 257.

INDEX

NB – page numbers in **bold** indicate information found in graphics

www.ingramcontent.com/pod-product-compliance
Ingram Content Group UK Ltd.
Pitfield, Milton Keynes, MK11 3LW, UK
UKHW020247290926
15470UKWH00002B/791

9 781509 980420